Queer(y)ing Kinship
in the Baltic Region and Beyond

Queer(y)ing Kinship
in the Baltic Region and Beyond

Edited by
Ulrika Dahl, Joanna Mizielińska, Raili Uibo & Antu Sorainen

Södertörns högskola

Södertörn University
Library
SE-141 89 Huddinge
www.sh.se/publications

Cover layout: Jonathan Robson
Cover image: composite by Jonathan Robson
Graphic form: Per Lindblom & Jonathan Robson

Södertörn Academic Studies 92
ISSN 1650-433X

ISBN 978-91-89504-20-2 (print)
ISBN 978-91-89504-21-9 (digital)

Contents

Acknowledgements

This volume has been long in the making and has along the way involved many people, conversations, and collaborations. We want to take the space to give thanks.

First, we want to thank the Foundation for Baltic and East European Studies for funding the project "Queer(y)ing Kinship in the Baltic Region" and the Centre for Baltic and East European Studies for funding the 2017 workshop from which this volume emerged, Joakim Ekman for creating such a rich and exciting research milieu over many years. A special thank you Vit Kysilka and Raili Uibo for providing administrative assistance and logistics coordination for the workshop. Above all, we would like to thank the contributors for their patience and faith that eventually this book would come together, despite a range of challenges. We also thank all the participants in our 2017 workshop, including those whose brilliant contributions did not make it into this volume: Varpu Alasuutari; Gosia Kot; Doris Leibetseder; Elisabeth Lund Engebrektsen; Ruth Preser; Olga Plakhotnik; Marcin Stasińska; Agata Stacinska; Johan Sundell and Alisa Zhabenko. Our conversations and networking at this and several other workshops around Europe animate this volume and all our work in this area.

For the final push into completion, post COVID-19, job changes, sick leave, and thesis completions, we are grateful to the Centre for Gender research at Uppsala University, in particular colleagues in the Family and Kinship research group, for their encouragement and material support. We would also like to thank the two anonymous reviewers for excellent and helpful feedback on the manuscript and the Publications Committee at Södertörn University for approving it for publication and Jonathan Robson and David Payne for their meticilous work to turn the manuscript into a book; for proof reading, typesetting and design, that ensures the book now exists in the world.

Ulrika would like to especially acknowledge her amazing co-researchers Joanna Mizielińska, Antu Sorainen and Raili Uibo for many years of excellent collaborations and meetings in both Stockholm, Helsinki and Warsaw, as well as at conferences in among other places, Lisbon, Athens, Helsinki, Copenhagen, Cracow, Warsaw, Stockholm and Uppsala. She would also like to thank long term colleague Jenny Gunnarsson Payne for close collaborations over many years and research assistant Johan Sundell for invaluable contributions in the first few years of the projects and for theoretical brilliance. For ongoing conversations, feedback on drafts and overall brilliance when it comes to queer kinship, Ulrika would also like to thank Varpu Alasuutari, Rikke Andreassen, Veronica Berg-Hultén, Jenny Björklund, Pako Chalkidis, Evangelia Elenis, Jacqui Gabb, Johanna Gondoin Lundström, Jack Halberstam, Helena Wahlström Henriksson, Sofia Klittmark, Anjelika Kjellberg, Del Lagrace Volcano, Matilda Lindgren, Giselle Newton, Jens Rydström, Samuel Girma, Anna Malmqvist, Petra Nordquist, Anna Nordqvist, Ana Cristina Santos, Lena Sawyer, Lina-Lea Zimmerman, and last but not least, Asynja Gray and all of our queer family.

Joanna, Antu and Raili also join Ulrika's above acknowledgements, but would also like to extend thanks to Ulrika herself, for her fiercely brilliant and bright directing of the project and her amazing patience in working on this book, and furthermore for creating this exciting and unique opportunity for us to be able to meet and talk and laugh and simply enjoy each other's company. Joanna wants to thank, in particular, all participants of her project on queer families in Poland who entrusted her with their stories, and of course, Agata Stasińska for her presence in her life and constant support. Antu wants to express her gratitude to the Academy of Finland for providing a salaried research fellow position while the project was active, and the book initially went into making; she would further like to thank her Academy of Finland research project team CoreKin in the Gender Studies Unit at the University of Helsinki, and especially Aliza Zhabenko for her insightful comments and intellectual companionship. Raili wishes to thank Ulrika, Joanna and Antu for their generous guidance and support on her path as a PhD student in the joint research project, along with Ulrika and Jenny Gunnarson Payne's brilliant supervision.

Raili would further want to thank the participants of her research project for sharing their lives and their stories about kinship and care practices in Estonia.

We dedicate this book to all the LGBTQ+ activists and families across Europe who are persisting in their fight against the right-wing tidal wave, thriving in spite of many obstacles and queering the future of the region and the world. With queer scholar Jose Esteban Munoz, let's envision queer as a kind of utopia, lodged in the "not yet" and hope that we will not only survive but actually live and thrive in better times; where all the queer(y)ing kin formations, relationships, attachments, care loyalties, families and also solo lives out there will be culturally encouraged, properly materially supported and socially and politically accepted equally, no matter their types and structures.

Stockholm, Warsaw, and Helsinki
October 2022

Introduction

Ulrika Dahl, Joanna Mizielińska, Raili Uibo & Antu Sorainen

Queer(y)ing Kinship in the Baltic Region and Beyond

> A kin-ship is a strange little vessel. She is small yet sea-worthy and abides by a comforting yet troubling set of codes that determines who gets in and who stays out of the boat. Like most ships, she lists. She lists between a company of kin that can sit down to breakfast with one mother or two fathers and their brood of loved but unrelated ones, and one that holds fast to blood that draws a line at the family table; between a block that parties and a party that blocks; between unruly affinity occupying all streets and the systematised sameness that holds office. (Weaver 2013, 43).

In the decades around the millennium, ideas that have been seen as self-evident in European modernity and essential to the building of nations, e.g., that kinship, family and parenthood are rooted in and based on heterosexual marriage, bloodlines and law, have come under considerable contestation, and for several overlapping reasons. Demographic changes, including growing divorce rates, increasing numbers of blended and recombined families, and significant new migration patterns, alongside increasing numbers of single parents, solo mothers by choice and LGBTQ+ people with children, have called the stability of life-long marriage and naturalised connections between kinship, race and nation into question. The emergence of assisted reproductive technologies (ARTs) such as In-vitro fertilization (IVF), gamete- and embryo donation and insemination and gestational surrogacy have since their conception in the 1980s developed into a global science and market, with both private and public healthcare providers as key actors in assisting people in achieving parenthood. With more than 8 million babies born conceived with IVF, the literal and conceptual use of assisted third party reproduction has decentred the function and meaning of heterosexual intercourse and reproduction as the basis for family, while simultaneously raising a range of ethical questions about "the facts of life" (Franklin 1997), including kinship, citizenship and affinity. Alongside feminist, queer and other critical perspectives, including scholarship on reproduction, these changes have contributed to changing understandings of family and kinship. Yet, few issues are more affective, at once deeply private and intensely public, but also inherently political, than those that pertain to reproduction, kinship and family and how they ought to be organised and regulated. Differently put, reproductive politics, and the meaning of family and kinship, remain as Donna Haraway (1997, 37) expressed it 25 years ago, "at the heart of questions about citizenship, liberty, family and nation."

On the one hand, the increasing visibility of gay and lesbian families and expanded laws that both recognise and enable same-sex family-making in a range of countries can be understood as both a form of progress towards greater equality, even if in the terms of queer critics, they can also be understood to constitute a form of homonationalism wrapped up in the appearance of queer liberalism (Eng 2010; Puar 2007; Duggan 2002). That is, certain LGBTQ+ subjects are welcome to participate in the making of a certain kind of nation; one that is centred around those of the majoritarian population who embrace consumerist and middle-class sensibilities and express particular kinds of national values and above all, who are distinguishable from those who do not belong. Yet, as we shall discuss further in this volume, neither is it the case that far from all nations recognise LGBTQ+ rights or new family constellations, culturally or legally, nor is it so that all LGBTQ+ families, or people whose lives do not fit the concept of family, benefit equally from existing legal frameworks. At the same time, while there is a global market of reproductive technologies as well as a global political agenda towards greater recognition, access to assisted reproduction and citizenship of children and partners, remains deeply stratified in the national settings in which they are located. On the other hand, alongside growing recognition and possibilities, recent years have also witnessed growing hostility towards LGBTQ+ persons and families and a re-energised emphasis on "family values" across European nations and globally, concomitant with growing attacks on what the conservative and extreme right calls "gender ideology" (Graff & Korolczuk 2021; Kuhar & Patternotte 2017). In European nations such as Poland, Russia and Hungary, LGBTQ+ people and their families have been especially targeted by right wing national and religious agendas. All this points to how "the politics of sexuality, intimacy and gender have acquired new significance in global geopolitics" (Brown and Browne 2016, 68).

Queer(y)ing kinship and Reproduction: Lessons from the Baltic region and beyond is a collection of papers and essays that explores both queer (non-heterosexual) kinship formations and family practices and the cultural, social and legal conceptualisations and configurations that shape them in a range of geopolitical settings. To that end, the volume consists of work that builds on a rich tradition of scholarship on queer kinship and family across different geopolitical settings and contributes both to the study of queer kinship and to queer(y)ing kinship. By researching (queer) relationship constellations reproduction and family making through critical and intersectional perspectives, contributors place questions of power at the centre of geopolitics. This includes questions of how culture is reproduced and contested and how the future is imagined, both within and beyond particular locations and national borders, by for instance, placing questions of race at the centre of welfare state reproductive politics.

Originating in the editors' joint research project *Queer(y)ing kinship in the Baltic region* which aimed to make a geopolitically based contribution to interdisciplinary queer and feminist research on kinship and reproduction on the one hand, and, on the other, to an understudied dimension within Baltic and Eastern/Central European Studies, namely queer kinship, the volume has invited other scholars who all in their own ways address what we continue to see as obvious gaps in each field that we argue are related to the geopolitics of (queer) knowledge production. Empirically grounded and in critical dialogue with a rapidly growing field of international scholarship, it seeks to contribute to the decentring of Western, Anglo-American dominance within the fields of feminist

and queer kinship studies, by highlighting the theoretical importance of geopolitics to queer kinship, national identity, community
making and social life. Emphasising national specificities and
attending to both local and transnational activism and community
knowledges, the project and this anthology also wants to unsettle
hegemonic progress narratives that tend to cast the "East" as
"behind" the "West", with respect for example to lesbian, gay, bi,
transgender and queer (LGBTQ+) rights. At the same time, neither
our project nor this volume has aimed to be comparative. Rather,
the contributions focus on distinct and locally relevant research
questions and analytical frameworks, both reworking and reinventing concepts.

If, as Laura Briggs (2018) has proposed, "all politics are reproductive politics", with this volume, we boldly claim that questions
of (queer) family, kinship and reproduction are central to the
broader themes of democratisation, post-communist transition,
the neoliberalisation of Europe and (unequal) relations between
East and West that characterise much of Baltic, Central and Eastern
European Studies research. Indeed, as Susan Gal and Gail Kligman
(2000: 15) noted long ago, "the discursive and practical effects of
debates about reproduction provide one of the keys to understanding how politics is being reshaped in East Central Europe."
Even if, as scholars have since repeatedly argued, the post-socialist
context is far from homogenous, it is clear that, as Korolczuk (2020,
152) has noted, "reproductive citizenship practices and ideals have
been (re)constructed in the region."

While there is a growing robust tradition of feminist work
within area studies and specifically related to questions of reproductive and sexual rights, thus far, very little research has been
funded and conducted on *queer* dimensions of these topics; rather,
it seems that the heterosexual family and the assumed gendered
division of labour within it, is frequently taken as a naturalised
point of departure in discussions about regional, national and state
politics. Paradoxically, while matters of recognition of LGBTQ+
people and their rights are frequently central to geopolitical debate,
and while the livelihoods of sexual minorities – including family
making within and beyond legal recognition – are also at the centre

of contemporary political debate, within Baltic and Eastern European Studies, these matters remain understudied. At the same time, there is a growing body of work that explores queer kinship and family making in different national contexts in the region, including Poland (Mizielińska 2022; Mizielińska 2020; Mizielińska & Stasińska 2018; Mizielińska 2020; Mizielińska, Abramowicz, and Stasińska 2015; Mizielińska & Stasińska 2017), Slovenia (Sobočan 2013a; 2011; 2013b; Streib-Brzic et al. 2011; Švab & Kuhar 2005b; 2014), Czech Republic (Nedbálková 2012; Polaskova 2007; Sokolová 2009; Fojtová 2011; Turcan et al. 2020), Hungary (Béres-Deák 2019; 2011b; Takács 2018a); Croatia (Tadić & Štambuk 2019; 2019; Štambuk, Milković & Maričić 2019), Bulgaria (Roseneil & Stoilova 2011), Estonia (Aavik 2020; Uibo 2021) and Russia (Zhabenko 2019). This research points to the significance of historically specific national legal and social contexts for understanding how LGBTQ+ kin constellations, relationships and families are formed and for how these constellations are experienced and practised. On the one hand, these studies demonstrate that many LGBTQ+ parents have children from previous heterosexual relationships, but also that access to existing assisted reproduction technologies are increasingly desired. Many of these studies point to how paths to procreation and family life are shaped by (the absence of) legal recognition of LGBTQ+ rights.

This research also illuminates the continued importance of a shared regional CEE sociopolitical context on the experience of queer kin constellations and families, and in particular to how histories of state socialism and strong conservative movements continue to shape contemporary family practices. For instance, Béres-Deák (2020) argues that with regards to family practices in Hungary, there is no clear line between state socialism and its 2010s aftermath, and contends that understandings of the role of the family that were developed in state socialist times still matter. Yet, she finds that LGBTQ+ people's understandings of kinship and what makes it queer also largely involves reworking the main ideas of Euro-American kinship as famously outlined by classic kinship theorist David Schneider (1980), namely blood relations and legal relations which together produce what he called "diffuse and enduring solidarity." These findings suggest that rather than considering LGBTQ+ or queer kinship as an exception, it can offer a lens through which to understand the symbolic significance of kinship and reproduction to national and regional politics, more broadly.

Building on and contributing to this tradition, the authors in this volume are queer studies scholars working within and across our respective locations in Sweden, Poland, Finland, and Estonia, who know that there is much to be gained by placing queer forms of making kinship and family at the centre of Baltic and East European area studies. While many more empirical examples could certainly be added here and hopefully will be in the future, the chapters in this volume point to some of the complexities, nuances and exchanges within different nation states and legal and cultural frameworks and thereby deepen knowledge of the socio-cultural and political situation of queer people in the 21st century. Core questions that are explored in this volume include: How are kinship and family bonds preconfigured and arranged, practiced and narrated among LGBTQ+ people, within and beyond the confines of the law? What challenges do queer family-makers meet and how are they negotiated? Does queerying kinship extend and reconfigure the meaning of kinship and family more broadly and if so, how? We hope that the volume will help readers further consider the implications of queer perspectives on queer relationality/relationships, families and reproduction for Baltic cohesion and collaboration.

Area studies, queer studies and critical kinship studies

> Area studies has always seemed to me rather queer. Queer in the sense that language is queer: promiscuous and ranging, given to misfires and infelicities, promising to reveal more than it can access or represent. Queer in the sense that its objects are queer: messy and incommensurable, irreducible to identitarian categories yet occasioned by identity, boundaried yet open, unbounded yet self-referential. Queer in the sense that interdisciplinarity is queer: a knowledge project premised on destabiliz-

> ing its own objects, which points to the social, historical, and political construction of the disciplines between and against which its labors are situated. Queer in that it is antinormative. Queer in that it is impossible. (Srinivasan 2019, 125)

It is no secret that whilst scholars frequently insist on the importance of academic freedom, that is, the intellectual right to pursue topics of our own interest, not all topics are considered equally important; the broader political and economic climate always shapes the conditions of research. In this context, the lives and families of lesbian, gay, bisexual, transgender and queer people are frequently understood as at best minoritarian exceptions to questions of broader importance and at worst, as dangerous, irrelevant or unworthy of funding or study. This means that both historically and presently, research on the lives of sexual minorities is often conducted without funding or by scholars who remain marginalised within many social scientific and humanities disciplines, with the possible exception of interdisciplinary gender studies. It is clear that opportunities for funding shape both the questions we ask and the collaborations we can create, and moreover, that the material conditions of research shape the geopolitics of knowledge production. In this respect, as researchers with a long-term interest in how European queer and feminist research is shaped by geopolitics, and by historical and ongoing relations often cast as matters of "East" and "West" (cf Mizielińska & Kulpa 2011; Dahl et al. 2016; see also Kulawik & Kravchenko 2020), we understand area studies, such as Baltic and East European studies, as a particularly interesting and complex formation of knowledge to intervene in, especially since as queer theorist Nikki Sullivan (2004,1) notes, "regionality, as a categorizing logic that makes meaning and identity possible, does so in and through the instituting of boundaries." Put otherwise, interdisciplinary area studies are far from neutral; indeed, with deep roots in colonialist knowledge practices, in the 20th century and following the second world war, area studies have also reflected and been the product of particular historical and global power relations (Said 1979; Chow 2006).

Like all research, this anthology and the project in which it has been conceived reflects a particular moment in time and space. It is, in turn, an effect of historical power relations that also shape our research. In 1994 the conservative Swedish government decided to end two decades of Social Democratic attempts to place a part of taxes into building employee funds (also called wage earner funds), which were originally managed by labour unions and which were created to contribute to collective benefits from and ownership of corporate wealth, and transform these by then substantive funds into research funds. At that time, only a few years since the "fall" of the Soviet Union, the Baltic states Estonia, Latvia and Lithuania had just regained independence, and Poland, which also borders the Baltic Sea, had recently broken off from the communist bloc. At the same time, it was clear that the Baltic Sea itself was in dire condition after hundreds of years of over-fishing, trade and pollution.[1] There was, in short, from the point of view of Swedish politicians at that time, an urgent need to better understand the "new" political (and environmental) situation in the Baltic region, meaning the nations bordering the Baltic Sea. The Foundation for Baltic and East European studies was thus established, and with it came statutes stipulating that research funded by the foundation "must be related to the Baltic Sea Region and Eastern Europe," where the former refers to the body of water itself as well as "surrounding areas" and the latter refers to post-communist parts of central, Southern and Eastern Europe. This funder has since literally created a material base for area studies insofar as it requires that funded research makes "a concrete contribution to our knowledge of this area" and also stresses that it does not fund theoretical research in which the area called the Baltic region is not "reflected in the main question."[2] The foundation and its intimate links to Södertörn University, has played a significant role in the development of Baltic and East European Studies, while simultaneously

---

[1] https://ostersjostiftelsen.se/wp-content/uploads/2019/12/jubileumsfolder-19-2.pdf; last accessed 2022-10-01.
[2] https://ostersjostiftelsen.se/en/for-researchers/research-relevance-for-baltic-sea-region-and-eastern-europe/; last accessed 2022-10-01.

actively encouraging scholars at Södertörn University to engage in empirical research within this interdisciplinary field.

As Srinivasan notes in the quote that opens this section, and as the brief story shared above suggests, there is indeed something queer – that is, strange – about geopolitically defined objects of study, which, like all concepts and categories, are historically and politically constituted. As critical queer scholars we are used to both querying and queering what is taken for granted, and as scholars in this field and editors of this book we understand it as one of our tasks to trouble what can be encompassed within the boundaries of area studies, by bringing critical perspectives on the geopolitics of knowledge production into focus. Needless to say, the "Western" invention of area studies reflects particular geopolitical stakes and interests, and themselves often reflect a power relation. Yet, as the 2010s have clearly rendered visible, queer subjects are frequently at the core of debates about how neoliberal capitalism should be managed, and as the 2022 Russian neo-imperial invasion of Ukraine attests to, geopolitical entities are never fixed and always reflect relations of power.

The term geopolitics is often attributed to Swedish political scientist Rudolf Kjellén, who in the early days of the previous century was of the view that "states, and particularly great powers, were the true actors that determined the field and history of international relations" (Kinnunen 2019, 23). As a concept, geopolitics tends not only to require a great amount of generalisation about entire populations in order to construct its view of states as singular actors in international relations, it also tends to privilege masculinist understandings of political economy, and to rely on and reproduce an often naturalised distinction between public and private domains, which also often depoliticises the private while highlighting the public. Since at least the early 2000s, a distinct *feminist* geopolitics has been built out of the broader field of critical geopolitics, a field which emphasises that power relations shape meanings and experiences of place, and research therein has demonstrated that not only are the seemingly naturalised domains of public and private deeply gendered (Hyndman 2001, 215), and that geopolitical categories and narratives need to be interrogated and historicised rather than assumed and taken for granted.

For us this means that while we see the value in and wish to contribute to institutional modes of producing knowledge such as area studies, these are not simple or taken-for-granted scholarly sites of belonging or "home," rather, they necessarily need queering. As we approach queer kinship and family making around the Baltic Sea, we depart from feminist geopolitics, and aim to attend to "the ways in which relations of power at different scales (global, national, urban) are linked" and how "global processes, whether economic, political, or socio-cultural, are experienced in localized, every day, embodied ways" (Hyndman 2001, 212). As Dixon and Marston (2011, 445) note, a feminist critical approach to conventional geopolitical categories, involves an active "questioning of their normativity" and "their role in the production of marginality and the everyday struggles of people to make sense of and negotiate their geopolitical existence." Indeed, a queer feminist geopolitics cannot simply be concerned with "adding" women or LGBTQ+ people, but rather "attends to the gendered, racialized, classed, sexualized, and otherwise differentiated everyday spaces previously ignored in geopolitical analysis" and furthermore, advocates "for a situated epistemological and methodological framework that recognizes the embodied and partial nature of knowledge production and the complicated and power laden relationship between the researcher and researched" (Massaro & Williams 2013, 570).

From this approach, questions of queer family, reproduction and kinship are not marginal questions of relevance to queer people, rather they are simultaneously highly political matters and deeply private affairs, insofar as they are both subject to international political debate and at the heart of how LGBTQ+ people find meaning, organise their everyday lives and imagine their futures. That is, we go beyond challenging foundational ideas in Kjellén's notion of geopolitics where the private realm is 'apolitical' or 'feminine' (Kinnunen 2019) and instead attend to how spatial categories such as nations and regions are also everyday spaces in which (queer) people live and, shaped by multiple relations of power, what is required are intersectional analyses, including how sexuality comes to matter. To put it in other terms: what is taken for granted for the for the dominant and normative view on kinship arrangements and frequently placed in the 'private arena' is precisely what makes the subjects of our research central to larger geopolitical debates. We contend that by asking how non-heterosexual, or queer, families are made, represented and treated in several nations around the Baltic Sea and in (Northern and Southern) Europe in the 21st century, we are not simply adding empirical data on an understudied population, we are addressing questions that are at the core of contemporary regional and global politics and culture. To us, queer(y)ing kinship and reproduction means asking questions about what is often taken for granted or naturalised, such as what family, kinship and reproduction means in everyday relations, intimacies and social reproductions in different geotemporal locations as well as in encounters with different state institutions, borders and laws. In this respect, we look to queer kinship as a "looking glass" (Franklin 2013) or as a "repro lens into multiple dimensions of social life" (Inhorn 2020).

In order to queer the geopolitics of area studies, we draw on queer theory/studies, an interdisciplinary field in which matters of (hetero)sexuality and gender diversity are studied in a range of ways. Immediately, we must point out that this is a field also entangled in geopolitics. Most narratives about the emergence of the field of queer studies place the very origins of queer and of queer studies in the US (cf. Dahl 2011; Kulpa & Mizielińska 2011). Indeed, the field remains heavily dominated by Anglo-American scholarship. In many of the main sites of scholarly conversation, including anthologies and academic journals, conferences and courses, this means that there is a tendency for both queer empirical phenomena and queer research, which is produced in and about other geopolitical settings, to always relate to a hegemonic Anglo-American understanding of queer and to meanings of LGBTQ+ politics as defined in the North/West. As Anjali Arondekar and Geeta Patel (2016, 152) put it in a special issue on queer geopolitics that starkly critiques US intellectual imperialism, "the citational underpinnings that provide the theoretical conduit for such explorations were and continue to be resolutely contemporary and drawn primarily from the United States; that is, geopolitics provides the exemplars, but rarely the epistemologies." This critique shares much with decolonial feminist Madina Tlostanova's critiques of European gender studies and other fields of interdisciplinary research. Building on her work with Walter Mignolo, Tlostanova has thoroughly interrogated how the coloniality of knowledge invented and continues to shape knowledge production in area studies, including Baltic, Central and East European/Post-Soviet studies. On the one hand, in a critical and inspiring text on geopolitical epistemic differences, Tlostanova usefully draws on postcolonial feminist Gayatri Spivak's notion of "sanctioned ignorance" of the West towards an often homogenised non-West, including its periphery and semi-periphery, and notes that "powerful critical interventions have not so far changed the general modern logic of knowledge production which is still grounded in rigid taxonomies, effective annihilations and sly appropriations" (Tlostanova 2015, 44). Tlostanova on the other hand calls for continued self-scrutiny and reflection and for Post-Soviet social science in particular to engage in the difficult process of decolonialising knowledge in order "to disavow the epistemic grounds of the rhetoric of modernity" and for a university that can foster researchers who are "truly and unselfishly interested in the world around in all its diversity and striving to make this world more harmonious and fair for everyone and not only for particular privileged groups" (Tlostanova 2015, 54).

In critical dialogue with international scholarship, and inspired by critiques of "Western" dominance in knowledge production, our research and this anthology thus aims to make an empirically based intervention on the level of theory that might decentre the Western, Anglo-American dominance of feminist and queer kinship studies as they relate to national identity, community making and social life. In developing our contribution to Baltic and East European Area studies then, we have drawn on both queer feminist theoretical framings, previous research in the field, and on contributions from post socialist and decolonial scholars such as Tlostanova to simultaneously gather empirical data, interrogate existing frameworks, and present new questions and findings to a research field that remains both imaginatively and quantitatively heavily dominated by Anglo-American research.

Queer(y)ing reproduction and kinship: terminologies, conceptual frameworks

Queer theory has always been a theory of kinship

(Bradway & Freeman 2022, 1).

As an interdisciplinary research field, queer studies consists of empirical and theoretical scholarship that centre on non-normative genders and sexualities on the one hand and that, on the other, develop critical perspectives on heterosexuality and binary gender as organising principles. Queer studies take as a starting point that gender, sex and sexuality (both as historical concept/category and as practice) are intrinsically entangled. The normative script suggests that humans are assigned sex upon being born and thereafter tend to be treated and read differently, are assumed to relate to the humans who raise them through gendered idioms of parenthood, and are expected to orient themselves towards the "opposite" sex and to desire a heterosexual reproductive futurity. Indeed, as Raewyn Connell and Rebecca Pearse (2002) point out, most understandings of gender pivot around a dichotomy based on presumed biological differences between people defined as male and female. Connell and Pearse propose that gender instead can be defined as "the structure of social relations that centre on the reproductive arena, and the set of practices that bring reproductive distinctions between bodies into social processes" (ibid., 10). In this process then, desiring someone of "the same gender" presumably has significant consequences for one's ability to procreate and make a family, and the ways in which one parents.

Kinship has long been a central question for fields such as anthropology and sociology; and typically refers to matters of classification, genealogy, structure, and organisation, but also to everyday practices and processes of identity formation. Modern Euro-American kinship, as cultural anthropologist David Schneider (on whom several contributors in this book rely) famously outlined, tend to rely on two main areas: nature/blood and culture/law. For Schneider kinship is premised both on "shared bio-genetic substance" and "enduring diffuse solidarity" organised via heterosexual intercourse as its key symbol (Levine 2008, 376). While the growing numbers of new and changed family forms since at least the 1990s has been presumed to radically alter how kinship is understood and practiced, it is clear that in an era where great significance is placed on diagnosing and medicalising deviance and on biogenetics, ideas of origin are not likely to decrease in significance. At the same time, it is very clear that new family forms, at least in the Western context "draw equally on conventional ideas and radical ones, and often draw on ideas about kinship that reference biogenetic connections." (Levine 2008, 377).

Insofar as kinship, family and reproduction are central to constructions of gender and sexuality, queer studies and theory, as well as research on LGBTQ+ communities have arguably always to some extent involved these themes (cf., Rubin 1975; Butler 1990; 2002; Freeman 2007; Bradway & Freeman 2022). If we follow Connell and Pearse's definition, we can also immediately see that these reproductive distinctions are related to how families are and can be made, and also that new forms of families, including those conceived through assisted reproduction, also have a bearing on our understandings of gender. At the same time, queer reproduction and parenthood cannot be reduced to a simplistic "same-sex" model. Rather, as many articles in this volume will show, it has specific gendered implications, for instance, lesbian parenthood might challenge the presumed connection between biological female sex, gestation and motherhood, whereas gay fatherhood may challenge the emphasis on mothers and growing numbers of trans-male pregnancies challenge dominant societal conceptions of how gender and gestation are linked.

In her work on queer phenomenology, Sara Ahmed (2006, 2010) has detailed how "coming out" as non-heterosexual often tends to impact people's relationship to kin and to shape one's life course and possibilities for reproductive futurities. Queer/ying kinship is complicated, as both Kath Weston's (1991) ground-breaking work and our own research has shown in this project; many LGBTQ+ people understand family and kinship as both encompassing those with whom one is related to by blood and law, and those who are "chosen" as family and with whom one makes everyday life. At the same time, as has long been documented by sociologists and anthropologists working in queer studies (Weston 1991; Lewin 1993; Weeks et al. 2001), as well as by scholars working on LGBTQ+ families in the CEE region mentioned above (Mizielińska 2022; Uibo 2021), many LGBTQ+ people do have children as well as other forms of intimate relations and families, and in the new millennium, increasingly through using various forms of assisted reproduction (Mamo 2007). At the same time, the hegemonic discourse of "coming out" and what it means to live a queer life, has been contested, not least by scholars who situate themselves in the Baltic and east European region, including researchers in this project. Raili Uibo (2021), has recently shown how in the context of Estonian neoliberal precarity, queers practice close relations partly through opacity; a kind of presence that, for many, affords for many different kin relations.

In the 2000s, one theme that has become increasingly central to conceptualisations of queer family and kinship is the degree to which and under which circumstances LGBTQ+ people can have children of their own, including through access to adoption and assisted reproduction, either via state healthcare or through the market, and the extent to which same-sex relationships and families are legally recognised. While this is a foundational question that shapes livelihoods and reproductive futurities across different geopolitical settings, it is also clear that research on and definitions of queer families and kinship is not reducible to what is legally recognised or what this signifies. As the literature from Poland, Hungary, Czech Republic and Croatia shows, this also means that we cannot only attend to how states view queer families or how LGBTQ+ movements advocate for recognition of various forms of queer kinship in various kinds of nation-political contexts, we also need to attend to the everyday practices of queer family making and to the differentiated impact of new forms of assisted reproduction (see Svab & Kuhar 2014; Beres-Deak 2020; Mizielińska all; Uibo 2021).

The growing size and complexity of a global fertility industry is another matter of urgent concern. Indeed, with the rise and spread of assisted reproductive technologies during the past decades, we have seen a veritable explosion of qualitative feminist and queer scholarship around how new forms of conception and procreation both challenge and reproduce normative ideas of kinship and relatedness (e.g., Edwards 2000; Franklin 2008, 2013; Franklin & Ragoné 1998; Kroløkke 2011; Kroløkke et al. 2016; Mamo 2007). Of particular interest to kinship theorists is so-called third-party reproduction, that is, assisted reproduction with donated gametes and gestational surrogacy, because it radically de-links sperm, egg and womb from parenthood (Thompson 2005; Franklin 2013; Gunnarsson Payne 2016; Ryan-Flood & Gunnarsson Payne 2018; Mohr 2018). To that end, many contend that assisted reproduction not only calls ideas of what is "artificial and natural" into question, it also renders reproduction itself queer (Franklin 1997, 2008, 2013; Mamo 2007), thereby showing how flexible kinship categories are, since terms and relations can be highlighted or downplayed, depending on parental intent, legal frameworks, resources and cultural understandings (Bryld & Lykke 2002; Franklin 2013; Nordquist & Smart 2014; Gunnarsson Payne 2016, this volume; Stuvøy 2018; Sorainen 2018). Gunnarsson Payne (2016) has proposed the notion of grammars of kinship as a way to conceptualise the diverse ways that assisted reproduction is worked into kinship and indeed, many note that parents tend to "rationalize the procedures they have initiated by naturalizing them" (Levine 2008, 382) or simply put by highlighting different dimensions of relatedness; be it gametes, gestation or the social practice of parenting. For queer scholars of kinship, all this means that there are a range of ways to conceptualise what is queer about family, kinship and reproduction.

As the fertility "industry" becomes one of the most rapidly growing sectors of the world economy, a central theme in the past decade has also been the growing transnational dimension of reproduction (Ryan-Flood & Gunnarsson Payne 2018; Lie & Lykke

2016; Dahl & Andreassen 2021). While families, that is, parents and children continue to live and "do" family in particular locations and circumstances, achieving parenthood increasingly involves gametes, surrogates and parents-to-be travelling across national borders within a global market for fertility biomedicine (Mamo & Alston-Stepnitz 2015; DasGupta & DasGupta 2014; Pande 2016; Twine 2015). Even if different nations have different understandings of what constitutes parenthood, and some recognise same-sex marriage and parenthood and others do not, possibilities for realising one's dreams of parenthood and family are not only dependent on national laws, but largely dependent on resources and privileges that exceed citizenship. Stated otherwise, in an age of assisted reproduction, family-making reflect global inequalities that go beyond queer constellations, while also frequently reinscribing race and nation in new ways (Lie & Lykke 2016; Luna & Luker 2013; Rudrappa 2015; Smietana, Thomson & Twine 2018; Mizielińska 2020a).

At the intersection of emerging queer studies, critical kinship studies and studies on assisted reproduction, in the new millennium there has also been a veritable explosion of work on LGBTQ+ families, queer kinship and reproduction (Dahl & Gunnarsson Payne 2014; Dahl & Björklund 2020; Dahl & Gabb 2019; Levine 2008; Mizielińska all; Gabb & Stasińska 2018; Parks 2013; Riggs & Peel 2016; Wahlström Henriksson & Goedecke 2021). While a full review of this extensive literature is quite difficult to conduct and beyond the scope of this introduction, we want to draw attention to a couple of identified themes. The first is the difficulty of defining queer kinship. It can refer to the kinds of kinship and families that lesbians, gay men and other queers, as in non-heterosexuals, make (Malmquist, all; Mamo 2007; Park 2013; Riggs & Peel 2016). In this connection, frequently research centres on the difference that legal recognition of non-heterosexual relations (or lack thereof) make. A second theme that emerges across a range of research is that rather than dismiss the principles of Euro-American kinship, that is the largely heteronormative logics of biogenetics (blood) and law, LGBTQ+ families retain and rework these understandings in a variety of ways, from maintaining close relations to their own birth-families, to creating families with children of their own through reproductive technologies, using both their own and donated gametes (Weston 1991; Lewin 1993; Hayden 1995; Carrington 1999; Levine 2008; Béres-Deák 2019; Mizielińska 2020b, 2022).

Queering kinship and reproduction thus inevitably open up for new definitions of family and how they relate to broader questions of intimacy and practices of care (Wahlström Henriksson & Goedecke 2021). Following Butler's (2002) crucial intervention in the article "Is kinship always already heterosexual?", which urges us to conceptually move beyond the significance of same sex marriage and reproduction unfolding from/within it, many queer researchers argue for expanding our understanding of (queer) kinship beyond procreation and parenthood to a consideration of how kinship both dictates and reflects practices of care and inter-dependency. Butler proposes an understanding of kinship that highlights how the needs that arise from the human condition of vulnerability are organised. If humans are fundamentally depend-ent on other people in order to meet our various needs kinship might be understood as way of instituting and organising relation-ships that meet those needs (Butler 2002, 15). Even if such relation-ships are not formed at random, different (kinship) positions and relations are the result of drawing boundaries between those who belong (our kin) and those who do not. Kinship is classificatory – it defines various ways of connecting and disconnecting, inclusion and exclusion (Franklin & McKinnon 2001, 15), it also marks the dividing line between those who are encompassed by our care and those remaining outside. The cultural expectation to take care of those who are familiar (and familial to us) leaves out others deemed strange and foreign, thus creating both family and nation as an effect of belonging to such units (Rodriguez 2014, 47).

Understanding kinship through interdependency and care brings attention to the interpersonal and corporeal practices of care, as queer theorist Elisabeth Freeman's (2007) definition of kin-ship proposes. Accordingly, kinship might be understood as "a set of representational and practical strategies for accommodating all the possible ways one human being's body can be vulnerable and hence dependent upon that of another, and for mobilising all the possible resources one body has for taking care of another" (Freeman 2007, 298). Such an approach thus focuses on both the emotional and practical labour that goes into sustaining people and relationships, and less on the legal and institutional frameworks that undeniably also shape kinship networks. In a more recent volume, Freeman together with Taylor Bradway contend that "queer theory has always been a theory of kinship" (2022, 1) and together with contributors, mostly from the US, return to questions of race, sex, belonging and form and how they come to matter in queer kinship. Bradway and Freeman here warn against expanding the grammar of kinship too far and losing track of how kinship remains "an idiom of state power, white supremacy, and Western modernity" (ibid.).

In a geotemporal context of growing neoliberal precarity and the ongoing dismantling of welfare states, taking care of each other is increasingly a matter of survival rather than a manifestation of particular emotional closeness. As argued by Uibo (2021) in her research on queers doing intimate relations in Estonia, in a harshly neoliberal post-Soviet setting, obligation, duty and dependence are frequently equally important reasons for maintaining bonds and relations of care, apart from any sense of belonging and emotional attachment. What her study makes visible is the obvious limits of a discourse of queer kinship as a matter of "choice". Even if Weston's (1991) original discussion of how queers make families beyond hetero-repro-normative frameworks is quite far from how it has been taken up in contemporary discussions of assisted reproductive "choices" that emphasise intent and neoliberal ideas of self-realisation through family-making, reconsidering kinship as practices of care might offer a better framework for understanding how differently situated LGBTQ+ people create what Schneider famously described as "diffuse and enduring solidarities" in a hostile world. Indeed, as Eng (2010), Rodíguez (2014) and others have noted, a framework of queer liberalism may only be relevant for a limited privileged few who benefit from recognition in a market-driven and neoliberal state.

In practice, differently situated queers in the Baltic region and beyond are involved in complex relationships that are not only tied together through positive feelings of kinship, such as love and connection or solved by legal recognition, but are also shaped by negative affects (cf Dahl 2014). When we discuss kinship then, we need to consider not only love, solidarity, family and belonging but also anger, guilt, shame and failure. As Raili Uibo's (2021) research shows, precarious living conditions or legal obligations may force some queers to become involved in practices of care towards people (or states) that may in fact not reciprocate the care, or in fact be actively negative. Even though care practices are closely linked with intimacy and belonging, these are not necessary or natural links, but are rather continuously shifting. To be encompassed in a circle of care is often itself quite conditional and precarious. While LGBTQ+ people are sometimes included in the nation (and thus in its self-image) or have rights recognised, such as currently in the Scandinavian welfare states, these rights can easily be rescinded and queer subjects purged, when political winds change, as they have for instance with regards to partnership in Estonia, marriage in the US, or reproductive rights in Spain. LGBTQ+ people can also become the scapegoats of the far right, as they have in Poland and Hungary in recent years. Differently put, that strange little vessel called "kin-ship", which set its sails at the beginning of this intro-duction and indeed at the beginning of our project, continues to be buffeted between various waves of negotiations in the stormy seas of meaning. Pulled in different directions at once, it is a ship that frequently changes its course, that both picks up and throws off passengers, as it is thrown against age-old rocks and kinship blocks, and only occasionally seems to be sailing smoothly towards an imagined perfect sunset in an equally romanticised West.

This volume

Like many projects of a collective nature, this volume has been long in the making, for reasons both geopolitical and queerly personal. It began as a workshop at Södertörn University in 2017, hosted by the editors of this volume who have worked together within the project *Queer(y)ing Kinship in the Baltic Region*. Involving around 25 participants from around the Baltic Sea and beyond, it reflected a wide range of new and emergent scholarship within the field, including all contributors to this volume alongside a significant number of PhD students. The main aim was to share insights and build networks, with the additional aim of putting together a volume. For various career and life specific reasons, workshop contributors had differentiated possibilities for contributing to the volume at hand. Some had to prioritise completing PhD theses and many felt the growing pressure from institutions to opt for fast publications or to choose peer-reviewed journals over anthologies. Indeed, anthologies are often slow in production and always involve personal, professional and creative challenges and differentially situated pressures and stakes. We mention this in part to render the real conditions of collective knowledge production visible and to point to how not only geopolitical location but also career trajectories, disciplinary conventions and personal matters always inform the work we do.

As indicated above, the rationale behind the volume is thus not so much to offer a geopolitically diverse smorgasbord of LGBTQ+ kinship and family making; in fact, this volume can hardly be seen as "representative" of the Baltic region or any nation as such. Rather, beyond reflecting and representing the collective work of us as editors, it includes work by scholars with whom we have been in conversation and to whom we are indebted in various ways. Part of what makes this volume queer is the broad and eclectic range of topics and themes presented and the empirical and theoretical contributions they make to the broader field. While few contributions explicitly theorise geopolitics, we contend that as a volume they show the value of considering LGBTQ+ family making at the intersection of area studies and critical kinship studies.

Even if the contributions speak to one another across a range of different themes, for the sake of organisation, the book is divided into three sections. With significant thematic overlaps, all of them, we feel, contribute to the core objective of the project, namely to intervene on the level of theory in these debates. The first part is entitled "Queer/ing reproduction and the grammars of kinship" and consists of three chapters that consider how kinship is reconfigured and reproduced in the context of national frameworks. Ethnologist and kinship theorist Jenny Gunnarsson Payne's chapter "Re-queering Reproduction: Queer Kinship, 'Reproductive Third Party' and the Incest-taboo" reconceptualizes and nuances the specific position and role of the reproductive third party in order to allow for reproductive visions that would bring about greater reproductive justice. In particular, Gunnarsson Payne, a leading kinship theorist, here discusses the active process of de-kinning that takes place when a third party is involved in the reproductive process (in surrogacy, adoption, gamete donation), where the third reproductive party is constructed as something else than a parent. Because of this need to actively de-kin the potential relationship, Gunnarsson Payne proposes that the third party cannot be understood either as non-kin or as kin, but instead occupies an ambiguous third position – the "un-kin". She thus introduces the idea of theorising the position of the un-kin through the lens of the incest taboo. There is the constant danger that the dormant potentiality of an un-kin relationship could be reactivated, and that the process of (re)-kinning could happen in the "wrong way". Sexual prohibition, in other words, governs these potential relationships to un-kin, marking this position differently from that of the non-kin, to whom the incest taboo would not apply. In addition to addressing an underlying fear of assisted reproduction with donated gametes, i.e., the risk of transgressing the incest taboo, Gunnarson Payne's intervention has political consequences insofar as it dares to acknowledge the ambiguous position of the third party in ways that might open up for differently queer and less hierarchical reproductive futures.

The second chapter, by queer anthropologist Pako Chalkidis, is entitled "Vanilla Democracy: Sexuality, Parenthood and Kinship in Greece" and develops a sharp critique of queer kinship theory in Europe that has invested much scholarly work in questions of reproduction and family-making but at the same time has neglected the ways in which ideas about sexual pleasures and practices shape meanings of parenthood. Through a close reading of the Greek context, Chalkidis argues that the institutionalised parenthood for which the LGBTQ+ movement attempts to make claims, is always already predicated on the exclusion of non-normative and non-respectable sexuality. In the Greek cultural imaginary, heterosexuality is intimately tied to the right to family and legitimate parenthood, whereas queers are expelled from any reproductive vision of the nation. Queer sexuality is not only seen as a threat to parenthood and to the nation but it is also linked with racialised ideologies of perversion. Chalkidis thus demonstrates how heterosexual vanilla sexuality – supposedly cleansed of any perversion – becomes naturalised as the normative position in the hierarchical web of sexual, gender and kinship structures.

The third chapter, "Queer kinship in Swedish numbers: Reproducing National Whiteness", by queer ethnographer and project coordinator Ulrika Dahl, discusses the findings of the first national survey on LGBTQ+ people's paths to and experiences with parenthood in Sweden. The demographics here suggest that while same-sex marriage and family law in Sweden might indicate an inclusive and progressive context for family making and results show a wide range of family practices and imaginaries, there is a quite clear norm. Dahl contends that the experiences of those LGBTQ+ family makers who responded reveal similar values to those of other middle-class subjects, and that paths to parenthood are increasingly and deeply shaped by the privatisation of the welfare state, a growing fertility industry and a legal framework within which privileged queer subjects have a clear sense of their rights (and lack thereof), not only as parents but as consumers of fertility medicine.

Following this opening part's attempt to offer conceptual and methodological richness to the field, section two, entitled "Assisted reproduction, queer parenthood and the nation state" goes deeper into empirical investigations of the national and legal frameworks in which queer kinship is imagined in different locations. This part consists of four articles, each taking a critical approach to core matters of individual Nordic welfare states, namely equality. These critical investigations are specifically explored through the lens of access to assisted reproduction, highlighting how questions of gender, race, and nation organise queer kinship. In the section's first chapter "Room for All: Equality, Race, and Reproduction in the Norwegian Social Democracy," feminist cultural anthropologist Suraiya Jetha draws on ethnographic fieldwork on donor siblingship in Norway, as well as on media and document analysis, and offers a rich cultural analysis of how the Norwegian state understands or rather erases the significance of race and racialisation in the process of donor insemination and thus how the discourse of equality produces *inequality*. In a chapter that contributes to the growing field of research on race, nation and (queer) reproduction Jetha demonstrates how the colour-blind donor insemination policies produce discriminatory effects for non-white Norwegian citizens such that non-white Norwegian citizens are excluded from the Norwegian welfare state in the process of donor insemination. Jetha also analyses the various claims made about the process of recruiting and choosing sperm donors. In cutting edge research, Jetha illustrates how these claims and frameworks differ widely depending on whether they are made on behalf of intended parents, the fertility clinics or civil society actors. While the intended parents define equality as the right to have access to donor sperm that would make their child resemble their own ancestry, the fertility clinics treat any such wishes as requests for differential treatment and thus in contradiction to equality. Thus, the meaning and role of equality, belonging, kinship and the (Norwegian) welfare state are negotiated through the process of choosing donor sperm. Jetha's cutting edge work calls attention to themes we expect will become increasingly important for how scholars conceive of assisted reproduction involving a range of choices in increasingly diverse nations.

The next chapter, "Altruism and Built-In Nationalism: The Surrogacy Debate in Finland 2013–2019," by Finnish gender studies scholar Anna Moring, approaches the issue of surrogacy from the Finnish national context through a nuanced analysis of public debate in the 2010s. Based on media and document analysis, Moring outlines the different ways in which surrogacy is framed in the public sphere and their respective consequences. In a significant contribution to the field, Moring illuminates how the Finnish surrogacy debate is deeply ingrained in nationalism; local altruist surrogacy is constructed as more ethical and preferable to the looming dangers of foreign commercial surrogacy. Moring contends that the nationalist framing of the surrogacy debate goes hand-in-hand with its intrinsic whiteness and lack of discussion about race and ethnicity. The Finnish debate is also deemed heteronormative and gendered, since any discussion about potentially allowing altruistic surrogacy refers only to heterosexual married couples, actively excluding other subjects such as lesbians and gays, as well as other single or unmarried people. Finally, Moring's chapter problematises the strict dichotomy between altruistic and commercial surrogacy reproduced in the Finnish surrogacy debate. She instead calls for a nuancing of the debate on the ethics and practices of surrogacy, while taking into account the complex racialised, sexualised, gendered processes taking place both locally and transnationally. Moring's contribution adds significant perspectives here that have direct bearings on emerging Finnish feminist discussions around assisted reproduction and surrogacy (see also Eriksson 2021; Homanen 2018; Honkasalo 2018), both in the research field and beyond academia.

In "The mediation of commercial transnational surrogacy: The entanglement of visual, colonial, and reproductive technologies," Danish queer feminist scholar Michael Nebeling Petersen scrutinises the entanglement of technologies that participate in commercial transnational surrogacy. This chapter extends the author's many crucial interventions in the field of critical kinship studies (Nebeling Peterson 2018; Nebeling Peterson & Myong 2015; Nebeling Peterson et al. 2017) and is based on an online ethnography in various online communities where gay fathers display their surrogacy journeys. Here Nebeling Peterson shows how these journeys are shaped by the intersection of reproductive technologies, media technologies and technologies of power and global and local power inequalities. Surrogacy, he argues, allows gay men to reshape gay male subjectivity and approach reproductive generational kinship by orienting themselves towards fatherhood. Online mediation of every step on this path to parenthood contributes to the possibility of embodying both fatherhood and pregnancy as 'real' and their own, while both exploiting and erasing the reproductive labour of surrogate mothers. The reproductive and media technologies that are involved in transnational commercial surrogacy journeys of gay men are not only about coming to fatherhood, but an imaginary deeply embedded in colonial legacies and power technologies.

Last but not least in this section, in her "Swedish lesbian mothers arrange parental leave: Idealizing equality, sharing (more or less) evenly" Anna Malmquist, leading Swedish scholar on lesbian motherhood and parenthood, discusses the under-studied field of parental leave arrangements among lesbian mothers in Sweden. After conducting interviews with 94 lesbian mothers in the early 2010s, Malmquist identified three main ways of arranging parental leave between birth mothers and non-birth mothers, all of whom relate in different ways to the rarely questioned ideal of equality. Malmquist's research shows that while a majority of lesbian parents in Sweden share available parental leave, most of the birth mothers use the first part of parental leave with only a minority choosing to take parental leave simultaneously from early on. The third group of lesbian mothers consist of couples where the birth mother takes out the majority of parental leave. The chapter shows various ways of reacting to the ideal of shared parental leave and dissects the different meanings of equality that are at stake, along with the normative and naturalised order in which mothers are expected to take parental leave. The chapter is an important contribution to theoretical debates on gendered (in)equality and parenting. Moreover, it also introduces various practical implications for institutions that support lesbian mothers. The chapters in this section, like the rest of the anthology, are not meant to present national case studies; rather they explore how becoming and being parents is a journey deeply entangled with state imaginaries, colonialist legacies, ideas about parenthood as altruistic and equal, as well as fantasies of sameness and difference, at the core of kinship.

The anthology's final section entitled "New directions in the temporalities and geopolitics of queer kinship" is a cluster of texts that in a sense return us to core themes of both the research project and this volume, namely, the meaning of queer, and the significance of temporality, and materiality. What is queer about queer relations? In their joint chapter "The Legacy of Age Gap as a Decisive Difference in Lesbian Relationships", project members Joanna Mizielińska and Antu Sorainen offer a reconsideration of what counts as kinship by attending to the queer, that is, intriguing topic of age differences within lesbian relationships through ethnographic examples from their respective research settings – Poland and Finland. They show that lesbian age gaps in intimate relationships have a long history in for instance famous characters in history to cultural representations. However, the authors contend that as a specific pattern of desire and difference in lesbian relationships, what they call the "age gap" has been under-discussed among feminist and queer theorists. To look closer at the nuances of the lesbian age gap as a decisive difference across historical and national borders, Mizielińska and Sorainen direct a contrastive spotlight on the question of how a significant age dissimilarity relates to agency, personal lives, and power relations in two different lesbian landscapes of intimacy. Post-socialist Poland and Nordic (post)welfarist Finland are, albeit in divergent ways, both on the periphery of the dominant Western sexuality knowledge production. Thus, they also produce diverging answers to the question of how rooted assumptions of age relating to "female desire" are reimagined and lived out in these two different geographical and national scenes for lesbian relationships.

The next chapter, "Mourning with Rainbow Kin: Approaching Queer Kinship from New-Materialist Perspectives" by leading Nordic feminist theorist Nina Lykke also explores how temporality and materiality shape kinship and returns us to the level of theory. In a poetic essay, Lykke paves the way towards a new-materialist approach to queer kinship. Joining other scholars who increasingly discard the families of choice framework as voluntaristic, Lykke instead focuses on the corporal and affective moments involved in the process of mourning for her lesbian life partner together with her rainbow kin. Through an innovative and creative autho-phenomenographical account of her experiences, Lykke attends to the process of change that took place in her way of relating to her partner's family in time of her partner's illness and death. Here we learn that the immediate affective void that emerged through her partner's death not only brought her rainbow kin closer together through collective grief and mourning practices, but Lykke also experienced a personal shift from identifying as a lesbian co-mother towards filling the void of a mother that had passed. The shift involved "corpoaffective" intimacies and intensities that transgressed the families of the choice framework. By paying detailed attention to the queer temporalities that are involved in the formation of queer rainbow families, Lykke presents a beautiful and nuanced contribution to a theory of queer kinship-making that is both deeply grounded in new materialist and affect-theoretical approaches and that illuminates the power of storytelling as central to making kinship.

As has been outlined in this introduction, neither the project *Queer(y)ing Kinship in the Baltic region* nor this volume are concerned with practices of comparison. Rather, we have let our respective theoretical and empirical approaches inform sustained discussions and have learned from one another's approaches, at times through a more contrastive lens. At the same time, work on this anthology has also pointed to the habitual ways in which scholarly knowledge production often tends to either take the national framework for granted whilst simultaneously giving our conceptual and methodological frameworks more mobility than we afford our subjects. We often end up engaging in unconscious forms of comparison.

Extending the intellectual kinship between us as project participants and with many of the contributors here over the past decade, we have aimed to take seriously the different geopolitical and intellectual milieus in which we are located, our respective trainings, and so on. We have sought to engage both one another's respective theoretical and empirical work and to bring together work that we have undertaken in separate projects alongside our own joint project. Indeed, over the past decade, the project and the work on this anthology has been much like the "kin-ship" described by Lois Weaver in the opening epigraph of this introduction: it has taken us across the Baltic Sea between Estonia, Poland,

Finland and Sweden and beyond, it has indeed been guided by and yet has been thought critically about; "a comforting yet troubling set of codes about who gets in and who stays out", both with respect to this research project and as a theme in our empirical projects. Rather than smoothing over the productive epistemological and geopolitical differences in our respective approaches and empirical settings and creating a joint and seamless framework and a unified set of conclusions, the volume wants to draw attention to these, perhaps, unsolvable matters.

Thus, we end the book with "Yours in Struggle: Baltic Dialogues," an extensive conversation where Ulrika Dahl and Joanna Mizielińska discuss their respective and overlapping interests in queer kinship and the ways in which geopolitics continue to shape their scholarly work. This chapter reflects the process of collaboration and knowledge production, the rhizomatic paths, sore points, and stories and stakes that place us in this field. While we expect readers to find use for the respective chapters of the volume depending on distinct interests, we hope that as a collection, this book will offer readers both with an interest in Baltic and East European and Nordic area studies, on the one hand, and in studies of queer kinship and reproduction, on the other, new perspectives and insights, as well as inspiration to continue to build an inter-disciplinary field of queer and critical kinship and reproduction studies and to de-centring "Western" and "Anglo-American" perspectives.

References

Aavik, K. 2020. "Negotiating Uncertainty: Sexual Citizenship and State Recognition of Same-Sex Partnerships in Estonia," in *LGBTQ+ Activism in Central and Eastern Europe*, edited by R. Buyantueva and M. Shevtsova, 127–55. Cham: Palgrave Macmillan.

Ahmed, S. 2006. "Orientations: Toward a Queer Phenomenology." *GLQ: A Journal of Lesbian and Gay Studies* 12 (4): 543–574.

Ahmed, S. 2010. *The Promise of Happiness.* Durham: Duke University Press.

Andreassen, R. 2021. "From the families we choose to the families we find online: media technology and queer family making." *Feminist Theory.* doi: 10.1177/14647001211059517

Arondekar, A. & Geeta P. 2016. "Area Impossible: Notes toward an Introduction" *GLQ: A Journal of Lesbian and Gay Studies* 22 (2): 151–171

Béres-Deák, R. 2011a. "'I Was a Dark Horse in the Eyes of Her Family': The Relationship of Cohabiting Female Couples and Their Families in Hungary." *Journal of Lesbian Studies* 15 (3): 337–55.

–––. 2019. *Queer Families in Hungary: Same-Sex Couples, Families of Origin, and Kinship.* London: Palgrave Macmillan.

Bradway, T & Freeman, E., eds. 2022. *Queer Kinship: Race, Sex, Belonging, Form.* Durham: Duke University Press.

Briggs, L. 2018. *How all Politics Became Reproductive Politics: From Welfare Reform to Foreclosure to Trump.* Oakland: University of California Press.

Brown, G. & Browne, K. 2016. *The Routledge Companion to Geographies of Sex and Sexualities.* New York: Routledge.

Bryld, M. and Lykke, N. 2002. "Cyborgbabyer og den politiske debat om 'det naturlige,'" in *Homo Sapiens 2.0*, edited by G. Balling, 195–215. Copenhagen: Gads forlag.

Butler, J. 1990. *Gender trouble: Feminism and the subversion of identity.* New York: Routledge.

–––. 2002. "Is kinship always already heterosexual?" *differences: A Journal of Feminist Cultural Studies* 13 (1): 14–44.

Carrington, C. 1999. *No place like home: Relationships and family life among lesbians and gay men.* Chicago: The University of Chicago Press.

Chow, R. 2006. *The Age of the World Target: Self-Referentiality in War, Theory, and Comparative Work.* Durham: Duke University Press.

Connell, R. & Pearse, R. 2002. *Gender in World Perspective.* Cambridge: Polity Press, 1st edition.

Dahl, U. 2011. "Queer in the Nordic region: Telling queer (feminist) stories" in eds., *Queer in Europe: Contemporary case studies*, edited by L. Downing & R. Gillet, 143–157. London: Ashgate.

Dahl, U. 2014. "Not gay as in happy, but queer as in fuck you: notes on love and failure in queer(ing) kinship." *lambda nordica* 19 (3/4): 143–168.

Dahl, U. & Andreassen, R. 2021. "Donors we choose: race, nation and the biopolitics of (queer) assisted reproduction in Scandinavia." *Biosocieties.* doi: 10.1057/s41292-021-00256-2.

Dahl, U. & Björklund, J. 2019. "Editorial: Queer Kinship Revisited." *lambda nordica* 24 (2–3): 7–26.

Dahl, U. & Gabb, J. 2019. "Trends in Contemporary Queer Kinship and Family Research." *lambda nordica* 24 (2–3): 209–237.

Dahl, U. & Gunnarsson Payne, J. 2014. "Introduction." *lambda nordica* 19 (3–4): 11.

Dahl, U., Liljeström, M. & Manns, U. 2016. *The Geopolitics of Nordic and Russian Gender Research 1975–2005.* Stockholm: Södertörn University.

DasGupta, S. & DasGupta, S. 2014. *Globalization and Transnational Surrogacy in India: Outsourcing Life.* Lexington Books.

Dixon, D. P. & Marston, S. A. 2011. "Introduction: feminist engagements with geopolitics." *Gender, Place & Culture* 18 (4): 445–453.

Edwards, J. 2000. *Born and Bred: Idioms of Kinship and New Reproductive Technologies in England.* Oxford: Oxford University Press.

Eriksson, L. 2021. "Outsourcing Problems or Regulating Altruism? Parliamentary Debates on Domestic and Cross-Border Surrogacy in Finland and Norway." *The European Journal of Women's Studies.* doi: 10.1177/13505068211009936

Fojtová, S. 2011. "Czech Lesbian Activism: Gay and Lesbian Parental Rights as a Challenge to Patriarchal Marriage". *Journal of Lesbian Studies* 15 (3): 356–83.

Franklin, S. 1997. *Embodied Progress: A Cultural Account of Assisted Conception.* London: Routledge.

Franklin, S. 2008. "Reimagining the facts of life." *Soundings: A Journal of Politics and Culture* 40 (3): 147–156.

Franklin, S. 2013. *Biological Relatives: IVF, Stem Cells, and the Future of Kinship.* Durham, NC: Duke University Press.

Franklin, S. 2013. "Conception through a Looking Glass: The Paradox of IVF." *Reproductive Biomedicine Online* 27 (6): 747–755.

Franklin, S. & McKinnon, S. 2001. "Introduction. Relative values: Reconfiguring kinship Studies," in *Relative values: Reconfiguring kinship studies,* edited by S. Franklin & S. McKinnon, 1–26. Durham: Duke University Press.

Franklin, S. & Ragoné, H. 1998. *Reproducing Reproduction: Kinship, Power, and Technological Innovation.* Philadelphia, PA: University of Pennsylvania Press.

Freeman, E. 2007. "Queer belongings: Kinship theory and queer theory," in *A companion to lesbian, gay, bisexual, transgender, and queer studies,* edited by G. E. Haggerty & M. McGarry, 295–314. Malden, MA: Blackwell. Pp. 295–314.

Gal, S. & Kligman, G. 2000. *The Politics of Gender After Socialism: A Comparative-Historical Essay.* Princeton: Princeton University Press.

Graff, A. & Korolczuk, E. 2021. *Anti-Gender Politics in the Populist Moment.* New York, NY: Routledge.

Gunnarsson Payne, J. 2016. "Grammars of Kinship: Biological Motherhood and Assisted Reproduction in the Age of Epigenetics." *Signs: Journal of Women in Culture and Society* 41 (3): 483–506.

Haraway, D. J. 1997. "The Virtual Speculum in the New World Order." *Feminist Review* 55 (55): 22–72.

Hayden, C. 1995. "Gender, genetics and generation: Reformulating biology in lesbian kinship." *Cultural Anthropology* 10 (1): 41–63.

Homanen, R. 2018. "Reproducing whiteness and enacting kin in the Nordic context of transnational egg donation: Matching donors with cross-border traveller recipients in Finland." *Social Science and Medicine* 203 (April): 28–34.

Honkasalo, J. 2018. "Unfit for parenthood? Compulsory sterilization and transgender reproductive justice in Finland." *Journal of International Women's Studies* 20 (1): 40.

Hyndman, J. 2001. "Towards a feminist geopolitics." *The Canadian Geographer/Le Geographe canadien* 45 (2): 210–222.

Inhorn, M. 2020. "Where has the quest for conception taken us? Lessons from anthropology and sociology." *Reproductive biomedicine & society online* 10: 46–57.

Kinnunen, T. 2019. "Ellen Key and Rudolf Kjellén on war, peace, and the future of post-First World War Europe." *Scandinavian Journal of History* 44 (2): 150–168.

Korolczuk, E. 2020. "Making babies and citizens: reproductive technologies and citizenship in Poland," in *Borderlands in European Gender Studies: Beyond the East-West Frontier*, edited by T. Kulawik & Z. Kravchenko, 151–169. London: Routledge.

Kroløkke, C. 2011. "Biotourist performances. Doing parenting during the ultrasound." *Text and Performance Quarterly* 31 (1): 15–36.

Kroløkke, C., Myong, L. Adrian, S. W. & Tjørnhøj-Thomsen, T., eds. 2016. *Critical Kinship Studies*. London: Rowman and Littlefield.

Kuhar, R. & Paternotte, D. 2017. *Anti-Gender Campaigns in Europe: Mobilizing Against Equality*. London: Rowman & Littlefield International, Ltd.

Kulawik, T. & Kravchenko, Z., eds. 2020. *Borderlands in European Gender Studies: Beyond the East-West Frontier*. London: Routledge.

Kulpa R. & Mizielińska, J., eds. 2011. *De-Centring Western Sexualities: Central and Eastern European Perspectives*. Farnham: Ashgate.

Leibetseder, D. & Griffin, G. 2018. "Introduction: Queer and Trans Reproduction with Assisted Reproductive Technologies in Europe." *Journal of International Women's Studies* 20 (1): 1.

Levine, N. E. 2008. "Alternative Kinship, Marriage and Reproduction." *Annual Review of Anthropology* 37: 375–389.

Lewin, E. 1993. *Lesbian mothers: An account of gender in American culture*. Ithaca: Cornell University Press.

Lie, M. & Lykke, N., eds. 2016. *Assisted Reproduction Across Borders: Feminist Perspectives on Normalizations, Disruptions and Transmissions*. New York, NY: Routledge.

Luna, Z. & Luker, K. 2013. "Reproductive justice." *Annual Review of Law and Social Science* 9 (1): 327–352.

Malmquist, A. 2015. "Women in Lesbian Relations: Construing Equal or Unequal Parental Roles?" *Psychology of Women Quarterly* 39 (2): 256–267.

Mamo, L. 2007. *Queering Reproduction: Achieving Pregnancy in the Age of Technoscience.* Durham, NC: Duke University Press.

Mamo, L. 2013. "Queering the fertility clinic." *Journal of Medical Humanities* 34: 227–239.

Mamo, L. & Alston-Stepnitz, E. 2015. "Queer intimacies and structural inequalities: New directions in stratified reproduction." *Journal of Family Issues* 36 (4): 519–540.

Massaro, V. A. & Williams, J. 2013. "Feminist Geopolitics: Redefining the Geopolitical, Complicating (in)Security" *Geography Compass* 7 (8): 567–577.

Mizielińska, J. 2020a. "'Is She Still a Family or Rather Some Stranger?' – Relative Strangers and Kinship Plasticity in Families of Choice in Poland'. *Journal of Homosexuality* 68 (11): 1899–1922.

–––. 2020b. "The Limits of Choice: Queer Parents and Stateless Children in Their Search for Recognition in Poland." *Gender, Place & Culture* 0 (0): 1–24.

–––. 2022. *Queer Kinship at the Edge? Families of Choice in Poland.* London: Routledge. Available Open Access.

Mizielińska, J., Gabb, J. & Stasińska, A. 2018. "Editorial Introduction to Special Issue: Queer Kinship and Relationships." *Sexualities* 21 (7): 975–82.

Mizielińska, J. & Kulpa, R. 2011. "'Contemporary Peripheries': Queer Studies, Circulation of Knowledge and East/West Divide," in *De-Centring Western Sexualities. Central and Eastern European Perspective,* R. Kulpa & J. Mizielińska, eds. Farnham; Burlington, VT: Ashgate. Pp. 11–26.

Mizielińska, J. & Stasińska, A. 2018. "Beyond the Western Gaze: Families of Choice in Poland." *Sexualities* 21 (7): 101–23.

–––. 2020. "Negotiations Between Possibilities and Reality: Reproductive Choices of Families of Choice in Poland." *European Journal of Women's Studies* 27 (2/4): 1–16.

Mizielińska, J., Abramowicz M. & Stasińska A. 2015. *Families of Choice in Poland. Family Life of Non-Heterosexual People.* Warsaw: IP PAN. familiesofchoice.pl.

Mohr, S. 2018. *Being a Sperm Donor. Masculinity, Sexuality, and Biosociality in Denmark.* New York/Oxford: Berghahn.

Nebeling Petersen, M. 2018. "Becoming gay fathers through transnational commercial surrogacy". *Journal of Family Issues* 39 (3): 693–719.

Nebeling Petersen, M. & Myong, L. 2015. "(Un)liveabilities: Homonationalism and transnational adoption". *Sexualities,* 18 (3): 329–345.

Nebeling Petersen, M., Kroløkke, C. & Myong, L. 2017. "Dad and daddy assemblage: Resuturing the nation through transnational surrogacy, homosexuality, and Norwegian exceptionalism" *GLQ* 23 (1): 83–112.

Nedbálková, K. 2012. "Rendering Gender in Lesbian Families: A Czech Case," in *De-Centring Western Sexualities: Central and Eastern European Perspectives*, Mizielińska, J. & Kulpa R., eds. Farnham; Burlington, VT: Ashgate.

Nordqvist, P. 2006. "Att tala om familj: Lesbiskas berättelser om planerat föräldraskap." *lambda nordica* 11 (4): 63–81.

Nordqvist, P. 2009. "Feminist heterosexual imaginaries of reproduction: Lesbian conception in feminist studies of reproductive technologies." *Feminist Theory* 9 (3): 273–292.

Nordqvist, P. & Smart, C. 2014. *Relative Strangers: Family Life, Genes and Donor Conception*. 2014 edition. Basingstoke New York: Palgrave Macmillan.

Pande, A. 2016. "Global reproductive inequalities, neo-eugenics and commercial surrogacy in India." *Current Sociology* 64 (2): 244–258.

Park, S. M. 2013. *Mothering Queerly, Queering Motherhood: Resisting Mono-maternalism in Adoptive, Lesbian, Blended, and Polygamous Families*. Albany: State University of New York Press.

Polaskova, E. 2007. "The Czech Lesbian Family Study: Investigating Family Practices," in *Beyond the Pink Curtain: Everyday Life of LGBT People in Eastern Europe*, Kuhar, R. & Takács, J., eds. Mirovni Institut. https://www.academia.edu/7982842/Beyond_The_Pink_Curtain_Everyday_Life_of_LGBT_People_in_Eastern_Europe.

Riggs, D. & Peel, E. 2016. *Critical kinship studies: An introduction to the field*. New York: Palgrave MacMillan.

Rodríguez, J. M. 2014. *Sexual Futures, Queer Gestures, and Other Latina Longings*. New York: NYU Press.

Roseneil, S. & Stoilova, M. 2011. "Heteronormativity, Intimate Citizenship and the Regulation of Same-Sex Sexualities in Bulgaria," in *De-Centring Western Sexualities. Central and Eastern European Perspective*, R. Kulpa & J. Mizielińska, eds., 167–90. Farnham; Burlington, VT: Ashgate.

Rubin, G. 1975. "Traffic in women: Notes on the 'political economy' of sex," in *Toward an anthropology of women*, Reither, R. R., ed. New York: Monthly Review Press. Pp. 157–210.

Rudrappa, S. 2015. *Discounted Life: The Price of Global Surrogacy in India*. New York, NY: New York University Press.

Ryan-Flood, R. 2009. *Lesbian Motherhood: Gender, Families and Sexual Citizenship*. London: Palgrave Macmillan.

Ryan-Flood, R. & Gunnarsson Payne, J., eds. 2018. *Transnationalising Reproduction: Third Party Conception in a Globalised World*. London: Routledge/Taylor & Francis.

Said, E. W. 1979. *Orientalism*. New York: Vintage Books.

Schneider, D. M. 1980. *American Kinship: A Cultural Account: David M. Schneider*. 2nd ed. Chicago: University of Chicago Press.

Smietana, M., Thompson C. & Winddance Twine, F. 2018. "Making and Breaking Families – Reading Queer Reproductions, Stratified Reproduction and Reproductive Justice Together." *Reproductive Biomedicine & Society Online* 7 (November): 112–30.

Sobočan, A. 2011. "Female Same-Sex Families in the Dialectics of Marginality and Conformity." *Journal of Lesbian Studies* 15 (3): 384–405.

–––. 2013a. "Same-Sex Families (in Slovenia): The New Minority?" *Calitatea Vietii*, no. 1: 31–46.

–––. 2013b. "Two Dads / Two Moms: Defying and Affirming the Mom–Dad Family. The Case of Same-Gender Families in Slovenia." *Confero Essays on Education Philosophy and Politics* 1 (2): 90–122. https://doi.org/10.3384/confero.2001-4562.13v1i21f.

Sokolová, V. 2009. "Otec, Otec a Dítě: Gay Muži a Rodičovství." *Sociologický Časopis/Czech Sociological Review* 45 (1): 115–46. doi:10.13060/00380 288.2009.45.1.06.

Sorainen, A. 2018. "How the Inheritance System Thinks? – Queering Kinship, Gender and Care in the Legal Sphere," in *Law, Politics, and Gender Binary*, Agha, P., ed.,. London: Routledge, 81–103.

Srinivasan, R. T. 2019. "Possible Impossibles between Area and Queer." *GLQ* 25 (1): 125–130.

Stasińska, A. 2018. *Socjologia Pary. Praktyki Intymne w Związkach Nieheteroseksualnych*. Kraków: Nomos.

–––. 2020. "Tender Gestures in Heteronormative Spaces. Displaying Affection in Public by Families of Choice in Poland." *Gender, Place & Culture* 29 (2), 177–200.

Streib-Brzic, U., Quadflieg, C., Zavirsek, D., Sobočan, A., Schmitt, I., Gustavson, M. & Pan, M. 2011. *School is Out?! Comparative Study "Experiences of Children from Rainbow Families in School" Conducted in Germany, Sweden, and Slovenia*. Berlin: Humboldt-Universität.

Stuvøy, I. 2018. *Parenthood at a Price: Accounting for the Viability of Transnational Surrogacy*. Doctoral dissertation, NTNU, Trondheim, Norway.

Sullivan, N. 2004. "Being-Exposed: 'The poetics of sex' and other matters of tact" *Transformations* 8, Regions of sexuality. http://www.transformationsjournal.org/wp-content/uploads/2017/01/Sullivan_Transformations08.pdf

Štambuk, M., Milković, M. & Maričić, A. 2019. "Motivation for Parenthood among LGBTIQ People in Croatia: Reasons for (Not) Becoming a Parent." *Revija Za Sociologiju* 49 (September): 149–73. https://doi.org/10.5613/rzs.49.2.2.

Štambuk, M., Tadić, M., Milković, M. & Maričić, A. 2019. "Pathways to Parenthood among LGBTIQ People in Croatia: Who Wants to Become a Parent and How?" *Revija Za Sociologiju* 49 (September): 175–203. https://doi.org/10.5613/rzs.49.2.3.

Švab, A. & Kuhar, R. 2005a. *The Unbearable Comfort of Privacy: The Everyday Life of Gays and Lesbians*. Ljubljana: Peace Institute, Institute for Contemporary Social and Political Studies.

–––. 2005b. "The Unbearable Comfort of Privacy – the Everyday Life of Gays and Lesbians." *Social Analyses*. 1 January 2005. http://pdc.ceu.hu/archive/00003433/.

–––. 2014. "The Transparent and Family Closets: Gay Men and Lesbians and Their Families of Origin." *Journal of GLBT Family Studies* 10 (1–2): 15–35.

Tadić, M. & Štambuk, M. 2019. "LGBTIQ Parenthood in Croatia: Experiences and Perceptions." *Revija Za Sociologiju* 49 (September): 143–48.

Takács, J. 2018. "Limiting Queer Reproduction in Hungary." *Journal of International Women's Studies* 20 (1): 68–80.

Thompson, C. 2005. *Making Parents: The Ontological Choreography of Reproductive Technologies*. Cambridge, MA: MIT Press.

Tlostanova, M. 2015. "Can the post-Soviet think? On coloniality of knowledge, external imperial and double colonial difference." *Intersections* 1 (2): 28–58.

Turcan, P, Prochazka, M., Pokorny, P., Kvintova, J., Sigmund, M. & Sedlata Juraskova, E. 2020. "Desire for Parenthood and Associated Trends in Czech Lesbian Women." *Sexual Medicine* 8 (4): 650–59

Twine Winddance, F. 2015. *Outsourcing the Womb: Race, Class and Gestational Surrogacy in a Global Market*. New York, NY: Routledge.

Uibo, R. 2021. *"And I don't know who we really are to each other." Queers doing close relationships in Estonia*. Stockholm: Södertörn University.

Wahlström Henriksson, H. & Goedecke, K., eds. 2021. *Close Relations: Family, Kinship, and Beyond*, S.l.: Springer.

Weeks, J., Heaphy, B. & Donovan, C. 2001. *Same sex intimacies: Families of choice and other life experiments*. London: Taylor and Francis.

Weaver, L. 2013. "Kinship." *Contemporary Theatre Review* 23 (1): 43–4.

Weston, K. 1991. *Families we choose: Lesbians, gays, kinship*. New York: Columbia University Press.

PART 1
Queer/ing Reproduction and the Grammars of Kinship

1. Re-queering Reproduction:
Queer Kinship, 'Reproductive Third Party'
and the Incest-taboo

Jenny Gunnarsson Payne

Since Judith Butler (2002) published her seminal text "Is kinship always already heterosexual?" we have seen an increasing number of nation states in different parts of the world legalising same-sex marriage, often (but not always) granting these couples equal formal rights to form families by way of adoption or assisted reproduction. Third-party reproduction (reproductive arrangements using either a gamete donor or a surrogate or both)[1] has become an increasingly accessible and normalised way of forming a family in many regions – especially in the West – not just for heterosexual couples but also single people, same-sex couples and (albeit to a much lesser extent) other relationship constellations. On the one hand, this development has helped many involuntarily childless people of different genders and sexualities to reproduce and form families that include children and having these relationships legally recognised. As such, it has doubtlessly contributed immensely to de-naturalising – and, some would say, queering – cultural conceptions of parenthood, reproduction and family. In terms of kinship, we may say that this development has diversified the meanings of what can be counted as kinship and who can count as kin by de-naturalising biology and "the genetic link". Some voices have argued that this has led to a "reproductive imperative" by further universalising the desire to have one's

---

[1] For lack of a better term, this text uses the terms "third reproductive party" and "third-party reproduction" as an umbrella term for all reproductive arrangements that involve the gametes or reproductive labour of persons outside of the parental constellation (regardless of how many parents are involved). Another term that has been proposed to name what I here call reproductive third parties is "reproductive collaborators". As we shall see, I would like to reserve this term to specific situations where the relationship between the reproductive parties is one characterised by a more equal relationship than e.g., most transnational commercial surrogacy arrangements today are.

"own", preferably, biological children through the contribution of one's own DNA or through gestation. As noted by several scholars, the last few decades have seen the emergence of stronger normative incentives to reproduce, for straight and queer people alike (Duggan 2002; Franklin 1997; Mamo 2007; Gunnarsson Payne 2016; 2018; Dahl & Gunnarsson Payne 2014; Dahl 2018).[2] The field of empirical and theoretical research investigating kinship in this new bio-cultural context has virtually exploded, often under headings such as "new kinship studies", "critical kinship studies" and "queer kinship studies". Within this plethora of research, much attention has been paid to how kinship and family is "made" through processes of what adoption scholar Signe Howell (2007) calls "kinning" and "de-kinning", that is, the set of practices that link one person to another, thereby making their relation into a relation of kinship – and vice versa, disconnect any reproductive third party from the kinship constellation (e.g., a donor, surrogate, birth mother in adoption). Many empirical studies have focused on gamete donors and surrogates, offering crucial insights into the varied and complex experiences of the persons occupying such positions in this new global "reproscape" (e.g., Inhorn 2010; Mohr 2015). Despite this, I argue, the positions of reproductive third parties remain significantly under-theorised, not least in relation to the queer kinship constellations which they make possible. It is with this in mind that this chapter shall focus especially on theorising the position of the "reproductive third party", how the process to "de-kin" the third party from the donor or surrogacy conceived child may actually serve to preclude a development towards more equal – and "queerer" – ways of creating queer kinship formations that include children.

---

[2] As some commenters of this text have noted, even more recently, a reverse trend can be discerned, especially in light of climate change, but also major ongoing more or less overlapping crises in Europe and elsewhere (including Russia's full-scale invasion of Ukraine, the energy and fuel crises, soaring food prices and inflation). Moreover, in the wake of rising illiberalism and anti-gender politics, assisted reproductive technologies are in some contexts demonised from religious and ideological perspectives. At the time of writing, however, it is too early to know the extent to which such counter movements and tendencies will influence current repro-normative discourses.

I shall begin by introducing the theoretical framework of kinship grammars I have previously developed in my work on kinning processes in egg-donation and surrogacy (Gunnarsson Payne 2016a & 2016b). Thereafter I shall proceed to discuss how currently predominant forms of kinning in third party reproduction more often than not strive for the simultaneous de-kinning of the reproductive third-party, with the end goal to "disambiguate" the relationship between the reproductive third party and the offspring; to render it, if not always a complete non-relationship then at the very least a non-kinship relationship, as it were.

Importantly, I shall interrogate the extent to which the relationship between off-spring and a third party can ever be entirely disambiguated, and propose that this relationship should rather be called an un-kin position, that is, a third position between parental kin and non-kin, one which is determined precisely because of its inherent ambiguity. Inspired by Claudia Fonseca's (2011) work on Brazilian adoption, I shall also discuss the fact that kinning and de-kinning processes in third-party reproduction on the global fertility market is generally partisan in relation to the intended parents, thereby confirming and perpetuating already existing economic, racial and national inequalities. Through the lenses of ambiguity and partisanship, this essay seeks to unpack and reactivate the queer radical potential of third-party reproduction. I am particularly interested in exploring ways in which queer third-party reproduction can be practiced in a way that is more compatible with reproductive justice, and concomitantly with an intersectional approach, which goes beyond naïve notions of reproductive "choice" (see e.g., Smietana, Thompson & Twine 2018). In doing so I argue that we urgently need to look beyond new forms of "homonormativity", queer liberalism and reproductive imperatives and ask ourselves what can be gained by reintroducing ambiguity into the discussions, and how might this permit us to imagine queer reproduction differently.

In arguing that the position of the "un-kin" occupies a specific position which is neither kin nor non-kin, I shall return to the classical kinship-issue of the incest taboo and argue that it is only by reading third-party reproduction through the lens of this cultural phenomenon that we can adequately begin to theorise the position that reproductive third parties occupy in our contemporary post-IVF culture (Franklin 2013). Finally, I shall argue why acknowledging the inherent ambiguity of the reproductive third party is a necessary step for beginning to explore queerer, less partisan and more just reproductive practices and visions for the future.

What kinship can be: The theory of kinship grammars

In Butler's formulation, kinship is described as "a set of practices that institutes relationships of various kinds which negotiate the reproduction of life and the demands of death". This includes practices that "emerge to address fundamental forms of human dependency, which may include birth, child-rearing, relations of emotional dependency and support, generational ties, illness, dying and death (to name a few)" (Butler 2002: 15). As such, kinship is not only about relationships and practices of love and care, but is also related to issues of property and ownership – including such where persons may be another person's property, and nationalist and racial ideas of "bloodlines" (Butler 2002: 15). While scholars such as Charis Thompson have shown us that kinship is flexible (2005), we also know that it is by no means random, but rather tends to be governed by a set of cultural and legal principles, classificatory systems, or grammars that are "generative of the kinds of material, relational, and cultural worlds that are possible, and for whom" (Franklin & McKinnon 2001: 15).

In my previous work, I have taken the lead from these theoretical ideas and have begun developing a theory of kinship grammars that, I argue, offers a framework through which it is possible to retain the idea that kinship is indeed contingent and flexible, while at the same time it tends to be governed by contextually determined articulatory principles that have decisive consequences for human relationships, including its legal, social and emotional aspects. As such, the theory of kinship grammars does not intend to offer a "grand theory" removed from everyday experiences and cultural practices. Rather it is formulated with the aim to, as Clifford Geertz has put it, stay "close to the ground" in a way that allows us to produce "thick descriptions" of the ways in which kinship is actually lived (Geertz 1973), while at the same time offering concepts that have explanatory value valid beyond the specific local setting of an individual study.[3] The "ground" to which my formulation of this theory originally refers – that is, the empirical reality and experiences through which it theorises – is mainly my research in the field of kinship and assisted reproduction. This includes my own empirical research on the Nordic region (Sweden in particular), but also on readings of the vast empirical literature in the fields of kinship studies and third-party reproduction that has been produced mainly (but not exclusively) in the Euro-American context.[4] Importantly, however, the framework is formulated to be flexible enough for other scholars to "take it and run with it" in other empirical contexts. Indeed, it is only by trying it out that its more general interpretative utility can be confirmed or contradicted.

I argue that conceptualising kinship in terms of contextually determined grammars helps us to see how the types of relationships that we call kinship are "governed by a set of historically and culturally contextual articulatory principles" (Gunnarsson Payne 2018: 68). Put differently, these articulatory principles govern

---

[3] This is why the identification of a specific kinship grammar must necessarily be retroductive in character (Howarth & Glynos 2007) and entails a movement between empirical material as well as extensive contextual research into the emergence and possible transformation of a specific kinship grammar.

[4] Despite its limitations, for the purpose of this text, I have chosen to use the term Euro-American kinship as an umbrella term to designate the *dominant* ways in which kinship has commonly been regulated and oftentimes (but far from always) practiced and understood. As such, it is not meant to capture all the different ways in which human beings in the region form kinship and affinity, but should rather be understood as an overarching hegemonic discourse (with some internal variations) that has a major impact on cultural norms, legislations and policy, which in turn affect people's everyday lives in multiple ways (including access to assisted reproduction and recognition as actual or potential parents). Although there are certainly individual, local, national and regional variations within this overarching discourse, the similarities are striking enough, and, indeed a crucial condition of emergence for the transnational fertility industry and the ways in which its services are practiced and marketed. For a good discussion on the complexities, usefulness and problems of thinking in terms of Euro-American kinship, see Edwards (2006).

articulatory processes that "link together" specific persons and establishes lines of demarcation between, first, those who are included in this specific kinship constellation and those who are excluded from it (that is, between kin and non-kin), and, second, to differentiate between various kinship positions in a specific kinship constellation. These demarcations and differentiations, in turn, have consequences not only for which legal rights and responsibilities these persons have to each other (including inheritance rights, and responsibilities of care and provision), but also for affective ties and social expectations in a given historical, political and cultural context (see also Butler 2002; Strathern 1996).

Despite the use of the linguistic term "grammars", then, the concept seeks to capture how kinship emerges, how it is sustained or interrupted through practices that articulate a plethora of linguistic and symbolic (e.g., biological and kinship vocabularies and symbols), material elements (e.g., biological substances and processes, technological equipment), and affective investments (e.g., romantic love, parental attachment). The practices through which kinship may be articulated include, but are not limited to, medical and legal practices, monetary exchange and responsibility, practices of care and love, and practices of conflict, discipline and punishment. Considering the complex entanglements that constitute kinship, it is no wonder that kinship has turned out to be so flexible (see Thompson 2005)!

Kinning as rule-following

In my own work, I have previously discussed how kinship grammars such as *genetics, epigenetics, gestation* and *parental intent* are negotiated in different ways when determining parenthood (and "natural motherhood") in egg-donation and surrogacy in different legal and cultural contexts. In this work, I have shown that kinship grammars might be best understood as providing a set of principles that can be differently applied in various settings to disambiguate the inherently ambiguous phenomenon that is kinship (see also Thompson 2005).[5] Drawing on Ludwig Wittgenstein and political theorist Aletta Norval's Wittgensteinian notion of political grammars, we can say that kinship grammars can never tell us what kinship "really" is, but rather tell us how we shall delimit "what may *count* as possible descriptions" of kinship (Norval 20017: 7, emphasis added, see also Gunnarsson Payne 2016: 488). Though not an idealist concept in the philosophical sense, it is certainly anti-essentialist; for Wittgenstein, the very essence of an object is determined by grammar: "Grammar tells what kind of object anything is." (1953/2001: §371, 373). In other words, kinship grammars tell us what "counts" as kinship, and who "counts" as kin in a given context (e.g., historical, cultural) or specific domain (e.g., legal, medical).

Such grammars, then, provide us with the rules to determine the "sameness" of objects (or subjects): in order to point out, for instance, that my mother has a quality of "sameness" in relation to other mothers in the world, I need a rule to apply in order to determine what this "motherness" consists of. Depending on what "rule" we will apply in determining who "counts" as a mother, we will simply draw different conclusions. A crucial contribution of the Wittgensteinian perspective is his notion of *rule-following*. This allows us to consider how the application of a "rule" is not external to the rule, but rather how, through being "applied", the rule itself changes (Wittgenstein [1953] 2001). Importantly, it is through the application of a certain rule in a new context that grammars may evolve over time, and through which the need for new ways of thinking kinship may create new grammars, for instance in the form of hybrid-grammars. Different kinship grammars may peace-fully co-exist within a specific context or even within the same family, or sometimes grammars may conflict and a decision on which rule should be applied may be necessary (for example through legal processes, or psychological or relational processing). It is very easy to see how this is related to queer kinship, whereby

[5] It is precisely because kinship is inherently ambiguous that such grammars are necessary to determine the relationships between people, and this is also why the very application of a grammar is never mere "repetition" but rather *iteration*, in the Derridean sense of the word, including both repetition and alteration in the same move (Derrida 1988: 7).

previously existing principles of kinship have been practiced by non-straight people (most often couples), thereby changing the meaning of what "counts" as family and who "counts" as a parent. As scholars of queer kinship and reproduction have shown, this is applicable not least when it comes to the emergence of new ways of forming kinship- and family bonds through the use of medically assisted reproduction (see e.g., Mamo 2007; 2013; Dahl 2018; Nordqvist & Smart 2015). By utilising treatments such as donor insemination, egg-freezing, culturally available kinship grammars that determine parenthood have become rearticulated, and some-times – though far from always – normalised and sedimented in law (see e.g., Tinnerholm Ljungberg 2015).

The partisan flexibility of kinship and
the position of the "un-kin"

By coining the term ontological choreography, Charis Thompson describes the "dynamic coordination of the technical, scientific, kinship, gender, emotional, legal, political and financial aspects of ART clinics" (2005: 8). She shows that the articulation of pro-creative intent in third-party reproduction necessarily requires a lot of labour, often over an extended period of time. As she writes, it "is made manifest and followed when kinship is sufficiently dis-ambiguated to pre-empt conflict" (Thompson 2005: 147–148, em-phasis added). In egg-donation, for example, it is common that the kinship grammar of genetics is downplayed in favour of kinship grammars of parental intent, reproductive labour (such as mother-ing practices, pregnancy and childbirth) or even epigenetics. In gestational surrogacy, the situation is the opposite; the repro-ductive labour involved in surrogacy is not intended to function as a kinning process at all – especially not from a legal or commercial point of view. What both of these kinship grammars share, how-ever, is that they "disambiguate" parental kinship bonds not only by kinning the intended parents with the child (legally, socially and emotionally) but also by de-kinning the reproductive third party as well as this person's offspring from other parental constellations, who, were another kinship grammar to be applied, would have been potential parental or sibling candidates. As Thompson shows in detail, such disambiguation requires what can best be described as emotional, linguistic and psychological labour that mobilises various ideas of kinship (including ideas of genetics, gestation or ethnicity and race) so as to establish the intended parents as the "real" parents (Thompson 2005).

That kinning processes to establish parental kinship in third-party reproduction is an emotional process that may take place over an extended period of time is also evident in Helena Ragonés pioneering work on US surrogacy whereby surrogates and intended mothers continuously perform "kinship work" to disambiguate the relationship between mother, surrogate and child (Ragoné 1994: 352–353, see also Kroløkke & Hvidtfeldt Madsen 2014; Teman 2010). Indeed, the whole vocabulary that has emerged in the wake of assisted reproduction – such as "donor", "gestational carrier" and "diblings" – serves a crucial purpose in disambiguation processes to determine who is kin and who is non kin (see e.g., Cahn 2013: 7). The naming and re-naming of different positions of relatedness is a crucial aspect of renegotiating "the extent to which kinship is part of the pregiven natural order of things and the extent to which it is shaped by human engagements" (Carsten 2004: 6, 9).

As Claudia Fonseca has argued in her work on adoption, in practice, the flexibility of kinship tends to be interpreted and practiced in partisan ways, in favour of adoptive parents rather than the birth mother (2011: 7). While adoption and third-party reproduction (whether it involves a donor or a surrogate, or both) are not fully comparable due to differences in initial reproductive intent, there are still some useful lessons to be drawn from Fonseca's observation surrounding the "partisan flexibility" of kinship also for the context of third-party reproduction. In commercial surrogacy, contractual agreements and monetary transactions, support disambiguation by rendering invalid the surrogate's potential claims to be a parent. Some previous research shows that some parents through surrogacy speak of the wish for a "clean transaction" as a way of cancelling out any felt obligations for a future relationship with the surrogate (Murphy 2015; Thompson 2005).

Complexifying this picture somewhat, Marcin Smietana (2017; see also Strathern 1992), has argued that payment does not necessarily exclude the possibility of continued relationships that resemble a form of non-parental kinship relations, or "affinity ties". He has argued that in his research on gay fathers through surrogacy in the US, affective narrative frames of altruism and gift-giving coexist with neoliberal frames of agency, thereby serving to actually facilitate commodification. In other words, one might say that what is disambiguated through payment is not necessarily the surrogate's kinship – or kinship-like – position *per se*, but rather the parental rights and responsibilities that come with it, as well as the intended parents' obligations towards the surrogate. In this sense, while such relationships might on many levels – precisely because they acknowledge the third party – be less violent than surrogacy arrangements (or adoption processes for that matter) with starker economic inequalities between the parties involved and "cleaner" breaks between them, they cannot be said to be any less partisan. The proverbial cards, are, so to speak, in the hands of the commissioning parents, who because of the partisan nature of commercial surrogacy can decide whether they would like to form such affinity ties with the surrogate who bore their children or not. Considering that we also know from research that many surrogates do prefer some kind of relationship or continued contact after pregnancy, and that moreover there is evidence that some experience disappointment and grief when this does not occur (e.g., see Teman 2019), any scholar who argues for reproductive justice and believes that surrogacy may, at least under certain circumstances, play a role to achieve it, needs to take this evidence seriously.

The similarity between all of these cases is that the applied kinship grammar does not only serve to "kin" the intended parents with the offspring, but it also simultaneously disarticulates, or de-kins, the reproductive third party, thereby constituting the reproductive third party as, precisely, a "third party" rather than a parent. Unlike the ways in which birthparents in adoption have often been construed as unfit for parenting or even "'unnatural', 'irresponsible', or 'shameful'" as a way to normalise adoption practices (including the norm of the "clean break"), in third-party reproduction, donors (especially egg-donors) and surrogates tend to be represented as altruistic and selfless, which in turn often serves to "gloss over disturbing inequalities" on the global fertility market (Fonseca 2011: 312; 334).

But regardless of whether we speak of "clean break" adoption, contractual surrogacy or gamete donation, and entirely regardless of whether the relationship is exploitative or not, the most important point to make here is that the very fact that a de-kinning has to take place in order to disambiguate their position, means that the position of the third party cannot be understood as merely non-kin, but something that perhaps would be better described as un-kin. The "un-" in the term "un-kin" is meant to denote a similar meaning as in "un-done", meaning that we cannot ignore the fact that what it now "is" has been preceded by something else, even if that something else might only have been an unrealised potential. The consequence of this is that this "before", or this "unrealised potential" that gave rise to the need to disambiguate the relation-ship to begin with can never be entirely forgotten, but only "repres-sed" insofar as its potential may, under certain (contingent) condi-tions, be re-activated. In Jeanette Edwards' words:

> Kinship is not neutral. As Marilyn Strathern remarks, it has 'certain built-in effects' (1999: 69). It connects persons to other persons in their absence, and in so doing can disconnect them from others who are present. It is not merely information which can be used or not used to good or bad effect but a thread of identity which once known cannot be unknown. (Edwards 2004: 768)

With this in mind, I argue that it is necessary to re-think the posi-tion of the reproductive third party, as well as any offspring that has been produced by this third party as part of a different repro-ductive constellation to get away from simplified "either-or" models of kinship in third-party reproduction. Identifying and acknowledging the position of the third party, I believe is a crucial step towards visualising alternative reproductive visions using medically assisted reproduction, ones that are more compatible with a reproductive justice approach and which are truly based on arrangements between reproductive collaborators (rather than buyers and sellers of reproductive tissue and labour).

The un-kin and the incest-taboo: Bringing sex back into kinship (at least for a moment)

What constitutes the position of the un-kin? What, precisely, is it that demarcates it from simply non-kin? One aspect of this can be seen in the possibility of "reactivation" of a previously unrealised potential of kinship (which would differ from, say a marriage, where the union is what activates such a bond to begin with). Some aspects of "reactivated" kinship connections have been discussed in relation to donor-conceived people searching for donors or donor-siblings, as well as the consequences caused by the medicalisation of kinship.

Empirically, we know from examples of donor-conception that donor-conceived people and their parents have for some time organised through online tools – the most well-known being the US-based Donor Sibling Registry (DSR) – to identify their anonymous donors as well as other people conceived with sperm from the same donor. For a significant number of these people, the motivation for searching for genetic relatives and/or the new relationships with genetic relatives to which the search has given rise have been framed in positive terms of identity and kinship (e.g., Turner & Coyle 2000; Freeman et al. 2009; Jadva et al. 2010; Andreassen 2017). Another form of "reactivation" of forgotten or repressed kinship based on genetics has been discussed in Kaja Finkler's work on the medicalisation of kinship. She argues that this development has constituted new forms of kinship relations based solely on biogenetic connections, rather than love and choice. Biomedicine, she claims "insists on uniting those who may not choose to be connected" (Finkler 2001: 239).

In order to theorise the position of the un-kin, we also need to take a look at the hitherto under-researched yet very specific aspect that firmly sets the un-kin apart from the non-kin, and this is the incest taboo. Indeed, following Edwards again, it is clear that "Incest acts as a conceptual break to biotechnological manipulation of gametes, which are already related, outside of bodies" (2004: 768). The reason to look at third party reproduction through the lens of the incest taboo – despite the term's uncomfortable connotations with norm-breaking, scandal, abuse, and sexual misconduct – is that it helps us to understand what in a specific cultural and historical context is understood as something that is "too close", or "close in the wrong way" (Edwards 2004), and that this tends to be regulated through cultural norms of sexual prohibition.[6]

It's the sex that makes the parents – or is it?

As Aaron Goodfellow has pointed out so poignantly "one could argue that the very predicaments associated with determining the relationship between sex and kinship" has haunted kinship studies since its very beginning (or, as Goodfellow states, this conundrum even launched the discipline of anthropology itself) (2015). It is commonly said that in our post-IVF world, sex and reproduction have ultimately become disconnected (e.g., Braidotti 1994) – and there are certainly examples of people who have created well-functioning (though rarely – or at least normally involving considerable strategising – legally recognised) family constellations with children without sexual relationships between every adult involved. Nonetheless, parental kin is still largely regulated around an assumption that there is a sexual relationship between the parents (Dahl 2014). Consider, for example, David Schneider's now classical formulation of cognatic and conjugal kinship: while the norm prescribes that there "should be no sexual intercourse between blood relatives, for their love is cognatic ... there should be, as a sign of love, *and* as love itself, sexual intercourse between husband and wife, for their love is conjugal" (Schneider 1980: 60). Although this definition today, especially in cultures that recognise legal

---

[6] Importantly, norms concerning what is considered incestuous behaviour varies across historical and cultural contexts, which not least becomes clear when taking into account different views on cousin marriage, or legal regulations between in-laws in different historical times (see e.g. Åkesson 2000).

unions (marriage or partnerships) between persons legally considered "of the same sex", the assumption of a sexual relationship is often a pre-requisite for access to medically assisted reproduction and/or legal recognition of a non-biological parent's parental status (Dahl 2014: 150). For instance, it is quite obvious that legislation on adoption and assisted reproduction generally assumes a sexual relationship between two persons who seek to become parents (it is generally not possible to apply for either if explicitly done so as platonic friends). And, contrary, a person who has a sexual relationship with an intended parent is generally not legally considered a donor or a surrogate, but rather a parent, if a child is conceived as a result of their intercourse. Indeed, the parental status after, for example, a one-night-stand can be legally imposed regardless of any parental intent.

Conversely, while Schneider discusses the symbolic centrality of the heterosexual coitus in the constitution of kinship, the position of the reproductive third party is determined by the opposite, namely, that this person may not be a sexual partner of either or both of the intended parent(s); this is generally one of the criteria that makes the third party into a third party rather than a legally recognised parent. To be clear, it means not only that there is no assumption or expectation of a sexual relationship between parent and third party, but rather that the position of the third party requires an assumption – or even a strict prohibition – of such a relationship. But at the same time, just as the parental kinship relation between parents and offspring is defined by sexual prohibition, so is the relationship between third party and offspring, as well as any offspring between, for example, donor siblings (and in Edwards' example as discussed below, between genetically unrelated offspring who have been gestated by the same surrogate).

What determines the relationship between children conceived by the same donor or surrogate not-kin in relation to each other's parent(s), then, is the absence of a sexual relationship, but what determines their position as un-kin in relation to each other, as well as any reproductive third party, is sexual prohibition. This dual sexual prohibition constitutes the reproductive third party as not-quite-kin – and one which in hegemonic understandings of the reproductive third party disqualifies them from being included in any form of, to use Schneider's (1980) expression, "enduring solidarity" (diffuse or not), even though gratitude towards the third party is often expressed in publicly available narratives. Needless to say, these hegemonic understandings of third-party reproduction do not prevent some from forming alternative, or queerer, parental kinship constellations that transgress these norms, but these very norms and their materialisation into structures, such as legislation and social security systems, generally require ample negotiation among the reproductive parties, often causing social confusion, with agreements rarely recognised by law.

Traces of ambiguity: The incest-taboo at the interface of biological inheritance and intimacy

In donor-conception, the incest-taboo most often makes itself known in terms of anxieties about possible relationships between donor-conceived offspring. This anxiety also underpins many regulations that limit the number of donations that can be made, and to how many families. On the one hand, considering the actual risks of inbreeding, regulations that prevent two persons who are closely genetically related from reproducing using their own gametes makes sense. On the other hand, as Jeanette Edwards has demonstrated in her study of European kinship (with English and Latvian ethnographic data), the incest taboo as manifested in her interviewees' narratives is also articulated with symbolic and moral meanings that far exceed "purely" medical risks. Worries about the consequences of inbreeding among donor-conceived people who may not know of their shared genetic ancestry were often expressed in her interviews, and she draws the following conclusion:

> It is said that offspring, from such a union, will inevitably display some kind of deformity (physical or mental). It is as if the child not only acts as a receptacle for the transgressive relationship of its parents (embodying that relationship), but it also makes it manifest (and known). The child embodies the freight of its parents' transgression, incubates it and makes it explicit and visible. Furthermore, the effect is enduring. (2006: 135)

The fear of incest is also commonly manifested in the popular press, when gamete donation is discussed; the widespread use of sperm donation is often said to have caused a "ticking time bomb". In one example, "the ticking bomb" is seen as caused by a man who donates sperm privately, outside of the medical system.

The British tabloid newspaper, *The Sun*, for example, reported that "Family campaigners have slammed Declan Rooney, 43, calling him a 'ticking time bomb' because his work is not overseen by medics" and explained that because he donates within a radar of 50 miles around the town of Middlesbrough, there is a risk that the children born as a result of his donations will "potentially live close to each other, meaning that they may go on to have kids". In response to the criticism, Rooney is said to have insisted never to sleep with his clients, or to receive any monetary compensation apart from travel costs for delivery (Warrander, 7 December 2015). This reassurance can be read as an attempt on behalf of Rooney to calm the reader that this is a respectable practice, and one that further disambiguates his relationship to the recipients precisely as a donor rather than a parent.

But the fear of unintended incest features also in articles on the more controlled fertility industry. In another article on the topic of sperm donation Ross Clark writes in the conservative magazine *The Spectator* that "[i]t is hard to think of a code of behaviour which is common to all societies on earth, let alone to most other species too – except, that is, for the avoidance of incest." He adds that "even cockroaches" have developed a strategy to avoid inbreeding but that despite the human species, despite our increased understanding of the risks of genetics, are dismantling "the social infrastructure that guards against it" (Clark, 25 August 2018). This article – which is tellingly entitled "Sperm donors and the incest trap: When one man can anonymously father up to 800 babies, what happens if those children meet?" – sees not only the anonymity and quantity of sperm donation as the main risks, but also argues that the chances of these specific children meeting and falling in love is further heightened by something called genetic sexual attraction (GSA).

In short, GSA is the idea that genetic relatives who have not grown up together are more likely than others to experience an overwhelmingly strong sexual attraction to each other, because unlike those who have, they have not become habituated to each other and therefore not developed the sexual aversion that normally acts as a deterrent protecting against incest. This type of "negative sexual imprinting" between family members is known as "the Westermarck effect", after the Finnish anthropologist Edward Westermarck, who was the first to substantially investigate the phenomenon (1921). While there has been further evidence for the Westermarck effect (negative sexual imprinting) the existence of GSA has been scientifically questioned (Rantala & Marcinkowska 2011).

Despite this, however, anecdotal evidence of GSA between adoptees and their birth family is repeatedly reported in the media and is intermittently mentioned in articles using the metaphor of the ticking bomb. For instance, *The Telegraph* reported in September 2016 about an alleged case of GSA between a birth mother and her adoptive daughter in the US, where they had ended up marrying each other (Gill, 9 September 2016). In this article, which is entitled "Disgusted by incest. Genetic sexual attraction is real and, on the rise", Charlotte Gill uses known examples of when birth mothers' parents and their adopted children meet and fall in love to warn for the dangers of gamete donation:

> Perhaps one of the biggest causes for concern is egg and sperm donation. Over the last few decades, it has never been easier for organisations – and individuals – to dish out large quantities of eggs and sperm to different locations. The last Human Fertilisation & Embryology (HFEA) report shows that sperm donations, especially, have been rising since 2005 – with many coming from the US and Denmark.

> This seed sprinkling will essentially mean lots of children go through life without ever knowing their biological father and/or mother, and other important close relatives, in the time where the desenticisation effect[7] should happen.
>
> Should they never meet with their (unknown) biological family, then they will never put themselves at risk of experiencing GSA. But such reunions have become much easier – especially as new rules brought out by the HFEA mean that any child conceived on or after April 2005 can now seek information on their parents when they turn 19. (Charlotte Gill, *The Telegraph*, 9 September 2016)

To be clear, what interests me here is neither whether GSA is a valid scientific term nor whether the reported cases of the phenomenon are true. Rather, it serves as an example of how the relatedness of the de-kinned donor as well as offspring of the same donor is being reactivated through the incest taboo, where the definition of persons that are "too close" to engage in a romantic or sexual relationship are defined by applying the kinship grammar of genetics.

Furthermore, based on her ethnography, Edwards proposes that the incest taboo was also manifest in her interviews in relation to intra-family gamete donation, where no genetic birth defects were at stake. Instead, her interviewees express reservation against such a practice because it is felt to upset the clear distinctions between kinship positions, thereby making the role of the child as a "glue" that binds the parents together ambiguous by risking to connect the "wrong" persons with each other. She argues that in both Lithuanian and English kinship, childlessness – whether voluntary or involuntary – is therefore tenuous (2006: 135). Hence, she argues:

---

[7] "The desenticisation effect" here refers to the argument within GSA-theory that e.g., genetic siblings who grow up together are "desenticised" from feeling any sexual attraction to each other. Conversely, the proponents of these ideas argue, genetic siblings who do not grow up together, or a child and a birth parent who are separated and re-united after the child has grown up, risk feeling a strong attraction to each other, which risk turning to a strong sexual attraction (and hence incest). This is what is also referred to as "negative sexual imprinting" or "the Westermarck effect", as mentioned above.

> If the child embodies the relationship between its parents, it has
> the potential of creating a relationship between where there was
> no relationship before. Thus the possibility of a brother donating
> sperm to his brother gives people pause for thought partly
> because the ensuing child both contains, and develops from, the
> mingled body substances of its father's brother and its mother.
> (2006: 135)

Based on this, Edwards concludes that the incest taboo is not so much about sex, but rather the creation of a child – with or without genetic risks of inbreeding. I agree with her that this calls for more detailed ethnographic research on different articulations of the incest taboo and assisted reproduction, and how it is played out in different contexts that may differ from the ones she studied (not least in relation to non-heterosexual kinship constellations). Although, to my knowledge, the research on this topic is virtually non-existent, there is anecdotal evidence to the contrary, that rather supports Edwards' hypothesis that the incest taboo designates what is seen as "too close" (or, I would argue, "close in the wrong way") – and that this may indeed involve same-sex relationships. The fact that none of the media reports referred to in this essay mention that the risk of GSA would only be a problem for heterosexual couples who might reproduce using their own gametes may speak in favour of Edwards' hypothesis, yet anecdotal evidence of more "scandalous" stories of GSA between genetic relatives of "the same sex" (as referred to above) speak to the contrary.

Based on this, it is safe to say that even when the rule of the incest taboo is articulated within a kinship grammar of genetics, it is genetic relatedness that defines who is considered "too close" or "close in the wrong way" – even if more research is needed to investigate its various permutations in non-straight or non-reproductive relationships. But interestingly, Edwards' interviewees also express a similar disgust against potential sexual relationships between people who have been conceived using the same surrogate, even in the absence of a genetic link (Edwards 2004: 769–770). Rather than being an issue of either sex or reproduction, therefore, the separation between the two in third-party reproduction seems to have given rise to a complexification of the incest taboo that allows for a sliding between them, to the extent that we can today speak of a "fragmentation" not only, as is commonly said, of motherhood, but also of the incest taboo. This, fragmentation, I argue, needs to be thoroughly investigated empirically in order to better understand that the new reproductive relationships (e.g., surrogates, gamete donors, donor siblings) cannot simply be considered non-kinship relations. Existing research on how people engaging in or being conceived through third party reproduction themselves describe their relationships (or non-relationships) to each other therefore needs to be complemented with substantial research on the different permutations of the incest taboo, since this will help us to shed further light on the consequences of current practices of de-kinning in third-party reproduction, and perhaps to open up for a debate surrounding the direction of future policies that better take into account the complexities of kinship and third-party reproduction. While we know from decades of research on queer kinship that a surrogate is indeed not simply "a mother", and a gamete donor not a parent, it seems to me that current Euro-American cultural understandings, legislations, and policies of parenthood that merely allows for the recognition of a relationship as either one of kin or one of non-kin is inhibiting rather than supporting the subversive potential of queer kinship.

Re-ambiguating the third party, requeering reproduction

As Claude Lévi-Strauss famously argued, the fact that "the prohibition of incest constitutes a rule need scarcely be shown". Reminding us that "the prohibition of marriage between close relatives may vary in its field of application according to what each group defines as a close relative" he argues that the incest taboo is on the one hand universal because it exists in all known groups and is "sanctioned by no doubt variable penalties, ranging from immediate execution of the guilty parties to widespread probation, sometimes merely ridicule", but on the other hand that the definitions of what constitutes incest as well as its consequences varies widely between different cultural contexts (Lévi-Strauss 1969: 8–9). Expanding on Lévi-Strauss' insights, then, the incest taboo can be read as a rule that is applied differently depending on cultural and historical contexts – and considering the Wittgensteinian notion of rule-following, it only becomes logical if the very application of it in the context of third-party reproduction ends up transforming the rule itself. Considering that queer reproductive practices using gamete donation and surrogacy have become commonplace in large parts of the Euro-American world, it follows logically that these practices have transformed the very rules that govern what kinship "is".

Entangled within this process are two parallel and sometimes contradictory processes whereby discourses of biological kinship have become at the same time more *and* less predominant. On the one hand, the desire for "biological" children (predominantly articulated through the kinship grammar of genetics, or "blood") is a crucial "motor" for the fertility industry and treatments such as IVF, egg freezing, surrogacy and donation (in order to ensure a "genetic tie" to one of the parents). On the other hand, there has been an increased tendency to downplay the significance of biological kinship – not least in non-heterosexual parental constellations – in favour of a kinship grammar of parental intent, and an emphasis on parenting as practice and parental love. While the latter serves to de-kin the reproductive third party from the offspring (and, as a consequence, from the parents) the result of the de-kinning, I argue, is however better described as an *un*-kinning, constituting the reproductive third party as un-kin, and as such as only temporarily and partially dis-articulated from the offspring and whose (physical, imaginary or affective) presence is always "threatening" to re-emerge, thereby revealing the fundamental undecidability of kinship in a dislocatory, sometimes conflictual way. Such previously unrealised potential kinship bonds continuously make themselves known in empirical cases of donor-conceived people searching for donors and donor siblings, in donor conceived or adopted people searching for genetic relatives for medical reasons, or even narratives where donors and surrogates in different ways resist the narratives which write them out of the child's lineage (as a surrogate in Amrita Pande's research expressed it, "[i]t might be her egg, but it's my blood", 2009). All of these cases speak of an imagined or felt "closeness" based on a potential kinship bond that has had to be repressed to disambiguate other relationships.

In this chapter, however, I argue that a surer way to identify such relationships – those I have called the un-kin – is to be guided by the incest taboo. Indeed, as opposed to existing examples of reactivated kinship relationships, the incest taboo tells us also where the potential, but not (yet) reactivated kinship relationships are, regardless of whether they are acknowledged by anyone as such or not. It tells us, who in a given context, is rather to be considered un-kin than non-kin – and according to which kinship grammar (be it blood, genetics, gestation, intent or something else which in a given context counts as a kinning-principle). By closely investigating the incest taboo, then, we can learn more about what kinship "is", also in our post-IVF world where sex and reproduction are said to be disconnected and queer reproduction is becoming increasingly normalised. Following from this, I propose to conceptualise the ambiguous positions in third party reproduction, the un-kin, as following:

First, unlike mere non-kin, the un-kin is always a result of a potential ambiguity concerning the kinship bond, whereby one culturally available kinship grammar has been applied in favour of another. The act (or, rather, repeated set of acts) of applying one kinship grammar rather than another is always an act of exercising power, and cannot as such be separated from societal hierarchies, cultural norms, and forms of reproductive stratification. Second, because the un-kin, unlike the position of non-kin, has always emerged as a repression of other potential alternatives, there is always a risk (or chance, depending on perspective) that the position becomes "re-ambiguated" and therefore in need of re-negotiation. Third, the un-kin position always show "traces" of its repressed potentiality and these traces can be empirically observed in the cultural norms of behaviour relative to the un-kin, and particularly so in norms of sexual prohibition (the incest taboo).

Acknowledging the un-kin as an existing albeit ambiguous position in queer kinship, I argue, is an important first step to begin learning to confront, in Claudia Fonseca's words "deeply disturbing processes that speak of living together with others or, on the contrary, of relegating these others to the realm on the non-human" (Fonseca 2011: 334). Even is such de-humanisation far from necessary in third party reproduction, we cannot ignore that it does occur, especially on the global fertility market where inequalities are stark and exploitation does take place. By acknowledging the reproductive third party – by welcoming ambiguity back in – we can begin to visualise other, less stratified and more multifarious reproductive futures. Considering the partisan nature of kinship, which in third party reproduction tends to be flexible mainly in favour of the intended parents, it is worth considering Schneider's formulation of expectations "for how relatives should behave towards each other" – namely through enduring though sometimes diffuse solidarity (Schneider 1980: 61). By daring to acknowledge the un-kin, we might be able to open up and invite them to be included in the expectations of such enduring – more or less diffuse – solidarity. The disambiguation of the reproductive third party as it is generally (though not without exceptions) practiced today, serves precisely to ensure that no such obligations exist between the reproductive third party and the family they contributed to forming. But, may we ask, what does it mean that an increasing number of queer families are made this way (some would say, at the detriment of other, previously more prevalent alternative queer family constellations, with or without children)? What might have been lost on the way? And how can we visualise different reproductive futures? While there is nothing intrinsically "queer" or "conservative" to any type of kinship formation I think there are many good reasons to interrogate and de-naturalise the necessity of disambiguating the reproductive third party altogether. We need to ask ourselves whether there are other ways of constructing "queer kinship", where acknowledging ambiguity may serve as a route to re-queering kinship, as well as the expectations of solidarity that comes with it, in more inclusive and less hierarchical ways.

References

Andreassen, R. 2017. "New Kinships, New Family Formations and Negotiations of Intimacy via Social Media Sites." *Journal of Gender Studies* 26 (3): 361–371.

Braidotti, R. 1994. *Nomadic Subjects: Embodiment and Sexual Difference in Contemporary Feminist Theory*. Cambridge: Cambridge University Press.

Butler, J. 2002. "Is Kinship Always Already Heterosexual?" *differences: A Journal of Feminist Cultural Studies* 1(13): 14–44.

Cahn, N. 2013. *The New Kinship: Constructing Donor-Conceived Families*. New York: New York University Press.

Carsten, J. 2004. *After Kinship*. Cambridge: Cambridge University Press.

Clark, R. 2018. "Sperm Donors and the Incest Trap." *The Spectator* (25 August 2018). Available: https://www.spectator.co.uk/2018/08/sperm-donors-and-the-incest-trap/ (Accessed 12 August 2019).

Dahl, U. 2014. "Not Gay as in Happy, but Queer as in Fuck You: Notes on Love and Failure in Queer(ing) Kinship." *lambda nordica* 19 (3–4): 143–168.

––– 2018. "Becoming Fertile in the Land of Organic Milk: Lesbian and Queer Reproductions of Femininity and Motherhood in Sweden." *Sexualities* 21 (7): 1021–1038.

Dahl, U. & Gunnarsson Payne, J. 2014. "Queer kinship in Europe: Quest editor's Introduction." *lambda nordica* 19 (3–4): 11–28.

Derrida, J. 1988. Limited Inc. Evanston, Illinois: Northwestern University Press.

Duggan, L. 2002. "The New Homonormativity: The Sexual Politics of Neoliberalism," in *Materializing Democracy: Toward a Revitalized Cultural* Politics, Castronovo, R. & Nelson, D. D., eds. Durham, N.C., London: Duke University Press, 175–194.

Edwards, J. 2004. "Incorporating Incest: Gamete, Body and Relation in Assisted Reproduction." *Royal Anthropological Institute* 10 (4): 755–774.

–––. 2006. "Reflecting on the 'Euro' in 'Euro-American' Kinship: Lithuania and the United Kingdom," in *Defining Region: Socio-Cultural Anthropology and Interdisciplinary Perspectives, Part 2*, V. Čiubrinskas & R. Sliužinskas, eds. Vilnius: Acta Historica Universatis Klaipedensis, 129–139.

Finkler, K. 2001. "The Kin in the Gene: The Medicalization of Family and Kinship in American Society." *Current Anthropology* 42 (2): 235–263.

Fonseca, C. 2011. "The de-kinning of birthmothers: Reflections on maternity and being human." *Vibrant: Virtual Brazilian Anthropology* 8 (2): 307–339.

Freeman, T., Jadva, V., Kramer, W. & Golombok, S. 2009. "Gamete Donation: Parents' Experiences of Searching for the Child's Donor Siblings and Donor." *Human Reproduction*, vol. 24: 505–516.

Franklin, S. 1997. *Embodied Progress: A Cultural Account of Assisted Reproduction*. London & New York: Routledge.

–––. 2013. *Relative Values: IVF, Stem Cells, and the Future of Kinship*. Durham: Duke University Press.

Franklin, S. & McKinnon, S. 2001. "Introduction," in *Relative Values: Reconfiguring Kinship Studies*, Franklin, S. & McKinnon, S., eds. Durham: Duke University Press.

Geertz, C. 1973. *The Interpretation of Cultures*. New York: Basic Books

Gill, C. 2016. "Disgusted by Incest? Genetic Sexual Attraction if Real and on the Ruse," *The Telegraph* (9 September 2016). Available: https://www.telegraph.co.uk/family/relationships/disgusted-by-incest-genetic-sexual-attraction-is-real-and-on-the/ (Accessed 12 August 2019).

Goodfellow, A. 2015. *Gay Fathers, their Children and the Making of Kinship*. Fordham: Fordham University Press.

Gunnarsson Payne, J. 2016a. "Grammars of Kinship: Biological Motherhood and Assisted Reproduction in the Age of Epigenetics." *Signs: Journal of Women in Culture and Society* 3 (41): 483–506.

---2016b. "Mattering Kinship: Inheritance, Biology and Egg Donation, Between Genetics and Epigenetics," in *Critical Kinship Studies*, C. Krøløkke et al., eds. London: Rowman & Littlefield: 33–47.

---. 2018. "Autonomy in Altruistic Surrogacy, Conflicting Kinship Grammars and Intentional Multilineal Kinship." *Reproductive Biomedicine and Society Online*, vol. 7: 66–75.

Howell, S. 2007. *The Kinning of Foreigners: Transnational Adoption in a Global Perspective*. Oxford UK: Berghahn Books.

Glynos, J. & Howarth, D. 2007. *Logics of Critical Explanation in Social and Political Theory*. London: Routledge.

Inhorn, M. C. 2010. "'Assisted' Motherhood in Global Dubai: Reproductive Tourists and Their Helpers," in *The Globalization of Motherhood: Deconstructions and Reconstructions of Biology and Care*, W. Chavkin and J. M. Maher, eds., 180–202. New York: Routledge.

Jadva, V., Freeman, T., Kramer, W. & Golombok, S. 2010. "Experiences of Offspring Searching for and Contacting their Donor Siblings and Donor." *Reproductive Biomedicine Online* 20 (4): 523–532.

Kroløkke C. & Hvidtfeldt Madsen, K. 2014. Moderskab(elser): Slægtsskabsøkonomier og moderfølelser i transnational surrogatmoderskab, *Kvinder, Kön & Forskning* 1–2: 70–81.

Lévi-Strauss, C. 1969. *The Elementary Structure of Kinship*. Boston: Beacon Press.

Mamo, L. 2007. *Queering Reproduction: Achieving Pregnancy in the Age of Technoscience*. Durham & London: Duke University Press.

Mamo, L. 2013. "Queering the Fertility Clinic," *Journal of Medical Humanities*, 34 (2): 221–239.

Mohr, S. 2015 "Living Kinship Trouble: Danish Sperm Donors' Narratives of Relatedness." *Medical Anthropology*, 34 (5): 470–484.

Murphy, D. A. 2015. *Gay Men Pursuing Parenthood Via Surrogacy: Reconfiguring Kinship*. Randwick: University of New South Wales Press.

Norval, A. 2007. *Aversive Democracy: Inheritance and Originality in the Democratic Tradition.* Cambridge: Cambridge University Press.

Nordqvist, P. & Smart, C. 2014. *Relative Strangers: Family Life, Genes and Donor Conception.* Basingstoke: Palgrave McMillan.

Pande, A. 2009. "It May Be Her Eggs But It's My Blood: Surrogates and Everyday Forms of Kinship in India." *Qualitative Sociology* 32 (4): 379–397.

Ragoné, H. 1994. *Surrogate Motherhood: Conception in the Heart.* Boulder, Colorado: Westview Press.

Rantala, M. J. & Marcinkowska, U. M. 2011. "The Role of Sexual Imprinting and the Westermarck Effect in Mate Choice in Humans." *Behavioural Ecology and Sociobiology* 65 (5): 859–873.

Schneider, D. M. 1980. *American Kinship: A Cultural Account.* (Second edition) Chicago & London: The University of Chicago Press.

Smietana, M. 2017. "Affective De-Commodifying, Economic De-Kinning: Surrogates' and Gay Fathers' Narratives in U.S. Surrogacy." *Sociological Research Online* 2 (22): 1–13.

Strathern, M. 1996. "Cutting the Network." *The Journal of the Royal Anthropological Institute* 3 (2): 517–535.

Teman, E. 2010. *Birthing a Mother: The Surrogate Body and the Pregnant Self.* Berkeley: University of California Press.

–––. 2019. "The Power of the Single Story: Surrogacy and Social Media in Israel." *Medical Anthropology* 3 (38): 282–294.

Thompson, C. 2005. *Making Parents: The Ontological Choreography of Reproductive Technologies.* Cambridge, Massachusetts: MIT Press.

Tinnerholm Ljungberg, H. 2015. *Omöjliga familjen: Ideologi och fantasi i svensk reproduktionspolitik.* [The Impossible Family: Ideology and Fantasy in Swedish Politics of Reproduction]. Stockholm: Stockholm University Press.

Turner A. J. & Coyle, A. 2000. "What Does it Mean to be a Donor Offspring? The identity Experiences of Adults Conceived by Donor Insemination and the Implications for Counselling and Therapy." *Human Reproduction,* vol. 15: 2041–2051.

Warrander, R. 2015. "UK's Biggest Sperm Donor and Dad of 54 'Has Created an Incest Ticking Time Bomb'." *The Sun,* 7 December 2015. Available: https://www.thesun.co.uk/archives/news/829942/uks-biggest-sperm-donor-and-dad-of-54-has-created-an-incest-ticking-time-bomb/ (Accessed 12 August 2019).

Westermarck, E. 1921. *The History of Human Marriage.* London: Macmillan.

Wittgenstein, L. 1953/2001. *Philosophical Investigations: The German Text with a Revised Translation.* Translated by G. E. M. Anscombe. Oxford: Blackwell.

Åkesson, L. 2000. "Blodsband som förenar och förskräcker. Släktbegreppens komplikationer," in *Arvets kultur. Essäer om genetik och samhälle,* S. Lundin & L. Åkesson, eds. Lund: Nordic Academic Press.

2. Vanilla Democracy:
Sexuality, Parenthood, and Kinship in Greece

Pako Chalkidis[1]

This is not (just) a blowjob[2]

A few years ago, in spring 2014, I followed lengthy discussions on social media about reforms to the Civil Union Act to include same-sex couples, to institutionalise gay marriage and, most importantly, to recognise the same-sex couples' right to parenthood and thus to a family.[3] I came upon an old provocative gay motto posted by one of my Facebook friends that revealed the underlying tension between respectability, perversity and sexuality: "Try and say the word *respectability* with a dick in your mouth. You can't, can you?" Not being able to "say the word *respectability* with a dick in your mouth" refers to the visible and visceral processes of exclusion through which respectability acquires its meanings, in this instance, through, around, and in the throat of a sexualized queer

---

[1] Reprinted with permission from "Vanilla democracy: Sexuality, parenthood, and kinship in Greece," Chalkidou A., 2020. *Sexualities* 25 (5–6), 563–580, Copyright 2020 by SAGE Publications.

[2] This article is reprinted with permission from *Sexualities* and a previous version has been released in Greek at the online journal *Feministiqa* (2018) under the title 'Seksoualikoi thesmoi: Goneikotita kai politikes siggenias stin Ellada'. For constructive comments and important conversations, I thank Ulrika Dahl, Venetia Kantsa and Antu Sorainen. I also particularly thank the participants at *Queer(y)ing Kinship in the Baltic Region* at Södertörn University (2017) and *Shifting Kinship Relations Workshop on Marriage, Sexuality and Family*, University of the Aegean (2019) where versions of this article have been presented.

[3] The press release of the 10th Athens Pride reads: "Equal access to the family Law constitutes a fundamental obligation of a contemporary democracy. The exclusion of certain citizens from Civil Partnership, marriage, childbearing, adoption due to their sexual orientation or gender identity entails their essential and discriminating exclusion from state protection and the deprivation of the safety it involves. It impedes stability in personal life and constitutes an emotional and financial burden in everyday life. Adopting the slogan 'A Family Affair', Athens Pride 2014 highlights the singular concept of family, as it is defined by each LGBT person." The whole press release can be found *here* in Greek (accessed 25 March 2019).

body/mouth, so that certain sexual practices, forms of pleasures, connoted as perversion, effectively render the terms of respectability conspicuous. The tension between respectability, perversity and sexuality gets crystallised into the fleshy materiality of specific forms of sexual gestures that points to the pedagogies of knowledge saturating and spreading beyond the event of a sexual encounter. This motto is not (just) about a blowjob. It is indeed a shift towards viewing sex as one of the most emblematic battlegrounds in contemporary queer kinship politics and theory, in the fight for (the right to) queer parenthood.

Although in the past decade queer kinship theory in Europe has become deeply enmeshed in questions of reproduction and family-making practices, less scholarly attention has been devoted to how ideas about sexual practices and pleasures circulate to define the cultural meanings of parenthood. In this article, through a meticulous analysis of the Greek case,[4] I examine the extent to which notions of parenthood are underpinned by sexual ideologies, the pertinence of which continue to be undervalued even while ubiquitous, in that they imbue contemporary public policies and laws on and beyond kinship. I argue that untangling these knots which tie parenthood with notions of normative sexuality offers paths for further understanding and analysing the exclusion of gays and lesbians from all forms of institutionalised reproduction and thus provides threads for unravelling the very meaning of *institutionality* more broadly.

---

[4] In this article, I build on findings of an extensive policy analysis and the collection of published material of the printed and online publications on the uses of assisted reproductive technology by gay and lesbian people in Greece that I conducted in the context of a three-year research program (September 2012 to September 2015). (In)FERCIT, ((In)Fertile Citizens: On the Concepts, Practices, Politics, and Technologies of Assisted Reproduction in Greece: An Interdisciplinary and Comparative Approach) was co-funded by the European Social Fund and the General Secretariat of Research and Technology, Greece. The research project focused on the detailed, multisided ethnographic account of assisted reproduction concepts, practices, politics and technologies in Greece, relating them to legal issues and human rights on (in)fertility and reproduction.

My theoretical orientation follows and adds to the intersecting trajectories between ethnography on sexuality and research on kinship as they have emerged within the context of anthropological scholarship in Greece in the past decades. Sexuality is still devalued as a field of study in social sciences and humanities in the Greek academy (Yannakopoulos 2006a, 9) and sexuality studies is restricted to "the existence of a few single courses in undergraduate and postgraduate level, thus giving a picture of only partial engagement with the subject and the absence of a systematic academic discourse" (Kantsa 2010). At the same time, kinship remains a recognised and scientifically legitimate field in ethnographic research and theoretical analysis, evidenced by the wide-ranging academic publishing on kinship, courses at the undergraduate and postgraduate levels in anthropology and other social sciences departments, the establishment of permanent teaching posts for kinship-related topics and, consequently, greater allocation of research funding. While scholarship on kinship and sexuality might seem to operate in separate spheres of scientific inquiry, what we witness in the body of academic knowledge production in Greece are narratives in which kinship and sexuality are inextricably intertwined, insofar as both lines of inquiry do not just co-exist but are co-dependent. The story of one inheres in the narration of the other.

Unlike in Western scholarship, where research into sexuality was undertaken primarily in the field of history and literature, the first sexuality research that emerged in Greece during the late nineties and into the new millennium was situated within the field of anthropology (Yannakopoulos 2006a, 10). According to Yannakopoulos (2006a, 10), "this is linked to the privileged – particularly in relation to the other social sciences in Greece – position of gender not only as a field of study but as an analytical tool of the anthropological research of Greek society." Yet, early Greek anthropology from the 1960s onwards focused on kinship and gender and the crafting of personhood through the "domestic model of gender". In other words, in the anthropological research on Greek society, gender and kinship prominently overlapped and operated as analytical mirrors to one another.[5]

In Greek society, where family is institutionalised across the social, cultural and political spectrum, the first ethnographers of sexuality in Greece, although interested primarily in sexuality, could not circumvent the category of kinship in their analysis. This period also witnessed the emergence of the field of "new kinship studies" in anthropology, especially in relation to same-sex relationships and reproductive technologies. Thus, research on sexuality offered an invaluable vehicle to reconsider kinship in Greek society (and the concept of personhood) for further discussion with international co-peers.[6] Indeed, "gender was grafted with sexuality" (Kantsa 2005) in Greek anthropological scholarship. Yet what remains undertheorised is how this "transplantation" in the field of anthropology took place in part through the overlapping spheres of gender, sexuality, and kinship. This epistemic kinning has crafted paths for the emergence of sexuality research in Greece, even as the field of queer/sexuality studies remains a non-institutionalized field in Greek academia. In other words, scholars in Greece created avenues for a hitherto unauthorised field of queer/sexuality studies by grafting sexuality and gender onto one of the most legitimised fields of knowledge in Greek academia and society, namely kinship.[7] Recognising those points of intersection

---

[5] An extensive account of bibliographic references on the study of kinship in Greece is beyond the scope of the present article.

[6] I am indebted to Venetia Kantsa for her invaluable insights.

[7] Ethnographers of sexuality in Greek academia queered the (hetero)epistemic grounds of kinship by including non-heterosexual subjects in research on/around kinship, family, and reproduction and reorienting kinship theorising to sexuality research and vice versa. For example, Venetia Kantsa's (2001) dissertation, the first ethnographic study on female same-sex erotic desires in Greece, emphasises on the invisibility and silence surrounding female same-sex practices. Kantsa highlighted silence as the primary means for sustaining relations with the family of origins. At the same time, she problematised the epistemic silence among anthropologists who have conducted fieldwork in Greece that shared the widespread opinions attributing the invisibility of female same-sex desires "to the linking of female sexuality to a fertility which is so powerful that there can be no perceived need for women to 'express' their sexuality in contexts which cannot lead to procreation" (Loizos and Papataxiarchis, 1991: 229, quoted in Kantsa 2001: 41). Athena Athanasiou (2001, 2006, 2007) has drawn to our attention the assemblage of gender, sexuality, reproduction and the nation by

is crucial for at least two reasons. First, because they constitute a form of epistemic kinning between unequally legitimised fields of academic knowledge production. Second, because they map avenues and terms of existing, envisaging a possible modality of inquiry despite the lack of institutional recognition.

In this article, I follow and add to these trajectories of kinning. Drawing on state policies on kinship and reproduction, public discourse, and the demand of the LGBTQ+ movement for institutional recognition and consolidation of families with same-sex parents, I scrutinise three central questions, each of which unfolds within the respective sections of this chapter. First, what does the tension between sexuality and respectability more broadly teach us about the sexual underpinnings of institutionalised parenthood and thus, about the terms of institutionality? Secondly, how does the analytical conjoining of sexual practices and pleasures with the right to family and parenthood weave together the normative fabric of kinship? Thirdly, what does it tell us about the racial[8] prerequisites of democratic inclusion, institutional recognition, and state protection in the face of "deviant" sexual desires, practices, and professions? Finally, what other crucial alliances and

focusing on discourses on the "highly politicized anxiety" over the population decrease in modern Greece. Athanasiou (2006) analysed the fantasies of endangered national sovereignty vis-a-vis demographic imaginaries as an idiom of gendered subjectivity and she demonstrated "its implication in the constitution of intimate subjectivities according to the cultural intelligibility of reproductive heterosexuality, familial generationality, and national continuity" (229). Stressing the entanglements of kinship, sexuality and (homo)sexual identity Kostas Yannakopoulos examined the destabilisation of the "natural" and "self-evident" nature of family love in the lives of homosexual men infected by HIV (2011) and emphasised the reconfigurations of kinship in the context of male same-sex desiring intergenerational erotic affairs (2010).

[8] According to the historian Efi Avdela (2017), the emphasis in recent decades on the historical study of nationalism has overshadowed the importance and influence of racial theories, with the result that "race remains hidden behind the nation" (19). I use the term race here (in Greek *φυλή*/fyli) to examine how national ideologies are reproduced through the racialisation of certain groups and populations by targeting them as dissenters in the otherwise violent fantasy of Greece's supposed cultural homogeneity. For relevant discussion on the usage of the term "racism" in the Greek context as an "umbrella term" extending to other forms of oppression not only based on race but also based on gender and sexuality see Carastathis (2019) and Riedel (2005, 2009).

trajectories of solidarity are brought about by the demand for institutional recognition of gay and lesbian parenthood?

The passion for anal sex is stronger than holy water blessed by the church[9]

While same-sex couples can now enter into a civil partnership in Greece, they continue to lack legal recognition as same-sex co-parents. As research on lesbian motherhood has shown, the legislators' refusal to include same-sex couples in Greek law on medically assisted reproduction in 2002 is intimately connected to the absence of a legal framework for same-sex marriage (Kantsa and Chalkidou 2014, 188). While accurate, Juana María Rodríguez (2014, 48) argues that "legal recognition alone is never enough to overcome the means through which affective relationships are legitimated or stigmatized." Indeed, as Rodriguez (ibid.) notes, keeping the space for recognition around kinship open "requires acknowledging multiple, and at times conflicting, investments that cannot be dictated by the rule of law." Moving in a similar direction, new kinship studies and queer kinship studies have focused on family law and state policies regarding new reproduction technologies, demonstrating how these policies regulate the reproduction of both human existence and ideas about gender, race, sexuality, nation, class, and able-bodiedness (Dahl and Gunnarsson-Payne 2014; Kroløkke et al. 2015; Lie & Lykke 2017). In other words, these scholars examine how policies about kinship and reproduction regulate not only bodies, but also the reproduction of certain ideas while muting others. In this section, I focus on the sexual ideologies invoked by reproduction policies to probe what they might tell us about the sexual terms of institutionalised parenthood and thus about institutionality more broadly.

Now let me take you some years back by mentioning two examples chosen out of countless others that reproduce common schemes regarding the interweaving of gender, sexuality, and parenthood. In 2002, gay men were legislatively excluded

[9] Famous Greek queer slogan.

from the possibility of contracting surrogate mothers to gestate their implanted offspring in Greece. During that period of public debate, the then-president of the Greek National Council for Radio and Television (NCRTV), Loannis Laskaridis, defended NCRTV's decision to censor a much-discussed TV series scene featuring two gay men kissing each other, declaring that "homosexuality is a peculiarity which lies outside the productive process of life." Some years later, in 2008, during discussions over gay marriage and the demands for institutional recognition of same-sex parenthood, the cleric of Greek Orthodox church Serafem (speaking as the metropolitan of Piraeus) issued a press release declaring that "the human body's alimentary canal of excretion can never be a life value", in reference to anal sex, widely known as "ottoman" in Greece, yet ironically known as "Greek" throughout the world.[10] According to Apostolidou (2017, 72), the "ostensibly odd analogy" between othomanikó and the act of anal sex (with reference to both same-sex and different-sex encounters) reveals collective agonies linked to the disavowal of the country's multi-ethnic history as a subordinated part of the Ottoman Empire. The sexual connotations of "Ottoman style" echoes the disavowal of national subordination and at the same time links to the desire to clear local same-sex history namely, the Greek antiquity's connotations to homosexuality.

These statements are typical and have great discursive potential not just because those who utter them are recognised as authoritative at local and national levels (be it as government or clerical representatives), but also because they reproduce and at the same time re-establish an exceptionally familiar national sexual fantasy surrounding parenthood and its constitutive outside. Tallying with the fields of sexual desire and kinship, the aforementioned fantasies evoke certain gestures of intimacy and sexual connection, the

---

[10] For the use of English terminology, see the subcategory "Greek-style" on international porn websites (e.g. Pornhub, Youporn). For Greek sex as a metonymy for anal sex, see *urbandictionary.com*. For the national-sexual connotations of the term *ottoman*, *greeklanguage.gr* writes "related to the Ottoman Turks: Ottoman state or Ottoman Empire, which was abolished in 1920 and replaced by the Republic of Turkey, Ottoman law. (As a noun., Vulgar) Ottoman, sodomy." (accessed 25 March 2019).

bodily and emotional labour in sexual pleasure, as is the case with anal sex and a kiss, in order to determine who can and cannot participate in the reproductive process of life, who is not worthy of reproducing life, and consequently of taking on the responsibility and care for a human life.

Here, the interweaving of gender, sexuality, reproduction, and parenthood does not constitute a matter of sheer juridical abeyance. Rather, it serves as a matter of authorising some sexual pleasure as legitimate and targeting certain sexual desires as outside the bonds of possible kinship. If queerness is associated with perversity and pleasure, and this is conceptualised in opposition to parenthood (Rodriguez 2014, 33), it would not be inaccurate to suggest that the criteria by which parenthood is defined are exceptionally sexual. Also, since heterosexuality is the only institutionally recognised sexual orientation of a parent in Greece, it becomes more than evident that on the level of legal, political, and everyday normative rhetoric, parenthood in Greece is by default a sexual category par excellence.[11] This very constitutive conceptualisation of parenthood as rooted in (normative) sexuality is underscored and articulated in the abovementioned ethno- sexual anti-reproductive fantasies. It is not a coincidence that the revision of the Civil Union Act of December 2015, to include same-sex couples, was based on the government's commitment to ensure that voting on this controversial bill would not serve as a "bridge" for adoption,[12] access to medically assisted reproduction, or for that matter the juridical recognition of families with same-sex parents. As a result, when a lesbian couple visited a clinic for medically assisted reproduction in Athens, after entering into civil union, the people in charge informed them

[11] My argument here is not new; from a different perspective, a quick browsing through websites of straight, gay and lesbian porn can be illuminating regarding the sexualisation of parental and other kinship symbolisms, such as Mummy or Daddy play, daughter, son, MILF, incest and so on.

[12] According to the 2018 revision of the Underwriting and Adoption Act by the Greek parliament, same-sex couples are excluded from the right to adoption, but they can foster. In a recent interview, members of the NGO Rainbow Families pointed to widespread stereotypes and fear of rejection by social services as key reasons for the low rates of fostering applications by same-sex couples

that in order to gain access to the medical services provided, they would have to void their partnership contract and be legally recognised as single women desiring to be mothers by bearing a child, rather than as a lesbian couple.[13] If, therefore, the right to medically assisted reproduction in Greece is not provided through recognition of same-sex sexuality but through the recognition of the desire of a "single", and thus an imagined straight woman to bear a child (Kantsa & Chalkidou 2014, 188), then in institutional terms this legal exclusion not only materialises the naturalised connection between reproductive heteronormativity and national identity (Athanasiou 2006, 2014; Halkias 1998, 2007) but also illuminates the extent to which in Greece sexual connotations, and thus the dimensions of sexuality, underpin the notion of parenthood itself.

Several approaches have critiqued this exclusion from the perspective of legal abeyance and human rights to highlight the fact that inclusion in civil unions acquired through the compulsory exclusion from any form of institutional reproduction constituted a legal void in family law. As has already been argued elsewhere, the absence of an institutional framework for the recognition of gay and lesbian parenthood does not signify a lack of framework, for the framework is established in different terms (Kantsa & Chalkidou 2014, 97). In other words, this is not about the exclusion of families with same-sex parents from the state authorised social body, but rather a political gesture of gay and lesbian inclusion into the social body predicated on their exclusion from institutionally recognised and legitimised forms of parenthood. This institutional(ised) "absence" constitutes the evidence of institutionalised homophobia (Kantsa & Chalkidou 2014, 97).[14]

---

[13] Personal communication with NGO Rainbow Families.

[14] I use the term institutionalised homophobia instead of anti-gay politics since the latter garners political value by targeting LGBT populations and discriminating against LGBT rights. Although institutionalised homophobia also reproduces discriminations against LGBT people/rights, it operates in a more silent or concealed way, often simultaneously with a minority rights' rhetoric or even through the adoption of inclusive laws such as the civil union extension to same-sex couples. While it is important not to equate institutionalised homophobia with anti-gay politics since that would mean erasing both how different

Considering that in the Greek collective imaginary, the notion of family is interwoven with the sexual fantasies of a heterosexually reproductive nation, the absence of the institutional legitimisation of families with same-sex parents in Greece constitutes a gesture of institutional nationalism articulated in sexualised reproductive terms. Consequently, the legislative void of family law is not a space with absent meanings; it is rather a dense space, infested with sexual fantasies over what is considered the constitutive outside of Greekness and parenthood, whereby that outside is imagined as seething with queer bodies, mouths, anuses and replete with sexual perversions and all the intimacies, socialities and pleasures these perversions connote. The ideologies circulating through and around this "void" are crucial in recognising how they relate to other forms of illegitimate kinship bonds that refer to other "deviants". In other words, it is important to understand how an imbrication of kinship and sexuality produced by this void is in dialogue with other legal forms of sexual and reproductive regulation and control. There is, for instance, a legal clause in the Greek labour law, according to which, for a sex worker to obtain a legal work license, they must present a certificate of marital status "whereby it is proved that they are unmarried, widowed or divorced." So, for sex workers to acquire state recognition as legally employed and hence receive social insurance and access to public medical treatment, they are institutionally excluded from certain family/ kinship bonds and relations of intimacy. More specifically, this legal clause that pertains to their labour rights essentially excludes sex workers from what is deemed marital life, the keystone of which is considered to be "love". At this point, we could argue that in the context of state recognition of sex work as work, this labour regulation targets sex workers as "unrespectable" and regulates family policies through the conjoining of labour, sexuality and respect-

politics of discrimination mark different trajectories of violence and their unequal effects against targeted populations, it remains crucial to recognise that they are in constant feedback. As Anna Carastathis (2018) argues, homophobic and transphobic violence and hostility in Greece reproduced through institutions and institutionalised means "legitimates and even encourages violent attacks occurring in streets, squares, and shops by citizens, fascist assault battalions, and also by police and military officers" (272).

ability. Moreover, this labour regulation sheds light on the ways in which heterosexual love, as an ideological apparatus, gets instrumentalised by the law and institutionally normalised through the deprivation of labour rights.

This law explicitly forces sex workers to choose between the basic rights of all workers or the right to marital life, structurally barring them from having access to both. Considering that the category of sex worker in Greece consists primarily of immigrant women and men and that the marriage of an immigrant with a Greek citizen is a path leading to their naturalisation, then this law specifically bars immigrant sex workers from accessing both their rights to work and their right to citizenship through marriage.

Approaching the exclusion of gays and lesbians from institutionally recognised forms of parenthood through the lens of sexuality enables scholars to investigate how the normative web of kinship and nation gets reproduced in Greece in terms of gender and sexual normativity. But it also goes further to inquiring into the ways in which the very notion of institutionality, namely institutional recognition and institutional inclusion, is shaped through prevalent understandings of sex and sexuality and hence reproduces certain ideological correlations in the form of sexual orientations.

Vanilla democracy

Institutional recognition entails legitimising the presence of certain bodies (and not others) within the context of biopolitical democratic governance by configuring the terms of otherness. For the purposes of this study, institutional recognition, configured in terms of sexuality, reproduces certain sexual orientations (and not others). Drawing on phenomenology, Sarah Ahmed (2007, 150) has described whiteness as an orientation, and more specifically as "an ongoing and unfinished history, which orientates bodies in specific directions, and affects how they 'take up' space." Associating the abovementioned points, we could ask: what kind of racial ideologies are reproduced by reproductive politics if we approach them as sexual policies that institutionalise/legitimise sexual orientations? Departing from the fact that "the democratic right" to create a family has surfaced as a rallying cry in the gay and lesbian political agenda and that the LGBTQ+ movement has claimed the institutional recognition of families with same-sex partners/caretakers to be a fundamental obligation of a contemporary democracy, we could possibly rephrase this question as follows: what do the sexual ideologies predicated on our desire for institutional recognition and state protection teach us about the prerequisites of democratic inclusion?

I will now attempt to follow this logical thread within a less obvious field, that of the educational institution. In the collective Greek imaginary, gays and lesbians are understood as a threat to the reproduction of the (heterosexual) nation. The emphasis put on anality, blowjobs and other sexual practices, widely perceived as "an abuse of the bodily organs of the human species"[15], links queerness with racialised ideologies of perversion, filth, and death, ideologies that have been attributed to people of colour but also to poor families and people who suffer from poverty and historically these projected fears have been crystallised in the demand for the protection of minors, the "forthcoming generation". The imagined progeny of the future becomes the site where the love for the nation is invested and the hope for recompensation for the state's investment is placed (Ahmed 2016).

An earlier version of this article was presented at a conference organised by the NGO *Rainbow Families* in Athens in February 2016, entitled "Love Creates Families". The title of the presentation, "What's a hard-on got to do with it? A discussion for the whole family" resulted in the prohibition of the distribution of the conference program in secondary schools in Attica by the office of secondary education, i.e., the office in charge of the administration and operational control of secondary educational institutions in Attica. As Ahmed (2012, 20–21) puts it, to explain institutions means explaining how they appear or are configured; it

---

[15] From a press release published by the Supreme Confederation of multi-child Parents of Greece against the civil union bill. The entire press release can be found https://racistcrimeswatch.wordpress.com/2015/12/15/1-68/ (accessed 25 March 2019).

means describing "not simply the activities that take place within institutions [...] but how these activities shape the sense of an institution or even institutional sense." Following Ahmed, we can interpret the prohibition of the distribution of the conference program as due to the problematic juxtaposition of the words *hard on* (as an embodiment of lust) and *family* in relation to parenthood as a constitutive gesture of the educational institution. This gesture of exclusion shapes both the notion of education and of parenthood at the same time by establishing which content is considered inappropriate. While the general title of the conference, which stressed love as the foundation of family, had already been approved by the office of secondary education in charge, the reference to hard on, which rendered sexual desire and pleasure visible within (same-sex)parenthood, activated a set of reflections that have to do with the disassociation of family from sexuality, as well as the protection of underage students from the allegedly unrestrained queer sexuality, sexual "excess," and threat of defilement brought about by gays and lesbians. It is worth focusing here more on the interrelation of kinship, love, and sex in order to invoke the poignant reading of Ulrika Dahl (2014) a feminist and kinship scholar, of anthropologist David Schneider's ([1968] 1980) *American Kinship: A Cultural Account.* Dahl (2014, 149) under-scores the fact that Schneider's kinship theory is built on the belief that the romantically involved couple is considered the basis for reproduction and family creation in a scheme where "love manifested or translated into sex (or sex into love) and this, in turn, is what gives rise to the product and object of love, a child." Dahl (ibid.) goes on to suggest that "both LGBTQ+ political activism and studies of queer kinship have naturalized the emphasis on love as the foundation of family."[16] If

[16] In an article on gay and lesbian families, Schneider has argued that cultural models, such as the model of the desire for family creation, are "hegemonic" and there can be no cultural differentiation between heterosexual and non-heterosexual people, in that when, for instance, one grows up in a social condition where heterosexual nuclear families prevail, they have to confront this experience, whether straight or gay (Schneider 1997). Kath Weston (1991), whose book *Families We Choose* is emblematic for queer kinship studies, has emphasised love as the cornerstone of gay and lesbian families of choice and has

we follow Dahl's argument that queer kinship theories/activism have naturalised the emphasis on love as the foundation of family, and if in the case of the romantically involved couple love "is translated into sex (or sex into love)" (Dahl 2014, 149) then queer kinship theories/politics have also naturalised sex by symbolising it as love. In this scheme, reproductive rights are demanded as love rights (Dahl 2014, 151), and by emphasising the aspect of love, the demand for institutional recognition and democratic inclusion shifts from the homosexuality of parents/caretakers to the affective qualities of their relationship. Considering the sexualisation of gay and lesbian parenthood through the public perverse fantasy regarding the "effects" of childbearing by non-heteronormative parents – evoking "love" does not constitute an avoidance of discourse about sex but instead translates sex into an act of love. Here, the very meaning of queer sexuality becomes naturalised in a way intended to protect it from automatic association with perversion, filth and fatality. In other words, we could be talking about the predication of a sexuality which, in its identification with love, is "cleansed", it goes unnoticed, as is the case with some of the best-known attributes of vanilla sexuality.

Here, I deploy the use of the term vanilla, drawing on the conceptual toolbox of Bondage and Discipline, Sadism and Masochism (BDSM), where vanilla practice or sexuality designates hetero-reproductive sex that does not include sadomasochistic (SM) and fetishist practices and pleasures, and in a broader sense, signals "a distinct lack of desire for deviation from the status quo."[17] The term vanilla might be considered problematic insofar as it suggests a rigid distinction between vanilla and non-vanilla sexuality, hence obscuring the sexual and cultural borrowings exchanged between what is considered "normal" and "perverse" sexuality. Nevertheless, since "BDSM scenes reflect real-world asymmetries of power" (Rodriguez 2014, 58), vanilla does not refer to the absence of

---

suggested that within the existing dominant cultural models, there is some differentiation and resistance, which nevertheless does not render them alternative models. In an article, Weston concludes that gay and lesbian ideologies of kinship have used common, shared categories and dominant symbols in order to create unusual concepts (Weston 1995, 106).

[17] BDSMWIKI.

asymmetries but rather to the lack of *conscious power exchange in relationship dynamics* (see note 16). The concept of vanilla, thus, draws attention to the naturalised and therefore non-consensual power differentials circulated through "normal" sexuality, including male dominance and heterosexuality, as the foundational presuppositions of gendered and sexual orderliness. Precisely because it conceals inequalities and naturalises the lack of consent, vanilla serves as a provisional tool for tracing the structural inequalities of democratic inclusion and its racialised components. Rather than engage power differentials, negotiate sexual roles, and establish clear terms for exercising consent, vanilla sexuality conceptually highlights the persistence of power dynamics as both natural and inevitable, mirroring the way the state similarly denies the structural inequalities that surround accessing the rights of citizenship, while suggesting that we have all freely consented to our subjugation. In her attempt to trace the origins of the term, Lynda Hart (1998, 220–221, note 5) ponders on the racialised ideologies circulating within the cultural notion of vanilla sexuality, which might signify whiteness and white supremacy in the collective imaginary of the West, in terms of sex and sexuality. As Hart (1998, 222) puts it, "I am not saying that vanilla white, but I am suggesting that it is an interesting choice of words that conjures certain racial associations." Hart, of course, is referring to the use of the term made by SM communities in the US during the 1970s and the 1980s, which were shaped by/within a particular racially defined American history and social condition. In Greece, the term vanilla is mostly used in the BDSM scene to denote the opposite of the perverse, SM, kinky, sexuality associated with BDSM. As shown elsewhere, in the Greek context, BDSM erotic practices are classified by state health policies as a sexual expression of a potentially psycho-pathological personality, while they are also evoked in public discourses as the sexual symptom of a fascistic, anti-democratic political ideology (Chalkidou 2015). Specifically, from the beginning of the so-called Greek financial crisis, BDSM has multiplied its visibility in political discourse and the public imagination as BDSM iconography, terminology, and paraphernalia have been used as a metaphor in the political commentaries on the debates between Greek politicians and the International Monetary Fund. Sadism has been outlined as a political sexualised expression for IMF's policies resulting in austerity and financial subordination, and thus have been used as a metaphor for anti-Greek ideology, while many Greek reports characterise consent to the austerity program, from the side of the then Greek government, as "an extreme fiscal masochism". These sexualised political fantasies derive from stereotypical equations of sadomasochistic desire with totalitarian regimes such as Fascism and Nazism (Moore 2005, 2011). In this sense, these representations comment on politics while using the metaphor of sexual perversion. Namely, "BDSM transcribes in terms of sex and sexuality the threat – not merely against sexual norms – but against the integrity and well-being of the nation" (Chalkidou 2015). These normative perceptions of BDSM, in and out of parliament, reflect the widespread argument that "a sexual anomaly creates the tendency for a political anomaly" (Papanikolaou 2012). In a rather suspicious reading of that scheme of the interrelation between sexuality and political ideology, a scheme where normative ideas on sadomasochism perceive it as the supposed sexual metonymy of fascism, patriarchy, financial subordination and social imposition, among other political woes, then what is silently implied, reproduced and projected on this perception is that vanilla sex, the opposite of BDSM, allegedly constitutes a sexual metonymy for democracy. Vanilla democracy assumes and naturalises the states' dominance by concealing the multifaceted lines of power that produce some as worthy recipients of the state's love, while silencing the continued structural inequalities and the subsequent social marginalisation that have occurred for those falling outside the confines of respectable sexual, gender and kinship structures.

Here, I do not aim to define vanilla or non-vanilla sexual practices as politically correct, liberating or reformist. Rather, I explore the ways in which these are normalised and instrumentalised by the law, institutions, definitions and imaginations of democracy and the social imaginary through policies on reproduction. There are multiple ways in which one can respond to the arraignment of queer sexuality as a threat, as the constitutive opposite of parenthood and it might be that the political predication of an unmarked vanilla sexuality, which is cleansed of any perversion, is one of them. For example, Athens Pride 2014, featuring the central slogan "A Family Affair", promoted "the right to family creation" as a central matter of equality and democracy for the LGBTQ+ community in Greece. The poster featured two white, young, able-bodied men, the archetypal couple of Adam and Adam (as a gay variant of the Christian couple Adam and Eve), keeping a safe distance between their bodies and being "united along with their child, Eros, as an example of an LGBT family".[18] As an institution, Pride constitutes a political gesture of visibility and collective claim, and it could be said that what is demanded through rights is access to another future, different from the present. Nevertheless, every explicit or implicit reference to a certain future navigates and negotiates connections with a certain past, a certain origin. And in this case, the depiction of a child as a metonymy for same-sex Eros is not accidental.

Historically speaking, Athens Pride is closely associated with the movement that followed the violent crackdown by the Greek police in 2003. On 20 February 2003, police forces staged an early morning raid on a party exclusively for men at the gay club, Spices. This raid was presented as part of an organised sting operation, allegedly intended to target paedophilia and the dissemination of child pornography on the internet. During this raid, the owner of the club, two employees, and three customers, who were found in the darkroom, were arrested. Moreover, another five people were arrested in a private residence. Five days later, after their names had been published in newspapers and on TV channels and they had been identified with unsubstantiated accusations of prostitution, paedophilia and distribution of child pornographic material, all those arrested were finally released, except one of the club's customers, who committed suicide in the holding cell at the General

---

[18] For the press release and the poster, see https://www.avgi.gr/koinonia/100857_oikogeneiaki-ypothesi-athens-pride-2014-ayrio-stin-pl-klaythmonos (accessed 25 March 2019).

Police Directorate of Attica.[19] After this raid, and as a response to police repression, collective actions were carried out by LGBTQ+ groups. The Colourful Forum was created in this context and featured various LGBTQ+ organisations and individuals. The following years also saw the establishment of the Homosexual Lesbian Community of Greece as a union (2004) and of Athens Pride (on an annual basis from 2005 onwards), which later took the form of a Pride Festival.[20]

Turning to Athens Pride's "Family Affair" poster, the representation of the "child" as a metonymy for Eros on behalf of the LGBTQ+ movement does not merely symbolise the reproductive outcome of non-heterosexual love. Rather, this representation constitutes the site on which the sexual load attributed to queerness is managed in a way that resonates and predicates a symbolic and political displacement from the desire for boy toys to the desire for children. Ironically, this displacement from sexual lust to reproductive love is predicated on the erasure of the historical origins that incited the very political processes that led to the establishment of Athens Pride in the first place. In the context of a vanilla democracy that grants the space of public representation to non-heterosexual sexualities, this erasure comes to designate the vanilisation

[19] For a report on the incidents written after the police raid at Spices by an LGBT website, see *Lesbian.gr* (in Greek, accessed 25 March 2019). For an analysis of the incident in relation to the wider context in which different forms of sexual sociality emerged, and especially the emergence of self-defining discourses on BDSM in Greece, see Chalkidou (2015, 84–106). For an approach to understand the Spices incidents through the lens of necropolitics, see Yannakopoulos (2011, 166–170).

[20] During the 1980s, there were some early attempts to organise public events on homosexuality. Loukas Theodorakopoulos (2005) has documented the first outdoor event organised by the Liberation Movement of Homosexuals in Greece (AKOE in Greek) against the bill entitled "On the protection against venereal diseases and the regulation of appertaining matters", according to which, homosexual people were threatened with one-year imprisonment and banishment in case they were arrested by the police while looking for a sexual partner in public. The relevant protests took place on 26 January 1981 at the Propylaea of the University of Athens and were attended by 500 people. Moreover, during the 1990s, Paola Revenioti and *Kraximo* magazine had organised days of "homosexual pride" in Athens in outdoor spaces, such as Strefi Hill, Pedion Areos and indoor spaces, such as Camel Club and Soda. For an account of the Gay Pride Parades that took place in the 1990s, see Thodoris Antonopoulos' article *here*, *10%*, June–July 2004 (in Greek, accessed 25 March 2019).

of LGBTQ+ politics; it legitimises the "white-washing" of the historicity of Pride, and perpetuates an ongoing historicity of oppression and normalisation. Moreover, it contributes to silencing the ways in which intergenerational relationships are continuing to constitute and have historically constituted valuable networks of survival and fields of socialisation for underage gay boys[21] and underage lesbians.

Queering stories of kinship

It remains crucial that we inquire about how we can respond to the stigmatisation of queer sexual practices and pleasures as the constitutive outside of parenthood, without naturalising heterosexual reproduction (Rodriguez 2014, 44), the sexual and gender hierarchies that compose the normative web of kinship and parenthood. What inevitably emerges at this point is the question of how politics and theories of kinship intersect with politics and theories of sexuality. In other words, how invaluable stories of upbringing, imbued with the everyday emotional and material labour required and the pleasures of parental/caretaking relationships gain their voice without erasing biographies of migrants, sex workers, underage youth, and those that fall outside the boundaries of respectable sexuality, without overcoming the sexual biographies carried within the broader spectrum of queer genders, desires, and bodies. These are stories in which sexuality and sexual practice are not only matters of pleasure; they do political work within groups, movements, collectivities, and initiatives, stories in which the very desire for sociality is born based on sexual yearnings, lust and erotic desire, spanning lesbian bars, queer parties and our beds, to parks, darkrooms and orgasms on keyboards. These are stories in which sexuality lingers persistently in the form of precarious and underestimated labour on the streets, at studios, massage parlours, saunas and erotic ads. While we must not forget or underestimate the significance of legal equality, we should also be able to consider demands to same-sex parenthood as a dynamic field of relations that brings about a number of affinities, which are interrelated not

---

[21] For male intergenerational erotic relationships in Greece, see Yannakopoulos (2011).

only in terms of reproduction, but also in terms of sexual and precarious biographies which are exposed to state and its laws. So, if the promise brought by the claim to institutional recognition and establishment of gay and lesbian parenthood is that civil rights will serve as a safer space and access to state services will function as a means of protection against social debasement and the violence it entails, then another promise, also brought by this claim, is that it will shed even harsher light on the question of what it means to live exposed to diverse forms of state violence. In fact, the selective promise of inclusion highlights more persistently what it means to live a dispossessed life, at the mercy of a discriminatory state, a life exposed to ongoing risk and danger.

An institutional logic, as Ahmed puts it, can be perceived as a logic of kinship, meaning as a way of relating to and reproducing social relationships (Ahmed 2012, 38). In this way, an institutional logic of exclusion can also be understood as a logic of kinship, to the extent that it also proposes certain modes of relating to and reproducing social relationships, which lead to exclusion. If we focus on the processes and rhetoric that justify the deprivation of rights, rather than the rights themselves, we can possibly imagine political kinship through the logic of institutional discrimination and differentially violent deprivation reproduced by it. Taking a certain stand regarding the institutional recognition of families with same-sex parents/care givers means being able to imagine a different future regarding what family means, to imagine the bonds made by kinships of affective, care-giving, and erotic association in a different way and being able to articulate the claim for domestic safety and family protection through various and varying stories. For instance, what does the notion of "domestic safety" mean to a trans person who, deprived of the legal recognition of gender identity, is often barred from renting a domestic space, e.g., a flat? What does the "right to marriage" means for a sex worker who has to mark under marital status unmarried, widowed or divorced in order to acquire a work license? What do "reproductive rights" mean, considering the coercive sterilisation to which trans people were subjected up until recently in order to complete the process of acquisition of state documents certifying their gender reassignment?[22] What does "equal access" to medically assisted reproduction technology mean, when the very notion of accessibility is a matter of everyday dystopia for LGBTQ+ and non-LGBTQ+ people with disabilities? These questions do not aim to undermine or replace the significance of the demands made by gays and lesbians for equal access to family law and equality of the law. Quite the contrary, they are gestures of recognition of the vital associations reproduced through reproduction if we narrate the story in a different way. They constitute an attempt to map other orientations, on which we can chart different political, sexual and theoretical kinships, alongside different origins, proximities and futurities.

References

Ahmed, S. 2007. "A phenomenology of whiteness." *Feminist Theory* (8): 149–168.

———. 2012. *On Being Included: Racism and Diversity in Institutional Life.* Durham, NC: Duke University Press.

———. 2016. "Fascism as love" Available at: https://feministkilljoys.com/2016/11/09/fascism-as-love/ (accessed 7 December 2019).

Apostolidou, A. 2017. "Greek nationhood and 'Greek love': Sexualizing the nation and multiple readings of the glorious Greek past." *Nations and Nationalism* 23 (1): 68–86.

Athanasiou, A. 2001. *Nostalgic futures, contentious technologies: Reckoning time and population in Greece.* Unpublished PhD Thesis, New School University, New York.

———. 2006. "Bloodlines: Performing the body of the 'demos', reckoning the time of the 'ethnos'." *Journal of Modern Greek Studies* (24): 229–256.

———. 2007. *Zoi sto orio: okimia gia to soma, to filo kai ti viopolitiki.* Athens: Ekkremes.

———. 2014. "To ethniko soma se katastasi ektaktis anagkis: oi dimografikes politikes kai ta oria tou politikou," in *Politikes tis kathimerinotitas: Sinoro, soma kai idiotita tou politi stin Ellada*, Papataxiarchis, E., ed. Athens: Alexandria, pp. 455–484.

---

[22] For an analysis of the coercive sterilization of trans people as a form of gender violence, see Anna Carastathis 2015.

Avdela E. 2017. "I aneksitili diafora: logi gia ti fyli stin Ellada," in *Fyletikes theories stin Ellada: proslipsis ke xrisis stis epistimes, tin politiki, ti logotehnia kai tin istoria tis tehnis kata ton 19o ke 20o aiona*, Avdela, E., et al., eds. Iraklio: Crete University Press, pp. 11–40.

Carastathis, A. 2015. "Compulsory sterilisation of transgender people as gendered violence," in *(In)Fertile Citizens: Anthropological and Legal Challenges of Assisted Reproduction Technologies*, Kantsa, V., Zanini, G. & Papadopoulou, L., eds. Athens: Alexandria, pp. 79–92.

–––. 2018. "'Gender Is the First Terrorist': Homophobic and transphobic violence in Greece." *Frontiers: A Journal of Women Studies* 39 (2): 265–296.

–––. 2021. "'Racism' versus 'Intersectionality'? Significations of Interwoven Oppressions in Greek LGBTQ+ Discourses." *Feminist Critique: East European Journal of Feminist and Queer Studies* (4): 37–58.

Chalkidou, A. 2015. *BDSM practices, socialities, sexualities: Anthropological approaches*. Unpublished Doctoral Dissertation, University of the Aegean, Greece.

Dahl, U. 2014. "Not gay as in happy, but queer as in fuck you: Notes on love and failure in queer(ing) kinship" *lambda nordica* 19 (3–4): 143–168.

Dahl, U. & Gunnarsson Payne, J., eds. 2014. "Kinship and reproduction [Special Issue: Introduction]." *lambda nordica* 19 (3–4): 11–27.

Halkias, A. 1998. "Give birth for Greece! Abortion and nation in letters to the editor of the mainstream Greek press." *Journal of Modern Greek Studies* 16 (1): 111–138.

–––. 2007. *To adio likno tis Dimokratias: Sex, ektrosi kai ethnikismos sti sichroni Ellada*. Athens: Alexandria.

Hart, L. 1998. *Between the Body and the Flesh. Performing Sadomasochism*. New York, NY: Columbia University Press.

Kantsa, V. 2001. *Daughters who do not speak, mothers who do not listen: Erotic relationships among women in contemporary Greece*. Unpublished PhD Thesis, University of London, UK.

–––. 2005. "Anatheorisis: Otan to filo boliastike me ti seksoualikotita," in *Conference proceedings*, Mytilene, Greece. Available at: http://www.aegean.gr/gender-postgraduate/ Documents/Fylo_Chrima_Antallagi/ Praktika_Synedriou_2005.htm (accessed 7 December 2019).

–––. 2010. "Poios fovate ti seksoualikotita?" *I Avgi tis Kiriakis*. Available at: https://enthemata.wordpress.com/2010/03/21/ποιος-φοβάται-τη-σεξουαλικότητα/ (accessed 7 December 2019).

Kantsa, V. & Chalkidou, A. 2014. "Doing family in the space between the laws. Notes on lesbian motherhood in Greece." *lambda nordica* (3–4): 86–108.

Kroløkke, C., Myong, L., et al., eds. 2015. *Critical Kinship Studies*. London/New York, NY: Rowman and Littlefield International.

Lie, M. and Lykke, N. eds. 2017. *Assisted Reproduction across Borders. Feminist Perspectives on Normalizations, Disruptions and Transmissions*. New York, NY / London: Routledge.

Loizos, P. & Papataxiarchis, E. 1991. "Gender, sexuality, and the person in Greek culture," in *Contested Identities: Gender and Kinship in Modern Greece*, Loizos, P. & Papataxiarchis E., eds. Princeton, NJ: Princeton University Press, pp. 221–234.

Moore, A., 2005. "Sadomasochistic desire as fascism." *Lesbian and Gay Psychology Review* 6 (3): 163–176.

———. 2011. "Sadism as social violence," in Toulalan, S. and Fischer, K., eds. *Bodies, Sex and Desire from the Renaissance to the Present*. Basingstoke: Palgrave.

Papanikolaou, D. 2012. "Eimaste olio kseskismenes aderfes?" *Unfollow Magazine*. Available at: https://enthemata.wordpress.com/2012/10/21/papanikolaoy-3/ (accessed 7 December 2019).

Riedel, B. S. 2005. *Elsewheres: Greek LGBT activists and the imagination of a movement*. PhD Dissertation, Rice University, USA.

———. 2009. "Homophobia as 'Racism' in contemporary urban Greece," in *omophobias: Lust and Loathing Across Time and Space*, Murray, D. A. B., ed. Durham, NC / London: Duke University Press, pp. 82–102.

Rodríguez, J. M. 2014. *Sexual Futures, Queer Gestures, and Other Latina Longings*. New York: NYU Press.

Schneider, D. [1968] 1980. *American Kinship: A Cultural Account*. Chicago, IL: University of Chicago Press.

———. 1997. "The power of culture: Notes on some aspects of gay and lesbian kinship in America today." *Cultural Anthropology* (12): 270–274.

Theodorakopoulos L. 2005. *'Amfi' kai apeleftherosi*. Athens: Polychromos Planetes.

Weston, K. 1991. *Families We Choose: Lesbians, Gays, Kinship*. New York, NY: Columbia University Press.

———. 1998. *Long Slow Burn: Sexuality and Social Science*. New York, NY: Routledge

Yannakopoulos, K. 2006. "Eisagogi," in *Seksualikotita: theories kai politikes tis Anthropologias*, Yannakopoulos, K., ed. Athena: Alexandria, pp. 9–15.

———. 2010. "Cultural meanings of loneliness: Kinship, sexuality and (homo)sexual identity in contemporary Greece." *Journal of Mediterranean Studies* 18 (2): 265–282.

———. 2011. "Zoes choris martyria," in *Glossa kai seksoualiko- tita, glossikes kai anthropologikes proseggiseis*, Canakis, C., ed. Athens: 21st Century Publication, pp. 161–179.

3. Queer Kinship in Swedish Numbers:
Reproducing National Whiteness

Ulrika Dahl[1]

> Quite honestly, I don't have a great need to meet other HBTQ[2] families. Possibly for my children to see that families look different. But I feel that I can show that through other families who are not HBTQ…there are a lot of different kinds of families that are not. We like the concept of rainbow family – that feels inclusive. That can include grandmother, grandfather and children, father and children, not everything has to have to do with sexual orientation or gender identity. (Survey respondent, 2017)

This quote is from one of many responses to a question concerning needs for meeting places for LGBTQ+ families in Sweden included in a national survey on paths to and experiences of parenthood among LGBTQ+ people conducted in 2017. While perhaps not "representative" of the whole data set of 645 respondents – indeed, the main majority of respondents, especially outside urban areas, stated that they *do* want places to meet other families like their own – it tells us something about how (queer) kinship is understood in contemporary Sweden. This chapter explores what a national survey might tell us about who is reproducing the (queer) Swedish nation, what they aspire towards and struggle with, and what it means to have and engage with children.

With a strong commitment to (gender) equality, after a century of strong social democratic welfare politics, Sweden has created a (self)image of itself as progressive and inclusive in terms of gender, sexual and even racial politics, or what researchers have called exceptionalism (cf. Habel 2012; Alm et al. 2017). In the aftermath

---

[1] Acknowledgements: For feedback on drafts of this chapter I thank Rikke Andreassen, Raili Uibo, Anjelika Kjellberg, Joanna Mizielińska and Antu Sorainen.
[2] As is discussed below, in Swedish the term 'HBTQ' (Homo, bi, trans, queer) is frequently used to refer to what in other contexts is often LGBTQ+, sometimes with several additional letters, including I and +.

of the AIDS epidemic, Sweden passed a law on same sex partner-ship in 1998, which in 2009 was transformed into gender neutral marriage (Rydström 2011). While partnership, unlike marriage, originally excluded reproduction and parenting (ibid., Dahl 2022), the number of existing same-sex families along with the rise of access to assisted reproduction technologies have led to a series of changes in Swedish family law, in order to make room for new families. Beginning with same-sex adoption – specifically, the inclusion of a partner's ("biological") child/ren in 2003 – lesbian couples gained access to assisted reproduction with donated gametes through state health care in 2004, and in 2014 single women[3] also gained that access. These seemingly progressive changes might, as the opening quote suggests, indicate that little distinguishes non-heterosexual families from heterosexual ones, with equality achieved. Indeed, a very large number of respondents describe their lives with children as "normal" and "ordinary."

As Butler (2002) has proposed, when we move beyond the question of recognition and rights, we might ask different ques-tions regarding queer kinship; including how conception matters, about what love and desire beyond the heterosexual matrix might mean, and about parenthood, care, and interdependency. In the 2000s, scholarship on LGBTQ+ families and paths to parenthood has grown significantly and, yes, today, we do know quite a lot, both about living with children conceived in heterosexual relations and sharing parenthood with friends (Zetterqvist 2006), about the growing numbers conceived through assisted reproduction and especially how LGBTQ+ families navigate heteronormativity in various ways (SOU 2001; Ryan-Flood 2009, Malmqvist 2016, Nordqvist 2006a and 2006b). This research and the changes it tracks, might indicate that being queer (as in non-heterosexual) is no longer an obstacle to family making in Sweden, or differently put, that what anthropologist David Schneider (1968) called love as the key symbol of kinship now includes the love that queers prac-tice: erotic, sexual, intimate, and romantic (cf Dahl 2014).

---

[3] And others with functioning uteruses, including transmen.

Yet, we might ask to what extent the existence of queer families actually changes our conception of kinship and for whom is it a possibility and how. As we shall see here, in many ways, Swedish family law maintains the "facts of life" central to heterosexual reproduction as the premise of parenthood and limits parents to two. Furthermore, parental status and recognition remains legally tied to a mode of conception and the status of the so called third party (or donor) is significant, if ambiguous. Furthermore, since access to fertility services through public healthcare is regulated in a range of ways and relies on assessments of both economic and social resources, many LGBTQ+ people continue to conceive at home or abroad through a growing private global fertility market (cf Dahl & Andreassen 2021). At the same time, by focusing primarily on how gender and sexuality, shapes family-making research in this field has tended to unflexively focus on the white majoritarian population and has rarely taken an intersectional approach to experiences and challenges of same-sex (lesbian) parents.[4]

In this chapter, I discuss what the national survey into Lesbian, Gay, Bisexual, Trans* and Queer persons' experiences of and needs in relation to parenthood and company of children in Sweden might tell us about *who* is reproducing the (queer) Swedish nation, *what* non-heterosexual family-making means, and about broader understandings of relatedness and kinship.

The survey, to my knowledge the first of its kind to be conducted in Sweden, was designed by staff at the Swedish Federation for Lesbian, Gay, Bisexual, Transgender, Queer and Intersex rights (RFSL) in 2017, loosely following the format of a regional survey conducted in Stockholm a few years earlier. Distributed nationally through RFSL's channels, it garnered 645 respondents and generated thousands of free text answers to many of its questions, making it a rich archive of reflections on (paths to) parenthood. Here I first give a brief background to the survey and discuss why qualitative researchers might benefit from looking at

[4] Research on "gay dads" is growing, see Malmquist 2022; Malmquist and Spånberg Ekholm 2019.

survey data, given the challenges involved in drawing on and creating statistical norms. Then I turn to 13 demographic questions that provide data which is difficult to obtain through normative census questions and discuss what this tells us about who is making family and how the legal frameworks shape (experiences of) family making. This is followed by a discussion of how kinship relations are described and how parenthood is understood and practiced, drawing on free text answers. Lastly, I turn to data on how the process of conception involves navigating legal frameworks that reflect particular biopolitical state interests as a context in which contemporary dreams and practices of LGBTQ+ family-making in Sweden are realised. With an intersectional approach to queer kinship, I discuss how gender, race, class, age and relationship status shape experiences of and hopes for family making, how queer kinship is entangled in broader racial, national and biogenetic understandings of relatedness, all which might reflect and contribute to certain "homo" norms.

As the opening quote suggests, there are many ways to make family in Sweden today. With growing divorce statistics, it is estimated that at least 1/4 of children in Sweden grow up with multiple parents due to parents' new relations. In an era of rights, which as research shows is the strongest indicator for growing "tolerance" (Takacs et al. 2016), it may not be self-evident that LGBTQ+ parents are in need of community or interested in meeting others "like" them. The respondent's feeling that sexual orientation and gender identity does not matter for parenting could suggest that the legal changes have indeed "succeeded" in obtaining sexual and gender equality for families. At the same time, while (queer) kinship and family might ultimately be about interdependent intergenerational bonds and relations, the meaning of kinship here remains lodged within a heteronormative logic where kinship terms (such as grandmother) are both always already deeply gendered, and intrinsically entangled with ideas of heterosexual reproduction and relatedness. I will here argue that the survey shows that the idea of Sweden as a place where LGBTQ+ people have "equal rights" is not quite a reality, and that indeed, in neoliberal times of growing segregation and inequality, sexual orientation/identity and gender identity, along with a range of other demographic factors including class, race and location matter in different and profound ways in paths towards and experiences of family making. In fact, we might say that LGBTQ+ reproduction tends to favour a certain segment of the population, white upper-middle class lesbians, who are thus bestowed with the opportunity to reproduce national Swedish whiteness.

The power in numbers

We might ask why queer qualitative researchers with an interest in theorising kinship through stories of lived experience and everyday life should care about demographic data and statistics. Isn't it enough to account for the complex ways in which people navigate heteronormative state apparatuses and succeed in manifesting their dreams of family? As a feminist cultural anthropologist, I admittedly have a preference for the rich complexities that emerge through qualitative interviews and an archive of cultural materials and representations over "big anonymous numbers." Yet, when I have presented findings from interviews and observations that point to norms and power relations embedded in and revealed by Sweden's allegedly "inclusive" family law and how it affects people differently, in particular trans and queer people of colour, my sample size is frequently questioned in terms of its "representivity". My view is that this response itself reveals a deep attachment to the idea of the tolerant and inclusive state that recognises LGBTQ+ subjects as parents and partners, adults.

Of course, we know that there is power in numbers; they can make or break social movements, political parties and even individual lifelines. Statistics (the result of research that collects, organises and analyses data according to certain premises and demographics) are often mobilised to demand representation, rights and recognition for different kinds of social groups. Consider the famous statement "we are everywhere", which drew on the idea that 10% of the US population is homosexual originating from Kinsey's large-scale studies of sexual behaviour (Spiegelhalter 2015). Here a statistical figure not only revolutionised gay and lesbian movement, it has been used to argue for the existence of LGBTQ+ people (and families) all over the world, in every school and village, ever since. Yet, as Joanna Mizielińska's (2022; this volume) work attests, it is not always sufficient to point to demographic "facts", such as that LGBTQ+ people *are* in fact raising children or living in familial arrangements, since questions can easily be raised about the representativity of a survey. Another dilemma is, as feminist, postcolonial and critical race scholars have long pointed out, the statistical instruments and categories themselves. Writing on the census, Mennicken and Espland (2019, 228) note that it is "often bound up with notions of identity, citizenship, and belonging" that not only depart from predetermined categories, but often (re)produce norms and medians, miss the messiness of reality and render invisible non-normative ways of living. At the same time, as research on racism and sexism frequently demonstrates, it is rarely enough to simply point to numbers (Ahmed 2013). Indeed, we know that demographic statistics also have documented strong ties to a history of eugenics where they have been used to perpetuate structural racism and pathologisation of certain groups (Zuberi 2001). Numbers, in other words, become both powerful and useful through the acts of interpretation and narration.

Given the fluidity of gender and sexual identities, it is not surprising that statistics on LGBTQ+ families have been difficult to create, find and interpret. Defining identities tends to fix them in ways that don't always reflect or tell us what we want to know. For instance, according to Statistics Sweden's (SCB) 2019 report on households, (i.e., people registered on the same address), 1,6% of the population live with a person of the same sex (about 150 000 people) and 6,000 of such households include children. Yet, these figures do not tell us what kind of relationships adults and children have in such households.[5] Indeed, at the end of 2017, according to census data, 6 837 women and 5 321 men were in same sex mar-

---

[5] *Ensam, med partner eller kompisboende? Vad säger hushållsregistret?* SCB Demografiska rapporter 2019, 1. https://scb.se/contentassets/cfe7690018d741798939bd8a6d087219/be0701_2015i2018_br_be51br1901.pdf. Last accessed: 2022-10-01.

riages or registered partners[6], and 3 155 children under 17 had two mothers, while 209 had two fathers as their registered legal guardians, a considerably smaller number. These figures also illuminate the fact that marriage and family is not numerically gender "equal" (i.e., more women than men are married and have children) but also that marriage to a great extent defines parenthood. In 2017, numbers of children adopted by one or two parents in a same sex couple increased significantly, to 161 or 14% of the total number of adoptions, with the vast majority being women adopting their partner's biological child/ren.[7] Yet, such figures do not tell us who is raising children, about multi-parent families by design or default, about children who live part time with multiple (gay) parents, or about people who have had children in heterosexual constellations and who "come out" later in life. In short, and as the public investigation that led to the changing family law (SOU 2001: 10) noted already 20 years ago, it is difficult to define and capture the size of the LGBTQ+ population with children. Here a national survey that offers an opportunity to outline in greater detail one's family situation and define one's own terms for kinship and its meaning can provide meaningful additional data.

Against this backdrop of limited national census data on LGBTQ+ families, it is valuable to know more about actual existing families. While it is difficult to fully ascertain the statistical representativeness of the national online survey entitled "HBTQ persons' experiences and needs connected to parenthood and engagement with children,"[8] discussed here, we get a sense at least in relation to the census data discussed above, to statistical methods and norms. This survey followed the questions of a previous regional survey and was designed, marketed and distributed by RFSL, a community organisation, both on their own websites and in social media, especially Facebook and Twitter. Using digital

---

[6] https://www.scb.se/hitta-statistik/artiklar/2018/samkonade-aktenskap-vanligast-bland-kvinnor/. Last accessed: 2022-10-01.

[7] https://www.scb.se/hitta-statistik/artiklar/2018/allt-fler-adopterar-styvbarn/. Last accessed: 2022-10-01

[8] In Swedish: Nationell enkät om hbtq-personers erfarenheter och behov kopplat till föräldraskap och umgänge med barn.

form and promotion, including a form of digital snowballing whereby a number of key actors, from midwives and clinics to activists and organisers of a range of groups on queer families were asked to spread the news of the survey, was a strategic choice for a number of reasons. Social media use is high in Scandinavia; at least half the population has a Facebook account, compared to 1/3 of the global human population (Andreassen 2018) and LGBTQ+ people increasingly use social media and digital technologies both to find and maintain relations and community, and to harvest information (cf. Lilieqvist 2020, Tudor 2018, Schwartz 2020), which suggests that this mode of distribution and participation was reasonable. We also know that people who are planning or living in queer families often use a range of discussion groups on social media (many with thousands of members) to gain and share information, and to construct and maintain community and kin relations (Andreassen 2018), which means it was likely to reach the target audience.

This survey consisted of 56 questions that offered both multiple-choice and free text answers and it was completed by 645 people from all counties in Sweden.[9] As the first national Swedish survey aimed to capture both "HBTQ people's" experiences and needs connected to parenthood *and* their broader engagement with children, the data offers a rich and complex picture. The majority of 103 comments to the final question expressed gratitude for the work of RFSL and found the survey important, even if a few found it too long and complex, and almost all participants completed the entire survey. In this analysis, the focus is, on the one hand, on the "big picture", that is, the demographics of the "community" that answered, and also hones in on particular narrative responses drawn from the rich data from free text answers. As we shall see, many of those give a rich sense of how several factors shape experiences, including gender, sexuality, age, mode of conception and so on, but it does not provide detailed insight into who is behind each narrative response.

---

[9] The Survey questions are included as an appendix at the end of this chapter.

The survey's focus on both experiences of parenthood and of other forms of interaction with children confirm the numbers offered by SCB Sweden that today many LGBTQ+ people have or desire to have children in their lives. What we get here is the richness of the free text questions and the nuanced views of relations and kinship terms. 58% of respondents were parents or legal guardian of children, 35% also identified as an "important adult" in a child's life, and 27% were godparents to children, with 30% also stating that they planned to have children in the future. This suggests a strong reproductive norm in the sample (indeed others might have felt discouraged), but also suggests that people engage with children in ways that exceed the nuclear family. Table 1 below shows gender and sexual orientation (questions 7 and 8) for respondents, and for both questions it was possible to choose several options, for instance both cis-person and woman:

Table 1. Gender identification and sexual orientation.

Gender identification	n	%	Sexual orientation	n	%
Transperson	33	5,12	Homosexual	393	60,93
Cisperson	91	14,11	Bisexual	154	23,88
Non-Binary	41	6,36	Heterosexual	7	1,09
Transvestite	1	0,16	Queer	149	23,1
Transsexual	13	2,02	Other	80	12,4
Intergender	5	0,78	I do not use any words for my sexuality/sexual orientation	47	7,29
Queer	110	17,05			
Woman	468	72,56			
Man	101	15,66			
Other words:	21	3,26			
I don't use any words to describe my gender identity	24	3,72			

A major finding here is the limitations of using the commonly used Swedish acronym "HBTQ" (homosexual, bisexual, transgender and queer) as it does not indicate gender differences. While 61% of respondents opted for the term homosexual and 23% for queer, 73% also identified as women and the most common free text word chosen was lesbian or dyke, which points to the significance of gender in terms of queer reproduction and kinship. As this chapter will show, if we are to understand the complexities of non-hetero-sexual parenthood, the "H" for homo or "same-sex" masks more than it reveals; especially given that only those with uteruses are helped by fertility medicine in Sweden, which along with the challenges of both domestic and international adoption leaves many having to either engage in transnational surrogacy arrangements or family constellations involving persons who can carry children. It is also noteworthy that 28% of respondents identify as queer, trans or non-binary and worth pointing out from the beginning that responses to the survey's different questions indicate that experiences of transgender parents differ significantly from those of cis-gendered parents (whether or not the latter identifies as such).

In this chapter I will use the acronym "LGBTQ+" to highlight that lesbians (and women) according to this survey are more likely to be/come parents; there is a strong lesbian "norm" and to mark these differences, even if these letters do not reflect stable categories as such. These demographics also demonstrate a theme throughout the survey and thus a key argument in this chapter, namely that in Sweden, differently gendered bodies with different capacities for sexual reproduction have very different paths to obtaining (legal) parental recognition and that this matters for how (queer) reproduction, kinship and family-making are understood.

Telling queer stories with demographic data

This national survey differed from previous regional surveys designed by RFSL staff and conducted in Stockholm on one important matter: it included a set of demographic questions. Beyond gender and orientation, it also included initial questions that asked about age, location, educational background, occupation and experiences of migration and racism. Here I paint an overall picture from the 13 demographic questions, and then offer a qualitative reading of this data in relation to the significant changes in Swedish law and assisted reproduction in the 21st century.

83% of respondents were between 26 and 45, 45% were under 36 and only 7 respondents were over 55.[10] As further supported by free text answers concerning paths to parenthood and what having children brings, this suggests that the survey might have been more successful in reaching the currently "fertile" population, that is, a majority have just had or are planning to have children. Table 2 shows how parenthood is practiced and imagined:

Table 2. Experiences of parenthood and future family imaginaries.

Experiences of parenthood	n	%	Future family imaginaries	n	%
Voluntary solo parenthood	60	9,57	I can imagine being a voluntary solo parent	106	16,85
Involuntary solo parenthood	36	5,74	I can imagine sharing parenthood with one other person	365	58,03
Sharing parenthood with one other person	339	54,07	I can imagine sharing parenthood with several others	134	21,3
Sharing parenthood with several persons	66	10,53	I can imagine my child/ren having multiple residences	124	19,71
Child/ren with multiple residences	122	19,46	Not relevant/cannot answer	205	32,59
Sharing residence with a different person than my child/ren's parents	74	11,8			

[10] Internet use is high across the board in Sweden.I In 2017, 98% of Swedes over 56 used the internet, even if the number of elderly users is lower than the national average. More than 50% of the population over 70 used Facebook daily in 2017 according to a report from the Swedish Internet Association. https://svenskarnaochinternet.se/rapporter/svenskarna-och -internet-2017/kommunikation-och-sociala-plattformar/. Last accessed 2022-10-01.

Shared residence with several others, including children	48	7,66				
Not relevant/cannot answer	209	33,33				

Interestingly, 54% of current parents shared parenthood with one other person, 16% were solo parents, with 9,5% voluntarily so, while 5,8% described it as involuntary. 19% do not live with their children full time, 8% share housing with others, including children and 12% share housing with others than the parents of their children. 10% share parenthood with more than one person. These figures suggest while there is a strong couple norm (supported by the law) there is also great diversity of family forms among LGBTQ+ people, including those not currently legally recognised.

30% of respondents plan families in the future, and while we know there is a difference between what one imagines and hopes for and what actually happens, the survey responses point to a range of conceivable "choices" in 2017, and above all perhaps, to the fact that reproductive futurity is conceivable and desirable; perhaps even expected (Mamo & Stieglitz 2014). 58% state that they plan to share parenthood with one person, which suggests that the dual parenthood norm remains strong. At the same time, 17% can also imagine solo parenthood with 21% able to envision multi-parent constellations with children dividing time between several households, which is a significantly higher number than existing families. Arguably, the former reflects solo women's access to assisted reproduction whereas the latter suggests that people do continue to imagine making family both within and beyond the law. Bearing in mind gendered differences, multi-parent constellations might both point to strategies chosen among those who cannot gestate (for different reasons) and to intentional alternative family-making practices.

The second question concerned location. While all counties in Sweden were represented in the survey, 72% of respondents were from Sweden's major cities of Stockholm, Gothenburg and Malmö.

Within (Western) queer studies, migration to urban areas in search of like-minded others is well documented (Weston 1995). Clearly, LGBTQ+ people are (still) drawn to cities, also reflecting broader domestic migration patterns relating to education and employment. Yet, research also suggests that both migration patterns and reasons for moving are changing, and that those born after marriage and family rights experience less stigma (Wimark 2015). Read alongside survey questions concerning encounters with health care and various state institutions and questions on needs of parents it is clear that there are significant differences between and great needs among those in smaller towns, and also that people (are willing to) travel great distance to achieve pregnancy and/or parenthood. They also suggest that LGBTQ+ families living in smaller towns have fewer networks, are more dependent on families of origin, but also, like the quote that opened this chapter, that some are less concerned with the LGBTQ+ community.

One significant survey insight concerns socioeconomic factors, and respondents diverge somewhat from the national demographic.[11] Table 3 shows education, income and employment:

Table 3. Education, income and employment.

Education	n	%	Income (SEK)	n	%	Employment	n	%
Basic	194	30,08	Under 100.000	63	9,77	State Sector	98	17,47
Gymnasium	241	37,36	100.000–200.000	96	14,88	Municipal sector	171	30,48
Professional	80	12,4	200.000–300.000	131	20,31	County sector	84	14,97
University	477	73,95	300.000–400.000	187	28,99	Cultural sector	47	8,38
PhD education	40	6,2	400.000–500.000	113	17,52	Non-profit sector	60	10,7

[11] Source: https://www.scb.se/hitta-statistik/statistik-efter-amne/hushallens-ekonomi/inkomster-och-inkomstfordelning/inkomster-och-skatter/pong/statistiknyhet/slutliga-inkomster-och-skatter-2016/. Last accessed 2022-10-01.

Other	34	5,27	Over 500.000	55	8,53	Corporate sector	103	18,36
						Other	43	7,66

National census data from 2018 indicates that 43% (49% of women) of the national population had some higher education while 28% were highly educated.[12] In contrast, 73% of survey respondents having a university education and 6% educated up to postgraduate level;[13] suggesting that as a 'cohort' LGBTQ+ parents have a higher level of education than the national population.

Of the 68% who were employed, the majority work within different parts of the public sector. This is in line with the national population, for which the most common job is the municipal sector, which largely involves forms of care work; 91% of this labour is performed by women. In terms of income, survey demographics diverge from national figures in interesting ways. While in 2016, the median income in Sweden was SEK 309 000; SEK 281 000 for women and SEK 342 000 for men, 55% of survey respondents earn above the national average, with 26% earning over SEK 400 000. Given the average age and that 73% are women, these figures point to a seemingly strong (upper) middle-class norm among respondents. At the same time, it is important to note that almost half the respondents are under the national average in terms of income.[14] More research is needed on how class and material resources inform modes of conception and paths to parenthood among LGBTQ+ people.

The two final demographic questions asked about experiences with migration and racism. While the Swedish population has

[12] https://www.scb.se/hitta-statistik/sverige-i-siffror/utbildning-jobb-och-pengar/utbild ningsnivan-i-sverige/. Last accessed 2022-10-01.

[13] Free text answers suggest that the most common additional form of education is folk school/community college.

[14] Space limitation prevents a needed longer discussion here about geography and income, especially in relation to age. It is likely that high salaries are concentrated to urban areas and to the strong middle age bracket in the data. The demographics section in this survey indicate that queer families (and their complexities) are rendered quite invisible in standardized census data (f ex SCB) due to the heteronormative framework of its statistical units.

diversified significantly in recent decades and despite documented growing discrimination and racism, most research on LGBTQ+ families has to date tended to focus on the majoritarian population and also to naturalise whiteness (Dahl 2018, 2020). Whereas 24% of the national population was born outside of Sweden in 2017, 7% of respondents had migrated to Sweden with 13% having at least one parent who had migrated. A majority of these had migrated from another Nordic or North European country, which suggests that the majority of respondents are white and lack migration experience. 8% reported experiences of racism and 6% said "maybe", which might suggest that the meaning of racism is not entirely clear to some respondents. 18% had family members who have experienced racism and 8% answered "maybe." While much more research is needed on this topic, the 97 free text answers where participants could elaborate on those experiences offer a glimpse of both how racism is understood and how it operates in respondents' lives. Interestingly, many also reported that they are "wholly Swedish" or "many generations Swedish." Read together, the free text answers show that proximity to white Swedishness in terms of familial history, appearance, language and names is crucial for avoiding racism. Whiteness can thus be understood as the absence of experiences of racism, which seems to be the case for 92% of respondents (see also Dahl & Andreassen 2021, Dahl 2018). Arguably, taken as a whole, LGBTQ+ family making in Sweden appears to be reproducing whiteness.

Among the 8% who experienced racism, many reported being adopted, pointing both to how transracial adoption is the "adoption norm" in a country that has little domestic adoption and also to the failure of an imagined "colour-blind" discourse tied to ideas of Swedish exceptionalism (cf Hübinette & Andersson 2012). According to the data, being bullied in school for not fitting into a blond, light, Nordic racial stereotype is frequent and anti-Semitic sentiments and racism against Sami and other national minorities persist. While many state that roots in other Nordic or northern European nations enables passing as white, a significant number account for experiences of not fitting in or being othered for having parents or grandparents from Finland. Respondents with Latinx heritage, describe both being able to pass as (southern) European and being othered as "immigrants." Consistent with other research,[15] anti-black racism stands out. Respondents describe derogatory language, comments on skin colour and features[16], as well as being exoticised, sexualised and celebrated for "mixed-raceness." In particular, there are many stories of racism at hospitals and clinics and through the process of assisted reproduction, as well as of partners and children experiencing racism due to being non-white and/or mixed race.

Given these stories, it is noteworthy that the Swedish system where doctors choose and match donated sperm with intended parents based on the idea of likeness is only brought up by non-white respondents. One writes that "we were questioned when we requested colours of the donor that would resemble my wife. 'What difference does it make? You would not be able to have a child together anyway,' they said". Consistent with what my interview data has suggested, it seems that non-white parents cannot always expect racial "matching" (cf Dahl 2018). Another respondent writes that "treatment at the clinic was good in terms of HBTQ competence but we had many strange discussions around choice of donor, which, according to staff, should be based on the partner's appearance/ background, and both me and my ex-partner were treated as very "special" because we are non-white and got many questions about colour and origin." As I have argued elsewhere (Dahl 2018; Dahl & Andreassen 2021), while whiteness is often rendered invisible among white people, there seems to be a strong white norm in assisted reproduction.

These survey demographics are largely consistent with existing census data that suggest a strong LGBTQ+ "family norm": parents (to be) are overwhelmingly urban, lesbian, cis-gendered white women who are highly educated with income above the national average. This is not surprising, given the challenges in both access-

---

[15] Simon Wolgast, Irene Molina & Mattias Gardell. 2018. *Antisvart rasism och diskriminering på arbetsmarknaden.* Länsstyrelsen i Stockholm. Rapport 2018:21.

[16] Here I have opted against repeating verbatim the violent language these respondents describe because in a climate of endemic antiblackness there is enough wallowing in black pain and suffering and it is not necessary to make the point here.

ing assisted reproduction and managing paths to legal recognition, couple with the high cost of assisted reproduction technologies, such as surrogacy arrangements (3% of respondents) and insemination or IVF abroad (25% of respondents). Similar demographics are found in the extensive national survey carried out by Mizielińska et al. (2015) on Families of Choice in Poland concerning LGBTQ+ experiences of family making, where the majority of respondents were highly educated and had a higher income than the average Polish person, and Henny Bos' (2004) questionnaire-based study comparing planned lesbian families to heterosexual families in the Netherlands. Bos' study showed that lesbians who plan families were highly educated. Bos points out that there is a tendency towards over-representation of highly educated people in surveys, but research on assisted reproduction also shows that lesbian mothers are typically more highly educated than heterosexual women. I would argue that a narrow focus on sexuality and gender as the main features of queer parents, which has tended to be the case in previous research both in Sweden and in the wider Western or Anglo-American context (Malmqvist 2015, 2016; Ryan-Flood 2009; Nordqvist & Smart 2014), can obscure class dynamics and naturalise whiteness and belonging in the majoritarian population as a point of departure in discussions of LGBTQ+ parenthood. It may also be that (proximity to) whiteness is helpful for inclusion in the heteronormative reproductive nation.

While the survey suggests a strong white middle class urban norm, it also importantly indicates that LGBTQ+ parents and families exist in all counties in Sweden, and are quite diverse; there are significant differences in both experiences and understandings of reproduction linked to gender identity and parental status, but also to paths to procreation or chosen family form. Free text answers show that geographic location, material resources and knowledge about options shape experiences with assisted reproduction and legal recognition of parenthood. LGBTQ+ people with children is not a socioeconomically homogenous group, and clearly access to state funded assisted reproduction does to some extent "democratise" queer family making, given that the costly reproductive technologies in the global fertility market via state-funded might to some extent serve to "democratise" queer family-making. This brief discussion of demographics indicates that much more research is needed on inequalities in LGBTQ+ paths to and experiences of parenthood, beyond the current focus on discrimination on the basis of sexual orientation and "same-sex" parenthood.

In your own words: Relations to children and the performativity of kinship terms

The survey aimed to capture a range of ways that LGBTQ+ people engage with children in their lives and the open-ended questions provide rich and nuanced descriptions of the meaning that being with children provides. The majority of respondents (58%) are parents or legal custodians to one or more children, with 6% stating that they are parents who lack legal recognition with 30% planning to become parents. Only 1% are grandparents, a figure likely explained by the age demographic, wherein only 7 people over 55 responded. However, respondents also engage with children in many different ways: 28% are godparents (*fadder*) for children of kin and friends, 35% state that they are important adults in children's lives and 20% work with and have other experiences involving children. The survey thus suggests that LGBTQ+ people increasingly have or desire to have children of their own and given the many other ways that they report engaging with children, that many children have significant people in their lives who are LGBTQ+ identified. This is a stark contrast to the idea that being queer means exclusion from contact with kin and children, again suggesting a certain "normalisation."

The survey also shows the complexities of kinship and the multiple roles people have; many report being both biological and legal parents, bonus parents and godparents. While this might seem obvious and while to respondents themselves, it may or may not matter for parenting, it is clear that these are not equal before the law.

An especially crucial finding is the level of involvement in relatives' and friends' children's lives; indeed, the survey suggests that LGBTQ+ people are not cut off from families of origin. To some, engaging with (others') children offers preparation: "it gives me a strong sense that I too would really like to have children and my own family, and that it is actually possible", one respondent writes. In other words, in 21st century Sweden, being gay or queer does not make family inconceivable. In this section I discuss what survey results might teach us about queer kinship, that is, about views on kinship and relatedness, what terms are used to describe parenthood and what having children does to a sense of belonging and identity in kinship terms.

For instance, the free text question "describe with your own words what kind of relation you have to the children in your life," generated 317 answers and points to how language matters for kinship. A "relation" is a noun, that both describes connections between people and things and according to the Free dictionary connotes "the mode or kind of connection, connection between persons by blood or marriage, a person who is related by blood or marriage, relative and finally the act of relating, narrating, or telling; narration."[17] Survey answers are examples of narration about connections between people in kinship terms. Narration of origin stories (how babies were made, what relations are between parents, etc) is crucial for understanding (queer) kinship, and can be understood as reflecting kinning practices, or "the process through which kinship is established by connecting one being to another" (Gunnarsson Payne 2016, 484). As the survey concerned parenthood rather than (romantic) relationships, we only learn about parents' relations to other adults and parents indirectly, from how they describe their relation to children (see Dahl 2022).

Coding free text answers also indicates what sorts of relations and terms are used to describe kinship.[18] The neutral but significant term "parent" (*förälder*) is used over 200 times across the survey, while the sometimes advocated for legal and equally gender-neutral term "caregiver" (*vårdnadshavare*) is used comparatively fewer, 15 times, suggesting that there is a preference for being

---

[17] https://www.thefreedictionary.com/relation, accessed 2022-08-31
[18] The data file was searched in order to identify certain key terms, such as parent (förälder), mother (mamma), father (pappa), etc, to get an overall sense of what terms are used.

viewed as a parent. To describe parenthood, the term legal (*juridisk*) is used 78 times, while biological (*biologisk*) is used 134 times in free text answers, which, if nothing else, suggests that respondents make distinctions between different kinds of parents based on modes of conception, legal possibilities and understandings of relatedness. The gendered kinship terms mother and father are used 55 and 35 times respectively, while surrogate is used 6 times and foster home (*familjehem*) 14, again indicating recognition as an important adult/person. I argue that these descriptions do not simply reflect a certain reality or demographics of conception, they also speak to the need and desire to navigate an existing kinship logic. Descriptions of intimate relationships with siblings' and cousins' children, partners' children from previous relationships, and professional relationships as teachers, childcare workers, coaches and descriptions of housing young refugees or acting as contact families all point to a range of ways of engaging with children that reflect the kinship and legal structures of contemporary Sweden.

This rich data set suggests that in Sweden, same-sex parenthood both challenges and reproduces normative Euro-American kinship, that is, one in which parents are gendered categories referring to the two who provide the genetic materials – sperm and egg – and are joined through love and reproduction. According to kinship theorist David Schneider (1980) love (which to him is the same as heterosexual intercourse in marriage) is the key kinship symbol and also the foundation of family law, and it generates two forms of kinship: consanguineal (kinship by blood) and conjugal (kinship by marriage). While reproduction can now occur in many ways that do not involve heterosexual intercourse, and the centrality of life-long (heterosexual) marriage has diminished, love remains a strong organising symbol for what Schneider called (1980, 61) kinship as a "diffuse, enduring solidarity," including among LGBTQ+ families.

While LGBTQ+ parents and families are sometimes treated as one group, it is very clear that kinship terms also speak of relations as well as modes of conception and that many make distinctions between relations by blood (parents-children, or what is called consanguinity) and relations by law (marriage, also called affinity), even if significant effort is also put into erasing differences between, for instance, biological and legal parents, sometimes by simply using the term 'parent' (see also Mizielińska 2021). At the same time, in contemporary Sweden, 25% of all children have divorced parents and one in ten split their time between two homes, which means that many children, beyond those with "same-sex" parents, have multiple parents/adult caretakers of the same gender. Yet new family forms, including co-habitation, "recombinant families," and legal recognition of same-sex families, almost always centre the couple and dual parenthood and also emphasise distinctions between "step-" or "bonus-" parents and "real parents." Similarly, in this data, terms that name relations frequently invoke the biological/legal definitions of kinship and are often further clarified through using adjectives that provide attributes to the relation (e.g., "co-", "legal", "adoptive", "birth-", etc).

The extent to which and how changes in family forms actually challenge heterosexual reproductive logic as a basic premise for kinship is up for debate. Feminist scholars who have studied third-party assisted reproduction have pointed to the de-linking of genetic contribution and parenthood and potentially challenges the normative dimensions inherent in this practice. Kinship, scholars have argued, is not so much about "facts" as it is a kind of grammar that is "generative of the kinds of material, relational, and cultural worlds that are possible, and for whom" (Franklin & McKinnon 2001,15; see also Payne 2016). As Payne (2016, 488) proposes, these kinship grammars "tell us what 'counts' as kinship; they provide us with the rules for who counts as kin." Kinship terms are thus not descriptions put on an existing material reality, rather, kinship is the site where an always shifting boundary between nature and culture gets drawn, which means that changes in kinship grammars are not merely semantic, they change kinship itself (Payne 2016). Differently put, kinship terms are performative.

New terms such as "mapa" (a term that challenges the gendered connotations of mother and father and makes room for queer, intersex and non-binary parents and that a few respondents use in the survey as well as in my interviews) matter for queer kinship insofar as they challenge the connection between (reproductive) sex and parental categories. Other respondents use the term "care person" (*omsorgsperson*) to describe and highlight the importance of persons who raise children rather than those who have bio-genetic relations to them, thus shifting the symbolic meaning of parent from blood relation to function or practice, and an emphasis on the care labour involved. Extending Payne's (2016) discussion of kinship grammars, I suggest that an emphasis on parenting as care (labour) rather than biological or legal relatedness might be called a grammar of practice. Both the survey results and my interviews suggest that a kinship grammar of practice is central to Swedish LGBTQ+ people's understanding of parenthood, and that a lack of practice can also break a kinship bond. Understood in this way, the term *omsorgsperson* might be understood in light of Butler's (2002) idea that kinship, like gender, is a set of practices rather than a predetermined property of certain relations.

As noted above, many respondents describe how children are central to family and to inter and cross-generational relations and intimacies, including with families of origin. They create a sense of belonging, or 'being long' (to use Freeman's 2007 terminology). One respondent writes: "my sister's kids give me a feeling of belonging with my biological family, and I hope that I have and will be an important person in their life. That gives me a sense of meaning." Another writes:

> I think it's so fascinating how the love for my *brorsdotter* (niece) just came when she was born. I thought it was only parents who felt that way…I have never wanted to be a parent myself, but I like having an (important, I think) role in a child's life. I would have really liked to have another grown up in my life when I was growing up.

Responses like this point to how kinship, here siblinghood, explains love for children (cf Dahl 2018c) and creates love and meaning. Many respondents describe being an important grown up for a child in relation to what oneself missed growing up; suggesting that children provide a sense of repair of one's own childhood. Many answers to a question concerning what children bring to their lives mention closer proximity to families of origin:

> I have a better relation to my family of origin. Unfortunately, also a worse relationship with my ex initially but that doesn't have to be due to children. Rather, a child made it clear to me that that relationship was not good enough. Greater pressure on myself to make relations, work and finances work. But also a desire to be more independent. I want to be able to control my parenting myself and this makes me appreciate being alone with my child and make my own decisions more than I did when me and her other mother lived together.

Respondents stress that having children alters decisions and priorities, rendering other dimensions of life, including romantic relations, secondary (see Dahl 2022). In the above quote and many other responses, having children is tied to "adulthood" (cf Halberstam 2005); having them contributes to self-discovery, requires work on the self and brings desires for independence and control. Yet, while a child can create better relations to biogenetic kin, a focus on children can it seems also result in dissatisfactions surrounding the romantic parental relationship. Tellingly, the survey results suggest that for queers, consanguineal love, love for one's children and biogenetic kin, seems to take priority over conjugal love. Interestingly, only one or two respondents describe children as improving happiness in relations with another adult. There is an almost complete absence of discussions about relations to co-parents, other than as challenges (see also Dahl 2022).

The data in many ways illustrate why legal recognition of parenthood is important to LGBTQ+ parents. While the main argument for adoption (and thus legal recognition) that I heard in my research is that of a child's right to its parents, often based on fears of a future death of a gestational/biological parent, a statistically more likely scenario is that of divorce. 23% reported having experienced divorce, 5% a custody battle, and 14% had sought professional support, while 6% have drafted so called moral contracts for future conflicts. In my ethnographic research, including in courses for parents to be as well as in interviews, people frequently said that lack of recognition of more than two parents was a strong reason not to form families with more than one person, as it would otherwise be a challenging constellation to change. The 79 free text answers on divorce largely described separations from heterosexual relations, but some concerned lack of legal recognition of parenthood, and how birth mothers are privileged in counselling services and by courts. Also, many stated that how to heteronormative kin, legal recognition of a co-parent does not always translate into cultural recognition; indeed, extended kin may or may not recognise lesbian family-making as a legitimate and equal form of parenthood. In addition, when multi-parent constellations seek help in solving divorce-related issues, the number of parents can be confusing for professional staff and some state that they do not disclose their "identity" in therapy. Several describe spending significant time educating professional staff, especially around multi-parent constellations. One respondent tellingly writes that

> We were two mums and two dads that went to counselling when the mums were separating and we had different ideas about living arrangements, and so on. During the third meeting the counsellor sighs and says 'so you are all calling yourselves parents'?

Difficulties also emerge as a result of a lack of legal parenthood and many describe how the person who has given birth tends to be privileged in meetings with family services or in legal debates.

In terms of the grammar of practice discussed above, most understand parenthood as a care practice or reproductive labour, and many report that parenting is the everyday work of caring for, playing with, and raising children. Over 51% see children every day and 10% several days a week. Many found the free-text question "what do you do with children?" odd, because, as they stated, what one does is "obvious"; "everyday things" or "what everyone does", and they list homework, cooking, playing, reading, talking, travelling, and teaching children things. Responses here point to the opening quote; there is nothing "unusual" about being a parent, even if it is part-time. It is seen as a normal part of life.

Many, however, do distinguish between what they do with "biological" and "bonus" children with whom they live, with children at work and at home, and between activities with siblings' children and godchildren, foster children and friends' children, again suggesting that relations matter to practices. A strong overarching theme is centring activities on the child's needs and interests. No survey answers indicate that children do what parents do (for instance, at work or socially) and only a couple mention "fighting" or "quibbling" as part of being with children. Put together, this suggests a clear separation between work and leisure, significant time devoted to children, and distinctions between family ties and other relations. They also suggest that children are central in LGBTQ+ people's lives (see also Dahl 2022). Despite significant diversity, parenting practices and different intensities and frequencies of parenting, it is clear that LGBTQ+ parenting involves engaging with heteronormative ideas of relatedness and belonging. It is in everyday encounters in public, with extended family and surrounding society, that they have to negotiate ideas about the links between gender, sexuality, race and kinship in particular. Many respondents report that they find being asked about their relationship to the child and how children have been conceived invasive and stressful and in particular, that long and complicated procedures to obtain both biological and legal parenthood quite frequently leads to poor health and anxiety, as well as inequality between parents. In short, the navigation of the kinship grammars of biogenetics, law and practice are central to how LGBTQ+ people experience their lives with children.

Having babies like ourselves: Reproduction with parents, donors, clinics and the state

Following legal changes and technological advancements, a veritable queer baby boom has occurred in the past twenty years (cf Dahl & Andreassen 2021). The above section suggests that to survey respondents' parenting and kinship to a large extent is a form of 'doing' and a matter of everyday practices, the social reproduction of family-making. If labour division both reflects and produces gender, doing family queerly might alter the meaning, value and division of social reproductive tasks. It may also reproduce certain ideas, partly through the assignment of kinship terms.

Queer conception and in particular assisted reproduction, offers another interesting arena in which to study how gender, sexuality and race are reproduced and challenged in contemporary forms of queer kinship. Since the millennium, growing numbers of queers wish to have families and as a result, they are willing to spend considerable time and resources to obtain access to fertility medicine, either via the state or through a growing number of private clinics, and to go through quite complex screening processes for approval, especially when using state care.

The survey results support the idea that having children is not only a possibility but perhaps increasingly expected among LGBTQ+ people (cf. Dahl 2018; Mamo 2013). While this does not mean that there are not significant numbers of people who have raised children before these legal changes, people born before 1970 are unlikely to have had state support in achieving pregnancy without disguising their orientation. Yet, whether accessed through the state or through private clinics, assisted reproduction is hardly straightforward: it requires passing a number of tests, evaluations, approvals and institutions over significant time periods and always involves "choices." Differently put, the queering of reproduction and kinship is deeply shaped not only by growing inequalities in access but also by biopolitics and significant forms of state control. Drawing on survey data, in this section I discuss paths to parenthood and what it tells us about the landscape in which LGBTQ+ people achieve their dreams of parenthood. Table 4 shows modes of conception and imagined forms of conception:

Table 4.

Modes of conception	n	%	Future plans	n	%
I/we have used home insemination once or several times	102	16,11	Own/home insemination	158	25,16
I/we have obtained assisted reproduction at a clinic in Sweden once or several times	190	30,02	Assisted reproduction at clinic in Sweden	272	43,31
I/we have once or several times obtained assisted reproduction at a clinic abroad	163	25,75	Assisted reproduction at clinic abroad	252	40,13
I have had sex with another person for the purpose of pregnancy once or several times	49	7,74	Sex with another person for pregnancy purpose	59	9,39
Not relevant/can't answer	248	39,18	Not relevant/can't answer	259	41,24

The different imaginaries of existing and planned families are indicative of the changing landscape of assisted reproduction. While a progress narrative in which multiple parents is a relic of a pre-rights past, might assume that the 16% who had used home insemination with a known donor did so when there were few options, 25% can imagine home insemination in the future. Given the numbers of queer families in which multiple and different constellations can feature and where people have different kinship roles in relation to one another, and given the different capacities of different bodies, this makes sense, also considering the strong emphasis placed on origins and genetics. At the same time, using a clinic in Sweden is much more likely in the future, which suggests greater availability in the present, and yet 40% also imagine going abroad, which is also an increase. Given the greater range of options, that 9% state they can imagine having heterosexual intercourse for the sake of pregnancy suggests a persistence of bisexual and queer orientations and livelihoods.

While there is a diverse range of possible paths to parenthood, each comes with its own set of costs and challenges. And even if, since 2005, access to insemination and IVF with donated sperm is covered by public health care and funded by taxes in Sweden, it is only available to couples (and since 2014, persons) with functioning uteruses who are between the ages of 25 and 38, and who are approved after an assessment of socioeconomic resources. The state uses only registered donors and strongly advises against both known and unknown donors. This suggests a historically specific understanding of kinship and of the relationship between biogenetics, law, and parenthood (See also Dahl & Andreassen, 2021). Due to ongoing sperm shortage, in some counties, the waiting period to access "free" ARTs can be several years, pushing those who have the means but perhaps not the (reproductive) time, to continue going abroad. In addition, while there is a growing push to use donors who are willing to be found, it is clear that not all counties can offer a "match", with some wanting anonymous donors.

Among parents, 42% were the recipients of donated sperm, 2,4% of donated eggs and 2% of donated embryos. While 2% have donated eggs, only 0,5% have donated sperm, which is interesting given that about 4% have used surrogacy arrangements abroad to become parents. At the time of the survey, it does not seem that LGBTQ+ people are particularly keen to donate for others, even if they welcome donation for themselves. Among parenthood planners, 45% may use donated gametes and 15% may donate eggs, whereas fewer, around 6%, state that they would donate sperm, with known donation slightly more likely than to a clinic. While still limited in Sweden, the international literature on reproduction with donated gametes is growing (Nordqvist 2014, 2017; Nordqvist & Smart 2014), and given the persistence of biogenetic models for understanding origin, it is likely to remain a complex matter.

In Sweden, different paths to procreation are intimately linked to how the state understands and establishes parenthood and thus to different legal frameworks. In brief, for children conceived through home insemination, there is one legal system that distinguishes between a known donor and conception with purchased or unknown donated sperm (a practice which in turn has been variously discouraged and made illegal). A known donor automatically becomes a parent and must denounce their status in order for a lesbian co-parent to adopt. When donated sperm acquired through the commercial fertility market abroad is used, a co-parent must also formally adopt the child and the procedure in turn differs if the purchased gametes come from an open or anonymous donor. Before the early 2000s, common paths to parenthood either involved multi-parent arrangements, known donors or anonymous donors from abroad, each with their own set of understandings of the role of a donor and a parent (cf Malmqvist, Novak & Zetterqvist Nelson 2016). This is illuminated in many survey responses, for instance one who wrote about experiences with assisted reproduction explaining that "he who is now the father of our child and a part of her life donated sperm to us through a state clinic, that is, 'we brought our own donor' and he did not donate to anyone else. We were discouraged from this both by letter and verbally." By contrast, many also report that they chose to go abroad, specifically to Denmark, because they desired anonymous sperm, which is not permitted in Sweden.

This form of discouragement suggests that the state wishes to determine suitable donors and create 'order' in LGBTQ+ kinship. Indeed, those who wish to be inseminated through the welfare state, or get their fertility treatments abroad compensated for, may not choose sperm themselves, rather it must be done by clinic staff, in conversation with intended parents. The number of children conceived through each donor and set of parents is also regulated by the state. One writes:

> We went through 4 inseminations in total, two each. In other words, we made sibling attempts and switched carrier. Sibling attempts are always self-funded. The only thing we think is sad is that you only get to make one attempt at siblings, that is, we cannot have more than two children (with the same donor) which we think is really sad. But we understand that this is a lux-

ury problem, we have two amazing children thanks to Swedish healthcare.

Across the survey, the state's involvement in the biopolitical regulation of the population (Foucault 1990) is quite striking. As Foucault famously proposed, biopolitics point to how ideas about the reproduction, health, sexuality of the population are always entangled with political and institutional aims that encourage and limit particular population's reproduction. Historically, race has been one central dimension of the management of reproduction (cf Russell 2018). Through assisted reproduction and the 'fragmentation' of gametes, wombs and parenthood, populations are now increasingly managed through technologies and the legislations that regulate access and outcome (see further, Andreassen & Dahl 2021). In this case, the respondent, like a very large number of others, is very satisfied with Swedish healthcare and the support they receive. At the same time, a significant number report that they have not been treated fairly or in fact have been met with ignorance with respect to what they call "HBTQ issues", and many share stories of failed attempts and disappointments that they do not get to try more, or were not allowed to do IVF with their partner's eggs. One respondent writes that "I so want my wife to carry my egg with the same donor as my daughter has" but in 2017 that was not an option.

Many describe experiences at Swedish clinics as formal, and staff as often insensitive, not only in terms of parental recognition but also around donor choices. One writes: "When they told us how they chose donor they said it is based on the partner's appearance but not in our case as we were two women. I've heard that others get different answers and that they do choose based on the partner to the extent that it is possible." The meaning of "choice", so central to LGBTQ+ kinship and often imagined as self-evident in Swedish reproduction, is severely constricted and changes over time. For parents who are racialised as non-white, it seems particularly tricky (see Dahl & Andreassen 2021). There is an expectation of gratitude, but whereas Malmquist (2015) contends that there is a tendency to present a "just so" story of how happy things are, these respondents are quite willing to articulate grievances.

Unlike private clinics who often get sperm from banks in Denmark, Swedish state fertility clinics solicit their own gametes. According to Swedish law, presumptive donors, like those who wish to become parents, must go through a number of health tests, respond to questions about how they view kinship and disclosure, and must be willing to be open for a future child to contact. Respondents describe donation processes as quite invasive and offensive, insofar as they are felt to assess one's reproductive fitness:

> I went through an investigation in order to donate eggs. They concluded that my bio-family's medical history didn't make me fit as a donor. Despite the fact that the heredity of psycho-social challenges has been questioned. It made me feel like my own decision around parenthood was questioned.

Clinics seem to make an assumed connection between gametes and parenthood and between inheritance and futurity, and in this case in a way leaves the queer parent feeling unfit to reproduce the nation. While there are no legal or other forms of bonds or expectations for either donor or child, the biogenetic relation is established and to some extent secured by the obligation to inform children both of donor-conception and of their right to information about the donor upon reaching adulthood. On the receiving end, relations are also secured. One describes how at the clinic, "the doctor we met got super irritated over our questions about donor choice and such. We were also saddened and irritated over the letters that donors write to their potential children. The letters are initiated by the clinic and focus on fatherhood rather than on why they wanted to be donors." Along with many reports of being asked about "male role models," this suggests that in the eyes of the state, a relation should be maintained between donor and potential children; one which parents are expected to cultivate through stories. Arguably, the state thus shapes kinship as an orientation towards genetic heritage.

Across the research on donor conception, it seems clear that donors maintain some kind of position in queer kinship. For many, it is important that children share donors, even if the gestating body is not the same and growing numbers of lesbian and solo mothers search for donor siblings (Andreassen 2018). Marilyn Strathern (1999: 68) notes that "because of its cultural coupling with identity, kinship knowledge is a particular kind of knowledge; the information (and verification) on which it draws is constitutive in its consequences." While ideas about relatedness and belonging are largely lodged within stories about kin, the possibility of verifying information about a donor via state records also reveals that the state has several kinship logics working at once. Indeed, as Janet Carsten (2007, 409) notes, "expressed in the language of needs and rights, information about origins has a constitutive force that derives both from the linkage between kinship and identity, and from its previously hidden status."

Prior to insemination or IVF, intended parents must pass through a series of tests, including psychosocial ones (cf Malmquist 2015). Survey results show that to the large majority this "interview" was less uncomfortable than expected. Many do report feeling worried beforehand, since they did not know what to expect, with many pointing to a lack of knowledge about same sex couples among health practitioners, even if an equal number said that clinical staff had knowledge of LGBTQ+ issues. It is clear from the data that knowledge is growing, presumably due to the growing numbers of people who wish to have children. Frequent questions have concerned the presence of "male role models" and many say that much of the interview concerned how to address the child's conception.

Those who report having gone abroad for insemination and IVF have first and foremost gone to neighbouring Nordic nations, Denmark and Finland, largely due to the limited options available in Sweden. Descriptions of Danish clinics are strikingly positive, especially in comparison to Sweden; they are seen to offer more options for treatment, less regulation with regards to BMI and age, shorter queues for insemination, as well as knowledgeable staff. One theme that also emerges in previous literature (Malmquist

2015, Malmquist et al. 2016) is Denmark's proximity, the possibility of choosing the donor including an anonymous one. Respondents also describe surrogacy arrangements in the US, India and Thailand, egg donations in Estonia and Spain, and IVF with partner's embryo in England. This data suggests that LGBTQ+ reproduction in Sweden remains transnational, but also that going abroad seems to largely be a matter of "the rules being suitable for our wishes for making a family than those in Sweden," as one respondent put it. Here again several express wishes to be able to order sperm or embryos from Denmark for treatment in Sweden, seemingly because they trust national health care more and it being in closer proximity. Several also state that they feel cultural affinities to Denmark or Finland, but the most common reason is that queues to donated sperm in Sweden are long and restrictions are perceived as more limiting.

As noted above, experiences of adoption of one's child or partner's child are not uniform, partly because there seems to be no standard process but very much up to the specific municipality where parents live and the competence of the particular investigator. While many describe the process as smooth and pleasant, a majority of respondents describe it as a time-consuming, confusing, and often degrading process. Instances with known donors appear to cause particular issues where parents are repeatedly asked about the donor's feelings and the child's rights to a 'father'. Some report that they either postpone the adoption process out of exhaustion or complicated legal procedures, or because they themselves wish to be able to go through insemination. One writes that she wants to avoid a conflict with her wife and thus has not gone through the process, even if it means that she is not a legal parent. In particular, constellations with multiple parents create significant challenges:

> My wife and I would have liked to avoid adoption as it would mean that the biological father must denounce paternity. He is present in our child's life and we have a wish for joint responsibility. We have a sibling from another father (also present) and for our children to be legal siblings, this is the only solution.

Again, we see how children become central to decision-making. At the same time, in some instances, legal challenges are such that the parents end up unable to agree, with serious impact for some parents and their children. One respondent writes:

> I married the legal guardian with the aim of adoption but the third parent who didn't have a legal tie to the child objected to my adoption so it was drawn out and then the adult relations were so bad that it resulted in divorce. I now have no way of adopting. The others have gotten married and thus the third person can adopt and I have no say legally speaking.

This brief discussion of complex data on paths to parenthood with assisted reproduction suggests that while the Swedish state permits single women and couples with uteruses access to assisted reproduction, they do not permit unregulated reproduction. Rather, it seems that the state (and sometimes also parents) wish to keep track of biogenetic heritage, described as "a child's right to origin" and thus aims to secure the possibility that the link between donor and kin/paternity is left open for (re)interpretation.

Conclusion

In this lengthy chapter, to date only the second publication to discuss the data from this unique national survey, I have aimed to theorise queer reproduction and kinship in Sweden. As a queer feminist with an interest in the biopolitics of welfare states, homonationalism and critical race and whiteness studies, I have challenged the notion of HBTQ people as a homogenous group benefitting from legal rights and technological developments in the past decade. Instead, I have argued that while there is great diversity, resourced white married couples with at least one uterus – that is, lesbians who are white and middle-class – seem to be the main beneficiaries of the expansion of family law and access to state sponsored fertility treatments and other reproductive technologies in Sweden. As such, data is consistent with previous research (Malmquist 2015), which has shown that already, by the end of the first decade of the new millennium, half of all lesbian couples in Sweden were living with children and these numbers have likely risen as new generations who have grown up with rights reach the age of fertility. Like in this survey, two thirds of Malmquist's (2015) lesbian research participants also lived in urban areas, but while hers were almost exclusively white Swedes, when asked the question, these survey participants also speak to experiences of racism and discrimination.

The survey shows that experiences of assisted reproduction and parenthood remain particularly challenging for trans and queer identified people on both individual and structural levels (cf Leibetseder 2018), and that those who themselves or whose family members are not white and Swedish encounter many more challenges. This points to the need to move beyond simplistic comparisons of national (legal) differences and to consider queer kinship in an intersectional framework. Indeed, socioeconomic, racial and gendered inequalities and differences in access are not "secondary" to questions of LGBTQ+ rights, they are often entangled with them, indicating that sexual citizenship is far from equal. If, as Puar and Eng (2020, 3) have argued, "LGBTQ alignments with nationalist and racist ideologies are in fact not aberrations but, rather, constitutive of a normative queer liberal rights project itself" then we might instead investigate how LGBTQ+ family making is entangled with the biopolitics of reproducing the (white) nation.

Even if this survey provides significant narrative data on contemporary experiences of parenthood and living with children, it tells certain stories and not others, and likely overrepresents those who have or desire children and who are interested enough in these questions to fill out a lengthy survey. Many appear highly educated; they know their rights and can articulate their grievances, especially in relation to healthcare, and offer these in rich, nuanced, and perfectly spelled out and articulated free text responses. The Swedish healthcare system, like that of many neoliberal welfare states, is not easy to navigate; it involves both public and private actors, a number of different authorities that rarely speak to one another, and it requires patience, persistence, access to social security, the ability to access and navigate complex websites, and certainly the ability to present oneself as a credible and reasonable parent (to be) in Swedish. That LGBTQ+ parents with significant cultural capital are best represented and most active in improving their conditions, as well as the most willing to participate in studies and express their views, in research, social media settings and in relation to state institutions is also evident from public debate, community discussions and various forms of political organising.

As Henny Bos (2004) has noted, planned lesbian parenthood within contemporary neoliberal welfare state settings requires significant planning, patience, and choices; values and practices clearly aligned with those of the middle class – indeed, Bos found no great differences between heterosexual and lesbian parents who use assisted reproduction. Seen in this light, the kinds of tastes and expectations on life with children that the survey respondents articulate are striking (see Dahl 2022), especially when placed in a historical perspective. Parents expect (and often receive) good treatment and know what to do when they are dissatisfied. They have access to resources and many do not view themselves as any different from other parents, aside from having to go through sometimes quite lengthy and challenging processes to obtain pregnancy and/or parenthood. This also supports David Eng's (2010, 7) contention that in late capitalism in the West, being or becoming a parent is for the white middle class increasingly central to self-worth and value; having children has become central to a feeling of full citizenship (cf Halberstam 2005).

That said, living outside of the heterosexual norm does continue to cause pain, frustration and exclusion for many. As the demographics of Sweden change, so too will the future of queer fertility. How the growing privatisation of health care and range of providers of fertility services will respond to and reflect these demographics is a question that needs further study, as does the clear regional differences in health care provision and experiences of community. It is not sufficient to research or politicise LGBTQ+ parenthood in Sweden as solely a question of deviation from the heterosexual norm; more research is needed on those who are socioeconomically and racially marginalised and whose possibilities of reproducing the Swedish nation remain limited. Furthermore, the survey illuminates that multi-parent or "rainbow families" and their various components, including donors and divorced and new parents, remain lodged in the kinship logics of heterosexual reproduction and legal recognition as central, both with respect to whom the state understands us to be and to what future we may have, whether together or apart. If there is one take home lesson from this survey, it is a fairly obvious one; the closer LGBTQ+ families are to dual parental norms, middle class values, and indeed, to their extended kin, the better they are treated by heteronormative society.

References

Alm, E., Berg L., Lundahl Hero, M., Johansson, A., Laskar, P., Martinsson, L., Mulinari, D., & Wasshede, C., eds. 2020. *Pluralistic Struggles in Gender, Sexuality and Coloniality: Challenging Swedish Exceptionalism.* Cham: Springer International Publishing.

Andreassen, R. 2018. *Mediated Kinship: Gender, Race and Sexuality in Donor Families.* London: Routledge.

Bos, H. 2004. *Parenting in Planned Lesbian families.* Amsterdam: University of Amsterdam press.

Carsten, J. 2007. "Constitutive Knowledge: Tracing Trajectories of Information in New Contexts of Relatedness," *Anthropological Quarterly* 80 (2): 403–426.

Dahl, U. 2014. "Not Gay as in Happy, but Queer as in Fuck You: Notes on Love and Failure in Queer Kinship." *lambda nordica* 19 (3–4): 143.

———. 2018a. "Becoming Fertile in the Land of Organic Milk: Lesbian and Queer Reproductions of Femininity and Motherhood in Sweden." *Sexualities* 21 (7): 1021–1038.

———. 2018b. "(the Promise of) Monstrous Kinship? Queer Reproduction and the Somatechnics of Sexual and Racial Difference." *Somatechnics* 8 (2): 195–211.

———. 2018c. "Moderskapande meditationer och variationer," in *Mamma hursomhelst: Berättelser om moderskap,* edited by Margareta Fahlgren & Anna Williams, 47–61. Stockholm: Gidlunds Förlag.

———. 2020. "Precarious Labourers of love: Queer Kinship, Reproductive Labour and Biopolitics," in *Bioprecarity: Body, migration and intimate labor,* edited by Gabriele Griffin & Doris Leibetseder, 61–78. Manchester: Manchester University Press.

Dahl, U. & Andreassen, R. 2021. "Donors we choose: race, nation and the bio-politics of (queer) assisted reproduction in Scandinavia," *Biosocieties.* doi.org/10.1057/s41292-021-00256-2

Dahl, U. 2022. "Happy ever after? Reproduction and Futurity under Swedish Queer Liberalism," in Kritiska blickar från marginalen: Reflektioner i spåren av Jens Rydström, edited by Andres Brink Pinto, Mikael Mery Karlsson & Irina Schmitt, 161–180. Lund: Lund University Press.

Dahl, U. & Gabb, J. 2019. "Trends in Contemporary Queer Kinship and Family Research." *lambda nordica* 24 (2–3): 209–237.

Eng, D. 2010. *The Feeling of Kinship. Queer Liberalism and the Racialization of Intimacy.* Durham: Duke University Press.

Habel, Y. 2012. "Challenging Swedish exceptionalism: Teaching while black," in *Education in the black diaspora: Perspectives, challenges and prospects*, edited by K. Freeman & E. Johnson, 99–122. London/New York: Routledge.

Halberstam, J. 2005. *In a Queer time and place.* New York: New York University Press.

Hübinette, T., & Andersson, M. 2012. "Between Colourblindness and Ethnicisation: Transnational Adoptees and Race in a Swedish Context." *Adoption & Fostering* 36 (3–4): 97–103.

Gunnarsson Payne, J. 2013. "Europeanizing Reproduction: Reproductive Technologies in Europe and Scandinavia." *NORA – Nordic Journal of Feminist and Gender Research*, 21 (3): 236–242.

Kantsa, V. & Chalkidis, P. 2014. "Doing Family 'In the Space Between the Laws'." *lambda nordica*, 19 (3–4): 86–108.

Leibetseder, D. 2018. "Queer and Trans Access to Assisted Reproductive Technologies: A Comparison of Three EU-States – Poland, Spain and Sweden." *Journal of International Women's Studies* 20 (1): 10.

Liliequist, E. 2020. *Digitala Förbindelser: Rum, riktning och queera orienteringar.* The Department of Culture and Media Studies, Umeå University.

Malmquist, A. 2022. *Pappa, Pappa, Barn: Gaypappors Vägar Till Föräldraskap Och Familjeliv.* Lund: Studentlitteratur.

---. 2016. *Lesbiska Småbarnsföräldrar: Utmaningar i En Tid Av Möjligheter.* Gothenburg: Makadam.

---. 2015 *Pride and Prejudice: Lesbian Families in Contemporary Sweden.* PhD thesis, Linköping University.

Malmquist, A. & Spånberg Ekholm, A. 2019. "Swedish Gay Men's Pursuit of Fatherhood: Legal Obstacles and Strategies for Coping with Them." *lambda nordica* 24 (2–3): 53–80.

Malmquist, A., Polski, A. & Zetterqvist Nelson, K. 2016. "No One of Importance: Lesbian Mothers' Constructions of Permanently Anonymous Sperm Donors," in *Doing Good Parenthood: Ideals and Practices of Parental Involvement*, edited by A. Sparrman, A. Westerling, J. Lind & K. I. Dannesboe, 29–40. London: Palgrave Macmillan Studies in Family and Intimate Life.

Mamo, L. 2013. "Queering the Fertility Clinic." *The Journal of Medical Humanities* 34 (2): 227–239.

Mennicken, A. & Nelson Espeland, W. 2019. "What's New with Numbers? Sociological Approaches to the Study of Quantification." *Annual Review of Sociology* 45 (1): 223–245.

Mizielińska, J. 2021. "'Is She Still a Family or Rather Some Stranger?' – Relative Strangers and Kinship Plasticity in Families of Choice in Poland." *Journal of Homosexuality* 68 (11): 1899–1922.

Mizielińska, J., Abramowicz, M. & Stasińska, A. 2015. *Families of Choice in Poland: Family life of non-heterosexual people*. Warsaw.

Nordqvist, P. 2006a. "Att Tala Om Familj: Lesbiskas Berättelser Om Planerat Föräldraskap." *lambda nordica* 11 (4): 63–81.

———. 2006b. "Önskat och oönskat föräldraskap: Kön och sexualitet i svensk lagstiftningshistoria om insemination." *lambda nordica* 11 (1–2): 30–46.

———. 2014. "Bringing kinship into being: Connectedness, donor conception and lesbian parenthood." *Sociology* 48 (2): 268–283.

———. 2017. "Genetic thinking and everyday living: On family practices and family imaginaries." *The Sociological Review* 65 (4): 865–881.

Nordqvist, P. & Smart, C. 2014. *Relative Strangers: Family Life, Genes and Donor Conception*. London: Palgrave Macmillan.

Pelka, S. 2009. "Sharing motherhood: Maternal jealousy among lesbian co-mothers." *Journal of Homosexuality* 56 (2): 195–217.

Ryan-Flood, R. 2009. *Lesbian Motherhood. Gender, Families and Sexual citizenship*. London: Palgrave McMillan.

Rydström, J. 2008. "Legalizing love in a cold climate: The history, consequences and recent developments of registered partnership in Scandinavia." *Sexualities* 11: 193–226.

———. 2011. *Odd couples: A history of gay marriage in Scandinavia*. Amsterdam: Amsterdam University Press.

Spiegelhalter, D. 2015. *Sex by Numbers: What Statistics Can Tell Us About Sexual Behaviour*. London: Wellcome Collection.

Takács, J., Szalma, I., & Bartus, T. 2016. "Social Attitudes Toward Adoption by Same-Sex Couples in Europe." *Archives of Sexual Behavior* 45 (7): 1787–1798.

Tudor, M. 2018. *Desire Lines: Towards a Queer Digital Media Phenomenology*. Media and Communication Studies, School of Culture and Education, Critical and Cultural Theory, Södertörn University.

Wade, P, ed. 2007. *Race, Ethnicity and Nation: Perspectives from Kinship and Genetics.* London: Berghahn Books.

Weeks, J., Heaphy, B. & Donovan, C. 2001. *Same sex intimacies: Families of choice and other life experiments.* London: Routledge.

Weston, K. 1995. "Get thee to a big city: Sexual imaginary and the great gay migration." *GLQ: A Journal of Lesbian and Gay Studies* 2: 253–277.

Zetterqvist Nelson, K. 2006. "Att vara pappa i homofamiljer: Berättelser om barn, mammor och familjeliv." *Socialvetenskaplig tidskrift* 13 (1): 66–86.

Zuberi, T. 2001. *Thicker Than Blood: How Racial Statistics Lie.* Minneapolis: University of Minnesota Press.

Appendix

In order to make the analysis more transparent, the full list of survey questions is included here, along with the number of answers received for each question. Some questions allowed for several options. For this reason, both the number of respondents and number of answers is documented. Of particular interest to the argument made in this chapter, is the extensive qualitative data yielded from the free text answers.

Nationell enkät om hbtq-personers erfarenheter och behov kopplat till föräldraskap och umgänge med barn

Questions

1. How old are you? 645 answers
2. In which county do you reside? 645 answers
3. What is your educational background? Tick all answers that apply to you. 645 respondents, 1056 chosen answers
4. What is your current primary occupation? 645 respondents
5. If you are employed, within which sector do you work? 561 respondents, 606 free text answers
6. What is your estimated annual income? 645 respondents
7. Which word(s) do you use to describe your gender identity? Tick any alternatives that fit. 645 respondents, chosen answers 908
8. Which word(s) do you use to describe your sexuality/sexual orientation? Tick any alternatives that fit. 645 respondents, chosen answers 830
9. Have you migrated to Sweden? 643 respondents
10. Has one or several of your parents migrated to Sweden? 649 respondents
11. Have you experienced racism? 641 respondents
12. Have persons who belong to your family experienced racism? 641 respondents
13. In your own words, please elaborate on your answers concerning migration and racism. 97 respondents

14. Which of the following statements describe your current life situation and/or experiences with respect to parenthood and engagement with children? Tick any alternatives that fit you. 645 respondents, 1493 chosen answers

15. Describe in your own words what kind of relation you have to the children in your life, for instance god parent, legal parent, biological parent, partner's children, grandchildren. 317 responses

16. Experiences of being one, two or several parents. 627 respondents, 954 choices

17. Future visions regarding being one or several parents 629 respondents, chosen answers 934

18. Experiences concerning (any) divorce or separation. 591 respondents, 710 chosen answers

19. If you have experiences with separation and/or divorce involving children, we are interested in how that has turned out. How did you experience the attitudes and hbtq competence of any professionals you and the person(s) from whom you separated encountered during the process (e.g., family therapy or court)? 79 respondents

20. How much time do you spend with the child/ren in your life? Tick the answers that best fit you. 645 respondents

21. What do you typically do with the children in your life? For instance, do you hang out after school, spend weekdays together, go to the movies, do homework, play, cook or something else. Please write in your own words. 403 respondents

22. What does engaging with children bring to your life? Please write in your own words. 410 respondents

23. Have your experiences of family creation affected your health in any way? Positively or negatively? Write in your own words. 326 respondents

24. Experiences of assisted reproduction (insemination or IVF treatment) 633 respondents, 752 chosen answers

25. Future visions concerning assisted reproduction (insemination or IVF treatment) = 628 respondents, 1000 chosen answers

26. Experiences with donation of gametes (eggs or sperm) 615 respondents, 672 chosen answers

27. Future visions concerning donation of gametes (egg or sperm) 626 respondents, chosen answers 814.

28. If you have experience of assisted reproduction at a clinic in Sweden, please tell us how you experienced it. Did everything go well or did you experience any practical/medical problems? How did you experience the encounter with and competence at the clinic? Write in your own words. 170 responses

29. When you receive donated gametes (sperm or egg) at a clinic in Sweden you have to undergo a particular assessment, sometimes called an aptitude test *(lämplighetsbedömning)* which involves one or several sessions with a social worker or therapist and a psychosocial assessment. Have you done this?
582 responses, chosen answers 596.

30. If you have undergone a particular assessment, we would like to know how you experienced this. Were you informed about the purpose of the assessment? How did you experience encounters with and HBTQ competence among staff? Write in your own words. 163 respondents.

31. If you have experience of assisted reproduction abroad, or if this may be of interest in the future, which countries/clinics have you or would you approach? Please also state why these countries/clinics are or have been of interest to you. Write in your own words. 166 answers.

32. Experiences of surrogacy/host pregnancy. 595 respondents, 599 chosen answers

33. Future visions regarding surrogacy/host pregnancy. 604 respondents, 675 answers.

34. If you have experience of surrogacy/host pregnancy abroad or if this could be of interest for you in the future, which nation(s)/clinic(s)/ surrogacy agencies would you contact and why have these particular nations been of interest to you? Please write in your own words. 35 respondents

35. If you are or have been or could imagine being a surrogate/host pregnant, we would like to know your thoughts around this. How does the agreement work out? Did everything happen as planned? If you could see yourself as a surrogate, what arguments lay behind your decision/ thoughts? Write in your own words. 34 respondents

36. Experiences of paternity investigation and related party adoption. 616 respondents, chosen answers 724

37. Future scenarios regarding paternity investigation and related party adoption. 602 respondents, chosen answers 837

38. If you have gone through related party adoption (i.e., you have adopted one/several of your children, or that your partner/coparent has done it), we would like to know how you experienced the process. How long did it take? How did you feel about the treatment and the HBTQ competence among clerks at, for example, the family court? 111 respondents.

39. Sometimes there are problems in related party adoptions. If you have experienced problems connected to your adoption, we would like to know more about it. It can concern starting a process that is not completed for different reasons. Or it could concern needing a related party adoption but choosing not to? Why would that have been? Describe in your own words. 21 respondents

40. Experiences of international adoption. 598 respondents, chosen replies 600

41. Future visions around international adoption. 607 respondents, chosen answers 731

42. If you have a plan to or would like to adopt internationally, please develop your answers. How far are you in the process? How do you experience treatment by and HBTQ competence among those who you meet in the process? Write in your own words. 48 respondents.

43. Which of the following authorities and organisations in Sweden have you had contact with in connection to your existing and/or desired parenthood? 645 respondents, chosen answers 1113.

44. Please tell us which authorities and/or organisations you have been in touch with in connection to parenthood and describe with your own words how you experienced their treatment and HBTQ competence. 189 answers

45. Which of the following types of care agencies in Sweden have you had contact with in connection to your existing and/or desired parenthood? 645 respondents, chosen answers 2041.

46. Have you actively sought out care agencies in Sweden that are profiled as HBTQ competent (for instance through advertising) connected to your existing or desired parenthood? 623 respondents

47. Please tell us with which care agencies you have been in contact, connected to parenthood, and describe in your own words how you

have experienced their treatment and HBTQ competence. 275 respondents

48. Those of you with experience of pregnancy (your own or a partner's/co-parent's). we would like to know what you think of the materials and information you received during pregnancy. To what extent do you think the information listed below was/is included when it comes to your path to parenthood? 599 respondents

49. If you have experience of pregnancy (your own or partner's/ coparent's), we would also like to know how your needs for social connections and your actual social connections were during pregnancy. Check all alternatives that fit you. 601 respondents, 755 answers.

50. Please tell us more about what needs for support, information, material and/or social connections you had during pregnancy. Did you lack some kind of support, information, material, books and/or social connections that you think would have helped you during pregnancy? 124 respondents

51. Since 2013 RFSL Stockholm has a social meeting space for rainbow families/HBTQ families. We are now investigating the need for similar spaces in the rest of Sweden. We are interested in what your needs for social meeting places connected to parenthood are like. Check all alternatives that suit you. 645 respondents, 1387 chosen answers.

52. Please develop your answers above. What kind(s) of social meeting spaces for rainbow families/HBTQ families do you have need for? 201 answers

53. Since 2014, RFSL Stockholm has courses for parents including practical and legal information relevant for HBTQ persons who want to become parents. We are now investigating what the needs are for similar courses in other parts of Sweden. If your nearest RFSL section was to hold such courses would you be interested in attending? 645 respondents, 662 chosen answers.

54. Please develop your answers above. Why would such a course be interesting? Or why wouldn't it be? 186 answers

55. Is there anything you would like to add or clarify when it comes to your need for meeting spaces, support or information connected to parenthood? Write with your own words. 48 responses

We want to extend a big thank you to those who have taken the time to answer our questions! Your answers are a great help to us in our continued work with HBTQ persons' parenthood and engagement with children. Finally, we wonder if there is anything that you would like to add that you think would be useful for us to know. Please write in your own words. 103 responses.

PART 2
Assisted Reproduction, Queer Parenthood and the Nation State

4. Room for All: Equality, Race, and Reproduction in Norwegian Social Democracy

Suraiya Jetha

> The purpose of this law is to ensure that medical use of biotechnology is utilized for the benefit of people in a society where there is room for all. This shall be done in accordance with principles of respect for human dignity, human rights and personal integrity, and without discrimination on the basis of heredity based on the ethical norms enshrined in our Western cultural heritage.
>
> – Norwegian Law on Medical Use of Biotechnology, LOV 1994-08-05-56

From the earliest days of their relationship, Mona had been open with Tine about wanting to have children. But it was not until nearly four years after they began dating that their nebulous plans to have children "someday" became more urgent. Tine's mother nearly died after suffering a massive stroke, and her mother's mortality became the impetus for Mona and Tine to begin talking about what their family constellation could look like and how they could go about becoming pregnant.

I met Mona and Tine in 2016 while conducting ethnographic research on donor siblingship – relations between people sharing a sperm donor – and kinship relations in Norway. As my fieldwork unfolded, it became evident that donor sibling networks, mainly facilitated by "solo mothers" who had conceived in Denmark without partners, both trespassed and reinforced the borders of the Norwegian nation. My attention turned to other ways that donor insemination instantiated the constitution of the Norwegian nation and the definition of membership to the Norwegian welfare state.

Like many other couples conceiving through the national healthcare system, Mona and Tine planned to request a sperm donor whose appearance resembled the non-gestational parent,

Mona. But because Mona is of Iranian descent, the national sperm bank's lack of Asian- and African-descendant donors presented a problem for them. This chapter discusses the attempts to conceive made by couples like Mona and Tine, wherein one partner is white Norwegian and the other is Norwegian of Asian or African descent, and the institutional practices which interrupt their creative use of biological substance to forge kin ties. By detailing couples' desires to make families and the challenges posed to realising those desires, I investigate how colourblind Norwegian state discourses of equality produce inequality on the basis of race.

My analysis draws on data collected from a range of research methods. Shuttling between the registers of national discourse and everyday intimate life, I analyse the nation and the idealisation of kin relations alongside people's actual kin-making practices. In doing so, I follow a tradition of feminist anthropological scholarship that investigates kinship and nation through analyses of legal discourse, media, and ethnographic analysis (Strathern 1992; Cannell 1990; Dahl 2018b; Fernando 2019). For eighteen months, I conducted ethnographic research with parents from Norway, Denmark, and Sweden who had used donor insemination in private Danish fertility clinics or in publicly funded clinics in their home countries; I also interviewed staff and toured sperm banks and fertility clinics in Denmark and Norway. Though my ethnographic analysis here focuses primarily on life history interviews conducted with a married Norwegian couple, participant-observation in Norwegian public life informs my reading of Norwegian and Scandinavian sociality.

Theoretical intervention: *Likhet* and equality

The starting point of my analysis is Norwegian biotechnology law's lofty promise to foster an egalitarian society with "room for all" (*plass til alle*) regardless of biological inheritance. Appearing in the opening of a law that went into effect in 1995, this pledge embodies a central belief investigated by scholars of equality and kinship in the Nordic region: that biology presents a threat to equality.

Anthropologists of Norway have analysed equality (*likhet*) as a cultural, moral, and political force guiding state redistributive policies or even shaping mundane social interaction (Lien and Melhuus 2009; Lidén, Lien, and Vike 2001; Gullestad 2002). As Marit Melhuus and Marianne Lien argue, the multivocality of *likhet* lends itself to multiple definitions depending on context:

> [*Likhet*] could refer to a redistributive economic policy that aims to some extent to neutralise economic differentiation, as implied in modern welfare states. It could imply a relative lack of stratified class-based hierarchies, with limited possibilities for class distinction through education for example. It could reflect an aesthetic and moral preference for everything 'ordinary' (*folkelig*), such as when the king, the prime minister, or the most successful business tycoons are imagined as 'one of us', (and even present themselves in ways that confirm this notion). Or it could imply that Norway is experienced by a majority of its inhabitants as a fairly homogenous society, where people tend to look the same, think the same, and live their lives in more or less the same way. (Lien and Melhuus 2009)

Lien and Melhuus' examples demonstrate the intertwining of *likhet* with notions of sameness: *likhet* is equality that is realised through the absence, or even elimination, of difference. Equality, here, is not only being of equal worth, but also being of the same kind (Gullestad 2006; Melhuus 2012, 17; Petersen, Kroløkke & Myong 2017, 84).

Analysts of *likhet* have also noted its relationship to individuality and autonomy (Melhuus 2012, 20; Jacobsen 2018, 316). Historian Lars Trägårdh's theory of "state individualism" posits that the Nordic state guarantees individual autonomy through ensuring the removal of constraints or dependency on other people (Trägårdh 1997). Within this framework, the state achieves equality through removing one's dependence on social and cultural institutions such as the family and organised religion. Though biology is not explicitly a part of this framework, state individualism proffers a model of society resonant with modernist narratives of societal evolution. Such narratives cast the development of the modern state as the conquering of the natural world by society (Rubin 1975); in supplanting a political order structured by blood-based kinship networks, the supposed impersonality of bureaucracies could provide a check on the tyranny of the patriarchal nuclear family. These narratives naturalise difference and power by framing gender, age, or ability as innate or inevitable forms of vulnerability, such that the modern state becomes a champion of women, children, and people with disabilities rather than a structure that produces and even exploits these subjectivities (Yanagisako and Delaney 1995). Thus, the entanglement of autonomy and equality relies on some essentialised notion of nature which poses a threat to equality.

On a more granular level than theories of Nordic state and society, the study of queer kinship has examined people's understanding of biology as a threat to equality in intimate care and kin relationships. In her study on parental equality and lesbian motherhood in Sweden, psychologist Anna Malmquist analyses the communicative repertoires on which mothers draw to describe parental equality and care labour (Malmquist 2015). Malmquist notes how some mothers confess previously held assumptions that their relationships with their co-parent partners would automatically be equal in the absence of heteronormative gender difference. Although one group of Malmquist's research respondents report that parental equality is self-evident in their households, bodily processes such as gestation, nursing, and shared genetic substance pose challenges to mothers' relations to each other and to their children. For a second group of respondents, equality is a goal that requires near-constant struggle to achieve. A third group describes parental equality as wholly unattainable due to the differentiation between gestational and non-gestational mothers. Malmquist cogently argues that the very belief in biological processes as a mechanism of kin-making leads parents to privilege and thereby strengthen the bond between the child and gestational parent (Malmquist 2015, 9). Put simply, Malmquist concludes that biology matters in kin-making only as much as people believe that it does. Though the stakes of Malmquist's research diverge from those of the scholarship on *likhet* discussed above, her argument's grounding in social constructivism positions biology as disruptive of equality.

I intervene in the scholarship discussed above by analysing how Norwegians of African and Asian descent engage with biological substance to articulate new notions of equality. My analysis draws on feminist science studies' insights regarding the multiplicity of scientific knowledge (Taussig 2009; Mol 2003; Strathern 2005). In the lives of the families discussed below, how biology matters (or does not) runs against the grain of essentialist and determinist notions of biological kin, resonating with the findings of queer kinship scholars who argue that the division between biology and love as kinship substances is less clear than we may think (Hayden 1995; Dahl 2018b). By showing how Norwegian institutions rebuff citizens' desires for reproducing racial difference, I further build on scholarship that has underscored the conditional limits to Scandinavian tolerance of queer intimacies (Dahl 2018a, 205; Jacobsen 2018, 322; Petersen, Kroløkke, and Myong 2017, 84).

Background: Fertility treatment and the privatization of healthcare in Norway

In Norway, local access to fertility treatment has been circumscribed by the increasing privatisation of healthcare. Initially intending to decrease patient waiting times for specialist treatment at public hospitals, legislative healthcare reforms, effective from 2015, allowed a patient referred for specialist care to choose between waiting months or even years for treatment at a public hospital with a low deductible payment or skipping the wait by paying for treatment at a private clinic and applying for reimbursement from public funds afterwards (Ringard, Saunes, & Sagan 2016; *"Eigendelar på sjukehus og poliklinikk"* 2019).

Regarding fertility treatments and donor insemination, the 2015 healthcare reform ostensibly gave patients an alternative to the long wait time for a donor. At public hospitals, the National Insurance Scheme partially covers fertility treatments for up to three attempts for every live birth; couples are responsible for paying a substantial deductible.[1] Waiting times for donor insemination can last up to eighteen months depending on donor availability, but if they can afford it, a couple can pay in full at a private clinic for treatment. As long as they would have been eligible for treatment at a public hospital, the couple can then apply for reimbursement for any expenses that would have been covered at a public hospital ("*Ufrivillig barnløshet og infertilitetsbehandling*" 2019). Effectively, the ability to pay in full at a private clinic and await reimbursement gives patients the ability to skip the waiting line. However, because the Norwegian national sperm bank services only public hospitals, private clinics must import donor sperm for their patients requiring donor insemination. Because imported donor sperm is not offered at public hospitals, couples cannot be reimbursed for the additional fees incurred to import donor sperm at a private clinic: the cost of shipping, cryogenic storage for donor sperm, and administrative fees from the sperm bank to ensure compliance with Norwegian law (*barnrett*). At minimum, these expenses can reach €1000[2] if a couple imports from Denmark, but if a couple wants to use the same donor for multiple pregnancies, these expenses can increase exponentially.

The privatisation of Norwegian specialist services potentially compounds social inequalities by giving priority access to those who can afford it; indeed, an analyst at the Norwegian School of Economics (NHH) found that even before the 2015 reform, decentralisation of hospital care disproportionately benefitted men and people with higher education, exacerbating gender and class distinctions (Sommerfelt Ervik 2014). In addition to benefitting those who can afford private services, the privatisation of healthcare has also given medical personnel justification for drawing boundaries around which people's health constitutes a matter of public con-

---

[1] As of 2020, the deductible is 18,000 SEK (approximately €1,800) per § 5–22 of National Health Insurance Act ("*Rundskriv til Folketrygdloven*").
[2] Shipping costs (€295), cryo-preservation storage costs at the clinic (€160 per year), VAT (€175, or 25% of the cost of the donor sperm) and an additional administrative fee for every child they plan to conceive (€500). Based on Livio Clinic's price list (https://livio.no/priser/prisliste-pricelist-pdf/) and European Sperm Bank's pricing (https://www.European spermbank.com/en-int/ordering/donor-sperm-prices)

cern and public funding in contrast to those whose health is a personal or private responsibility.

The Heteronormative Family Form

Whether one is treated at a public hospital or a private clinic, Norwegian biotechnology legislation closely regulates the use of fertility treatments and limits which people have access to treatments. Lawmakers sought to ensure that the use of in-vitro fertilisation (IVF), intra-uterine insemination (IUI), or any future reproductive technological advancements would not impact the lives of the children resulting from such technological intervention; the guiding ethos of Norwegian biotechnology law is what is in the "best interest of the child" (*barnets beste*) (Melhuus 2012). Though legislators believed they were preserving the nuclear family, biotechnology law, in fact, produced a new definition of the nuclear family that naturalised biological links between parents and their children (Strathern 1992).

Since its first iteration was passed in 1987, Norwegian biotechnology law has restricted the use of fertility treatments and gamete donation to married women or women in registered domestic partnerships; this effectively restricted access to heterosexual couples until 2009 when gender-neutral marriage legislation was passed. The law further requires doctors to evaluate the stability of their patients' relationships and general health before treating them with IUI or IVF, whether or not they use donor sperm or one's partner's sperm. Since 2005, all donor insemination in Norway is, by law, "open" donation: a donor must agree to release his identity to any donor progeny aged eighteen or older, and all sperm donors, whether their sperm is imported or collected within Norway, must be added to a national registry. Sperm donors must remain anonymous to the parents of their donor progeny.

The strict regulation of fertility treatment in Norway is still enforced for patients who avail themselves of services beyond the public hospital system per the free choice legislation discussed above and per the EU "Patients' Rights Directive," which allows patients covered by national health schemes in participating countries to access healthcare in EU and EEA member states.[3] To receive reimbursement for treatment outside the Norwegian public system, patients must acquire attestations from their doctors confirming that their treatment adhered to Norwegian law. Thus, accessing public funding to conceive abroad or at home still entails extensive evaluation to prove one's intimate life complies with Norwegian biotechnology law.

The language of biotechnology law does not distinguish between lesbian couples and heterosexual couples in terms of access and usage of fertility treatments and gamete donation, but the National Population Register requires additional paperwork for the legal recognition of non-gestational mothers (sg. *medmor*, pl. *medmødre*). A non-gestational mother must file an application for "co-mother" status, and in order to appear on the child's birth certificate at birth, one must submit the application as soon as possible after conception. The application requires supporting documentation verifying that the non-gestational mother agreed to her partner's conception and that an open donor was used. Norwegian law does not recognise anonymous sperm donation; if a couple cannot prove that they used an open donor, the gestational mother would appear as a "single mother" on the child's birth certificate. In order to add the non-gestational mother as the child's second parent, the couple would have to find the "biological father" such that he could relinquish his parental rights and the non-gestational mother could then adopt the child. In contrast, legal paternity is established automatically for heterosexual married couples or by declaration for unmarried couples; no biological testing is required. Thus, both the eligibility for reimbursement and for legal *medmorskap* ("co-motherhood") discipline lesbian couples disproportionately in comparison to heterosexual couples. Although biotechnology law does not distinguish between heterosexual and lesbian couples, the broader Norwegian bureaucratic apparatus requires that lesbian couples submit to additional documentary processes to become legible, literally, as parents on their children's birth certificates.

[3] See https://www.cleiss.fr/docs/directive_en.html.

The Fight: belonging, queer kinship and biological substance

The intricacies of Norwegian biotechnology legislation and clinical practice were, initially, not at the forefront of Mona and Tine's minds when they began planning their family. Once they decided to conceive, they mapped out their future family constellation, weighing the options available to them against the family form they wanted to create. Each decision they made drew on notions of intimacy shaped by their experiences growing up in Norway. For example, Tine and Mona decided that they would have two children and "take turns" gestating such that each would share biogenetic substance with one child. They explicitly agreed they would regard both children as belonging to both of them: "There wouldn't be this 'your child' and 'my child'," Tine said. Mona added, half-joking, "unless one of them misbehaves, then it's 'your child', but that's different." Since Tine and Mona were married, each would be the legal mother to the child she gestated and the legal "med-mor" or "co-mother" to the child she did not gestate. But their explicit statement that they would both be parents to both children suggested that they felt the pressure of Norwegian social conventions about biological relatedness and gestation as the "real" kinship ties in contrast to affective bonds. Even so, they used biogenetic substance strategically to map out their future family: they planned to use the same sperm donor such that their children would be biological half-siblings.

In one interview, I asked whether they considered alternatives to clinical donor insemination, such as asking one another's brothers to be sperm donors such that they'd each share some genetic substance with both children. They both cringed. Mona elaborated that knowing Tine's brother's sperm was "inside" her, "it would just feel weird!" Tine interpreted "feel" literally and laughed, "you don't really feel it in there, inside you, you know?" But nonetheless, neither woman could dissociate erotic intimacy from reproduction, and to some degree, the possibility of a bro-ther-in-law as a genitor seemed to present the problem of dis-tinguishing sibling intimacy, erotic intimacy, and reproduction.

Tine mused, "wouldn't it be incestuous?" Even using one another's brothers as donors seemed too "close," and the possibility that their future children could share genetic substance with them both did not outweigh or overshadow their discomfort.

One day, the topic of sperm donor choice arose in conversation, revealing a central assumption they had both made. Mona, born in Iran and raised from infancy in Norway, had always assumed they would try to find an Iranian donor, or at least someone from a country near Iran, a "brown" (*brun*) donor, as she put it. Although Tine, who is white Norwegian, had made the same assumption, she – as a thought experiment, she explained – believed it was worth questioning this assumption: "Do we need a brown donor? What if we used a white donor?" Tine questioned the normative assumption that the members of their nuclear family must resemble one another such that the appearance of biological relation would be maintained even in the absence of shared biogenetic substance. Was it necessary for their family to approximate biological relatedness and further reinforce the heteronormative template for the family in their own household? Mona reacted strongly and, as the non-gestational mother of their first child, asked whether it would be such a bad thing for their children to look like her. Was Mona's appearance so undesirable?

When I interviewed them separately, Tine and Mona both referred to this conversation as "The Fight" and elaborated on it to explain the significance of having children in the broader scheme of their social worlds in Norway. For Mona, a *brun* donor was tied to her understanding of belonging. Belonging was "everything," she insisted, "I've been looking for belonging, seeking it out, my whole life." Having a child, she explained, was a way of creating one's own belonging. Her understanding of belonging was deeply inflected by race – not to be the same race, but to be different in the same way.

When she was an infant, Mona's family moved from Iran to a town outside Oslo. Incidents punctuated her childhood and teen-aged years that sedimented the idea that she and her family were different from other Norwegians: the letters "KKK" spray painted on their house, threats shouted at her while she walked down the street, and, on a smaller scale, the open and seemingly inexplicable rudeness from total strangers. To Mona, these were constant reminders that she was not white and that if she were white, she would be treated differently. She would have the luxury of not being judged by strangers, of not feeling misunderstood. It took a long time, she explained, to grow out of that "insecure little girl."

For Mona, belonging in Norway was tied to a common experience of difference. As an adult living in Oslo, Mona built a local kin network of other Norwegian people of Asian and African descent, some queer and some heterosexual, with whom she felt she shared the common experience of being different in Norway. Mona's kin network mirrored those of anthropologist Ulrika Dahl's queer interlocutors of colour in Sweden for whom "affirming racial and cultural difference [was] as important as LGBTQ awareness" (Dahl 2018a, 204). In planning to become a parent with Tine, Mona had assumed they would use a donor whose appearance would approximate hers and her network's: if not an Iranian donor, then one of South Asian or Arab descent.

In contrast, belonging for Tine was not a horizon but a constraint. To attend college, Tine moved away from the city where she grew up, and a few years later, she began dating women. In our interview, she explained that moving away from home allowed her to come out to herself as queer and acknowledge her feelings for the woman who became her first girlfriend. If she had stayed in the same city, she mused, too many people knew her as heterosexual for her to know herself as anything else. The anonymity of a new city gave her the social freedom to "become herself," and the neighbourhood and the people with whom she felt she belonged were, in retrospect, necessary for her to leave behind.

Tine and Mona's fight and their divergent notions of belonging illuminate the tension between the bodily materiality of race and modes of kin making that reject biology's primacy (Dahl 2018a, 205). Tine's questioning whether the donor's race mattered drew from queer kinship traditions premised upon the social construction of kin, but in the predominantly white context of Norway, Tine's suggestion that the donor's biological race did not matter unwittingly animates discourses of colour-blindness that are further reinforced in common assumptions that white sperm donors are racially unmarked (Andreassen 2019, 20). However, as Mona's desire to find a *brun* donor demonstrates, the construction of race relies on "material bodily signs" like skin or hair colour, hair texture, or facial features (Andreassen 2019, 129); racial difference, in its corporeality, is tied to biological inheritance. In spite of Mona's expansive understanding of belonging through difference, Tine's suggestion effectively flattened Mona's desire to a biological one. Tine's proposition that she and Mona not trouble themselves to find a brown donor echoes Swedish anthropologist Ulrika Dahl's assertion that queer kinship, "despite all its utopian fantasies, can work as a reproductive technology for whiteness" (Dahl 2018a, 205).

Mona and Tine's fight reveals the intimate politics of sperm donor choice, but for couples seeking a donor of Asian or African descent, interfacing with the national healthcare system can constitute yet another fight. In the next section, I analyse debates between parents and Oslo University Hospital regarding donor choice and the onus of providing sperm donors of Asian and African descent.

Bordering the welfare state: Donor choice, race, and biology

In the years surrounding Tine and Mona's decision to conceive, larger scale disputes appeared in Norwegian public discourse that resonated with Mona's interpretation of biology, belonging, and race. Two years after I interviewed Mona and Tine, a series of articles in a daily newspaper featured a married couple, Nadette and Ingrid Narum, and the challenges posed in their attempts to find a sperm donor of African descent through the Norwegian national health system (Urbye 2018a; 2018b). Nadette, a Norwegian woman of Cameroonian descent, and Ingrid, a white Norwegian woman, hoped to find a donor whose appearance could approximate Nadette's. After visiting Oslo University Hospital's department of reproductive medicine, the Narums waited several months for a donor of African descent, only to be offered sperm from a white donor or a donor described as "Asian." The articles describe the Narums' attempts to recruit their own donor to the national sperm bank, only to be thwarted by a clause in biotechnology law that mandates that intended parents not know the identity of the sperm donor. With little recourse other than the hope that a donor of African descent enrolls in the national sperm bank, the Narums' imported donor sperm at great expense with the administrative assistance of a private clinic. The articles include brief interviews with staff members of Oslo University Hospital and the Organisation Against Public Discrimination (OMOD, *Organisasjon mot Offentlig Diskriminering*)[4] a local advocacy organisation.

In the summer before Mona and Tine decided to conceive, a woman filed a complaint with the Gender Equality and Anti-Discrimination Ombud (*Likestillings- og diskrimineringsombudet* or *LDO*).[5] Referred to as "A" in the complaint documentation, the woman was of West Asian descent and planned to conceive with her wife, a white Norwegian woman. Having decided that A's wife would gestate and provide the ovum for their pregnancy, A and her wife hoped to use sperm from a donor of West Asian descent. Like the Narums, A and her wife paid tens of thousands of Norwegian kroner to access sperm from a donor they felt was appropriate. A's complaint stated that the hospital should have either used more robust recruitment techniques or paid for the import of sperm from a West Asian donor. The Ombudsperson, who operates independently from the government in an advisory capacity, decided in favour of the hospital. A submitted a second complaint to the Anti-Discrimination Tribunal (*Diskrimineringsnemnda*), a four-person committee with the power to make legally binding decisions and award compensation. In agreement with the Ombudsperson, the Tribunal ruled in favour of the hospital and concluded that as long as their wish to have a child was satisfied, A and her wife had not experienced discrimination. Below, I detail the claims that the Narums and A made in favour of using non-white

---

[4] OMOD helps people file discrimination complaints against public agencies and works extensively with people of immigrant or minority background.

[5] See https://www.ldo.no/arkiv/klagesaker/klagesaker-2016/etnisitet/152549-behandlings tilbud-for-assistert-befruktning-var-ikke-diskriminering-pa-grunn-av-etnisitet/

sperm donors. I then analyse the rebuttals from the Oslo University Hospital Department of Reproductive Medicine.

The parents' perspective

In the public record of A's LDO complaint and in the article on the Narums, both sets of parents describe their motivations behind their choices of donor. Their explanations rely heavily on their ability to be identified as parents to their children. The Narums emphasise that they would feel the same way about their daughter Karla regardless of her hair and eye colour, but having used a donor of African descent, they wanted their child to be able to recognise herself (*kjenner seg*) in both of her parents. Ingrid explains that although she and Nadette look so different from one another, when either Nadette or Ingrid is alone with Karla in public, people say the same thing ("how sweet a daughter you have!") and that "no one can say, 'she's not your mum, is she?'" (Urbye 2018a)

Similarly, rather than arguing that she has a right to a child that resembles her, A frames her argument about donor choice in terms of her child's experience. A describes a hypothetical future in which she and her wife use sperm from a white donor; in this future, A's status as a parent to a white child is not a problem. Instead, the problem lies in her child's possible lifelong discomfort from having to explain A's visible difference from the rest of their family unit. In basing their claims on their children's experiences, both sets of parents appeal to the "best interest of the child." They each refrain from mentioning their own desire to have children who resemble them; rather, they emphasise the importance of their children having parents who visibly belong to them.

A's complaint also proffers an alternative reading of what shared genetic substance confers: physical traits that correspond to a shared social identity. Genetic substance is relational not in that it determines one's relationship to a donor, but in that it potentially produces visible signs of A's relation to her child. In A's complaint, A specifically states the importance of her relationship to her child being recognisable to strangers, but she also mentions in passing the importance of her child's affiliation to A's ethnicity. For A and her wife, their child's genetic substance and, by extension, physical appearance is a part of their child's link to broader kin- and non-kin social identities. For A and for the Narums, the best means to parenting ethically in the best interest of their children is to use donors of West Asian and African descent, respectively.

The Narums' and A's arguments rely on another common Scandinavian ideal: parental equality. Whereas studies like Malmquist's analyse parental equality in relation to care labour and gestation, for the parents discussed here, parental equality is not only a matter of household politics, but also of their ability to be socially recognisable as parents in public. Had either couple used a white sperm donor, the gestational and genetic mothers' status would be obvious in contrast to their spouses' appearances. Both families' arguments underscore that the best means to muddle the gestational mothers' biological ties to their children is the intentional use of a non-white donor. Here, biological substance and bodily processes are a means to effect parental equality rather than to undermine it.

More broadly, the Narums' and A's claims were not only about their ability to visibly belong to one another as a family, but also about their status as Norwegian citizens: their belonging to the Norwegian nation and the social democratic state. For each family, using sperm from donors of Asian- and African-descent entailed paying for their full fertility treatments at a private clinic and applying afterwards for reimbursement. Again, the costs eligible for reimbursement only include those that otherwise would have been borne by the public hospital; ineligible for reimbursement included shipping and storage of frozen sperm as well as sperm bank administration fees for documenting compliance with Norwegian laws on importing sperm. For the Narums, the costs that could not be reimbursed amounted to an additional 40,000–50,000 Norwegian kroner,[6] an amount that a white Norwegian couple would not have to pay because of the availability of white sperm donors within the national healthcare system.

---

[6] Roughly €4000–5000 in 2018.

Following the publication of the article on the Narums, the same periodical featured an interview with Akhenaton de Leon, a staff member of OMOD. De Leon identifies Oslo University Hospital's recruitment policies as a systemic factor contributing to the lack of Asian and African descendant sperm donors. The national sperm bank, he argues, recruits from blood donors, a pool limited by hospital policy to people who have not lived in sub-Saharan African for more than five years (Urbye 2018b). This practice, de Leon reasons, ensures that the national sperm bank would remain "free of African genes" (*fri for afrikanske gener*). In the LDO complaint, A makes similar claims, specifically emphasising the hospital's culpability in its lack of Asian- and African-descendant sperm donors. The hospital, she argues, could amend its recruiting practices or import donor sperm from abroad, but has chosen not to do so (*har valgt ikke å gjøre dette*). Drawing on the language of choice, de Leon and A argue that the sperm bank's failure to reflect the demographics of Norway's national population are a result of decisions made by the hospital.

De Leon's and A's arguments identify the same consequence of the hospital's recruiting practices. Though the Narums and A pay the same taxes as other Norwegians, they do not receive the same benefits. Beyond the economic injustice of this is the symbolic injustice of the social democratic state's denial of material support. Although the intended parents in question have made a contribution (*bidrag*) to Norway's social democracy by paying their taxes, their contribution to building the Norwegian nation is not reciprocated. The healthcare system, supported by the state apparatus, will not help them build their family. At stake in their desire to use non-white donors is both their belonging within their families and their belonging as equal citizens of the Norwegian social democratic state. A's appeal to the LDO states succinctly: "that the problem of not including many should not make it less unjust."

Institutional perspectives

In response to A's complaint and within the article about the Narums, the Oslo University Hospital Department of Reproductive Medicine rebutted the parents' claims about the best interest of the child, the recruitment practices of the sperm bank, and equality.

In defending its refusal to import sperm from abroad, the hospital issued a statement in response to A's complaint that reiterates legal guidelines about donor insemination. The statement emphasises that the "best interest of the child" shapes the hospital's clinical practices and that donor choice ultimately lies with the treating physician. An appropriate donor, per the hospital's statement, is "healthy, unselfishly motivated, is willing to disclose his identity to the future children, has appropriate sperm quality, and is not the carrier of hereditary or sexually transmitted disease." The best interest of the child, the statement continues, depends on parental care and social environment, not just "simple physical traits inherited from the sperm donor... the child cannot be created to meet the adult's expectations of appearance."

This section of the statement establishes the hospital's medical and bureaucratic authority through making a very specific claim about inherited genetic substance. Genetic inheritance is significant insofar as one must know the genitor or the specific individual from whom one inherits, but to engineer inheritance – to create a "designer child" – is inappropriate. The hospital statement does not consider the possibility that one's genetic inheritance or appearance could be a part of belonging to a broader group or claiming an identity; it reduces A's complaint to a superficial concern about appearance. Without explicitly referencing "race" or "ethnicity," it emphasises the importance of social environment. This argument is reminiscent of Norwegian attitudes towards difference: "race" refers to biological difference, but, per 1990's era public discourse on race, such biological differences are not "real" and ought not to have a bearing on social relations (Stolcke 1995). Scholars of kinship have identified how these discourses took root in Scandinavian imagination of transnational adoption (Howell 2006; Hübinette & Tigervall 2009; Yngvesson 2010; Myong & Bissenbakker 2021). The child's appearance, then, is of little importance with regard to their connection to their parents' ethnic backgrounds because social and ethnic conventions are learned and cultivated rather than innate.

The crux of the hospital's position is its particular framing of genetic substance and inheritance. At first glance, the hospital's claims about genetic substance seem to be contradictory: the donor and any "simple physical traits" inherited from him are unimportant in comparison to the social environment in which a child is raised, yet the release of the donor's identity to his donor progeny is central to the hospital's definition of an appropriate donor. With respect to the hospital's statement, the donor's appearance and its inheritance by the child are incidental to the making of a family, yet the child's access to his identity is a critical part of ethical sperm donation. One cannot request a specific donor, yet the donor is not just an anonymous nonentity.

Undergirding this tension within legal and medical discourse, I argue, is a particular idea about what kinds of subjects and relations are produced by shared genetic substance. Implicitly, the hospital's statement makes a claim about the appropriate use of shared substance. The shared genetic substance between the donor and the donor-conceived person is significant in that, in accordance with Biotechnology Law, the donor-conceived person is a subject bearing the right to knowledge about his or her genetic substance, and the donor, in sharing that substance, is a source of that knowledge. This understanding of genetic substance is co-productive of the donor-conceived person as a liberal rights-bearing individual. Accordingly, A's request for a donor of specific background is an attempt to engineer a "designer baby" with a particular appearance.

Addressing the demand for improved recruitment, the hospital claims that the national sperm bank does not discriminate, rather that it is difficult to reach men with "certain ethnic backgrounds." In the newspaper article, the hospital staff assert that some cultures have "different views on sperm donation," unlike Norway, "where the vast majority have no qualms about [it]," sentiments that echo conversations I had with hospital staff in 2016 (Urbye 2018a). These assertions are rather odd. Norway's intensive regulation of sperm donation and donor insemination, the concern with "the best interest of the child," and a chronic shortage of donor semen suggest that many Norwegians have, at least, some qualms about sperm donation. But the rhetorical force of this statement lies in the contrast between "certain ethnic backgrounds" and Norway; based on the hospital staff's reasoning, descendants from West Asia and Africa – the regions missing from the national sperm bank – are too different from Norwegians to want to enrol as sperm donors. By contrasting them to Norway, the hospital statement glosses over the heterogeneity of regions like West Asia and Africa, and through this comparison, it repeats a common refrain in Norway about immigrants and their Norwegian-born children: Norwegian society (and the national sperm bank) does not discriminate against them, they simple choose not to participate. Supported by the LDO Ombud and Tribunal, the hospital frames A's complaint and the Narums' plight as problems of their own making; the complainants' communities are to blame for the exclusion that they describe.

In response to A and the Narums, the hospital and the LDO justify the extra expense that the parents had to pay by arguing that meeting the needs of couples like A and her wife and the Narums would disadvantage the majority of the Department of Reproductive Medicine's patients. The "differential treatment" (*forskjellsbehandlingen*) experienced by couples seeking non-white sperm donors is not actually discriminatory in that the needs of many more patients are fulfilled under the current system of donor insemination; treating couples differently by importing sperm from donors of Asian and African descent would mean disadvantaging couples who need a Nordic donor or who do not need donor sperm at all.

Whereas the parents' claims draw on relational notions of genetics and biological substance, the hospital frames its response using a definition of genetics premised on a rights-bearing individual. In doing so, the hospital's statement effectively ignores the parents' assertions about the possibility that biological substance could confer some kind of shared experience, an argument which echoes Mona's hope that her child be different in the same way as she is. The parents' desires for a family are reduced to a selfish wish for a child with a specific appearance, and African- and Asian-descended communities are referenced only in their alleged reluctance to donate sperm, redirecting the parents' complaints to their own communities. Appealing to the national ideal of equality, the parents make claims premised on their status as Norwegian citizens, but the hospital's rebuttal frames their complaints as requests for special treatment. Such treatment, in line with the hospital's position, would disadvantage the majority of their patients over the parents' claims, drawing a boundary between which citizens' reproduction is a matter of national concern.

Conclusion: the price of belonging

In 1995, anthropologist Unni Wikan argued the following about Muslim immigration to Norway:

> Every choice has its price, and the price for living in Norway is that one must accept that one's children become Norwegian – if they themselves so wish. For no one 'owns' his or her children… for me it is also unacceptable that people who have come here and benefitted from Norwegian possibilities, such as freedom and material welfare, so readily denounce aspects of the 'culture' we have built up, and that provides the basis for the welfare which immigrants take advantage of. The majority of immigrants to Norway have had a choice – they were not among the worst off in their home country… They have also had the possibility to return: to go back home. The choice they have made bears its obligations. (Wikan 1995b; 1995a; Gullestad 2002, 52)

In scholarly and popular publications, Wikan has been openly critical of immigration and multiculturalism in Norway (see, for example, Wikan 2001; 2006). Her commentary here echoes a perception that I heard mentioned casually throughout my time conducting fieldwork: that nonbelonging results from people choosing not to adopt Norwegian social and cultural conventions. For Wikan, the welfare state is inextricably tied to Norwegian "culture" and society; it is inappropriate for people to claim material support from the social democratic state without also choosing ("choosing") to adopt Norwegian ways of life, to become like other Norwegians. Implicitly, Wikan reinforces the belief that sameness, or being of the same kind, is a central part of belonging in Norway.

For Wikan, if one takes material support from the social democratic state, an equal exchange entails giving of oneself or, at least, accepting that one must "give" one's children to the Norwegian nation. As anthropologist Marianne Gullestad has remarked, Wikan makes a subtle elision in her invocation of "we" who "have built up" the culture in which the social democratic state is founded (Gullestad 2002, 52). Wikan's "we" includes young white Norwegians who were born well after the founding of the welfare state and therefore did not participate in the very foundation of social democracy that Wikan describes.

The underlying message from the hospital and the LDO resonates with Wikan's writing even a generation after its original publication. If couples want to avail themselves of the Norwegian welfare state's material support to conceive, they must do so on the terms of the Norwegian state itself. By the arguments of the authorities, intended parents' refusals of the donors available at the Norwegian sperm bank represent rejections not only of white Norwegian genetic substance but of the Norwegian nation and welfare state itself.

However, in this chapter, I have offered an alternate reading of sperm donor choice. In arguing for their choice of sperm donor, the Narums and A drew on Norwegian parenting ideals: they prioritised the best interests of their (unconceived) children and parental equality. In contrast to the hospital's position, A argues clearly that she and her wife, like the Narums, are asking for the same treatment granted to other parents using donor insemination through the national system. One could argue that using a white Norwegian sperm donor through the national sperm bank would even result in each couple compromising their ability to parent "Norwegianly."

Like other families using reproductive technologies and gamete donation, the parents discussed here make creative use of biological substance. For Mona and Tine, A and her wife, and the Narums, biological substance is not an essential or deterministic source of national or personal identity. Instead, these parents harness the work of biological inheritance in hopes that their children's appearances would allow them to be "different in the same way," as Mona put it poignantly. However, whereas queer white Norwegian families may reinstate the nation in reconfiguring kinship formations (Petersen, Kroløkke & Myong 2017), the kinship practices of parents discussed in this chapter are definitively rejected by institutional actors. The Narums' and A's encounter with Oslo University Hospital and the LDO (re)produces the Norwegian nation, but it is at the expense of the Narums' and A's connection to the nation. Because of their desires to reproduce racial difference, the Narums, A, and her wife are conclusively on the outside of the border instantiated by the hospital and the LDO.

These families' use of biological substance, I have argued, runs against the grain of Scandinavian scholarship that frames biology as antithetical to equality. The mothers' engagement with biological substance becomes a means to achieve parental equality within their family household. In contrast, the impulse to reject the significance of biology unwittingly becomes a technology of reproducing the white nation. However, as I have demonstrated, the mothers' interpretations of equality are at odds with its institutional definitions. Their requests for equal treatment are interpreted as demands for special treatment, marking how racial difference constitutes the limits of the Norwegian state's acceptance of queer kinship.

References

Andreassen, R. 2019. *Mediated Kinship: Gender, Race and Sexuality in Donor Families*. New York: Routledge.

Cannell, F. 1990. "Concepts of Parenthood: The Warnock Report, the Gillick Debate, and Modern Myths." *American Ethnologist* 17, no. 4: 667–86. https://doi.org/10.1525/ae.1990.17.4.02a00040.

Dahl, U. 2018a. "(The Promise of) Monstrous Kinship? Queer Reproduction and the Somatechnics of Sexual and Racial Difference." *Somatechnics* 8, no. 2: 195–211.

–––. 2018b. "Becoming Fertile in the Land of Organic Milk: Lesbian and Queer Reproductions of Femininity and Motherhood in Sweden." *Sexualities* 21, no. 7: 1021–38. https://doi.org/10.1177/1363460717718509.

"Eigendelar på sjukehus og poliklinikk." 2019. Helse Norge. December 30, 2019. https://www.helsenorge.no/betaling-for-helsetjenester/betaling-pa-sykehus-og-poliklinikk/.

Fernando, M. L. 2019. "Family Resemblances: Binational Marriage, Muslim 'Communalism,' and the Patriarchal State," in *Deepening Divides: How Territorial Borders and Social Boundaries Delineate Our World*, edited by D. Fassin. London: Pluto Press.

Gullestad, M. 2002. "Invisible Fences: Egalitarianism, Nationalism and Racism." *Journal of the Royal Anthropological Institute* 8, no. 1: 45–63. https://doi.org/10.1111/1467-9655.00098.

–––. 2006. *Plausible Prejudice*. Oslo: Universitetsforlaget.

Hayden, C. P. 1995. "Gender, Genetics, and Generation: Reformulating Biology in Lesbian Kinship." *Cultural Anthropology* 10, no. 1: 41–63.

Howell, S. 2006. *The Kinning of Foreigners: Transnational Adoption in a Global Perspective*. New York: Berghahn Books.

Hübinette, T., & Tigervall, C. 2009. "To Be Non-White in a Colour-Blind Society: Conversations with Adoptees and Adoptive Parents in Sweden on Everyday Racism." *Journal of Intercultural Studies* 30, no. 4: 335–53. https://doi.org/10.1080/07256860903213620.

Jacobsen, C. M. 2018. "The (In)Egalitarian Dynamics of Gender Equality and Homotolerance in Contemporary Norway," in *Egalitarianism in Scandinavia: Historical and Contemporary Perspectives*, edited by S. Bendixsen, M. B. Bringslid & H. Vike, 313–35. Cham: Palgrave Macmillan. https://doi.org/10.1007/978-3-319-59791-1_14.

Lidén, Hilde, Marianne E. Lien, and Halvard Vike, eds. 2001. *Likhetens paradokser: antropologiske undersøkelser i det moderne Norge*. Oslo: Universitetsforlaget.

Lien, M. E., & Melhuus, M. 2009. "Norway: Views from the Interior." *Ethnologie francaise*, vol. 39, no. 2: 197–205.

Malmquist, A. 2015. "Women in Lesbian Relations: Construing Equal or Unequal Parental Roles?" *Psychology of Women Quarterly* 39, no. 2: 256–67. https://doi.org/10.1177/0361684314537225.

Melhuus, M. 2012. *Problems of Conception: Issues of Law, Biotechnology, Individuals and Kinship*. New York: Berghahn Books.

Mol, Annemarie. 2003. *The Body Multiple: Ontology in Medical Practice*. Durham: Duke University Press.

Myong, L., & Bissenbakker, M. 2021. "Attachment as Affective Assimilation: Discourses on Love and Kinship in the Context of Transnational Adoption in Denmark." *NORA-Nordic Journal of Feminist and Gender Research*, 1–13. doi: 10.1080/08038740.2021.1891133

Nebeling Petersen, M., Kroløkke, C. & Myon, L. 2017. "Dad and Daddy Assemblage: Resuturing the Nation through Transnational Surrogacy, Homosexuality, and Norwegian Exceptionalism." *GLQ: A Journal of Lesbian and Gay Studies* 23, no. 1: 83–112. https://doi.org/10.1215/10642684-3672312.

Ringard, Å., Sperre Saunes, I., & Sagan, A. 2016. "The 2015 Hospital Treatment Choice Reform in Norway: Continuity or Change?" *Health Policy* 120, no. 4: 350–55.

Rubin, G. 1975. "The Traffic in Women: Notes on the 'Political Economy' of Sex," in *Toward an Anthropology of Women*, edited by R. Reiter, 157-210. New York: Monthly Review.

Sommerfelt Ervik, T. 2014. "Fritt Sykehusvalg Viser Klasseskille." Forskning. No, March 8, 2014, sec. helse. https://forskning.no/helsepolitikk-norges -handelshoyskole-partner/fritt-sykehusvalg-viser-klasseskille/575404.

Stolcke, V. 1995. "Talking Culture: New Boundaries, New Rhetorics of Exclusion in Europe." Current Anthropology 36, no. 1: 1–24.

Strathern, M. 1992. Reproducing the Future: Anthropology, Kinship, and the New Reproductive Technologies. New York: Routledge.

———. 2005. Kinship, Law and the Unexpected: Relatives Are Always a Surprise. Cambridge: Cambridge University Press.

Taussig, K-S. 2009. Ordinary Genomes: Science, Citizenship, and Genetic Identities. Durham: Duke University Press.

Trägårdh, L. 1997. "Statist Individualism: On the Culturality of the Nordic." In: *Cultural Construction of Norden*, edited by Oystein Sorensen and Bo Strath, 252–85. Oslo: Scandinavian University Press.

"Ufrivillig barnløshet og infertilitetsbehandling." 2019. Helse Norge. December 27, 2019. https://www.helsenorge.no/refusjon-og-stotte ordninger/ufrivillig-barnloshet-og-infertilitetsbehandling/.

Urbye, F. F. 2018a. "Ønsket afrikansk donor – tilbudt asiatisk." *Dagsavisen*, June 26, 2018. https://www.dagsavisen.no/nyheter/innenriks/2018/06/ 26/onsket-afrikansk-donor-tilbudt-asiatisk/.

———. 2018b. "Nei Til Blod, Ja Til Sæd." *Dagsavisen*, June 30, 2018. https:// www.dagsavisen.no/oslo/nyheter/2018/06/30/nei-til-blod-ja-til-saed/.

Wikan, U. 1995a. "Kulturfundamentalismen." *Samtiden* 5: 21–33.

———. 1995b. *Mot en ny norsk underklasse: Innvandrere, kultur og integrasjon.* Oslo: Gyldendal.

———. 2001. *Generous Betrayal: Politics of Culture in the New Europe.* Chicago: University of Chicago Press.

———. 2006. "Ingen vei utenom." *Morgenbladet*, November 10. https://morgen bladet.no/boker/2006/ingen_vei_utenom.

Yanagisako, S. J., & Delaney, C. 1995. "Naturalizing Power," in *Naturalizing Power: Essays in Feminist Cultural Analysis,* edited by S. J. Yanagisako and C. Delaney, 1–24. New York: Routledge.

Yngvesson, B. 2010. *Belonging in an Adopted World: Race, Identity, and Transnational Adoption.* Chicago: University of Chicago Press.

5. Altruism and Built-In Nationalism:
The Surrogacy Debate in Finland 2013–2019

Anna Moring[1]

The 2019 Finnish Governmental Program states that "an investigation shall be made about allowing non-commercial surrogacy in cases defined specifically in the law." No background, no further information, just this statement. The program is the action plan of the Finnish government for the next four years. This statement means that the debate on surrogacy will be reopened in Finland, and that there may be a possibility to open a legal space for non-commercial surrogacy in certain cases.

Surrogacy[2] has been an issue of debate in many of the Nordic Countries in recent years (Nebeling Petersen 2018; Nebeling Petersen et al. 2017; Sudenkaarne 2018a; Lie & Lykke 2016; Kivipuro 2015). As late as in the summer of 2019 the Swedish Supreme Court gave a decision, which will clarify practices of transnational commercial surrogacy in Sweden (Ö 3462-18).[3] In Finland, however, surrogacy has been something of a non-issue in public debate. The last more profound public discussion on the theme was in

---

[1] I wish to thank the editors of this book, as well as the anonymous reviewers, for comments and suggestions that have greatly improved this chapter. An especially warm thank you to the exceptionally wise Raili Uibo for generous comments and revisions. The writing of this chapter was made possible by the project, "Contrasting and Re-Imagining the Margins of Kinship" (Academy of Finland 2016–2020), directed by Antu Sorainen at the University of Helsinki.

[2] In this article, surrogacy refers to any arrangement where a person with a functioning womb bears a child for another person/persons with the intention that the child be handed over after birth (See Cook, Sclater & Kaganas 2003, 1 n1).

[3] The case was about whether a mother through surrogacy, whose motherhood was legalised in a court order in the United States, could, in accordance with Swedish law, have her motherhood confirmed. The Supreme Court ruled that even though the case was not in accordance with Swedish regulations, nor was there grounds in Swedish family law to acknowledge the mother's legal parenthood, the best interest of the child and the child's right to have their family relations acknowledged by law was to be prioritised. For an account on the legal details on surrogacy arrangements in Sweden, see Mägi & Zimmeman 2015, 189–193.

2011–2013, but after that, mostly NGOs representing stakeholders have discussed the matter publicly.[4]

This chapter focuses on the Finnish public discussion on surrogacy from 2011 to 2019. It maps the rhetoric of discussing surrogacy arrangements in the context of a Nordic welfare state and asks how the complex and contradictory issue of surrogacy has been understood in the Finnish context. The discussions are approached through the concept of frames and framing (Markens 2007; Pande 2014), which helps one address the importance of ethical, moral and cultural understandings that come into play when trying to make sense of this issue.

The chapter is based on an analysis of the media coverage in Finland on surrogacy and surrogacy arrangements between the years 2011–2019.[5] The material was collected through a search with the media search engine Retriever on the Finnish words *sijaissynnytys* (surrogacy), *sijaissynn** (surroga*, a search, which would show also the Finnish inflected forms of the word, as well as the Finnish word for surrogate), and *kohdunvuokraus* (rent of womb – a concept previously used in Finnish to signify surrogacy). The search was complemented with a Google search with the same search words, and in addition, with a pdf-article from 2011, which was not found on the media research, but posted on the website of the NGO *Kohtuuttomat*. Altogether, the media search resulted in 25 published articles from 2011 to the end of 2019. In addition to these articles, all public statements from NGOs, as well as reports of ministries and other official documents were analysed. These were found through on-line searches, as well as by looking at previous research targeting these specific types of documents in

---

[4] Statements have been given by organisations such as the association for women lacking a womb, Kohtuuttomat ry, the association of involuntarily infertile people, Simpukka ry, and the association for LGBTIQ-families, Sateenkaariperheet ry.

[5] The time period chosen is based on the cycle of governmental programs in Finland: in 2011 the newly elected government ordered a statement from the ministry of justice on the possibilities of regulating surrogacy. This statement was completed in 2012 (OM 2012) and raised some public attention to the issue. It did not, however, lead to any further legislative action. This article was written during the summer of 2020, so the logical endpoint of the timeframe was the end of 2019.

Finland, such as Kivipuro 2015, Rintamo 2016, and Sudenkaarne 2018b.

The analysis focuses on the ways surrogacy is discussed in Finland – how is it framed, from whose perspective are surrogacy arrangements represented in media, what parts of the issue are considered ethically problematic, and what, if any, are the suggested solutions? Attention is also paid to the aspects that are omitted in the media coverage, for example, the question of gay men as commissioners of surrogacy arrangements, or questions of race or ethnicity. These issues are not widely debated in Finland. This chapter will trace the silences that are constructed in the debate, and ask, what parts of the picture are left outside the frames. The omissions are especially interesting in that they point at the nodes of conflicting interests, where it is not easy to find one ethically sustainable solution.

There is a vast body of medical, social, feminist and queer bio-ethical research on surrogacy, both from the perspective of the surrogate mother-worker,[6] the intended parent(s), and the children born through surrogacy arrangements. Also, the differences of commercial or altruistic surrogacy are widely debated (e.g., Markens 2007; Strathern 2011; Pande 2014, Söderström-Anttila 2013; Sudenkaarne 2018a; Nebeling Petersen et al. 2017; Leibetseder 2018; Kähkönen & Sudenkaarne 2018).

These aspects are essential for knowledge-based decision making in the question of surrogacy. This chapter will focus on how these questions are framed in the discussions around surrogacy in Finland. The question of how we look at it, how we frame it, becomes crucial to our understanding of the issue, and thus also our opinion formation (Lane 2003).

---

[6] This concept is used by Michael Nebeling Petersen et al. to make visible both the aspects of (paid or unpaid) work, and the aspects of (biological, genetic, or pre-surrogacy) motherhood, related to the figure of the surrogate in surrogacy-related discussions. See Nebeling Petersen et al. 2017. note 1. I find this concept relevant and useful and will employ it here throughout the text.

Surrogacy in Finland

Surrogacy has been discussed in Finland as part of a prolonged political, legal and media debate on assisted reproduction from the early 1990s. The Finnish process of legislating assisted reproduction took over 20 years, during which time the discussion centered on different issues.[7] Because of the prolonged process, Finland did not specifically regulate assisted reproduction before the Act on fertility treatments (1237/2006) that came into force in 2007. As a result of profound political disagreements, Finland thus has a long history of non-legislation in the issue of fertility treatments, as well as surrogacy.[8] Before this, Finland was something of a lawless zone with regard to fertility treatments in general, and surrogacy in particular. There was no legal framework in place, regulating the practices of fertility treatments, but the clinics providing treatments had ongoing ethical discussions, based on which they would decide what kind of treatments they would offer and to whom.

During the period of legal vacuum around fertility treatments, 18 well-documented cases of altruistic, domestic surrogacy took place in the fertility treatment clinic of Väestöliitto, the Family Federation of Finland, and 10 children were born through these arrangements.[9] There is thus practical experience and evidence of domestic altruistic surrogacy arrangements in Finland, and the ethical as well as practical issues involved. These experiences are a reoccurring reference point in the Finnish public discussion on surrogacy in the 2010s.

The 2007 act of assisted reproduction banned all fertility treatment related to surrogacy arrangements (Salminen 2007). Since then, up until 2011, surrogacy was a non-issue in the political debate. In 2011, however, then minister of justice Tuija Brax asked the Finnish national ethical committee of social and healthcare (ETENE) to investigate the situation and give a statement about the

---

[7] For a detailed analysis of the process and the phases of the discussions, see Burrell 2003.

[8] See Eriksson 2018 for a thorough account of the legal history.

[9] See Söderström-Anttila in annex two, ETENE 28.9.2011, for a detailed account of these cases.

ethics of surrogacy. ETENE commissioned a workgroup to investigate the matter, and as a result, stated that non-commercial surrogacy could be an ethically sustainable solution in certain, strictly regulated circumstances.

ETENE's statement led to an investigation by the ministry of justice (OM 52/2012), which was submitted for a round of statements.[10] The ministry received 64 responses from ministries, NGOs, courts etc. Based on these responses, the then minister of justice Anna-Maja Henriksson decided to stall all legal development of surrogacy and leave to the next government to decide what to do about the issue. The next government turned out to be composed of three of the more value-conservative parties of the Finnish political field, and thus surrogacy never came up for legal reconsideration during the period 2015–2019.

The analysis in this chapter will focus on public discussion on surrogacy in Finland between 2011–2019. I will first discuss the official public discussion consisting of the statement of ETENE (28.9.2011), the report by the ministry of justice (OM 52/2012), and related statements (summarised in OM 6/2013). Then I will proceed to an analysis of the media discussion from 2012–2019, and conclude with some remarks on the status of the discussion at the end of the analysed period.

The data for this article consists of public documents, statements, ministry reports and media coverage. The documents, statements and reports were gathered from the websites of the ministry and different NGOs mentioned in the ministry reports. Through an online media search, using the media search service Retriever, and a completing Google search-engine-based search, I have found 25 articles, public opinions, or TV-program manuscripts in Finnish from different sources,[11] published between 2011

---

[10] This is a form of public consultation, where stakeholders, ministries, NGO's, and legal and medical experts are asked to give a statement on the issue at hand. The statements are then considered in the further development of legislation in the question.

[11] Including: the archives of the organisation for women lacking a womb, *Kohtuuttomat ry*; the media following tool Retriever (from 2015 onwards); my own archives; sources mentioned in Finnish research on the issue, and Internet Search Engines.

and2019. The articles are listed in detail in the list of sources at the end of this chapter.

The material consists of articles in national newspapers, local newspapers, journals, and online media sites, such as the public broadcasting company YLE. In the material, surrogacy is portrayed variously from the perspective of the commissioning parents, surrogacy agencies, surrogate mothers, and Finnish authorities and legislators. Many of the articles include several of these perspectives.

By analysing these documents, my aim is to highlight some of the controversies, conflicting interests, morally or ethically problematic divisions and omitted frameworks of the discussion up to 2019. These issues are not unique to the Finnish discussion. Similar themes and framings will be and have been present in attempts to regulate surrogacy, both locally and globally (cf. Markens 2007 on the discussion in the US; Pande 2014 on discussions concerning global regulations and movements; Nebeling Petersen et al. 2017 on the situation in Denmark; Mägi & Zimmerman 2015 on the situation in Sweden). Finland, being a small country with clear political and legal structures and media discussions, provides an excellent example of how the framing of different aspects of the issue affects the outcomes of public discussion.

Method: framing surrogacy

Anxiety, ambivalence, and controversy are words that appear often in both research and political debates on surrogacy. In addressing these ambivalences, the concept of *framing* has proven useful in different contexts (see Markens 2007; Pande 2014; Rao 2003; Cook, Sclater & Kaganas 2003). In this text, I follow Susan Markens' (2007) conception and methodological use of the concept. By frame, I refer to a set of discursive, rhetorical and ethical choices preceding, and thus guiding, the formation of a political stance towards a given issue.[12] When it is unclear how an issue should be approached, the choice of frame becomes crucial. Understood as a tool for opinion-formation, the concept of frames is useful in

[12] See Markens 2007 and Pande 2014 on further discussions about this concept.

understanding the logic behind complex arguments and reactions, evident in public discussions around surrogacy (Markens 2007, 8).

Surrogacy is a question that reveals the tensions between conflicting ideals. For example, reproductive freedom and empathy for the infertile are emphasised by some proponents of surrogacy, while some opponents express concerns about the commodification of reproductive policies, and ultimately of women and children (Markens 2007, 56–60). In most discussions, however, there is a thorough understanding of the many aspects of the issue, and the opinion is formed by emphasising or prioritising some frames over others. International research on surrogacy shows that there is no clear or unanimous answer to the bioethical, moral, or political questions it raises. This, of course, is true of most issues, but in the case of surrogacy, the ambivalence is explicit (Markens 2007; Ragoné 2003; Pande 2014; Sudenkaarne 2018b). The moral evaluation of surrogacy ultimately depends on the choice of the frame or paradigm one chooses to emphasise (Lane 2003).

Discussions on surrogacy contain a set of different frames that vary across contexts and discussions. Susan Markens (2007, 56–75), for example, shows how discussions around commercial surrogacy in the United States frame the question as a women's issue – more specifically within the frame of the freedom of choice. At the same time, there is profound ambivalence in the conclusions that different women's rights advocates reach. On the one hand, surrogacy can be seen as the right for the surrogate to decide to utilise their own body as means of labour. On the other hand, the entire concept of choice can be put into question, arguing that the rhetoric of choice fails to recognise socioeconomic, race, or class related inequalities, and that no real choices can be made unless the effects of these inequalities are thoroughly accounted for.

According to Markens (2007, 182), "investigating the frames used in reproductive politics is an essential part of understanding how we as a society respond to developments in reproduction and biomedicine." She claims, that the diverse and competing framings related to surrogacy offer evidence of the plasticity of the problem – the diversity of interpretations and possible reactions to the question. The frames through which surrogacy is viewed change significantly once the discussion turns from commercial surrogacy arrangements to altruistic surrogacy. I claim, that one pivotal framework that this change has to do with, is a transition of the "location" of surrogacy from the public sphere of state-regulated commercial arrangements to the private sphere of friendship, kinship and altruism.

The Finnish discussion is explicitly built on the following dichotomy: Legalising surrogacy is only even contemplated in relation to altruistic[13] surrogacy arrangements, where the surrogate is assumed to be a close relative (e.g., mother or sister) or friend of one of the intended parents (Etene 2011; OM 28.6.2013). Commercial surrogacy, on the other hand, is utilised as a necessary counter-rhetorical framework also in the Finnish discussion, as I shall proceed to show.

I will begin my analysis with a brief discussion on the official documents of the Finnish discussion on surrogacy, and start with ETENE's statement, the Finnish national ethical committee of social and healthcare. This statement is the one of the most influential documents in the entire process of restarting the public discussion on surrogacy in Finland during the 2010s.[14] It is the founding paper on which the Ministry of Justice based its 2012 report (OM 2012), and it is also referred to in several other public statements and reactions in the discussion.

Official ethic and legal debate

> Surrogacy treatments require that the issue is ethically considered from the perspective of the situation and rights of different parties; the child, the surrogate and their family, and the married couple [sic] hoping for a child. It is important that all

---

[13] The dichotomy of altruistic / commercial surrogacy arrangements has been contested (e.g. Sudenkaarne 2018b), but in the discussions around surrogacy it is a crucial line of division. Altruistic arrangements refer to situations in which the surrogate mother-worker is a close friend to or relative of the intended parent/s, and usually reference to altruistic arrangements also contains the idea that the surrogate is not financially compensated for her work. On the other hand, commercial arrangements usually involve a surrogate previously unknown to the commissioning parent/s, who is also financially compensated.

[14] For a more thorough account of this specific statement, see Sudenkaarne 2018b.

parties' basic and human rights are respected, and that no harm is done to any party.[15]

ETENE bases its statement on the ethics of surrogacy arrangements in Finland on the ground of human rights and the principle of no harm. The task of the statement, then, is to define what is meant by rights, what is considered harm, and what is the relationship of rights vs. potential harm in different contexts of surrogacy. According to ETENE, no harm has been caused to children born through surrogacy with respect to the way they were born (ETENE 2011, 2). The family [sic] that wishes for a child, is not under immediate risk of being harmed either. Thus, the question of harm is concentrated on the surrogate mother-worker.

In considering the possibility of harm for the surrogate, two frames are posed against each other: first, the freedom and self-regulation of the surrogate, and two the possible threats of mistreatment through for example commodification, submission or forcing the arrangement. Possible health risks for the surrogate are also considered but they are discussed separate from these opposing frames.

After thorough argumentation on the different perspectives of all parties involved, ETENE concludes that it will support fertility treatments leading to surrogacy in Finland, but only in altruistic arrangements, with permission from an authority, and with the treatment performed under public healthcare. "Issues should not be forbidden because they are difficult or complicated, or can result to malpractice, if there has not been a true effort to seek positive alternatives", ETENE concludes (28.9.2011, 6).

In its statement, ETENE proposes first, that surrogacy would be accepted only for married couples, where the woman suffers from malfunction or absence of a uterus. In 2011 marriage in Finland was only open for heterosexual couples, so this statement effect-

---

[15] Etene 28.9.2011, translation AM. "*Sijaissynnytyshoidot edellyttävät, että asiaa eettisesti tarkastellaan eri osapuolien; lapsen, sijaissynnyttäjän ja hänen perheensä sekä lasta toivovan avioparin oikeuksien ja aseman pohjalta. On tärkeää, että kaikkien osapuolien perus- ja ihmisoikeudet, kaikkien etu ja vahingon välttäminen toteutuvat.*"

ively excluded same-sex couples. Also, the malfunctioning of the uterus was defined to be of medical nature, which can be assumed to exclude trans women.

Next, ETENE proposes that treatments should be subject to permission, and that all surrogacy arrangements should be altruistic – commercial surrogacy by default would be unethical (Sudenkaarne 2018b, 121). The conditions of surrogacy would be strictly regulated, and the terms would exclude for example couples suffering from other forms of incurable infertility than lack or malfunction of a uterus, and single or unmarried parents of all genders, sexualities, and backgrounds.

Based on the statement by ETENE, the Ministry of Justice started investigating the issue and consequently wrote a report, in which it proposed three different ways to regulate surrogacy:

1. Continuing the prohibition against surrogacy based on artificial insemination,
2. Allowing non-commercial surrogacy without restrictions, or
3. Allowing non-commercial surrogacy in individual cases.[16]

This report was then sent out for a round of statements, inviting stakeholder NGOs, legal and medical experts and organisations, and ministries to participate.[17] There were 64 statements given (OM 6/2013). A majority of the respondents took a stance for allowing surrogacy in limited, non-commercial cases. The second-most popular opinion was to continue the prohibition of all arrangements. Only two respondents considered an unrestricted allowance of non-commercial surrogacy preferable. However, a significant number of respondents were ambivalent on the question, and refrained from taking any stance, most of them wishing for more research and a more long-term experience to be gained

---

[16] OM 52/2012

[17] These rounds of statements are open also for organizations not invited and for any interested individual, if they are alert on the issues being prepared and find the information on the round of statements.

from international development. Importantly, not a single respondent wanted to allow commercial surrogacy in Finland.[18]

Both the Child Ombudsman and the Evangelical Lutheran Church opposed the legalisation of surrogacy arrangements in Finland. In their statements, they point to possible risks in allowing any form of surrogacy:

> As the memorandum and several articles have noted, it is extremely challenging to make solid legislation around surrogacy, which would secure the rights of all parties. The law should solidly secure the right of the child born through a surrogacy arrangement. Attention needs also to be paid to the children belonging to the family of the mother functioning as surrogate.
>
> – The Child Ombudsman of Finland in their statement 12.11.2012.

> Treatment given in Finland is of a medically high standard. Globally, however, the fertility treatment industry is commodified. Legislation can cause problems that are difficult to foresee, as well as human suffering. If people cannot receive the service in their own country, they may go abroad for treatment. In this case, the wealth of the family becomes even more significant. The child threatens to become even more commodified, and the attractiveness of illegal measures rises. Prohibition by law does not end, nor necessarily even diminish, the volume of the industry, as it moves to countries where there is no legislation on the issue.
>
> – The Finnish Evangelic-Lutheran Church, the Church Board, statement 11.12.2012.

These quotes capture the central dichotomy present in the statements in general: making legislation that accounts for the rights of all parts is difficult. Many of those objecting to the legalisation of surrogacy argue that because it is such a complicated issue, it is best left prohibited. On the other hand, several statements point out

---

[18] OM 6/2013. See also Kivipuro 2015 (diss.) for a thorough analysis of all the statements given to this memorandum.

that in the absence of Finnish national legislation, the arrangements are moved abroad. This is seen as a risk for the security of the child, as well as a route to the even further commodification of surrogacy, and illegal measures.

The risk of arrangements abroad is recognised in a majority of the statements, and it is a crucial argument for legalising arrangements in Finland. Crucially, this is a risk that also dominates the public discussion on the issue, and strongly affects the rhetoric of many of the proponents of allowing surrogacy in Finland, as I shall now show.

After the round of statements, the issue was left undecided, and a long silence on the official front ensued. However, some media discussion did take place in the years 2012–2019, and this discussion is the focus of the next part of this chapter.

Framing surrogacy in the media

The media coverage of surrogacy in Finland in the 2010s has been scarce, but surprisingly uniform. There have been a couple of major efforts in the mainstream media to cover the issue: In 2012, *Helsingin Sanomat,* the biggest daily newspaper in Finland, wrote a long piece on a heterosexual couple, where the woman lacked a womb but who got twins through a surrogacy arrangement in Russia. The piece also featured an interview with the surrogate, the agency, as well as people from the Russian fertility clinic (*HS Kuukausliite* 9/2012).

In 2018, the public discussion intensified for a while, when *Helsingin Sanomat* published an article about a gay man who was pursuing a surrogacy arrangement in Albania, acting as the official representative of an international surrogacy agency in Finland (HS 19.7.2018). In September 2018 YLE, the Finnish National Broadcasting Company, published a series of articles, an investigating TV-program (30 minutes) and a discussion program (45 minutes) on surrogacy, all within a couple of days 22.–25.9.2018. This spawned some shorter stories in other newspapers, and some discussion in the editorial column of *Helsingin Sanomat.*

Even with the publication of some longer articles in major media, however, the public discussion around surrogacy in Finland cannot be called extensive. Rather, the issue has risen in some individual articles over the years, without awakening much further discussion. This is unsurprising, given the fact that nothing much new has been happening around surrogacy in Finland during this period. What is interesting, however, is the uniformity of the coverage, the perspectives, and the way that the issue is presented.

The 2018 coverage of surrogacy, both in *YLE* and *Helsingin Sanomat,* centred on Finns who were making international surrogacy arrangements in Russia, Ukraine or Albania. The following quote from the *YLE* article in 2018 is a good illustration of the ways that the mother-worker's perspective surrogate is framed:

> The war broke out in Ukraine in the spring of 2014. The forces of the Ukrainian government fought for power against forces supported by Russia. In the middle of the war, Maria's family tried to cope. Her husband had a job, but his salary was small. It was not enough for everything: food, a home, and children's schools. The family had to move from apartment to apartment. The situation was desperate. When Maria noticed an advertisement of a surrogacy clinic on the Internet, she saw a solution.
>
> – Maria, a surrogate mother-worker, YLE 23.9.2018a.

In the *YLE* stories from 2018, surrogate mother-workers were interviewed, and their perspective conveyed. Their situations were explained through the frame of economical strain and the need to escape an escalating conflict in the area. Importantly, in both of these texts, the women are still portrayed as having agency of their own – as making an active choice and choosing to become surrogate mother-workers. Tiia Sudenkaarne explains how, in the context of surrogacy, especially surrogates in the Global south, tend to be "either demonized as purveyors of so-called commercial motherhood, or patronized as mindless victims by white, middle-class academic feminism" (2018b, 122). The media discussion in Finland avoids the pitfall of this dichotomy, since it frames the surrogacy arrangements as understandable, economically moti-vated, and voluntary by all parties. The stories attempt to explain the situation of the mother-worker, emphasising her agency and the understandability of her choice in a difficult situation. All sur-rogate mother-workers interviewed in the material were reported to have made the decision by choice, and supported by their family members in the process. An example of how the support of family is framed, is this quote from *Helsingin Sanomat* – the most read newspaper in Finland – from 2012. Maša is the single mother of a small child, and she has decided to become a surrogate mother-worker in order to be able to provide for herself and the child.

> The seventh month of pregnancy was about to begin, but Maša had not told anyone about it, except her mother and a friend who lived in the United States. Her mother had approved of her solution, even though otherwise she thought that her adventur-ous daughter had made mistakes in her life. – Maša, a surrogate mother-worker, in Helsingin Sanomat Kuukausiliite 9/2012.

In this quote, Maša is framed as an "adventurous" person, who "has made mistakes in her life." Although these framings could be read as negative, they also provide Maša with agency and power, show-ing that she is capable of breaking norms, and has previously gone against her mother's advice or opinions. In the question of surro-gacy, however, Maša's mother approves of her choice, thereby framing surrogacy as an understandable solution to a difficult economic situation.

The accounts of the surrogate mother-workers are one side of the story. On the other side are those of the potential intended parents or commissioners of surrogacy arrangements. These two sides are held both textually and discursively clearly apart in the media coverage of surrogacy. This is also true when they co-appear in the same article. In the texts, the change of perspective is marked by a clear break, a subheading, or the two perspectives are repre-sented in different articles (as in *YLE* 23.9.2018a and *YLE* 23.9.2018b). This is indicative of the process of international surro-gacy itself, where the extent of communication and common understanding between the surrogate mother-worker and the intended parents is often framed as an essential marker of the power differences involved in the process. (cf. Pande 2014).

The media coverage portrays the situations of potential commissioners of surrogacy through a frame of longing for parenthood: "I had a wonderful childhood friend, who immediately suggested that she could carry a baby for us. She has children of her own, and she knows how it feels to long for a child. I had to tell her that it is illegal in Finland." – Anne, a woman without a womb, in YLE 23.9.2018b. This is an unusual way of becoming a father – and it is also illegal in Finland. In another article, Erkko Välimäki, a single man, says that he intends to go through with the process in spite of its illegality, because it seems to be his only way to have a child. Välimäki has always wanted to be a father. "I find this an extremely important, fun and interesting period in a person's life. A child changes your entire life, and I look forward to that change with excitement." – Erkko Välimäki in Helsingin Sanomat 19.7. 2018. In both these stories, surrogacy becomes "the only possible option" to have a child. On the other hand, the legal problems of the process, both internationally and in Finland, are emphasised, and in many of the texts the interviewees explicitly state, that their considering of international (commercial) arrangements is only due to the fact that surrogacy is illegal in Finland. The discussion thus creates a tension between empathy towards the infertile on the one hand, and concern about legal issues, commodification of reproductive practices and commodification of children, on the other (Markens 2007, 8).

Having a child is not yet actual for 21-year-old Carolina Nystén. But the intention to do so is unwavering. She hopes that surrogacy will be allowed in Finland before she turns 30. "If this is not the case, I have to consider an arrangement abroad." – Carolina Nystén in Helsingin Sanomat 12.3.2014.

There are three frames present in the above quotes, which I identify as the most prominent in the Finnish public discussion around surrogacy from the perspective of the potential commissioners of surrogacy. These are first, an intensive wish to have a child; second, the legal difficulties of doing so in Finland, and third, the "threat" of being "forced" to consider (assumedly commercial) arrangements abroad if the situation in Finland will not improve. Sometimes a friend, sister or other close relative is mentioned, who would be willing to consider altruistic surrogacy, were she only allowed by Finnish law (cf. *YLE* 23.9.2018a). From the child's perspective and that of the intended parents, a prominent frame is that of legal and bureaucratic difficulties. These difficulties cohere around re-entering Finland – the child acquiring a passport and visa, and the intended parents having to prove their legal parenthood.

This set of frames constructs a dichotomy between the safe and secure domestic arrangements, and the dangerous, partly illegal and unethical surrogacy arrangements abroad. Altruistic surrogacy in Finland, now prohibited by law, is portrayed as ethical, egalitarian, safe, and preferred by the potential commissioners. Commercial arrangements abroad, then again, become suspect, legally and socially precarious, potentially taking advantage of women in difficult economic situations. The last part, however, is downplayed by representing the surrogate mother-workers' decisions as voluntary and informed.

While the Finnish legislators and official statements clearly dismiss commercial surrogacy, and while legalisation is only actual for non-commercial arrangements, the media coverage of surrogacy in Finland has put significant focus on Finn-initiated commercial arrangements abroad, as well as on the prospect of potential commissioners to pursue said arrangements. The official statements and the media coverage is united in posing international surrogacy as a threat that will loom large if Finnish legislation does not adequately deal with the situation of involuntary infertile.

Empty frames: race[19] and ethnicity

Reading international research on surrogacy, one is bound to encounter deeply rooted discussions on the role of race and ethnicity. As Susan Markens (2007, 10–11) points out, it is impossible

---

[19] I use the concept with the usual precautions of essentialism and with knowledge of the colonial history of the concept.

to discuss surrogacy without discussing race. Or so one would think. In the Finnish discussion, questions of race and ethnicity are in fact absent. In none of the hundreds of pages of documents and media coverage I have analysed, have I found a single mention of either race or ethnicity. The discussion is absurdly colour blind, but also blind to questions of ethnic background. Socio-economic inequalities, on the other hand, are well accounted for in many of the documents, and the possibility of economic exploitation is often mentioned, also in relation to altruistic arrangements. This intensifies the colour-blindness of the discussion. In many contexts it would be impossible to discuss socio-economic inequality without the perspective of race.[20] For example, the research by Susan Markens (2007, Amrita Pande (2014) or Michael Nebeling Petersen et al. (2017) show extensive debates on the racial issues related to surrogacy in the contexts of the US, India and Denmark. The absence of this framework in the Finnish discussion indicates that the question of race is, perhaps consciously, or in the absence of a common discourse, hidden under the concept of socio-economic inequality, thus highlighting the thorough whiteness of the discussions generated within the Finnish public sphere.

The ways of discussing race and ethnicity in the Finnish media are developing, with ethnic diversity slowly surfacing (Horsti and Hulten 2011). At the same time, the countries from where Finns pursue international commercial surrogacy, are also predominantly white – Ukraine and Russia, for example. The fact that Finns reach to these specific countries is mainly due to the geographic location of Finland: the fact that it shares a border with Russia, and that agencies offering services to Finns largely market Russian and Ukrainian, and now also Albanian services (see *MOT* 24.9.2018; *Helsingin Sanomat* 19.7.2018). Not many Finn-originated surrogate arrangements are known to happen in for example India, contrary to the Danish cases Michael Nebeling Petersen (2018) has been researching.

Even in a wholly white context, however, whiteness would still be relevant to discuss. According to Amrita Pande (presentation,

---

[20] I owe thanks to Raili Uibo for this important insight.

Turku 2018) the business of surrogacy is globalising, and Ukraine is one of the internationally most used sources of white donated egg cells. After 2018, the global COVID-19 pandemic made international travel very hard for a long period of time, causing problems for international surrogate arrangements.[21] In the present situation, in September 2022, the war in Ukraine is influencing surrogacy arrangements in Ukraine. In an article dated September 8th 2022, *The Economist*[22] reports that surrogacy agencies based in Ukraine have evacuated the pregnant mothers to Poland or the Czech Republic. Because of legislation in these countries, however, the surrogates will have to return to Ukraine to give birth, in order for the commissioning parents to have legal rights to the child when it is born. These developments show the fragility of international surrogacy arrangements in the face of global or local crises, changes in national legislation or conditions of travel. However, such accounts also show that the agencies are keen on finding ways to overcome these obstacles. Changes in the global or local surrogacy landscape do happen, but the business finds new ways and places to surface.

In the Danish context, Michael Nebeling Petersen (2018) mentions that some of the gay men he has interviewed have used specifically white egg donors to have as much resemblance as possible between the fathers and the child/ren. On the other hand, one gay couple, who had used the egg cells of the Indian surrogate mother-worker, sometimes used the assumption of international adoption to hide their surrogacy-arrangement – something that the difference in appearance of the parents and the children made possible (ibid.). The need to hide the initial surrogacy arrangement would spring from the stigma associated with surrogacy in Denmark, as well as the legal prohibition against commercial surrogacy in Denmark, which the couple would have had to work around to complete the arrangement.

---

[21] For example, a report from BBC 15.5.2020 on the situation in Ukraine states that surrogate babies are stranded in the country because the commissioning parents have not been able to travel: https://www.bbc.com/news/av/world-europe-52673225.

[22] https://www.economist.com/europe/2022/09/08/the-war-has-thrown-ukraines-surrogacy-industry-into-crisis

Race is a crucial factor also in all white surrogacy arrangements, even though it is not openly discussed. Whiteness is assumed in case of potential intended parents – the prospect of a non-white intended parent is not discussed in any of the media coverage I analysed.[23] Whiteness is thus intrinsic to the Finnish discussion on surrogacy.

Whiteness, and thus the possibility of being colour blind, is a controversial factor in relation to a certain built-in nationalism visible throughout the Finnish discussion. When reading personal accounts of surrogacy in relation to, for example, India or Thailand (Pande 2014; Vora & Iyengar 2017; Engh Førde 2017, Nebeling Petersen 2018), but also in the United States (Markens 2007), race, and the genetic question of racial inheritability, are essential in thinking about the ethical perspectives, power differences and potential exploitative (or empowering) aspects of surrogacy arrangements.

In the Finnish discussion on commercial arrangements in Russia, Ukraine or Albania, this aspect is missing. Thus, surrogacy can be portrayed as happening between semi-equal, voluntary subjects, closely resembling the conditions of domestic arrangements, save its commercial part. The absence of a discussion of race or ethnicity also enables the downplaying of the socio-economic differences between the commissioning parents and the surrogate mother-workers. What it enables is Finnish media representations of surrogates as non-desperate voluntary actors, that is, as not victimised, but looking for a better standard of living.

A similar pattern can be found among the gay couples that Michael Nebeling Petersen (2018) has interviewed. His interviewees articulated a distinction between those who could afford the "more ethical" – but also more expensive – surrogacy arrangements in the United States, and those who perceived themselves as less-moneyed, and who would have to resort to the cheaper (around 1/3 of the price) arrangements in India. Here too, we can find a (racialised) distinction between voluntary surrogates in a

---

[23] Please also see Suraiya Jetha's chapter [Chapter Four] in this volume, which deals with a similar question surrounding race and colour blindness, but in the Norwegian context.

country with high legal standards of surrogacy, versus potentially abused extremely poor surrogates in a country with high poverty and no legal framework in place for surrogacy arrangements.

Despite the representations of the Russian and Ukrainian surrogate mother-workers as equal and largely voluntary, there is still a drastic differentiation between international commercial arrangements, and non-commercial domestic ones in the Finnish public discussion. But rather than being based on differences of race or ethnicity between the surrogate mother-worker and the intended parents, or indeed instead of an analysis of power-imbalances and victimisation of the surrogate mother-workers, this differentiation is based on the legal and bureaucratic difficulties related to international arrangements. They are portrayed as semi-illegal, difficult, somewhat dangerous and with potential catastrophic consequences for the surrogate, in the case of for example miscarriages or pregnancy complications. (See *MOT* 24.9.2018.)

I suggest that a subterranean issue in present discussions is the construction of Russia, Ukraine and Albania as lawless territories, where local surrogacy agencies offer their services to desperate Finns, forced to act because of the strict Finnish legislation prohibiting surrogacy in Finland. This undercurrent is visible for example in articles that depict surrogacy arrangements in Russia. There is for example a vivid image of threatening Russian border guards, whose approval is needed in order to take the baby born in Russia back to Finland. The fear is whether or not the guards will let the baby pass to Finland with its intended parents; born during the parents' "vacation", the child has no visa (YLE 25.9.2018).

Again, the general sense in the discussion is that domestic non-commercial arrangements would be safer and more ethical, less threatening, and bureaucratically clearer, unless they were prohibited by law. Thus, the nationalist framework serves to construct commercial arrangements abroad as a threat, the solution of which is to permit domestic altruistic arrangements to take place. This would, several parties argue, lessen or even remove the need for international surrogacy (YLE 23.9.2018; Kohtuuttomat 2013; Lindfors & Jämsä 2013).

However, in for example Great Britain, where domestic altruistic surrogacy is allowed, evidence suggests that the need for international commercial arrangements has not diminished after the domestic legislation was in place. Rather, the contrary is the case (Crawshaw, Blythe & van der Akker 2013). Thus, this line of argument can be contested, specifically because there is no quantitative data available on the intentions, or even possibilities, of any potential Finnish commissioning parents to engage in altruistic arrangements according to the strict conditions suggested by ETENE and the Ministry of Justice.

Exclusions: Gender, marital status, and the gendered lack of a womb

In its memorandum from 2012, the Ministry of Justice tracks the legislative challenges of regulating surrogacy in any form other than a complete ban of the arrangements altogether:

> If one wanted to allow surrogacy arrangements, but only to a limited extent, as ETENE suggests in its statement, it would be challenging to draw a border between permitted and prohibited arrangements. It could reasonably be asked, why the arrangements would not be available to all those infertile couples, whose infertility is not due to themselves. [...] The border between permitted and prohibited would always be in some ways arbitrary. – Ministry of Justice, Memorandum on surrogacy, 52/2012.

The ministry here argues that due to the arbitrary nature of the borders between permitted and prohibited forms of surrogacy, no form of surrogacy should be made legal. This is a form of slippery-slope-argument, where opening one part of surrogacy would lead to a development, and where it would become increasingly hard to motivate banning other kinds of surrogacy arrangements.

This section of the chapter discusses limitations suggested about surrogacy arrangements in the public discussion on surrogacy in Finland. It addresses the explicit will to limit surrogacy to certain cases, thus limiting the eligibility for surrogacy. As the quote above exemplifies, the discussions on how, for whom, and in what situations, surrogacy should be legal, open up issues in several different directions. The central one being, *who* would be eligible for surrogacy arrangements under Finnish law and *on what premises*. This is a complex issue, but interestingly it is not widely debated in the official documents, nor in the public discussion. The above quote summarises the debate well – it suggests that surrogacy would only be allowed for mixed-sex (in the discussion usually referred to as heterosexual) couples, where the (assumedly cis-) woman suffers from malfunction or the absence of a uterus.

The ETENE statement takes this as given, referring from the very beginning only to "the couple" or "the married couple" wishing for a child. (ETENE 28.9.2011, 1–3, 5.) This given is not explained in any part of the statement, nor is it problematised in relation to any other potential persons, who could benefit from surrogacy arrangements. Tiia Sudenkaarne (2018b, 123) points out that "it is apparent that the case does not honour the diversity of families either inside or outside LGBTQI. Especially men, either as couples or single parents, are simply invisible."

This silence in the public discussion is only broken by the media coverage of the case of Erkko Välimäki, cited above, where it is explicitly stated that he is a single gay man, commissioning surrogacy in Albania and acting as the Finnish representative for the Israel-based surrogacy agency Tammuz (HS 19.7.2018; QX). However, this discussion is kept separate from the discussion of principles of regulating altruistic surrogacy through legislation.

Even the NGOs, who should be interested in promoting gay men's access to surrogacy arrangements, such as the Rainbow families' organisation *Sateenkaariperheet ry*, lay low in this question. It may be a strategic choice, but the organisation has chosen to act in this issue in unison with several other organisations, such as the organisation of involuntary infertile, *Simpukka ry*, the Network of Family Diversity, as well as the organisation for women lacking wombs, *Kohtuuttomat ry*. In their public statements, they emphasise formal equality of the legislation. "Legal regulation of surrogacy must be equal. The arrangements cannot be limited on for example the basis of the reason for infertility or confined only to the use of own gametes." (*Sateenkaariperheet, Monimuotoiset perheet-verkosto, Simpukka* and *Kohtuuttomat,* 19.11.2018.)

The issue of the willingness of male couples and single men to act as commissioners of surrogacy has thus far mostly been left out of the discussion. Michael Nebeling Petersen (2018) has interviewed several gay couples in Denmark, who have commissioned surrogacy and are in various stages of the process, some already parents. He describes the ambivalent feelings these men have in relation to the arrangements, but also the justifications that they give to their wish for a child of their own. What is evident in Nebeling Petersen's account, is that the issue spurs complicated feelings and reactions both in the men themselves, and in their environment.

In a heteronormative framework, it may be more socially understandable that there is a desire among mixed-sex couples to procreate in a way that replicates the norm as fully as possible. When the woman in such a couple lacks a womb, but is still able to produce ova, there is a possibility of the couple having a genetic child of their "own", thus passing as a "normal" heterosexual nuclear family. This is a case, where altruistic surrogacy is still relatively easy to regulate, and this is also the assumption built in all the official documents in the Finnish discussion.

However, as Tiia Sudenkaarne has argued, this discussion omits the suffering of "those involuntarily childless individuals, who are not a part of a (straight) married couple, and whose suffering could be greatly relieved by allowing surrogacy arrangements." (Sudenkaarne 2018b, 123.)

The lack of a functioning womb is considered an understandable condition, allowing for the wish to commission a surrogacy arrangement, but only in a situation where the lack of womb is due to an anomaly or illness, not where it is due to the gender of the person. Also, there seems to be an undiscussed will to limit the eligibility for surrogacy arrangements only to those female persons who lack a functioning womb *and* are married to a male person.

However, as I have suggested, part of this omission of any other situations may be a strategic move, not to politicise as a gay rights issue. The Finnish legislation includes strong anti-discrimination clauses, and when the process of legislating surrogacy is being considered, the non-discrimination of certain groups of people, allegedly eligible for surrogacy arrangements, may be a strong argument to include also those not part of a (mixed gender) married couple.

On the other hand, framing the discussion on equality to only include the use of a couples own gametes shows how fragile the trust is in the will to consider gay rights as part of legislative processes in Finland. By avoiding framing the question as a gay rights issue, the NGOs voice their lack of trust in the legislative process to be able to consider gay rights as an intrinsic part of legislating the complex issue of surrogacy. The near future will tell whether this non-politicising of the issue leads to the desired results.[24]

On altruism and regulation

In addition to being nationalist, colour-blind, gendered and heteronormative, the Finnish discussion also includes an omission of the complexity of the question of commercial versus altruistic surrogacy. Tiia Sudenkaarne (2018b, 121) points out that from a feminist bioethical perspective, the division between altruistic and commercial surrogacy is not at all clear, nor is it self-evident that altruistic arrangements are always more ethical. She notes that the definition of altruism in the ETENE statement means that the surrogate mother-worker is the only person not permitted to benefit economically from the arrangement. For example, the doctors, fertility clinics and sperm banks are allowed to gain financially from helping the intended parents – and they are also agents in the process. Thus, also altruistic arrangements always already involve commercial traits. However, in the Finnish discussion in

---

[24] N.B. While finalising this chapter, now in the fall of 2022, the issue of surrogacy is still not advancing in the Finnish legislative apparatus. There should be another memorandum published by the Ministry of Justice, but it has been postponed, and is due in April 2023. The COVID-19 pandemic has delayed many legislative processes and has also perhaps shed new light on the issue of surrogacy specifically. It is with great interest that we look forward to finding out what the ministry thinks and how the issue is further developed within the Finnish legal framework.

general, altruistic surrogacy is framed as non-commercial and being based on the goodwill of all parties involved.

In relation to the concept of altruistic surrogacy, Helena Ragoné (2003) asks who needs to diminish what aspect of genetics, biology, kinship or parenthood in order to justify the arrangement. This question is telling, in that it implicates that in surrogacy some aspects must be foregrounded, and some have to be omitted or diminished. This is true even in altruistic arrangements, where the surrogate mother(-worker) must diminish the worth of her labour, reduce it to a gift of love, to be allowed to carry the child of her friend or kinsperson.

In the United Kingdom, where altruistic surrogacy arrangements have been regulated by law since 1985, courts have repeatedly ruled that the best interest of a child exceeds the prohibition of payment to the surrogate (Rintamo 2016, 30). Thus, even when the payment exceeds reasonable expenses, which the law would not permit, intended parents' claims to parenthood have still been approved. This development would not be unlikely in Finland either, if one considers previous court decisions regarding parenthood of children born through surrogacy.[25] Thus, regardless of the way that altruistic surrogacy arrangements are defined by the law, in practice the border between commercial and altruistic arrangements have been and will be blurred.

Radhika Rao (2003, 23) identifies four categories of legal ordering of surrogacy in legislations across different states in the United States. These are:

1. Prohibition
2. Inaction
3. Status recognition and
4. Contractual ordering

---

[25] See for example HelHO:2013:4, where the right of the child to their family, as an integral aspect of the best interest of the child, was prioritised over the letter of the law. https://oikeus.fi/hovioikeudet/helsinginhovioikeus/fi/index/hovioikeusratkaisut/hovioikeusratkaisut/1377032400034.html

Of these, Finland is currently legally standing in a complex balance between the three first ones. Officially, the law prohibits fertility treatments for the purpose of surrogacy, but technically, surrogacy is not prohibited if it does not require fertility treatments. In the face of a growing commercial surrogacy industry in proximal countries, as well as a growing number of agencies offering their services to Finns, a politics of legal inaction is becoming less and less feasible. In practice, applications by intended parents have forced the courts towards different levels of status recognition – that is, in practice children born through surrogacy will gain the right to legal parents, based on the principle of the best interest of the child.

Now, the government has recognised the complexity and legal uncertainty of the current situation, which has led it to restart the process of regulating surrogacy. The regulation will need to be as ethical as possible and consider the interests of all parties while, one might hope, most powerfully protecting the weakest ones.

The question of regulation is framed throughout the public discussion as a dichotomy between commercial and altruistic surrogacy. The sedimentation of this dichotomy, as discussed previously in the first parts of this chapter, stagnates the discussion in two separate frames, where the fear is that allowing altruistic arrangements will somehow lead to these arrangements spilling out into commercial ones. This process, however, is already in progress because international commercial arrangements are now being recognised in Finland. In order to reach a balanced discussion, the static dichotomy would need to be reconsidered and a more refined discussion would be necessary on the many diverse aspects that surrogacy as a phenomenon may involve.

Conclusion: Questions of reproduction, commercialism, and queer bioethics

Tim Dean writes that the failure to reproduce the family in a recognisable form is simultaneously a failure to reproduce the social (Dean in Caserio et al. 2006, 827). What lies behind the need for surrogacy arrangements is specifically this: the need to reproduce family in a recognisable form. For some mixed-sex couples, where the woman lacks a womb, this means having genetic offspring, even if that offspring is gestated by someone else. For some same-sex couples, where neither partner has a womb, it means having a child just the two of you, without mixing in (lesbian) mother(s) or going through the process of international adoption, which in many countries, like in Finland, is practically impossible to success-fully complete as gay male couples (Smietana 2016).

Surrogacy as a phenomenon is not simple, nor is it easy to regulate. It is globalised, transnational, internationally unregulated, complicated, gendered, racialised, and includes different power imbalances – economic, genetic, physical, legal, and moral. There is no one good way to solve the problematic mesh of surrogacy. If there were, it would be done already. However, in regulating the issue, there are attempts to do this as ethically solid as possible.

This article has reviewed the Finnish discussion on surrogacy and pointed to some of the ways surrogacy is framed here. By analysing frames present in the discussion, but also what is left out-side the frames, this chapter has asked about what issues are *not* considered. It has pointed out some of the more simplified or prob-lematic distinctions in the discussion, such as the heteronormative basis of defining who is eligible for surrogacy, and the gap between altruistic and commercial arrangements, which in practice is quite unlikely to remain clear and possible to regulate.

The coverage of international surrogacy arrangements in Fin-land, as well as parental orders that Finnish courts have approved, already show that there is both will and an ability among Finnish citizens to commission international surrogacy arrangements. Sources from NGOs indicate that unofficial altruistic arrange-ments are constantly being made, usually with the fertility treat-ments carried out in Estonia or other neighbouring countries, with the pregnancy and delivery taking place in Finland.[26]

This chapter has analysed the framing of the argumentation in the public discussion on surrogacy in Finland. It has shown how such discussions build on distinctions and dichotomies that are not

---

[26] Personal inquiry, May 2019.

necessarily based on evidence or data, but rather on assumptions that foreground the ethical supremacy of domestic and altruistic arrangements. In a simultaneous move, international and commercial arrangements are problematised.

In addition, the analysis has shown, how questions of race and ethnicity are hidden under a frame of socio-economical differences. Attempts to exclude gay, lesbian, and unmarried people from the scope of surrogacy regulation, as well as strategies for counter-argumentation, show the fragility of equality as a basis of Finnish legislative processes.

Finally, the dichotomy of altruistic versus commercial surrogacy is cemented, and ultimately stagnates the discussion. A more nuanced and less stagnated discussion would be needed to enable the question of surrogacy to be handled as a complex and complicated ethical issue, and to find the most ethical legal solutions possible.

Overall, the need for an inclusive, ethical, and informed legislation on surrogacy in Finland is becoming quite evident. According to international experiences and a vast body of research, exclusions and omissions will only result in continuation of present unofficial or semi-legal arrangements. With its status as a liberal Nordic welfare state, Finland is in a position where it could become an example country internationally in how to approach this complex and delicate issue – including sufficient counselling and support for all parties, protection of the weakest and most vulnerable, an equality- and gender-conscious regulatory framework, and measured processes in case of complications.

References

Burrell, R. 2003. *Naisia ja sikiöitä: Avustetusta lisääntymisestä ja sikiön oikeuksista.* Helsingin yliopiston oikeustieteellisen tiedekunnan julkaisuja. Helsinki: Forum Iuris.

Caserio, R. L., Edelman, L., Halberstam, J. et al. 2006. "The Antisocial Thesis in Queer Theory." *PMLA*, Vol. 121, No. 3, 819–828.

Cook, R., Sclater, S. D. & Kaganas, F. 2003. "Introduction". In: Cook, R., Sclater, S. D., & Kaganas, F., eds., *Surrogate Motherhood: International Perspectives,* 1–16. Oxford: Hart Publishing.

Crawshaw, M., Blyth, E. & van den Akker, O. 2012. The changing profile of surrogacy in the UK – Implications for national and international policy and practice. *Journal of Social Welfare and Family Law* 2012:3. 267–277.

Engh Førde, K. 2016. "Fair Play in a Dirty Field? The Ethical Work of Commissioning Surrogacy in India". In: Lie, M. & Lykke, N., eds., *Assisted Reproduction Across Borders: Feminist Perspectives on Normalizations, Disruptions and Transmissions.* 37–48. New York & London: Routledge.

Eriksson, L. 2016. "Finland as a Late Regulator of Assisted Reproduction. A Permissive Policy Under Debate." In: Lie, M. & Lykke N., eds., *Assisted Reproduction Across Borders: Feminist Perspectives on Normalizations, Disruptions and Transmissions.* 124–136. New York & London: Routledge.

Horsti, K. & Hulten, G. 2011. "Directing diversity. Managing cultural diversity media policies in Finnish and Swedish public service broadcasting." *International journal of Cultural Studies.* Vol. 14 (2): 209–227.

Kivipuro, K. 2015. Sijaissynnytys ja Vanhemmuuden Normalisointi. Lisääntymisoikeuksien Rajaaminen Lainsäädäntöaineistossa. Unpublished Dissertation. University of Helsinki, Sociology. (diss.).

Kähkönen, L. & Sudenkaarne, T. 2018. "Queer, Biopolitics and Bioethics." *SQS Journal of Queer Studies.* 1–2/2018. XI–XIX.

Lane, M. 2003. Ethical Issues in Surrogacy Arrangements. In: Cook, R., Sclater, S. D. & Kaganas, F., eds., *Surrogate Motherhood: International Perspectives,* 121–139. Oxford: Hart Publishing.

Leibetseder, D. 2018. "Queer reproduction revisited and why race, class and citizenship still matters: A response to Cristina Richie." *Bioethics* Feb 32 (2). 138–144.

Lie, M. & Lykke, N. 2016. "Editorial Introduction." In: Lie, M. & Lykke, N., eds., *Assisted Reproduction Across Borders: Feminist Perspectives on Normalizations, Disruptions and Transmissions.* 1–21.

Markens, S. 2007. *Surrogate Motherhood and the Politics of Reproduction.* Berkeley & Los Angeles: University of California Press.

Mägi, E. & Zimmerman, L.-L. 2015. *Stjärnfamiljejuridik. Svensk Familjelagstiftning ur ett Normkritiskt Perspektiv.* Stockholm: Gleerups.

Nebeling Petersen, M., Krolökke, C. & Myong, L. 2017: "Dad and Daddy Assemblage: Resuturing the Nation Through Transnational Surrogacy, Homosexuality and Norwegian Exceptionalism." *GLQ: A Journal of Lesbian and Gay Studies.* Vol. 23:1. pp. 83–112.

Nebeling Petersen, M. 2018. "Becoming Gay Fathers Through Transnational Commercial Surrogacy." *Journal of Family issues.* Vol. 39 (3) 693–719.

Pande, A. 2014. *Wombs in Labor.* New York, NY, Columbia University Press.

Ragoné, H. 2003. "The gift of Life: Surrogate Motherhood, Gamete Donation, and Constructions of Altruism. In: Cook, R., Kaganas, F. & Sclater, S. D., *Surrogate Motherhood. International Perspectives,* 209–226. Oxford: Hart Publishing.

Rao, R. 2003. "Surrogacy Law in the United States: The Outcome of Ambivalence." In: Cook, Rachel, Sclater, S. D. & Kaganas, F., eds., *Surrogate Motherhood: International Perspectives*, 23–34. Oxford: Hart Publishing.

Rintamo, S. 2016. Regulation of Cross Border Surrogacy in Light of the European Convention on Human Rights & Domestic and the European Court of human Rights Case Law. Unpublished dissertation, University of Helsinki, Faculty of Juridics. (diss.)

Salminen, S. 2007. Sijaissynnytys – sallitusta kielletyksi. *Oikeustieto* 1/2007, 17–19.

Smietana, M. 2016. "Families Like We'd Always Known?" Spanish Gay Fathers' Normalization Narratives in Transnational Surrogacy. In: Lie, M. & Lykke, N., eds., *Assisted Reproduction Across Borders: Feminist Perspectives on Normalizations, Disruptions and Transmissions*, 49–60. New York and London: Routledge.

Strathern, Marilyn. 2011. "What is a parent?" *Hau: Journal of Ethnographic Theory 1:1.* 245–278.

Sudenkaarne, T. 2018a: "Considering Unicorns: Queer Bioethics and Intersectionality." *SQS Journal of Queer Studies.* 1–2/2018. 35–50.

---. 2018b: "Queering Bioethics: A Queer Bioethical Inventory of Surrogacy." *Ethics, Medicine and Public Health* 2018: 6. pp. 117–125.

Söderström-Anttila, V. & Vilska, S. 2013. Sijaissynnytys hoitavan lääkärin näkökulmasta. Presentation at the Finnish Association of Medical Law and Ethics. 14.3.2013. www.sloes.fi

Vora, K. & Iyengar, M. M. 2016. "Citizen, Subject, Property. Indian Surrogacy and the Global Fertility Market." In: Lie, M. & Lykke, N., eds., *Assisted Reproduction Across Borders: Feminist Perspectives on Normalizations, Disruptions and Transmissions.* 25–36. New York and London: Routledge.

Official documents and statements:

ETENE 28.9.2011. Sijaissynnytyshoito Suomessa. Lausunto Oikeusministeriön pyynnöstä

OM 52/2012. Arviomuistio sijaissynnytysjärjestelyistä.

OM 6/2013. Arviomuistio sijaissynnytysjärjestelyistä: Lausuntotiivistelmä.

Supreme court of Sweden, case Ö 3462-18 on acknowledging a court order from a foreign country (*Erkännande av utländsk dom*), 13.6.2019. http://www.hogstadomstolen.se/Domstolar/hogstadomstolen/Avgoranden/2019/2019-06-13%20%c3%96%203462-18%20Beslut%20till%c3%a4gg.pdf

The Finnish Governmental Program: Hallitusohjelma 2019–2023: Osallistuva ja osaava Suomi – sosiaalisesti, taloudellisesti ja ekologisesti kestävä yhteiskunta. (*A participating and knowing Finland – a socially, economically and ecologically sustainable society.*) 6.6.2019 http://julkaisut.

valtioneuvosto.fi/bitstream/handle/10024/161662/Osallistava_ja_osaava_ Suomi_2019_WEB.pdf?sequence=1&isAllowed=y

Evangelic Lutheran Church 11.12.2012: https://evl.fi/documents/1327140/ 43353795/Lausunto+arviomuistiosta+sijaissynnytysj%C3%A4rjestelyihin +liittyvist%C3%A4+oikeudellisista+kysymyksist%C3%A4+ja+s%C3%A4 %C3%A4ntelyvaihtoehdoista/10ce2f66-758d-d998-22a4-397137854b51

Child Ombudsman of Finland 12.11.2012: http://lapsiasia.fi/tata-mielta/ lausunnot-2/lausunnot-2012/lapsiasiavaltuutetun-lausunto-sijaissyn nytysjarjestelyista/

Simpukka, Kohtuuttomat, Sateenkaaiperheet Statement 29.9.2018: https:// www.sttinfo.fi/tiedote/ulkomaisille-sijaissynnytysjarjestelyille-on- mahdollista-kehittaa-eettisesti-kestava-kotimainen- vaihtoehto?publisherId=64150464&releaseId=69843042

Simpukka, Kohtuuttomat, Sateenkaaiperheet Statement 18.11.2018 https:// www.sttinfo.fi/tiedote/jarjestot-sijaissynnytysten-kotimainen-saantely- on-ainoa-eettisesti-kestava-ratkaisu?publisherId=64095818&releaseId= 69846770.

Ministry of Justice, statement 28.6.2013 https://kohduton.fi/2013/09/sijaissyn nytyskysymysta-tulee-viela-harkita-huolellisesti/

Media coverage

Ilta-Sanomat 6.8.2019: https://www.is.fi/kotimaa/art-2000006195854.html? fbclid=IwAR17VE20vorLM5TMeRtzLZbprJFunu4jDcHQMvsL6ZzTmU iIb6wdSJdBAWU.

Demokraatti 6.8.2019: https://demokraatti.fi/uutissuomalainen-puolet-suoma laisista-sallisi-sijaissynnyttamisen/

QX 12.6.2018: Erkko halusi isäksi, mutta se oli homomiehelle vaikeaa – ratkaisuksi löytyi sijaissynnytys.

MOT. 24.9.2018: Vauvani maksaa 70 000€: käsikirjoitus. Yleisradio.

YLE 25.9.2018 https://yle.fi/aihe/artikkeli/2018/09/25/suomalaiset-ovat- matkustaneet-vuosia-venajalle-sijaissynnytyshoitoihin

YLE 23.9.2018a https://yle.fi/aihe/artikkeli/2018/09/23/epatoivo-ajoi-ukraina laisen-marian-ja-georgialaisen-ketin-sijaissynnyttajiksi

YLE 23.9.2018b https://yle.fi/uutiset/3-10411364

YLE 22.9.2018 https://yle.fi/uutiset/3-10404517

YLE 22.5.2018 https://yle.fi/uutiset/3-10217519

Söderström-Anttila & Suikkari, Duodecim 3/2016 https://www.terveysportti. fi/xmedia/duo/duo13371.pdf

Simpukka journal 1/2017 https://kohduton.fi/uploads/2017/03/Simpukka- 2017_sijaissynnytys.pdf

Länsiväylä 25.7.2014 https://www.lansivayla.fi/artikkeli/228616-sijaissynny tyskielto-koskettaa-satoja

Helsingin Sanomat 19.7.2018 https://www.hs.fi/elama/art-2000005761526.html

Helsingin Sanomat 12.3.2014 https://www.hs.fi/kotimaa/art-2000002715934.html

Helsingin Sanomat 14.3.2014 https://www.hs.fi/mielipide/art-2000002716502.html

Helsingin Sanomat 12.3.2014 https://www.hs.fi/kotimaa/art-2000002715973.html

Tuima 4.7.2014 http://tuima.fi/kohduttoman-unelma-elaa-yha/

Helsingin Sanomat 12.5.2013 https://www.hs.fi/mielipide/art-2000002637998.html

Lindfors & Jämsä, *Helsingin Sanomat* 12.5.2013 https://www.hs.fi/mielipide/art-2000002638012.html

Helsingin Sanomat 6.1.2013 https://www.hs.fi/kotimaa/art-2000002604027.html

http://metku.net/~pesu/artikkelit/lainakohtu.php

https://kohduton.fi/2013/01/sannantarina/

Helsingin Sanomat Kuukausiliite, 9/2012 https://jurconsult.ru/smi/print/finland/helsingin_sanomat_babies.pdf

https://docs.google.com/viewer?url=http%3A%2F%2Fstatic.kohduton.fi%2Fuploads%2F2014%2F02%2Flailla-suljettu-kohtu-apu-lehti-2013-30-hein%25C3%25A4kuu.pdf

Meidän Perhe 9/2011 https://kohduton.fi/2013/03/tanjan-tarina/

6. The Mediation of Commercial Transnational Surrogacy: The Entanglement of Visual, Colonial, and Reproductive Technologies

Michael Nebeling Petersen

> Basically, I wish I was the one who could be pregnant. And since that's not the case, I want to be as much a part of the pregnancy as possible. […] Both Shirley and Karen [the surrogate mothers] have sent us all numbers and pictures and scans. We've gotten everything! And it was actually like this… This is going to sound all crazy… But during the pregnancy I went through a hormonal change. My skin changed. And yes, I started crying over everything. For the life of me, I got so phantom pregnant! It's scary…
>
> (Morten, May 2015)

When I interviewed the Danish gay couple Morten and Karsten, we talked about the two surrogate mothers who had helped them become parents to three children. Morten was overwhelmed with gratitude, but he also talked about a feeling of imperfection, that his body could not become pregnant, or as he phrased it: "I wish I was the one who could be pregnant." At the same time, he told me about his actual bodily pregnancy, the hormonal changes which were initiated by the many pictures, scans, and other information the couple received via email, Skype, and telephone from the surrogate mothers and the doctors on the other side of the Atlantic.

While the interviews I have made with commissioning parents going through transnational surrogacy are neither the data nor the focus of this article, I open with the quote from Morten, since it invites questions about how and in which ways the embodiment of third-person pregnancy takes place. Third-person reproduction is characterised exactly by the fact that the pregnant body is different from the intended parent/s. But as exemplified in the quote, third-person reproduction radically challenges an understanding of the human as a self-evident entity whose boundaries are clearly demarcated. In this chapter, I argue that third-person reproduction and the embodiment of pregnancy by commissioning parents are intimately connected to and enabled by the use of media technologies that expand and blur the lines between the bodies as well as to technologies of power, most notably colonialism.

In order to analyse the processes in such a posthumanist or somatechnical (Sullivan & Murray 2009) vein, I am influenced by Kember and Zylinska's (2015) conceptualisation of mediation. In their book *Life After New Media –mediation as a vital process*, they argue that "we are obliged to recognize that we human users of technology are not entirely distinct from our tools. They are not a means to our ends; instead, they have become part of us, to an extent that the us/them distinction is no longer tenable. As we modify and extend 'our' technologies and 'our' media, we modify and extend ourselves and our environments" (ibid., 13). Thus, mediation is understood as "a key trope for understanding and articulating our being in, and becoming with, the technological world, our emergence and ways of intra-acting with it, as well as the acts and processes of temporarily stabilizing the world into media, agents, relations, and networks" (ibid., xv).

In this chapter, I turn to blogs written by gay men and to Facebook communities for gay commissioning parents, in order to understand and examine how gay fatherhood and third-person pregnancy are being narrated, made intelligible, and embodied to such an extent that a pregnancy in one part of the world becomes a physical experience of the gay male body in another part, as Morten explains in the opening quote.

The questions raised for this examination are firstly, how is gay fatherhood being narrated and negotiated, and thus how is a liveable subjectivity as a gay father created? I will show that subjectivity as a gay father is rehearsed online by narrating and visualising gay fatherhood embedded within intelligible and normative structures of temporal and affective kinship. Secondly, I ask how online communities, and the blogs in particular, are enabling the gay men to mimic the pregnancy "for real". I am especially interested in how media technologies entangle with other forms of (power) technologies, and will show how pregnancy is embodied as an entanglement of media, colonial, and visual technologies that disaggregate the surrogate mother from the pregnancy and allow the gay commissioning parents to assume the control and affective and visual ownership of the pregnancy, reproductive matter, and the foetus.

I analyse the blogs and Facebook communities in line with the posthumanist scholarship of blogs as a bodily extension. This includes a conceptualisation of the body and the human as some sort of assemblage of technologies, present in boyd's work on blogs. boyd describes the blog as a medium characterised by a form of bodily expansion following McLuhan's understanding of a medium:

> In McLuhan's terms (1964) a medium is an "extension of man" that allows people to express themselves. Blogs are precisely this; they allow people to extend themselves into a networked digital environment that is often thought to be disembodying. The blog becomes both the digital body as well as the medium through which bloggers express themselves (boyd 2006, 11).

Likewise, Louise Yung Nielsen argues, in her readings of fashion blogs, that

> real bodies of flesh and blood and other matters are interwoven with discourses about bodies, gender, food, and everyday practices. In this way, I understand the fashion blog as a phenomenon, not merely producing discourses, but also producing matters and bodies (Yung Nielsen 2016, 62, my translation from Danish).

In this sense, we can understand the blog (and other media) not solely as a medium *representing* the body, but rather as a performative medium *constituting* the body. In the readings I offer in this article, I will follow this line of thought, and will look more closely at how social media performatively constitute a body in conjunction with other forms of subjectifying technologies.

In what follows, I will situate surrogacy within gay reproduction and family-making, and then elaborate on how transnational surrogacy is inherently intertwined with the internet and digital media. I will then present the chosen material and reflect on its sampling of before turning to the analyses of blogs and Facebook communities.

Gay fatherhood through surrogacy

Despite vast national differences in legislation, in the Global North gay men are increasingly using commercial surrogacy as a reproductive technology for having children. In popular imageries, gay masculinity has previously been understood as barren and non-reproductive (Butler 1992; Nunokawa 1991; Edelman 2004), even though gay men have been fathers for a long time. Before, gay men most commonly became fathers as a result of prior heterosexual relationships (Bergman, Rubio, Green & Padrón 2010, 115). Even though adoption has been a possible option in North America, many adoption agencies have made it difficult for gay men to make use of it. But as the assisted reproductive technologies were medically developed and became more common, gay men have increasingly found new ways to become fathers (Berkowitz 2012).

Most significantly, gestational surrogacy offers gay men a pathway to (new) parenthood (Murphy 2013). In contrast to another popular gay male family form, the rainbow families where gay men match up with a single woman or a lesbian couple to create a family with multiple parents and where the mother and father do not have a traditional sexual relationship, gestational surrogacy enables gay men to create a family consisting of only two (legal) parents, though this is neither legal nor easy in most European countries. And in contrast to adoption, gestational surrogacy enables the gay men to have children that are genetically related and offers the men a larger control over the reproductive process, e.g., choice of egg donor, when and how to get pregnant, etc.

As homosexuality has become more culturally accepted and, in many places, legalised in the Western world, it has been recoded from being associated with degeneration, sickness, non-repro-duction, and death to increasingly becoming associated with love, reproduction, happiness, and family (Nebeling Petersen 2012). One only has to think of the campaigns for gay marriage that actively have recoded gay masculinity from a framework of danger-ous promiscuous sex to one of monogamous loving gender-con-forming couples. This new cultural intelligibility of gay masculinity as a gendered identity suited for parenthood combined with new technologies to become fathers is radically changing the subject-ivities and life worlds of gay men (Nebeling Petersen 2016).

Surrogacy through and in global online media

Surrogacy is intimately connected to the internet and globalisation. Firstly, as surrogacy is illegal in most countries, to purchase surro-gacy gay men have to cross borders to find destinations that allow commercial surrogacy, and that welcome gay men and couples. Also, surrogacy is a highly stratified form of assisted reproductive technology, one that is dependent on global inequalities and large differences in income in order to become accessible to middle-class demographics. Thus, to navigate the global markets for surrogacy (in the form of different national legislations and expenses), the commissioning parents are dependent on easy access to informa-tion from many different contexts that include commercial agents (agencies, medical facilities, legal advisers, and so on), journalistic and academic work as well as the many online forums and social media sites connecting commissioning parents to shared know-ledge, experiences, and advice. The accelerated flows of informa-tion on the World Wide Web are fundamental to transnational commercial surrogacy, or as one informant told me when asked how they had come to learn about surrogacy: "I Googled it!"

Secondly, the often-long process of initiating a transnational surrogacy arrangement – finding an egg donor, a surrogate, clinics, agencies, legal advisers, understanding rapidly changing legis-lations and practices, etc. as well as the pregnancy itself –would be almost impossible to do without fast, instant, and visual communi-cative technologies like Skype, email, photo messaging, etc. An agent from a Californian agency specialising in transnational surrogacy told me that she is on "Skype most of the day." Likewise, the Danish commissioning parents I have interviewed all stress the importance of visual digital communicative technologies to enable contracting with agencies, clinics, and reproductive workers. And maybe those technologies are most important during the pregnancy, when Skype and digitally sent pictures "are simply not to do without" in order for the commissioning parents to be able to partake in the long and often stressful process, as another agent told me. For instance, commissioning parents often Skype with the surrogate or the medical staff during or after the surrogate's medical visits and scans. And agencies and medical staff send pictures of scans, bellies, and medical journals to the commissioning parents.

Thirdly, the internet offers a possibility for gay men to connect, to share information and experiences. These online communities, by many users termed *the surro community*, help, as I already mentioned, the commissioning parents to navigate global markets. But they also help the commissioning parents to create new stories and cultural imageries about gay fatherhood and surrogacy. It is important to notice that encountering surrogacy is fundamentally different for gay and straight couples: When heterosexual infertile couples turn to surrogacy, it is often the last option after other reproductive technologies have failed. On the contrary, "gay fathers turn to surrogacy joyfully as a pathway to parenthood" (Berkowitz 2012, 78). This new pathway is increasingly being embarked upon. Gay men are becoming fathers through surrogacy, but these new subjectivities have no script, nor do the pregnancies have any storylines. Gay men are creating new paths to embodying both fatherhood and pregnancy.

Method and material

This article is part of a larger study I have conducted on gay men and transnational commercial surrogacy. For two and a half years I have been involved in gay men's surro communities: interviews were conducted with 15 gay couples who are already or are planning to become fathers through surrogacy. I have participated in meetings for gay men involved in surrogacy and consumer conferences in Denmark and London, and have undertaken field observations and interviews with staff members in ten surrogacy agencies in Southern California and interviewed five surrogate mothers in California. Besides these offline ethnographic studies, I have, inspired by online ethnography (Hine 2015), followed multiple Facebook groups, Instagram profiles, blogs, and online forums for gay intended parents, surrogate mothers, and agencies. In this online ethnographic work, I followed the ethical guidelines from the Association of Internet Researchers (2019). These guidelines do not give a fixed set of rules, codes, or methods, rather they invite the internet researcher to stay reflexive about their ways of collecting data, ways of doing research, what questions they ask, what positions they navigate, and how they frame and disseminate their findings. Overall, I distinguished between "open" and "closed" spaces; the latter are online spaces not open for the public, whether it be closed Facebook-groups, closed Instagram accounts and closed forums; while the former are blogs, open Facebook pages and groups, open Instagram accounts and open forums. In the closed spaces, I applied for access/membership and informed admins or owners with all details about my research interests and purpose of joining. Following being allowed access, I posted a message, if at all possible, in the group about my presence, thereby affording people the possibility to reach out to me with questions or concerns. In the open spaces, I did not ask for permission, but as far as possible, I made my presence visible by posting a message. In general, and specifically regarding the blogs I analyse in this article, I follow Heidi McKee and James Porter's questions of how ethics depend on what type of research one is conducting – is it text-based or person-based? (McKee & Porter 2009, 5, see also Nebeling Petersen & Raun 2022, 2) I consider this study text-based and for this reason have not asked for informed consent from the participants.

The materials for this article are the online communities. I have chosen three blogs to analyse: The first is called *Becoming a Family*

(BaF) and is written by Charlie, an American gay man. The blog started in January 2012, and though the blog is still open, Charlie has not posted a new entry since October 2013. Charlie and his partner Brent undergo a successful surrogacy arrangement in India just before the new rules for medical visa were introduced, making it illegal for non-heterosexual couples to obtain a medical visa to India. Their child is born on March 1, 2013. The second blog, *Two Guys vs. the World* (TGvW), is written by an American gay man, Justin, who together with his partner, undergoes a surrogacy arrangement in Thailand after their first try in India is cancelled due to the new rules. The blog is created in August 2013, and the last entry is posted in April 2014. During this time, the couple became pregnant with a Thai surrogate mother. However, the pregnancy was terminated due to a failed heart. In April 2014 Charlie writes that they are now expecting twins with another Thai surrogate mother. The blog has not been updated since. The third blog is called *Two Men and a Baby* (TMaB). It is written by an Australian gay man who with his partner undergoes a successful surrogacy arrangement in Thailand – he is now the father of a girl born in February 2014. The blog was created in February 2013, with the last entry posted in March 2014.

I chose the three blogs because they all cover the full 'surrogacy journey' from start to end, and all three blogs primarily, if not solely, are about the surrogacy. Among other 'full journey' blogs, these blogs were selected to represent different national contexts (the US, the UK, and Australia), include both 'successful' and 'unsuccessful' outcomes in terms of children, and reflect different writing patterns and aesthetics. In this way the three blogs I have selected for close analysis represent some range within the different experiences gay men have with transnational surrogacy and cross-national differences, while the three blogs still are typical gay surro blogs. It is, however, important to emphasise that the blogs neither cover *the* online surro community nor represent the full spectrum of gay male experiences with surrogacy. What the three blogs enable me to analyse is the ways in which surrogacy experiences are mediated, staged, and made discursively and affectively understandable and liveable.

Secondly, I will include posts from selected Facebook groups for gay men involved in surrogacy. Most surrogacy Facebook groups are closed groups only visible to invited members. I have learned about different Facebook groups from other sites and from interviews with gay fathers going through surrogacy. When applying for membership of the groups I have informed the administrators about my research and promised full anonymity to the groups and the members. I have followed one Danish, one Swedish/Scandinavian, two European, and one international group for more than two years, and in this article, I will include posts from these groups to show how the tendencies on the blogs are performed on Facebook as well. I have anonymised the Facebook groups and their users, as I have promised the admins to do so, and for this reason the participants write their posts and comments to each other and probably do not think about me being present as a researcher. I have not anonymised the blogs since the blogs are in the public domain.

To walk the path to parenthood

Like on blogs written by heterosexual couples about surrogacy, the process is metaphorically staged as a journey (Madsen 2012). When Charlie introduces himself and his partner in the first post on the blog, he writes: "Brent and I (Charlie) love to travel. It's probably one of the things that immediately drew us to each other when we met just a short couple of years ago. […] This blog is about a different type of journey – the journey to becoming a family" (30.1.12). Similarly, Sam writes in his first post: "I'll be booking in to see my GP in the next week or so for a fertility test and, depending on the result hopefully moving onto the next chapter in our journey" (18.2.13). Here the surrogacy process is staged as a journey as well as a literary plot by metaphorically referring to "chapter".

Using the metaphor "journey" points to parenthood being performed by following already given roads or paths. The metaphor "chapter" is referring to Sam as the writer, but also to the movement towards parenthood as an already given script that needs to be followed. But the gay bloggers also describe how the journey is a new one, one that has not been walked before and needs to be paved by the bloggers. For instance, Justin writes:

> So, how to introduce you to our lives and our journey? Let's try this, and stop me if you've heard this one: "A white boy from California and a South Asian guy from New Jersey walk into a fertility treatment center in Thailand...." Hmmm, no, that's not quite right. Ok, how about this one: "How many gay guys and straight women does it take to make a baby?" No, that's not it either (TGvW 1.8.13).

In the quote, the journey is established as one that has not yet been walked by ironically using the saying "stop me if you've heard this one." Justin does not have the words to describe the process, as his explanations do not express his intentions "quite right", showing that there is no available discourse to capture the process.

The bloggers use the online surro community to share knowledge and create new discourses and ways of life in progress. This is expressed by Justin who explains that he and his partner have "learned a lot about the process through many people who were generous enough to share their experiences to make it easier for those who follow the same path behind them" (BaF 30.1.12). Through the online surro community and by using the blog and other social media as tools for expressing and performing themselves, the bloggers reorganise their life temporality to make what seemed impossible possible. Charlie describes how he has struggled to come to terms with his homosexuality, and how he thought "that, if I wasn't straight and married one day, I couldn't be a dad. I thought that being gay meant that I would never have a family. [...] I thought I'd never be able to get married and have kids, but now here I am blogging about it to anyone who will listen. This blog is about the journey into becoming a family" (BaF 30.1.12).

It is worth noting that Charlie's understanding of *the family* is a nuclear family consisting of a couple with 'their own' children. This is quite different from the non-heterosexual families described by Weston (1991) as "chosen families". Charlie's ideal family rather resembles "blood families", or traditional Western heterosexual kinship patterns. The idealisation and privileging of straight kinship patterns show how gay family structures and gay identity are to be understood, as mentioned in the introduction, in an affective history as non-reproductive and without a future (Ahmed 2004, 155–159; Ahmed 2010, 88–89; Edelman 2004; Nebeling Petersen 2012, 16–22). So, when gay men realise that they can become both gay men and parents, it involves a renegotiation of the experiences of kinship marginalisation and exclusion. Where becoming a gay man at first oriented the bloggers towards an unhappy future as non-reproductive *queers*, the mere possibility of procreation, of becoming a 'real family', forms other futures for the bloggers. This promise of happiness (Ahmed 2010) in the form of a 'real' family with children orients the bloggers in new reproductive directions.

Straight orientations, straight temporality?

Ahmed notices that if one orients oneself within the logic of reproduction then one is also orienting oneself according to a straight temporality, a straight line of "birth, childhood, adolescence, marriage, reproduction, death" (2006, 554) that simultaneously, when performing straight, creates the queer as that which does not orient in the same straight line. This 'straight' or at least reproductive orientation seems to place the commissioning parents in another and more intimate relation with their families of origin. Take for instance Sam, who, after the surrogate mother has become pregnant, writes "I have always loved kids. Seeing my brother's two boys and girl has always made me happy. Listening to their stories, their tales and being silly with them has always made me feel good, much to my parents' annoyance" (TMaB 18.2.13). The reproductive desire and the possibility to have children seems to activate the 'old' family anew. Sam becomes closer to his brothers and their children. According to his parents, he becomes a child again, when he positions himself as "being silly" with the (other) kids. By enacting this infantility in regard to his parents, while presenting his brother's kids as happy objects (Ahmed 2010), Sam creates a straight generational timeline (Halberstam 2005, 5) backward in time that enables desired futures structured by "the time of reproduction" (ibid.).

But also, the future is rethought as the child-free life becomes redefined throughout the procreative process from something valuable to something bad. Sam writes: "The idea of growing old with Pete is wonderful and I am grateful that I have him to grow old with. However, the thought of bringing a child into the world to love and protect would complete me emotionally." Sam is organising different forms of kinship (and one might add happinesses and futures), and to have a family solely with Pete is wonderful to Sam, but imperfect. Thus, the reproductive orientation is not 'just' an orientation towards the object of a child, but also a change of life temporality and a lifeline. These other futures are embedded in a heteronormative context as well as a hostile homophobic reality, thus leaving little space for negotiation, which may explain why the bloggers seem to orient themselves in straight lines and straight temporalities (see also Andreassen 2016 and Nebeling Petersen 2016).

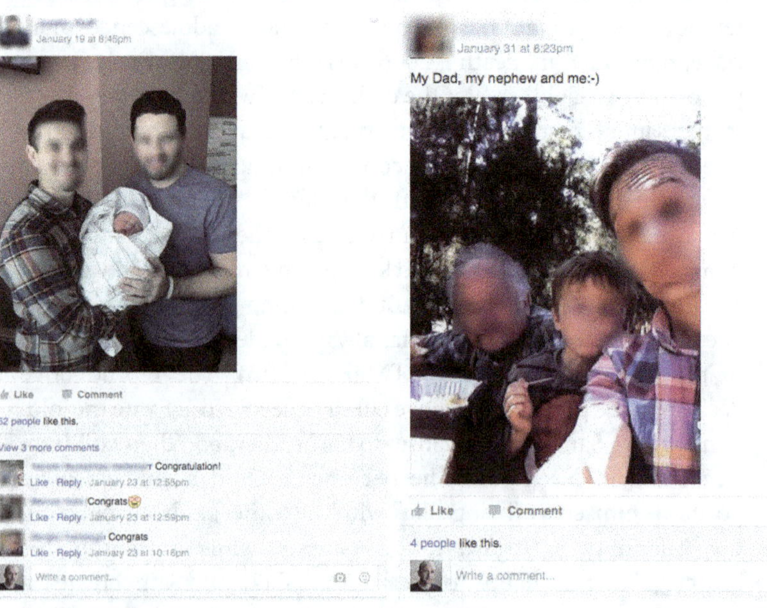

Picture 1 (left) and Picture 2 (right).

These new queer reproductive orientations and temporalities enable the former barren gay male subjectivities to be recoded into parental gay male subjectivities. In the Facebook group the recoding is visible by the many posts visually and textually representing the gay male father subjectivity. As represented in Picture 1, most pictures in the Facebook group include a happy male couple with the baby in the middle, thus visualising a classic portrait of a nuclear family, only this one is with the two men as the parents. Other users typically comment on these posts with hearts and congratulations. But the visuals also include the restructuring of kin, e.g., in Picture 2, where a user who a couple of days earlier posted that he was expecting a child uploads a picture of himself, his father, and his nephew. In this image, the gay man is writing himself into a generational line from father to son. Gay males have traditionally been excluded from this heterosexual generational kinship, because they have been understood as barren, non-reproductive, and represented as the end of the family line. In this way, online communities become a site of rehearsal (Raun 2010) of new kinship positions and form the contours of the parental gay male subjectivity.

Becoming real, mimicking the pregnancy

Charlie writes on his blog that the pregnancy feels "crazy" and unreal. But then the surrogate mother is hospitalised due to a series of irregularities in the pregnancy. Charlie and his partner are kept updated by email and text messages, resulting in many sleepless nights. The visual, real-time communication technologies work to affectively synchronise the commissioning parents to the pregnancy of the surrogate mother. The message beeping and calls from doctors with new information, scans, and medical records keep Charlie and his partner awake at night. And Charlie writes on his blog that this state of 'being-kept-awake' and his worries make the pregnancy feel more real for him.

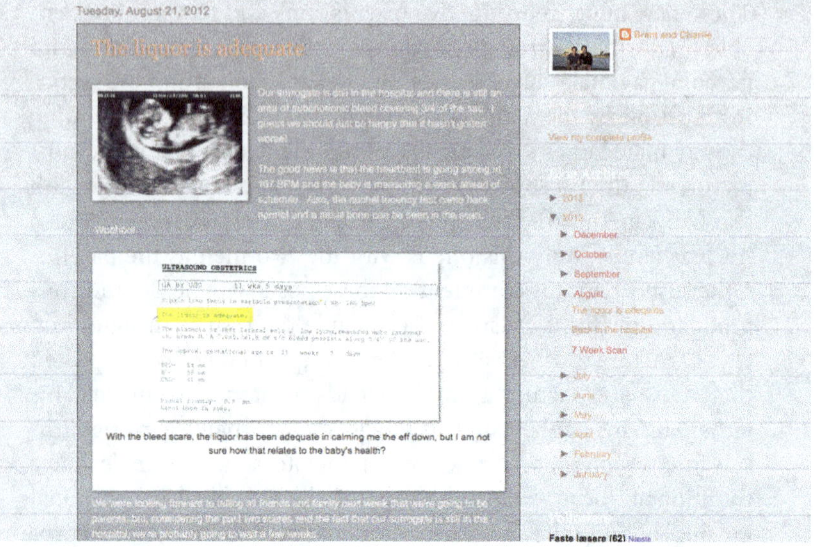

Picture 3.

Kalindi Vora analyses transnational surrogacy as affective and biological work that serve as "indices [of] new forms of exploitation and accumulation within neoliberal globalization" that "rearticulate a historical colonial division of labor" (2012, 683):

> The affective work and biological exploitation and accumulation represented in [...] commercial surrogacy depend as much on contemporary technologies that disaggregate and commodify discrete acts as they do on the longer colonial political economy within human "life" (as free, autonomous, self-willing and biologically healthy) has been supported in the First World by the labor and materials of the Third (ibid., 684).

The affective and biological work that Charlie's surrogate mother is doing – pregnant, bleeding, and hospitalised – is mediated through real-time, visual communication in the forms of scans of the foetus and journals, emails, and phone calls. It is mediated through reproductive technologies making the body of the surrogate mother disaggregated from the reproductive matter inside her, and it is mediated through colonial power relations that make the surrogate mother's body a necessary surplus.

When the irregularities end and the surrogate mother is healthy again, Charlie writes:

> For the first time in a long time, thoughts have been on things other than waiting for the next daily update, keeping fingers and toes and eyes crossed, hoping we don't get that phone call. Things are starting to feel more and more real. On Friday, I had to tell my boss that I had a conflict with a project I am currently leading because of a 'personal issue' (BaF 9.9.12).

And later on, Charlie writes:

> Telling my boss that I was going to have to stop leading the project, no matter what, was the first time that I felt like I was in control of something during this surrogacy process. It was the first time that I was able to do something parental for our future children. It's weird how it doesn't feel very real in the beginning of this surrogacy journey (BaF 9.9.12).

The anxieties and impatience Charlie felt during the hospitalisation of the surrogate mother result in a feeling of realness that gives Charlie the strength to tell his boss that he has to stop leading a project, as the project collides with the birth. Despite the fact that he does not tell his boss that he is pregnant, the act itself becomes yet another realisation of his parenthood. The acts Charlie does to balance work life and pregnancy, in his mind, become analogous to the pregnancy itself. Like a pregnant woman may experience physical and mental trouble doing her job while being pregnant, in the same way Charlie has troubles. These are troubles that he solves, and in this becoming pregnant *for real*, and coming closer, he orients himself more firmly in the pregnancy and towards the future child.

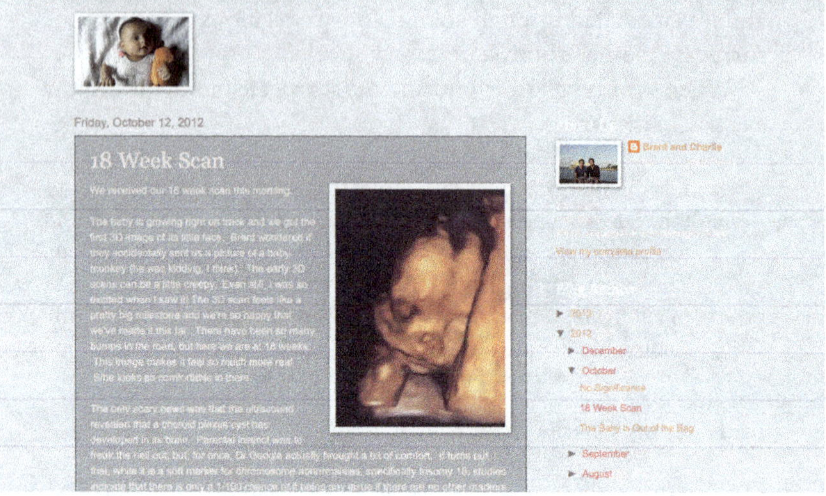

Picture 4.

The affectively and bodily mediated pregnancy is further represented on Charlie's blog. Already from the first scan, these scan
pictures, sent to Charlie by email, become the rhythm of the blog,
as one can see from the blog title "18-week scan" in Picture 4.
Charlie writes that given the many scans he receives compared to
the number of scans in a traditional pregnancy might make him
more unnecessarily worried – but at the same time the scans help
make the pregnancy real and physical. Charlie writes: "so because
you're not able to look down on your stomach or your spouse's and
see a growing belly, feel the baby kick, etc. having the frequent scans
helps the pregnancy feel real" (BaF 12.10.12).

The making real, the mimicking of the pregnancy, is doubled
through the blog. As we see in the quote above, the scans themselves make the pregnancy real and material. And when Charlie
posts these images online on his blog, then the pregnancy not only
feels real to him; it becomes visible to the surrounding world as
well. Just as the pregnant woman's belly grows, so does Charlie's
blog, with the many posts and scan images that slowly take the
discernible form of a child. A digital embodiment enabled by the
mediation of surrogacy, by the unequal power relations between

the surrogate mother and the commissioning parents, as well as by the mediation of reproductive technologies that disaggregate the surrogate mother from her body, and from the media technologies and the visuals they make possible.

The disappearance of the surrogate mother

Sam also uses the production of his blog as a way to materialise and embody the pregnancy. Sam does not write as often as Charlie or most other bloggers, but his posts have a rhythm: Every time the pregnancy is somehow present, he writes more than one post. When he and his partner decide to go for surrogacy, for instance, he creates a blog and writes three posts. Then he does not post for three months until he is in Bangkok to deliver the sperm. Here Sam writes four posts, each describing significant parts of the surrogacy process: the sperm donation, the egg donor, and the embryo transfer.

When Charlie is informed that the surrogate mother is pregnant, he changes the format of the blog: Now he posts every week, the titles of the blog posts are "week 7", "week 8" and so on, and each post is illustrated with scans as well as generic drawings from what could be a book about pregnancies.

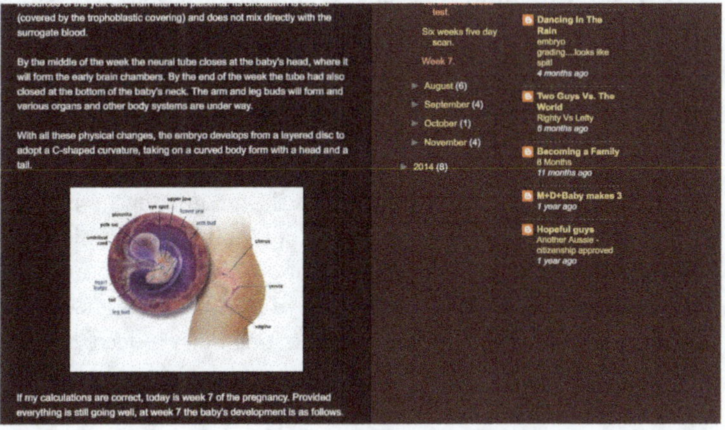

Picture 5.

Every week Sam describes in great detail how a typical pregnancy is progressing, while the drawings show the foetus slowly taking the form of a baby. At the same time Sam pays attention to the difficulties and problems that can arise in the specific week of the pregnancy, as well as to the well-being of the surrogate mother. The posts are illustrated with scans from the surrogate mother, but it is the generic drawings that take up most space at the beginning of the pregnancy.

In her critical analyses of the gendered aspects of reproductive technologies in general, Anne Balsamo argues that reproductive technologies isolate the womb from the female body and "promote [...] the rationalization of reproduction, such that the process of reproduction itself can be isolated into discrete stages: egg production, fertilization, implantation, feeding, and birthing" (1995, 91). This fragmentation of the reproductive process and the female body is further supported by visual monitoring techniques that disaggregate the woman from the pregnancy and foetus, and she concludes that "the same technological advances that foster the objectification of the female body through the visualization of internal functioning also encourages [sic] the 'personification' of the foetus" (ibid., 93).

After three months of pregnancy, Sam's posts start to become more personal. Bit by bit the generic descriptions are accompanied by more personal reflections. Slowly Sam embodies the pregnancy. By staging and visualising the generic pregnancy online Sam slowly embodies and takes ownership over the pregnancy. This process of embodiment can be seen in the different ways Sam articulates the pregnancy. When Sam is told about the pregnancy in July, he simply writes: "We have a pregnancy" (TMaB 6.7.13). This statement is in contrast to how Sam talks about the baby to come four months later: "We received some pics of our son. Yes, it's official, Pete and I are expecting a boy. Very exciting news indeed" (TMaB 7.11.13).

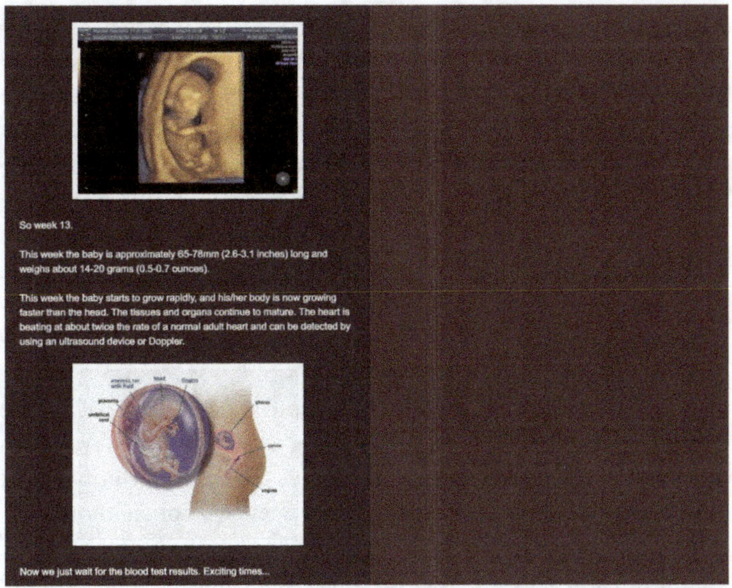

Picture 6.

The first description keeps the pregnancy inside the body of the surrogate mother by saying that "we have a pregnancy" instead of "we are pregnant." The second description, four months later, moves the reproductive action from the surrogate mother to Sam and his partner by calling the boy "our son," and by writing that they are "expecting a boy." In this way, the "boy" becomes a reproductive result of Sam and his partner and not of the surrogate mother, at the same time as the pregnancy moves from a generic one to a personal one, an embodied pregnancy. The fragmentation of the pregnancy into and the visualisation of specific stages entangled with the mediation on the blog enable Sam and Charlie not only to mimic the pregnancy, but to obtain ownership of the foetus and embody the pregnancy.

Many users in the online communities share the scans' visualisation of the foetus and pregnancy. Many share the images of the embryos before implantation, and throughout the pregnancy many users share the frequent scans. These posts are highly appreciated by other users, who congratulate and comment on the foetus' looks. In these textual responses to the visual scans, the surrogate mother is very rarely mentioned. Rather, the commissioning parent/s is/are wished "Good luck," etc.

In her ethnographic study of Indian surrogate mothers, Sharmila Rudrappa argues that the commodification of the surrogate mother and the pregnancy enables the commissioning parents to establish ownership of both foetus and pregnancy (2015, 126–135). She notices how the foetuses become persons while the surrogate mothers are dehumanised as nonpersons, and how the commissioning parents in this process erase the surrogate mother by making *her* pregnancy *their* pregnancy (ibid., 135).

In his blog, Sam turns the foetus into a person by *boying* the foetus, thus animating and humanising the foetus to a boy, which is underscored by Sam naming the foetus "Fossam", a composite of his and his partner's name. While the foetus becomes more prominent in the posts, the surrogate mother becomes more visible: her health and state are described in great detail, and images of her and her daughter, with their faces blurred, are posted on the blog (17.1.14 and 25.1.14).

Only due to the established and dominant narrative that *her* pregnancy really is *his* pregnancy can the increasing visualisation of the surrogate mother co-exist with the erasure of her. This process is not only visual, but also rhetorical. This is because the textual description of the surrogate mother is changing at the same time: she is increasingly described as a carrier without any emotions. Her bodily and visual presence seems to negate her emotional presence. As the foetus is humanised in order for Sam to become a parent to the baby, the surrogate is dehumanised and disaggregated from the pregnancy, and thus leaves affective space in her body for Sam to become a father and embody the pregnancy.

Conclusion

Media technologies
- Visual, real-time communication (skype, emails, mobile)
- Digital embodiment (blogging, Instagram, Facebook)
- Facebook communities
- Production of new scripts of sexual citizenship (e.g. new family possibilities)

Power technologies
- Global and local inequalities (e.g. gender, class, race, nation)
- Neo- and postcolonialism
- Gendered labor
- Bio- and necropolitics

Mediation of transnational commercial surrogacy

Reproductive technologies
- Innovative fertility treatments and the technologies of gestational surrogacy
- Pre-natal visualities and medical records
- Neoliberal scripts of reproduction (e.g. right to choose, buy, replace)

The phenomenon of transnational commercial surrogacy is emerging and taking form in the intersection and entanglement of different technologies. Firstly, the reproductive technologies: the technology of gestational surrogacy has become a much safer and successful technology due to innovations in fertility treatments, e.g., better technologies for the cryopreservation of eggs. But the reproductive technologies also include the ever improving and increasing ways of monitoring and scanning pregnant women, controlling and maintaining her hormonal cycle and development of pregnancy, e.g., treating the body heavily to prevent her body from rejecting the embryo. And technologies also include the prenatal visuals, the mediation of the pregnant body and foetus in the forms of scans, 3D scans, and different medical and discursive mediations of her health, body, and pregnancy. The reproductive technologies disaggregate the gestation of the pregnancy from the body of the surrogate mother. The commissioning parents obtain the ownership of the matter, i.e., the pregnancy matter, the foetus, and the baby, thus mandating that the surrogate worker submits herself to the technologies of routine surveillance. Embedded within a colonial division of labour informed by gender and race, the surrogate worker's bodily affective and biological work transfers vital energy and reproductive matter from her body to the commissioning parents in the First World.

Thus, these reproductive technologies are entangled with technologies of power in the form of both global and local power inequalities. Transnational commercial surrogacy is intimately connected to global and local divisions of class, race, nation, and gender. And this global division must be understood as part of colonial legacies, as Kalinda Vora (2012) argues. A globalised market enables neoliberal scripts to form surrogacy: the commissioning parents have the right and the possibility to choose, buy, and replace specific stages of the pregnancy, where the surrogate mother is just one (dehumanised) part of assembling the future baby.

And these reproductive and power technologies entangle with media technologies. First and foremost, visual and real-time communication technologies like Skype and FaceTime, MMS texting with pictures and emails with medical records and images of the surrogate's pregnancy. And they also include commissioning parents' mediation of pregnancy on blogs and in online communities. In these online mediations of surrogate pregnancy, the commissioning parents produce and unfold new scripts of pregnancy and parenthood, that is new forms of (surrogate) sexual citizenship, and mimic the pregnancy to obtain full ownership of both pregnancy and foetus.

References

Ahmed, S. 2004. *Cultural Politics of Emotions*. Edinburgh: Edinburgh University Press.

–––. 2006. *Queer Phenomenology: Orientations, Objects, Others*. Durham and London: Duke University Press.

–––. 2010. *The Promise of Happiness*. Durham and London: Duke University Press.

Andreassen, R. 2016. "Online kinship – Social media as a site for challenging notions of gender and family." *MedieKultur* 61: 76–92.

Association of Internet Researchers. 2019. *Internet Research: Ethical Guidelines 3.0*. https://aoir.org/reports/ethics3.pdf

Balsamo, A. 1995. *Technologies of the Gendered Body: Reading Cyborg Women*. Durham and London: Duke University Press.

Bergman, K., Rubio, R. J., Green, R.-J. & Padrón E. 2010. "Gay Men Who Become Fathers via Surrogacy: The Transition to Parenthood." *Journal of GLBT Family Studies* 6, no. 2: 111–141.

Berkowitz, D. 2010. "Gay Men and Surrogacy." In: *LGBT-Parents Families. Innovations in Research and Implications for Practice*, A. Goldberg & K. R. Allen, eds., 71–85. New York: Springer.

boyd, d. 2006. "A Blogger's Blog: Exploring the Definition of a Medium." *Reconstruction* 6, no. 4. http://reconstruction.eserver.org/064/boyd.shtml.

Butler, J. 1992. "Sexual Inversions." In *Discourses of Sexuality: From Aristotle to AIDS*, D. C. Stanton, ed., 344–361. Ann Arbor: The University of Michigan Press.

Edelman, L. 2004. *No Future. Queer Theory and the Death Drive.* Durham and London: Duke University Press.

Halberstam, J. J. 2005. *In a Queer Time and Place – Transgender Bodies, Subcultural Lives.* New York, London: New York University Press.

Hine, C. 2015. *Ethnography for the internet – embedded, embodied and everyday.* London and New York: Bloomsbury.

Kember, S. & Zylinska, J. 2015. *Life after new media – mediation as a vital process.* Cambridge and London: The MIT Press.

McKee, H. & Porter, J. (2009). *The Ethics of Internet Research. A Rhetorical, Case- Based Process.* New York: Peter Lang.

Madsen, K. H. 2012. "Rugemødre, rejser og nye reproduktions metaforer: Weblogs om transnationalt surrogatmoderskab." ["Surrogate mothers, journeys and new metaphors of reproduction: Weblogs on transnational surrogacy"] *K&K: kultur og klasse* 113, no. 1: 79–100.

Murphy, D. 2013. "The Desire for Parenthood: Gay Men Choosing to Become Parents Through Surrogacy." *Journal of Family Issues* 34, no. 8: 1104–1124.

Nebeling Petersen, M. 2012. *Somewhere, Over the Rainbow. Biopolitiske rekonfigurationer af den homoseksuelle figure [Somewhere, Over the Rainbow. Biopolitical reconfigurations of the homosexual figure].* PhD dissertation, University of Copenhagen.

–––. 2016. "Becoming gay fathers through surrogacy." *Journal of Family Issues.* First published Nov. 12, 2016.

Nebeling Petersen, M. & Raun, T. 2022. "Showing progress. Defining self-tracking as an aesthetic audio-visual genre." *Conjunctions. Transdisciplinary Journal of Cultural Participation* 9, no. 1: 1–16.

Nunokawa, J. 1991. "'All the sad young men': AIDS and the work of mourning," in *Inside/out: Lesbian Theories, Gay Theories*, D. Fuss, ed., 311–323. New York and London: Routledge.

Raun, T. 2010. "Screen-births: Exploring the transformative potential in trans video blogs on YouTube." *Graduate Journal of Social Science* 7, no. 2: 113–130.

Sullivan, N. & Murray, S. 2009. *Somatechnics. Queering the technologisation of bodies*. Cornwall: Ashgate.

Vora, K. 2012. "Limits of 'Labor': Accounting for Affect and the Biological in Transnational Surrogacy and Service Work." *South Atlantic Quarterly* 111, no. 4: 681–700.

Weston, K. 1991. *Families we choose: Lesbians, gays, kinship*. New York: Columbia University Press.

Yung Nielsen, L. 2016. *Indfoldede og udfoldede kroppe. En undersøgelse af kropslig performance på modebloggen [Convoluted and Unfolded Bodies. An examination of bodily performance on the fashion blog]*. PhD dissertation, Aalborg University, Denmark.

7. Swedish Lesbian Mothers Arrange Parental Leave: Idealising Equality, Sharing (More or Less) Evenly

Anna Malmquist

Lesbian couples divide both paid work and unpaid housework more evenly than other couples (Bauer, 2016; Brewster, 2017; Gotta et al., 2011; Kurdek, 2007; van der Vleuten et el., 2021). Moreover, lesbian couples with children also divide childcare more evenly than different-sex parenting couples, with both mothers generally spending more time with their children than fathers in different-sex couples (Bos & van Balen, 2010; Bos, van Balen & van den Boom, 2007; Ciano-Boyce & Shelley-Sireci, 2002; Goldberg, Smith & Perry-Jenkins, 2012; Patterson, Sutfin & Fulcher, 2004; Perlesz et al., 2010). Lesbian women's highly equal relations have been explained by their more egalitarian values, and by the fact that they experience less impact from gender-stereotyped expectations about division of labour (Patterson et al., 2004). However, these studies only show that lesbian women are more egalitarian than the couples with whom they are compared. When compared to one another within the couple, birth mothers engage more with childcare, while non-birth mothers put in more work hours outside the home, in particular when the children are young (Bos et al., 2007; Ciano-Boyce & Shelley-Sireci, 2002; Downing & Goldberg, 2011; Goldberg & Perry-Jenkins, 2007; Van Rijn-Van Gelderen et al., 2020).

For families with young children, access to parental leave is central to how childcare is arranged (Borrell et al., 2014). The present work focuses on how lesbian women in Sweden have arranged their parental leave. Many Swedish lesbian women idealise equality in their relationships and joint parenthood (Malmquist, 2015a). The focus on parental leave arrangements articulates an everyday life practice, which may or may not correspond to such values. The study draws on discursive psychology, where participants' accounts of their arrangements are scrutinised in detail. The analysis aims to answer the following research questions: How do the participants depict their arrangements of parental leave? How do they account for the parental leave for birth mothers and non-birth mothers, respectively? How are their descriptions of their arrangements related to notions of equality?

Previous studies on parental leave will be presented in the following section. Thereafter, the Swedish parental leave system will be described, in order to depict the specific context of the present study.

Studies on parental leave

Lesbian women's parental leave-taking is understudied, there is (to the author's knowledge) only a few statistical analyses on this topic (Evertsson & Boye, 2018; Moberg, 2016; Tegmyr, 2015), and an entire absence of qualitative studies. However, there is a body of research on parental leave in general, and its effects on equality in different-sex couples. Paid parental leave with job protection has been shown to increase women's labour market attachment in the long run (Lalive, Schlosser, Steinhauer & Zweimüller, 2014; Rønsen & Hege Kitterød, 2015). When parental leave is available to both parents, fathers' time spent with their children increases, particularly if part of the parental leave is reserved for fathers (Boll, Leppin & Reich, 2014). Fathers' share of parental leave also increases if the time home is paid and the benefit is high. Regulations on parental leave differ significantly between welfare states, and the length of paid leave is longer in most European countries than in the United States and Canada (Borrell et al., 2014). The Swedish welfare state has one of the most generous parental leave systems, and a number of studies have looked specifically at parental leave in Sweden. Before describing those studies, the Swedish parental leave system will be explained.

Sweden is often claimed to be at the forefront of gender equality and politics, with policies promoting a dual-earner/dual-care-pro-vider model (Ahrne, Roman & Franzén, 2003; Björk Eydal & Rost-gaard, 2011; Holli, Magnusson & Rönnblom, 2005; Magnusson, 2008; Ryan-Flood, 2009). Once a child has been born or adopted, the parents together have the right to 16 months of paid parental leave: 13 months of 80% earnings' compensation (up to a ceiling) and additionally 3 months at a low flat rate (*Försäkringskassan*, 2013). The parents may share the parental leave equally or may transfer days from one parent to the other, if they want one parent to stay home more than the other. Three months are reserved for each parent and may not be transferred. If the parents desire a longer total parental leave than 16 months, they may utilise lower levels of compensation, over a longer period of time. It is also optional to work part time and take part-time parental leave. Swedish law grants access to parental leave to all parents with legal custody. Thus, the parent's employer may never deny parental leave and may not discriminate against a person in a hiring process, wage determination, or promotion due to parental leave, or expected future parental leave.

For couples wishing to achieve equal engagement in their young children and equal career opportunities, Swedish policies offer a good head start. However, most couples utilise parental leave unevenly. When this study was conducted, mothers used 73% of the total paid parental leave, while fathers only 27% (Försäkrings-kassan, 2018, 21 March). Mothers' median time-off work was 12 months, and the vast majority had returned to work when the child reached two years (Evertsson & Duvander, 2011). Fathers often took out only the part of the parental leave they were not allowed to transfer to their partner (Duvander, 2014). Mothers generally explain their long parental leaves in terms of their family orientation, while fathers often give economic reasons for taking only short parental leaves (Duvander, 2014). Whereas men perceive parental leave as an option – accessible if they so desire – women are regarded as natural caregivers and are expected to take parental leave (Bekkengen, 2002). Division of parental leave has been somewhat more evenly spread in lesbian couples compared to different-sexed, with birth mothers taking 62% of paid parental leave and non-birth mothers the remaining 38% (Tegmyr, 2015). While no previous research has focused on lesbian women's ideals or thoughts on parental leave, they have focused on other aspects of lesbian women's family life in Sweden.

Lesbian parents in Sweden

For a lesbian couple in Sweden, the number of available paths to parenthood has increased since the turn of the millennium (Malmquist, 2015b). Since 2003, lesbian couples have been able to share legal parenthood through second-parent adoption, and in 2005 female couples were given access to insemination and IVF treatment at Swedish public fertility clinics. It was previously common for lesbian women to have children in shared parenting arrangements with gay men (Zetterqvist Nelson, 2007), but as options to become parents on their own have increased, many lesbian women today choose to have children within their intimate relationships only (Malmquist, 2015b). The author shows in another publication that Swedish lesbian parents commonly, though not always, idealise equality in their parenting roles (Malmquist, 2015a). Most couples want both women to form close parent-child relations and to share the role as primary caregiver. Still, most women also acknowledge a difference between themselves and their partner, which is tied to birth giving. They argue that the birth mother has an advantage in developing a close relationship to the child, while the non-birth mother initially has a secondary position. Some parents describe how they work hard on equalising their parental roles to overcome the early-established difference between them.

A lesbian couple with shared legal custody has the same access to 16 months of paid parental leave as any other couple, with all but three months being transferable between the parents (Försäkringskassan, 2013). In cases where the non-birth mother is not the custody holder already from birth, the birth mother may still transfer parental leave to her partner. Thus, it is fully possible for non-birth mothers to take parental leave as soon as the child is born.

Theoretical framework

Heterosexuality is generally privileged and construed as natural in hegemonic Western culture (Kitzinger, 2005; Land & Kitzinger, 2005). This heteronormativity is salient when it comes to expectations on family formation. Raising children is strongly associated with the nuclear heterosexual family, according to which a married wife and husband jointly raise their children conceived through sexual intercourse (Smith, 1993; Weston, 1991). As shown in the overview of studies on parental leave above, mothers' and fathers' relative contributions to the parental responsibilities generally differ. Caregiving mothers and breadwinning fathers represents a heteronormative way of doing family (Ryan-Flood, 2009).

Despite the heteronormative family ideal, contemporary families show great variation, causing family theorists to speak of "family practices" rather than "the Family" (Morgan, 1996, 2011). It has been argued that a lesbian woman becoming a mother reinforces the gendered cultural expectancies on women to nurture (Kawash, 2011). Thus, lesbian women's motherhood could be discussed in relation to heteronormativity and cultural ideals of motherhood. On the other hand, lesbian parenting could also be said to challenge family ideals, because parenthood is performed in a non-heterosexual setting (Clarke, 2005). When finding their paths to parenthood, it is reasonable to believe that specific norms on parenting would develop among lesbian women. For example, a great emphasis on relationship equality characterises many lesbian families (Bos & van Balen, 2010; Bos et al., 2007; Ciano-Boyce & Shelley-Sireci, 2002; Goldberg et al., 2012; Patterson et al., 2004; Perlesz et al., 2010).

Method

The present study was conducted as part of a larger research project on lesbian parenthood in Sweden (e.g., Malmquist, 2015a, 2015b, 2015c). Participants were recruited through personal data (e.g., names, social security numbers, and addresses) on second-parent adoption protocols. Many lesbian couples go through a second-parent adoption in order to establish legal parenthood for the non-birth mother (Malmquist, 2015c). Protocols from such adoptions are publicly accessible in Sweden and could therefore be harnessed to identify potential participants. As a first step, in 2009, the author collected second-parent adoption protocols established during the six years second-parent adoption had been available for lesbian couples, from all district courts in Sweden. A total of 185 unique lesbian families were found, with second-parent adoptions for 1–3 children in each family. After the exclusion of four families with whom the author had personal relations, parents in the remaining 181 families were invited by printed mail to take part in a study on lesbian parenting. The invitations included information about the study, and stated that participation was voluntary and that participants could withdraw from the study at any time. This recruitment procedure was approved by the Regional Ethics Board at Linköping University in Sweden. Among the invited families, 109 families responded and gave their informed consent to participate. During 2009–2010, the author conducted interviews with 96 parents in 51 of these families, selected to ensure a geographical spread among them (i.e., the geographical spread among the interviewees correspond to the geographical spread of all the initially invited families). In 45 interviews, both partners participated and were interviewed together. In the remaining six interviews, only one parent participated either due to conflicting schedules, or because the parents had separated. Joint couple interviews differ in many respects from individual interviews (Bjørnholt & Farstad, 2014). This is because joint interviews enable the couple to co-create their narrative and build on each other's reflections. However, in such contexts conflicts and dissatisfaction in the relationship may be more difficult to verbalise and may be toned down.

The interviews were conducted at a time and place that suited the participants, mostly during weekends, in the participants' homes. The interviews followed a semi-structured interview guide, where the parents were encouraged to provide their family narrative, from the time when the parents had first met until the time of the interviews. The interviews covered reflections on several topics, e.g., encounters with fertility clinics, maternal health care, antenatal education, donor choice, second-parent adoption processes, equality, and parental leave. The interviews differed in their focus, while some interviewees talked extensively on some of these topics, others focused on other issues. This applies also to the matter of parental leave: some interviewees described their arrangements and thoughts on this in depth, while others gave short responds and moved to other topics. Given the quite large data material, the total data on parental leave is rich, nonetheless. Parental leave was generally brought up by the interviewer using an open-ended question, such as "how did you arrange parental leave?" Each interview lasted between 41 and 101 minutes and was audio-recorded. All interviews were transcribed verbatim, including both the interviewer's and interviewees' voices. Names have been replaced with pseudonyms.

Participants

All 51 interviewed families were settled in southern and central Sweden, most of them in city areas and suburbs (n=36, 71%), while those remaining lived in middle size or small towns, or in rural areas. At the time of the interviews, the interviewees' mean age was 36 years (age range 24–58 years). Most of the 96 interviewees were currently working or studying (n=90, 94%), with a minority currently on parental leave, unemployed, or on long-term sick leave. One third (n=32, 33%) had an upper-secondary-level education, while two thirds had university-level degrees. Most of the interviewees were born in Sweden (n=86, 90%), but a few had migrated from other European countries. Of the 51 couples, 25 (49%) had one child and 26 (51%) had two children together. Three families also included children from a previous relationship, resulting in a total of 29 families (57%) with more than one child. In 19 (66%) of these 29 families, both parents had given birth, in contrast to 10 families (34%) where one mother had given birth to all children. In families with two birth mothers, the older partner had given birth to the first child, and the younger to the second. In families where one mother had given birth to all children, reasons for not switching birth mother varied. In some cases, this was due to the non-birth mother's infertility, in other cases the non-birth mother was not interested in becoming pregnant.

Analysis

Before conducting any detailed analysis of the interviews, the author read through the entire material and made an index of the content. This procedure ensured that the author gained an overview of the entire, quite extensive, data set. Thereafter, sequences that concerned parental leave were sorted into a separate document. Parental leave was discussed in 50 of the 51 interviews. Thus, the present findings are based on 50 interviews with 94 parents. At this point the author sorted the interview data into three different groups, based on how the parents had arranged parental leave. A discourse analysis was thereafter conduced on each data set (Potter & Wetherell 1987; Wetherell & Potter 1992). This process started with a detailed coding of each data set, where keywords and phrases were marked and copied into a separate document. Thereafter the codes were sorted thematically. Such thematisation provided a detailed and structured overview of the data.

In discursive psychology, close attention is paid to the details of the participants' rhetoric. The analysis aims to show how the mothers framed, argued for, and reflected on their parental leave arrangements, and these arrangements' benefits or deficiencies. When focusing on the details of a specific interview sequence, there is a risk that the analyst will lose the overall picture of the patterns in the data. The analysis therefore involved a cyclical process, where the author moved back and forth between the thematic overview and the detailed rhetoric. The author also carefully scrutinised how the depicted parental leave arrangements were accounted for in relation to ideals and values, principally the idea of equality. Excerpts were selected to clearly visualise the findings of the analysis, and detailed analyses of those excerpts are presented in the results section.

Results

After the interview data had been scrutinised, three substantially different ways of arranging parental leave could be identified among the interviewees. First, parents in 9 of the 50 families (18%) described an arrangement where the birth mother had taken a long parental leave (9–18 months), while the non-birth mother took either no or a very short parental leave (0–4 months). This arrangement is reminiscent of how parents in different-sex couples typically divide parental leave (Duvander, 2014; Ekberg et al., 2013;

Evertsson & Duvander, 2011), and (as will be shown in the following) when accounting for this arrangement, the participants drew on arguments similar to those generally made by different-sex couples (Bekkengen, 2002; Duvander, 2014).

Second, parents in 35 families (70%) described an approach that was by far the most common, namely, that both parents had taken long or fairly long parental leaves (5–18 months), arranged so that the birth mother stayed home for the first period, and the non-birth mother took over when the former ended her parental leave. In most of these families, both partners had taken equally long, or roughly equal, parental leave. Not only was this arrangement the most common among participants, but (as will be shown) it was also presented as the ideal or natural arrangement for lesbian couples.

Third, 10 families (20%) described a variety of arrangements where both parents stayed home for a long period (6–13 months) early on in the baby's life, either full- or part-time. These approaches were depicted by the interviewees as something novel and as challenging norms on parental leave, since they question the idea that the birth mother necessarily must stay home on a full-time basis while the non-birth mother must wait for her turn to come.

This, in total, amounts to more than 50 families. This is because four of the couples with two children had had different arrangements for each child. A more detailed analysis of the interviewees' accounts will be presented in the following.

Birth mother stays at home, non-birth mother continues working

Interviewees in 9 families (18%) described the most uneven division of parental leave, where the birth mother stayed home for a long period, while the non-birth mother took no or only short parental leave. Birth mothers in those families generally stayed home for between 1 year and eighteen months (only one of these birth mothers had stayed home for less than a year). A few of the non-birth mothers took no parental leave at all, while others stayed home for combined vacations and parental leave during the summer, and still others for a period worked part-time. Some of these non-birth mothers took their parental leave when their partner also was at home.

Non-birth mother's work is demanding

When these interviewees described how they had organised parental leave, they mainly focused on the non-birth mother's employed work. Some of them described her work as demanding, while others depicted her work as beneficial, with some highlighting both these aspects. A few also depicted the birth mother's work as being less demanding or less fun. Malin and Rakel had a 19-month-old son. One birth mother had Malin stay home for 16 months, while her partner Rakel stayed home for three months during the summer. Both partners had the same employer, and argued that their different positions at work had been crucial in determining their arrangement:

> Malin: Well you chose to, you wanted to have it during the summer too, so you could do as much as possible.
>
> Rakel: But I probably could have been home another month, maybe, then I knew that my being away would be a big problem at work, I shouldn't be away too long, so I also felt some pressure there, then it was easier for Malin to be home because I'm the safety representative, so they didn't want me to be gone so long, so that's how it turned out.

Malin claimed that Rakel preferred staying home during the summer, so that she "could do as much as possible." This framing gives the impression that Rakel's parental leave was a prolonged vacation, a leisure time rather than a responsibility. Rakel herself objected to this interpretation, claiming that she could have stayed home for another month. Instead, she brought up work demands and claimed that her absence from work was problematic for her employer. Rakel's account sounds defensive; she claims she felt pressure at work, where "they" did not want her to stay home too long. The uneven division of parental leave was in this light depicted as necessary, "so that's how it turned out." Rakel's account gives the impression that the uneven sharing was both undesirable and out of her personal control.

Non-birth mother's work is beneficial

While Rakel highlighted her work as demanding and hard to leave, Victoria and Karolina argued that Victoria's work had the benefit of long vacations, so she did not take parental leave. Both non-birth mother Victoria and her partner Karolina were teachers, with long vacations during the summer. In the excerpt below they talked about the parental leave for their first child, who was four years old at the time of the interview.

> Victoria: But it never felt like I sacrificed it [parental leave] because he was born in May, and I work as a teacher, so I worked there a week, then I was off for three months and then you were and home and then… […]
>
> Karolina: I was home for a year and then we had the whole summer again, we were together…
>
> Victoria: …I feel like I was home a lot with Ludvig anyway. And at that time you weren't at all happy with your job and I really liked my job.

Working as a teacher was depicted as an advantage, on account of the long vacations. Victoria's picture of having three months off work every summer is likely an exaggeration, however; teachers in Swedish schools usually have less than two months off work each summer, covering July, and parts of both June and August. The exaggeration is rhetorically effective, as it serves to provide a picture of Victoria being home a lot. Karolina contributed to this picture by adding that another summer soon arrived, when they were home together again. Time spent with the child was depicted as ideal in their accounts, as Victoria claimed that she never "sacrificed" parental leave, and that she had stayed home "a lot […] anyway." First thereafter she added another dimension, namely that she liked her work, while her partner did not.

Talk about work benefits and demands dominated the line of argumentation among the couples with the most uneven share of parental leave. Still, it was the time spent with children that was depicted as desirable. Uneven sharing of parental leave was seldom merely reported by the interviewees, rather it was justified through their accounts of their specific situation. Uneven sharing was rhetorically depicted as having been caused by work demands or benefits, not by disinterest in staying home with the children. None of these parents spoke directly of inequality or depicted their division as unfair. Rather, ideals of equality were visible through more subtle statements, such as when the arrangement was depicted as an unfortunate consequence of work demands.

It is worth noting that it was only the non-birth mothers' work situation that was rhetorically depicted as hindering parental leave. Birth mothers' parental leave-taking was generally depicted as self-evident. In a few cases, the birth mothers' work situation was depicted as obstructive, but in those cases the participants described how they had made efforts to enable her to take parental leave anyway.

Birth mother stays home first, non-birth mother waits for her turn

By far the most common arrangement among the interviewees was that both parents took long, or fairly long, parental leaves. The time off work was arranged so that the birth mother stayed home when the child was newborn, and the non-birth mother took over when the birth mother returned to work. Parents in 35 families (70%) described this arrangement. In most cases, both mothers had taken equally long (or roughly equal) parental leaves, e.g., each staying home for nine months. In other families, one mother had taken a significantly longer period off than her partner, but both had nonetheless been on parental leave for at least five months. In those cases, it was most common for the birth mother to stay home for the first year, and the non-birth mother for the following six months.

Shared parental leave creates equality

While families with a highly uneven arrangement generally high-lighted work demands and benefits when accounting for their arrangement, the parents with more equal shares talked less about work and more about the benefits of staying home. They argued that shared parental leave gave both parents a close relation to the child. Interviewee Kim claimed: "It really helps in bonding with the child. You don't have the same contact if you haven't had parental leave." Besides close parent-child relations, several interviewees also claimed that shared parental leave gave them a balance and equality in their relationships to each other. Nina and Alexandra have both given birth to one child (four and one years old, res-pectively, at the time of the interview) and both parental leaves were shared equally. Nina explained:

> We're like that for the most part, we're very similar. It's import-ant to have the same amount of time off, for both of us to get to, just the same. It shouldn't all be on one person, and we've appre-ciated that a lot and think it's actually really important, when you look back, that you get to understand each other, because I mean it's not, just being at home isn't easy and working isn't easy when you have a family at home. Also it's not the case that the person who's at home is just fantastic and the one who's working is just trying to escape, because it's not fun at all to work in the begin-ning, you don't suffice for either place, not at home and not at work, but then it's the same for both of you and you understand each other a bit better even though there are conflicts, there's a common ground that's really good.

Nina's account is replete with arguments about the benefits of equally sharing parental leave, arguments that draw on the import-ance of understanding each other's situation and sharing a com-mon ground. Both the stay-at-home period and the time at work were depicted as demanding. It is worth noting how Nina initiated her account, by stating that "We're like that for the most part, we're very similar." Equal sharing was not depicted as a topic of nego-tiation, rather equality was depicted as a point of departure, an important characteristic of their relationship. Unlike the couples with an uneven share, where employment was claimed to have caused the uneven division of leave-taking, parents with an even share presented their arrangement as an important active choice.

Birth mother stays home first

Although these parents drew heavily on a rhetoric of equality and balance, their arrangements were also characterised by a difference between them, in that the birth mother stayed home for the first period with the non-birth mother taking over the parental leave thereafter. The order in which they took parental leave was generally simply reported in the interviews, but not argued for. When the interviewer asked how this was decided, several interviewees appeared surprised, and their answers tended to be short statements. They referred to breastfeeding and/or a need to recover after the delivery. In the interview with Nina and Alexandra, Alexandra gave a short and simple answer to the question of why the birth mother stayed home first: "It's the breastfeeding that decided it."

Such short and clear statements give the impression that who should stay home first is natural and self-evident. However, some parents expanded on this topic as a response to direct questions, and these responses tended to challenge the idea that it is only a matter of breastfeeding or recovery. Jessica and Ellen had one child together, 17-month-old Sixten, to whom Jessica had given birth. At the time of the interview, Ellen was pregnant with their second child. In the interview, the parents displayed their disagreement on how to arrange the up-coming parental leave. Jessica said that Ellen was considering returning to work when the baby would be six months, something that Jessica claimed she would not have done as a birth mother. Jessica had stayed home for a year with Sixten, and claimed that going back to work at that time gave her "a lot of anxiety," because "I wanted to stay home with Sixten, you know, keep being at home with Sixten." At this point in the interview, the interviewer asked the interviewees about the arrangement where the birth mother stays home first.

> Interviewer: Is it important that the person who gives birth is home with the child during the first period?
>
> Ellen: I don't think there's really any alternative because the person who gives birth to the child does the breastfeeding and those kinds of things, and that's just part of it.
>
> Jessica: Actually, I think you could solve the breastfeeding somehow [Ellen: yes, somehow] but, no, I guess I think it's important. Like, I can't imagine if I'd have started working and that Ellen would've been home with Sixten. But then there's the part about bonding. Of course, we're both parents, but you notice with Sixten that I was home first because he, he's actually a real mommy's boy [Ellen: yeah, yeah, yeah]. […] it would've been difficult for me if Sixten went to Ellen and not to me.

Ellen's response to the interviewer's question, that breastfeeding sets the limits, is a familiar theme in the interview data. Jessica disagreed with this picture when she claimed that breastfeeding is not the issue, rather, she argued it is the bonding that is at stake. She argued that the child is primarily attached to the parent who is at home, and from her perspective this is desirable for a birth mother. Jessica's account sets focus on the difference between the mothers. Although equality is often presented as the advantage of sharing parental leave, the arrangement where birth mother stays home first gives the partners unequal starts as parents.

Another interviewee, Linn, problematised this inequality. Linn had stayed at home with their son since his birth, while non-birth mother Kristin continued to work. Linn described that she had wanted Kristin to reduce her working hours to part time when their son was a newborn, but Kristin had insisted on continuing her full-time work, and planned on taking full-time parental leave when Linn returned to her occupation. The child was nine months old at the time of the interview, and the parents were about to switch stay-at-home-parent.

> Linn: This is how we did it, you know, and now his attachment to me is stronger, or now he's started choosing me, or he's attached to both of us, absolutely, but when things get difficult

he wants me, that's how it is now. […] I had some kind of dream that we could do this being parents in a completely equal way. But that's not how it turned out, I guess you could say. It's not wrong either or like, well….

Kristin: But I think I only saw it from a traditional perspective, you know, that one parent is at home while the other works, that's what you do. I can't stop working, you're the one who's home now. I'll stay at home later, then I'll be home full time and you'll do something else. […] But then it was really hard, you know, to start full time and leave him the whole day. That wasn't fun at all.

Linn depicted her dissatisfaction with their arrangement, and explained that their son had been primarily attached to her as a result of her being at home. Unlike Jessica (in the previous excerpt) Linn depicted equality as an ideal, and claimed that she has had "some kind of dream" about having equal parental roles. Kristin argued, self-critically, that her choice to continue working full-time had been "traditional." Kristin depicted their arrangement as a normative way of sharing parental leave when she claims, "that's what you do". Despite this, Kristin acknowledged that she learned that it was "really hard" for her to leave the baby at home. The benefits and equality of this common arrangement were thereby challenged.

There is, however, a group of families who have found ways to arrange parental leave so that the non-birth mothers could stay home much earlier in the children's lives. These arrangements will be presented in the following.

Both mothers alternate work and parental leave, or they stay home together

Parents in 10 families (20%) had an arrangement where both mothers stayed home early on in the child's life, full time or part time. In four of those families, both partners had stayed home full time from the child's birth, because one of them was on long-term sick leave or unemployed, while the other took parental leave.

Benefits of staying home together

Most of these parents depicted the situation of staying home together as advantageous. Katri and Darja had stayed home when their five-year-old daughter was newborn, as Katri was on long-term sick leave when Darja took parental leave.

> Katri: It's been good.
>
> Darja: It wasn't so nice that you didn't feel well.
>
> Katri: No no, but if we look at the positive side of it all, then it's been good that we were home a lot together.

Rather than pitying herself and her situation, Katri stated that staying home together was positive. In these interviewees' accounts, what is depicted as an unfortunate situation of illness or unemployment is also claimed to have advantageous features. In this sense, the interviewees adhere to the previously shown idealisation of spending time with children. Such a value rhetorically compensates for the negative consequences of being sick or unemployed.

Alternating caretaking enables equal parental roles early on

While four of the families described how they had stayed home together due to one partner's sick leave or unemployment, six other families depicted how they had chosen an arrangement where both parents worked part time and alternated care taking of the baby. Maja and Desiree had two children, aged two years and four months, respectively. They stayed home from work every other week.

> Maja: It works great. Both with work and at home.
>
> Desiree: At home, I think it's good for both the children and parents. The children don't differentiate, it works with either one of us, and we understand each other much better, when both of us have tried being home and tried working.
>
> [...]

> Maja: Yes. It's really good because you get to be home with the children and bond with them, but you can still get away and work. We both think working is pretty fun, so. You think it's fun wherever you are. If you work full time, you get tired of that, if you're home all the time, you get tired of that too.

Maja and Desiree depicted the benefits of their arrangement, which are very similar to those described earlier by parents who had taken evenly periods of full-time parental leave. Maja and Desiree too emphasised close bonds with the children and a shared understanding for one another as parents. Maja also highlighted another aspect, namely that work is (also) "fun". Rather than work being depicted as demanding, as seen previously, Maja argued for the importance of balance in everyday life, where you "get tired of" too much work or too much parental leave. Maja thereby drew on a rhetoric where neither work nor staying home is idealised, but where balance is put forward as the ideal. The birth mother, Desiree, also comments on recovery after childbirth: "Of course you need a little time, a month or two or maybe three, to recover. But then it's pretty boring being at home, I mean there isn't that much to do." While Desiree did argue for the need to recover, her account also focused on full-time staying at home as tiresome. Desiree described as well how she continued providing breast milk for the baby during her working weeks: "I took a cooler and a pump with me to work, so I pumped and took it home." Desiree's claims were in sharp contrast to how other interviewees depicted breastfeeding as setting natural limits for how parental leave could be arranged. Thus, their non-normative arrangement challenges norms on parental leave-taking and offers alternative ways of negotiating the parental role of the birth mother.

Discussion

Current Swedish parental leave regulations offer a plethora of possible arrangements for new parents. While official politics promote equal sharing of leave between parents (Carlson, 2013; Duvander, 2014), the couples are able to transfer most of their assigned parental leave between themselves, and may arrange child caretaking unevenly (Försäkringskassan, 2013). Previous studies on parental leave in Sweden focus on different-sex couples and show that mothers take the lion's share of parental leave, while most fathers continue working full time when the children are young and often use only their non-transferable share of parental leave, not seldom arranged as a prolonged vacation during summer (Duvander, 2014; Duvander & Johansson, 2012; Ekberg et al., 2013; Evertsson & Duvander, 2011). Only in 2 out of 10 couples is parental leave shared equally. Thus, despite Sweden's reputation as a gender-equal society, caregiving mothers and breadwinning fathers constitute a normative way of organising family life during the children's infancy.

In the present study of lesbian women's parental leave, only a small group of families arranged parental leave in a way that is reminiscent of different-sex couples' typical arrangement, i.e., where the birth mothers took parental leave like the average Swedish mother, and the non-birth mothers like the average Swedish father. Instead, most couples shared parental leave far more evenly. Equally shared parental leave was depicted as an advantageous solution, where equal parental roles and an equal relationship between the partners were visible as ideals in the parents' accounts. As most parents shared parental leave evenly, their arrangements corresponded to the presented ideal. This result echoes findings in previous research showing that lesbian couples often share egalitarian values, and arrange both domestic and employment tasks more evenly than other couples do (Bauer, 2016; Bos & van Balen, 2010; Bos, van Balen & van den Boom, 2007; Brewster, 2017; ; Ciano-Boyce & Shelley-Sireci, 2002; Goldberg, Smith & Perry-Jenkins, 2012; Gotta et al., 2011; Kurdek, 2007; Patterson et al., 2004; Perlesz et al., 2010; van der Vleuten et el., 2021). When parental leave had been unevenly arranged, this was defended or excused as being the result of work benefits or demands, i.e., external factors rather than personal preferences were used as explanations for the arrangement.

Despite the fact that equality was generally highlighted as a benefit of splitting parental leave in equal periods, some parents pointed at the inequality built into the situation, namely the fixed order in which parents stayed home. This shows that equality is a complex notion. Sharing parental leave evenly does not automatically imply that the time spent at home gives the parents equal preconditions when it comes to bonding with the child. While many parents depicted it as natural that the birth mother stayed home first – for recovery and breastfeeding – some parents challenged the necessity of this particular order. Arrangements where both mothers stayed home from early on and alternated caretaking and employment tasks were not common among participants, but the few examples challenged normative presumptions that birth mothers must stay home with newborns while non-birth mothers must wait their turn.

Most previous research on parental leave-taking has been conducted on different-sex couples. In the heteronormative family, the birth parent is a woman, while the non-birth parent is a man. In lesbian families, both the birth parent and the non-birth parent are women. The lesbian non-birth mother's unique situation of being a woman and a non-birth parent offers a possibility to theoretically separate female gender from birth giving in the context of parental leave. The present study shows that, in most lesbian families, non-birth mothers took fairly long parental leaves. Thus, in terms of length, non-birth mothers' parental leaves are somewhat shorter than the average Swedish mother, but far longer than the average father (see Duvander, 2014). Being two women in a parenting couple may facilitate sharing parental leave evenly, given that women are generally expected to stay home from work when they have children (see Bekkengen, 2002). The non-birth mothers usually took their parental leave at the end of the total parental leave period and, thus, in terms of order, the non-birth mothers arranged parental leave like the typical Swedish father (see Ekberg et al., 2013). An arrangement with an even distribution of parental leave – in a fixed order – constitutes a normative ideal for lesbian families, which seems to be the result of the unique combination of there being two female parents, but only one birth parent (for each child). Staying at home for several months to care for one's child seems to be linked to the female parental role; it is desired and socially expected for mothers. Staying at home and caring for a newborn child, specifically, is generally perceived as the natural task of the birth-giving parent. This finding makes an important contribution to our theoretical understanding of gender and equality in lesbian families.

The perspectives of modern family theory consider family life to be performative (Morgan, 1996). Rather than discussing 'parenthood' as a fixed and stable notion, 'parenting' is depicted as something done through the everyday practices of parents. Today, families show great variation in their form and structure, with lesbian parenting couples being part of this plurality. Heteronormativity is being challenged, as two-mother units create their own, unique ways of doing parenthood. The present work shows how lesbian mothers develop norms and ideals concerning parental leave that draw more heavily on equality than the norms and ideals of different-sex couples (cf. Bekkengen, 2002). When a lesbian couple shares parental leave unevenly, however, they do account for their arrangement by drawing on arguments similar to those made by different-sex couples. This shows that heteronormativity affects lesbian families too, despite the unique norms developed within this group.

Practical implications

The present study has important implications for those who support lesbian couples in their parental roles or intimate relationships. Understanding the interplay between parenting partners as well as the effects of ideals and social expectations is central. It is important to acknowledge the equality ideals that are common among lesbian mothers. For a lesbian mother who desires to continue working while having young children, it is likely that ideals of equality and close parent-child bonding put social pressure on her to stay at home, in particular if she is the birth mother. On the contrary, non-birth mothers are generally expected to wait for their turn, i.e., not to take parental leave before the birth mother returns to work. As shown in the present article, some non-birth mothers were not happy about this division, but arguing against what is presented as natural or self-evident is not easy. For clinicians who support lesbian partners' communication, it is important to acknowledge the norms and expectations concerning child caretaking that may affect birth mothers and non-birth mothers differently. While equally shared parental leave was presented as desirable by most interviewees, it is unlikely that one way of doing parental leave suits all. Therefore, clinicians should be aware of the ideals and norms that exist as well as the variation and the uniqueness that exists between families.

The present work only concerns the women's reflections on parental leave once they already have children. It is possible that images of future child caretaking arrangements also affect lesbian women when they are planning to have children. Norms, ideals, and social expectations concerning parental leave may impact on the couple when they decide whether and when to have children, and which one of them will be the birth mother. Thus, parental leave options and norms may impact on lesbian women's relations and careers both before having children and once the child is born.

Politicians and policymakers who establish regulations on parental leave, have a great deal to learn from Swedish lesbian mothers. These mothers have the ability to share parental leave evenly, with most doing so. Given that lesbian women generally prefer to share child caretaking equally (e.g., Bos & van Balen, 2010; Bos, van Balen & van den Boom, 2007), it is likely that many non-birth mothers who do not have access to parental leave would be happy to use parental leave if given the opportunity.

Limitations and suggestions for further research

Lesbian mothers in Sweden have access to a generous parental leave system, available to birth and non-birth mothers alike. The present study has focused on Swedish lesbian couples in families, where the non-birth mother shares the legal parenthood. Possibly, other lesbian family formations in Sweden would arrange parental leave differently. As lesbian women in other parts of the world must adjust their child caretaking arrangements to the parental leave system to which they have access, the findings of the present study cannot be generalised to other contexts. Rather, additional research is necessary to address questions of lesbian women's parental leave in other countries.

A core finding of the present work concerns the differences between birth parents' and non-birth parents' parental leave. This raises the question of how parental leave is arranged in couples with no birth parent (e.g., adoptive parents or parents through surrogacy). Does the non-presence of a birth parent affect parental leave differently, in lesbian, gay, and heterosexual couples? This would be a subject of interest for further research.

References

Ahrne, G., Roman, C., & Franzén, M. 2003. *Det sociala landskapet.* Gothenburg: Bokförlaget Korpen.

Bauer, G. 2016. "Gender roles, comparative advantages and the life course: The division of domestic labor in same-sex and different-sex couples." *European Journal of Population* 32 (1): 99–128.

Bekkengen, L. 2002. *Man får välja: Om föräldraskap och föräldraledighet i arbetsliv och familjeliv.* Malmö, Sweden: Liber.

Bjørnholt, M. & Farstad, G. 2014. "'Am I rambling?' on the advantages of interviewing couples together." *Qualitative Research,* 14 (1): 3–19.

Björk Eydal, G., & Rostgaard, T. 2011. "Gender equality revisited: Changes in Nordic childcare policies in the 2000s." *Social Policy and Administration,* 45 (2): 161–179.

Boll, C., Leppin, J., & Reich, N. 2014. "Parental childcare and parental leave policies: Evidence from industrialized countries." *Review of Economics of the Household* 12: 129–158. doi: 10.1007/s11150-013-9211-z

Borrell, C., Palència, L., Muntaner, C., Urquía, M., Malmusi, D., & O'Campo, P. 2014. "Influence of macrosocial policies on women's health and gender inequalities in health." *Epidemiologic Reviews* 36: 31–48. doi: 10.1093/epirev/mxt002

Bos, H., & van Balen, F. 2010. "Children in new reproductive technology: Social and genetic parenthood." *Patient Education and Counselling,* 81 (3): 429–435. doi:10.1016/j.pec.2010.09.012

Bos, H., van Balen, F., & van den Boom, D. 2007. "Child adjustment and parenting in planned lesbian-parent families." *American Journal of Orthopsychiatry,* 77 (1): 38–48.

Brewster, M. E. 2017. "Lesbian women and household labor division: A systematic review of scholarly research from 2000 to 2015." *Journal of Lesbian Studies,* 21 (1): 47–69.

Carlson, J. 2013. "Sweden's parental leave insurance: A policy analysis of strategies to increase gender equality." *Journal of Sociology and Social Welfare*, 40 (2): 63–76.

Clarke, V. 2005. "Feminist perspectives on lesbian parenting: A review of the literature 1972–2002." *Psychology of Women Section Review*, 7 (2): 11–23.

Ciano-Boyce, C., & Shelley-Sireci, L. 2002. "Who is mommy tonight? Lesbian parenting issues." *Journal of Homosexuality*, 43 (2): 1–13.

Downing, J., & Goldberg, A. 2011. "Lesbian mothers' construction of the division of paid and unpaid labor." *Feminism & Psychology*, 21 (1): 100–120.

Duvander, A–Z. 2014. "How long should parental leave be? Attitudes to gender equality, family, and work as determinants of women's and men's parental leave in Sweden." *Journal of Family Issues*, 35 (7): 909–926.

Duvander, A–Z., & Johansson, M. 2012. "What are the effects of reforms promoting fathers' parental leave use?" *Journal of European Social Policy*, 22 (3): 319–330.

Ekberg, J., Eriksson, R., & Friebel, G. 2013. "Parental leave: A policy evaluation of the Swedish 'Daddy-Month' reform." *Journal of Public Economics*, 97: 131–143.

Evertsson, M., & Boye, K. 2018. "The transition to parenthood and the division of parental leave in different-sex and female same-sex couples in Sweden." *European Sociological Review*, 34 (5): 471–485.

Evertsson, M., & Duvander, A–Z. 2011. "Parental leave: Possibility or trap? Does family leave length effect Swedish women's labour market opportunities?" *European Sociological Review*, 27 (4): 435–450.

Försäkringskassan. (2013, November 13). Parental benefit. Retrieved from https://www.forsakringskassan.se/wps/wcm/connect/a8203012-839a-4602-abef-00dfed41885b/4070_foraldrapenning_enGB.pdf?MOD=AJPERES

Försäkringskassan. (2018, Mars 21). Det som är bra delar man lika på. Retrieved from https://www.forsakringskassan.se/!ut/p/z0/DccxDsIw DADAtzB4RAliY6sQH4Cl6lIZYsBKcCzbDd-H2y4taU6L4OAXBnf B9v_8fXxOivGGw3GCfO4SJHG7rFdy7eI8CLIaDwwlc8jPbtgKGeRCD feNK0J2Lii-2nY3rknrtPsBKrnI1g!!/

Goldberg, A., & Perry-Jenkins, M. 2007. "The division of labor and perceptions of parental roles: Lesbian couples across the transition to parenthood." *Journal of Social and Personal Relationships*, 24 (2): 297–318.

Goldberg, A., Smith, J. A., & Perry-Jenkins, M. 2012. "The division of labor in lesbian, gay, and heterosexual new adoptive parents." *Journal of Marriage and Family*, 74, 812–828.

Gotta, G., Green, R., Rothblum, E., Solomon, S., Balsam, K., & Schwartz, P. 2011. "Heterosexual, lesbian and gay male relationships: A comparison of couples in 1975 and 2000." *Family Process*, 50 (3): 353–376.

Holli, A., Magnusson, E., & Rönnblom, M. 2005. "Critical studies of Nordic discourses on gender and gender equality." *NORA – Nordic Journal of Women's Studies*, 13 (3): 148–152.

Kawash, S. 2011. "New directions in motherhood studies." *Signs: Journal of Women in Culture and Society*, 36 (4): 969–1003.

Kitzinger, C. 2005. "Heteronormativity in action: Reproducing the heterosexual nuclear family in after-hour medical calls." *Social Problems*, 52 (4): 477–498.

Kurdek, L. 2007. "The allocation of household labor by partners in gay and lesbian couples." *Journal of Family Issues*, 28(1), 132–148.

Lalive, R., Schlosser, A., Steinhauer, A., & Zweimüller, J. 2014. "Parental leave and mothers' careers: The relative importance of job protection and cash benefits." *Review of Economic Studies*, 81: 219–265.

Land, V., & Kitzinger, C. 2005. "Speaking as a lesbian: Correcting the heterosexist presumption." *Research on Language and Social Interaction*, 38 (4): 371–416.

Magnusson, E. 2008. "The rhetoric of inequality: Nordic women and men argue against sharing house-work." *NORA – Nordic Journal of Feminist and Gender Research*, 16 (2): 79–95.

Malmquist, A. 2015a. "Women in lesbian relations: Construing equal or unequal parental roles?" *Psychology of Women Quarterly*, 39 (2): 256–267.

––– 2015b. *Pride and prejudice: Lesbian families in contemporary Sweden.* PhD thesis. Linköping University.

–––. 2015c. A crucial but strenuous process: Female same-sex couples' reflections on second-parent adoption. *Journal of GLBT Family Studies*, 11 (4): 351–374.

Moberg, Y. 2016. *Är lesbiska föräldrar mer jämställda? Institutet för arbetsmarknads- och utbildningspolitisk utvärdering.* Rapport 2016:9, Uppsala: IFAU.

Morgan, D. 1996. *Family connections.* Cambridge: Polity Press.

Morgan, D. 2011. *Rethinking family practices.* Basingstoke: Palgrave Macmillan.

Patterson, C., Sutfin, E., & Fulcher, M. 2004. "Division of labor among lesbian and heterosexual parenting couples: Correlates of specialized versus shared patterns." *Journal of Adult Development*, 11 (3): 179–189.

Perlesz, A., Power, J., Brown, R., McNair, R., Schofield, et al. 2010. "Organising work and home in same-sex parented families: Findings from the work love play study." *The Australian and New Zealand Journal of Family Therapy*, 31 (4): 374–391.

Potter, J., & Wetherell, M. 1987. *Discourse and social psychology.* London: Sage.

Ryan-Flood, R. (2009). *Lesbian motherhood: gender, families and sexual citizenship*. Basingstoke: Palgrave Macmillan.

Rønsen, M., & Hege Kitterød, R. 2015. "Gender-equalizing family policies and mothers' entry into paid work: Recent evidence from Norway." *Feminist Economics*, 21 (1): 59–89.

Smith, D. 1993. "The Standard North American Family: SNAF as an ideological code." *Journal of Family Issues*, 14 (1): 50–65.

Tegmyr, H., 2015. *Parenthood and Sickness Absence: A Comparative Analysis between Opposite-Sex and Same-Sex Couples*. Master's thesis. Uppsala: Uppsala University.

Weston, K. 1991. *Families we choose: Lesbians, gays, kinship*. New York: Columbia University Press.

Van der Vleuten, M., Jaspers, E., & van der Lippe, T. 2021. "Same-sex couples' division of labor from a cross-national perspective." *Journal of GLBT Family Studies*, 17 (2): 150–167.

Van Rijn-Van Gelderen, L., Ellis-Davies, K., Huijzer-Engbrenghof, M., Jorgensen, T. D., Gross, M., Winstanely, A., Rubio, B., Vecho, O., Lamb, M. E., & Bos, H. M. 2020. "Determinants of non-paid task division in gay-, lesbian-, and heterosexual-parent families with infants conceived using artificial reproductive techniques." *Frontiers in Psychology*, 11: 914.

Wetherell, M., & Potter, J. 1992. *Mapping the language of racism*. New York: Columbia University Press.

Zetterqvist Nelson, K. 2007, *Mot alla odds: Regnbågsföräldrars berättelser om att bilda familj och få barn*. Malmö: Liber.

PART 3
New Directions, Temporalities and Geopolitics of Queer Kinship

8. The Legacy of the Age Gap as a Decisive Difference in Lesbian Relationships

Joanna Mizielińska & Antu Sorainen

Lesbian age gap – always out there but never quite here?

Lesbian relationships in which one partner is significantly older than the other, in this article called the lesbian age gap[1] relationship or lesbian relationship defined by age difference, exist as a specific and longstanding cultural phenomenon, from famous historical figures (i.e., Sappho and her young protégées, the British lesbian poet Michael Field[2], Simone de Beauvoir and Sylvie Le Bon, thirty-three years her junior), to more recent political and popular culture characters. For example, it is a central theme in the romantic movie *Carol* (US 2015), based on the ground-breaking novel "The Price of Salt" from 1952 by Patricia Highsmith, which portrays a lesbian couple with a significant age and life phase gap. Discussing the film with fellow academics on social media and in private conversations, we noticed that the age gap in lesbian relationships is taboo. Moreover, in a time when there is much attention on queer families with children and their intergenerational bonds, this is an interesting and under-researched phenomenon presenting, perhaps, a queer form of queer relationships.

Although the age gap might arise in many human intimate relationship patterns and kinship institutions from modern Western heterosexuality to Antique's pederasty and Russian Tzars, we do not treat it here as a merely general human feature but as something that always requires a specific analysis in the specific

---

[1] In this naming we do not want to focus on the gap *per se* but rather on differences related to age, which we understand broadly not only as biographical age. Simply put, we argue that age functions for some women as an important difference which attracts them to one another. And of course, with age some important points of attraction coalesce, such as a (stable) position in life, physical maturity and vitality, etc.

[2] Behind the pseudonym was a British aunt and her niece, life-long lovers.

sexual, political and historical context. In this vein, and in this article, we discuss the specificity and possible generalities of the lesbian age gap as a significant line of desire in lesbian relationships. We shed light on how the age gap plays out and might influence the lives and relationships of lesbian lovers by contrasting two recent case studies from two European countries with differing political histories: Poland and Finland.

Inspired as well as amazed by what could be construed as ignorance about, and a silencing of this topic in queer kinship and family studies, we attempt to show how lesbian age gap relationships are constructed and lived by their participants. By contrasting case studies from two different geographical and cultural European contexts we discuss how queer desire is entangled with the pre-conditions of how the social and emotional political space is gendered and sexualised (Mizielińska & Kulpa 2011). The spatial and geo-temporal specificities of two empirical research projects, both focusing on the margins of the Western and Anglo-American epistemological dominance in queer and feminist knowledge production bring new light to this cultural phenomenon.[3] We ask in which practical ways significant age gaps between women influence everyday concerns and supports decisions in lesbian relationships. By focusing on the everyday practices of two lesbian couples, we open a broader window to a landscape of the culturally and emotionally complicated worlds of lesbian desire. We do this in order to claim lesbian age gap relationships as an essential and productive phenomenon within queer worlds, with the potential to create new lines of desire in diverse cultural and geopolitical contexts.

[3] Acknowledgements and Funding Sources: this article originated during a research visit funded by the collaborative project Queer(y)ing Kinship in the Baltic Region funded by the Foundation for Baltic and East European Studies (dnr 54/13). The article draws on research carried out within "Families of choice in Poland", funded by Polish Ministry of Science and Higher Education, program Ideas Plus, grant number IdP2012000462 (PI: Joanna Mizielińska), CoreKin – Contrasting and Re-Imagining Margins of Kinship" funded by the Academy of Finland, grant number 297957 (PI: Antu Sorainen), and Wills and Inheritance in Sexually Marginalised Groups – A Multidisciplinary Study" funded by the Academy of Finland, grant number 277203 (PI: Antu Sorainen).

The chapter begins with a short description of the state of the art and the marginalisation of this topic in the relevant scholarship. After the brief presentation of our research projects and chosen case studies, we will examine how age functions as an object of attraction in chosen cases, a trigger of emotional, intellectual, and sexual drives. Then, we deconstruct the negative myth of "the lesbian seducer" focusing on women's narratives and demonstrating that the power dynamic in lesbian relationships with a significant age difference is constantly shifting, depending not solely on chronological age. One such important factor which profoundly influences the relational trajectory and dynamics is the geopolitical location discussed in the following part. The "Beyond the happy future" section provides original and novel accounts for research on how the future is imagined in lesbian couples with significant age differences. Here we argue that these relationships are founded on different kinds of expectations, where death is always already present; this does not imply that all these women stay together until one (or both) of them dies, but the fact that they acknowledge the expectation that the older partner might pass away earlier, would they stay together. This takes us to our next part, which examines how the lesbian age gap, disclosure strategies, and geopolitical location intersect. Then, we move to the critical questions of how kinship and families are enacted and displayed in such relationships. Focusing on our findings, we demonstrate that in these two cases, kinship gets a "messier" political and everyday meaning than it in the everyday use has, and the women create a complex web of kin and non-kin being brought together within their support and care network – or within the void of that. In the final section, we concentrate on fears and anxieties around ageing and ways of protecting the younger partners and their rights to mourning. Throughout the chapter, we argue that significant age differences in lesbian relationships influence how (and why) women build their relationships and kinship from the very beginning till death (or divorce) do them part. This might be the case in non-lesbian relationships too, but here we focus on the very particularities of lesbian relationships as gender and sexuality influence these relational bonds.

Silence, taboo, and anamnesis
around the lesbian age gap

A significant age difference between intimate partners has mostly been a subject of interest in the – not too many – quantitative studies focusing on straight couples (Lehmiller & Agnew 2011). These studies often tended to orientalise their topic, for example, in scholarly articles on some "far away" countries where girls are forced to marry much older men, or, in the pioneering anthropological studies on women-women marriages, treated as an economic necessity rather than desire, and as such, marginal to the liberal and modern Western societies (Oboler 1980).

However, diverse statistical data reveal a tendency towards an increase in a number of relationships with a significant age difference in Euro-American cultures (McKenzie 2015). It is noteworthy that the authors of quantitative studies have strongly influenced the nature of the lexicon commonly applied in research on age-different couples. Therefore, the usual conceptualisation in this field ranges from "age discrepant", "generational gap", "age-dissimilar" to "age heterogamy" or "May-December" relationships (Bruns 2008; Lehmiller & Agnew 2011; McKenzie 2015). These quantitative studies have also defined age-gap relationships (as romantic involvements) as those with a difference of greater than ten years in age between partners (Lehmiller & Agnew 2011).

In our view, the meaning and reference field of the age gap is constantly shifting, and it depends on multiple other factors than merely or exclusively the biological age, but also conceptions of the 'lesbian age' (or coming-out), gender and sexuality and thus power. However, qualitative studies focusing on age-gap relationships are scarce. Recently, Lara McKenzie[4] (2015) studied straight age-dissimilar couples. Guided by the individual respondents' understanding of their age-dissimilar relationships, she does not define these relationships and their meanings beforehand; such an approach is close also to our understanding of age gap lesbian relationships.

---

[4] It is so far the only academic book fully devoted to the issue of age dissimilarity in straight relationships.

Although according to statistics, age-dissimilar relationships may have been more prevalent among lesbians and gays than straight couples (Lehmiller & Agnew 2011), this fact is not reflected in the earlier, relevant literature. On the contrary, the issue of the age gap as a potentially decisive factor in lesbian relationships has been silenced both in the mainstream and queer scholarship on intimacy, kinship, and families. In our literature review,[5] we found only one scholarly article that discussed this question directly (interestingly enough, not based on any empirical research), entitled "May-December Lesbian Relationships: Power Storm or Blue Skies?" (Bruns 2008). As the title suggests, the essay discusses the problems that lesbian couples with age differences may experience but also the possible benefits of such relationships. Although it is primarily speculative and contains many therapeutic advice it also touches upon an important issue concerning the variable and fluid nature of power dynamics in such couples.

The topic of age gap in lesbian relationships is sometimes touched upon in anthropological and ethnographic literature on non-Western countries, such as the above-mentioned Oboler's (1980) article or, more recently, Wekker's (2006) book *Politics of Passion*. Wekker's study crosses the colonialist/colonised border and also brings the researcher herself into sexual age gap relationship configurations, partly through her descriptions of her own relationships and also by looking at different cultural understandings of desire.

On the other hand, the scarcity of academic literature on the lesbian age gap meets the abundance of other materials, from the lists of historical and contemporary famous lesbian figures to popular literature and movies. The first classic lesbian films are almost *all* about the age difference, from *Mädchen in Uniform* (1931, Germany) to *The Killing of Sister George* (1968, UK) and *Desert Hearts* (1985, US). Likewise, the classic lesbian novels and erotic lesbian pulp stories are often about teacher/student attrac-

---

[5] We looked for relevant literature using diverse keywords such as lesbian age gap difference, age-discrepant relationship, age gap relationship, spousal age gap, age-dissimilar relationships, age heterogamy, May–December (lesbian) relationships.

tion or other sexual relationships based at least, partly, on the age gap. The density of this theme reveals how age as a desired and desirable difference is central to the lesbian cultural imagination as well as in collective memory. Consequently, while such an important political, cultural, and social topic has always been there, in previous academic research, it has not been discussed in any depth. This theoretical and empirical void raises many questions, including the possible reasons or explanations for such silence or even "tabooisation" around the lesbian desire resulting from the age gap in queer studies.

One of the possible explanations for this academic amnesia might be connected with the ideal of lesbian relationships as loving, equal, and egalitarian. The first source of this idealised image of lesbian relationships as based on sameness (i.e., the idea of the "lesbian merge") and equality arises out of the psychoanalytical and sexological discourses during the latter half of the 19th century. For example, Ellis' and Symond's (1897) concept of the sexual invert was based on the assumption that homosexual relations deny difference and saw sameness as a barrier to real sexual desire or satisfaction of erotic life. This assumption (historically proven wrong) was carried on by Radclyffe Hall – who herself indulged in a series of lesbian age gap relationships – in *The Well of Loneliness* (1928), known as "The Lesbian Bible" in some circles in the English-speaking world. Later on, in the 1970s and the early 1980s, lesbian feminism also treated the issue of difference with great suspicion in its quest for egalitarianism.

The second possible explanation is the haunting fear of paedophilia around and in contemporary queer communities. This fear is connected to the massively failed 'paedophile liberation movement' in the US and the UK after the mid-1970s, when its advocates tried to gain positive publicity and raise 'awareness' by doing their own surveys and publishing books and magazines with some famous intellectuals' support in the wake of the successful GayLib movement. However, this attempt for liberation caused more moral contempt and forced the paedophile activists to go underground and the intellectuals to back up (Sorainen 2007, and based on her unpublished research data collected from Hall-Carpenter

Archives in the LSE). Consequently, the publicly advocated social, political, and media fears and anxieties around many complicated non-normative gender configurations and sexualities significantly rose after the late 1970s (Rubin 1992; Herdt 2009). These debates also landed in other European countries, even though they were localised and circulated in more or less adapted versions (Sorainen 2007). Seen from this perspective, relationships with significant age differences become a particular form of potential "deviation" in same-sex love, dangerously touching upon or hooking onto the fantasy of familial transgression (i.e., mother/daughter, sisters).

In order to provide greater depth to both the abovementioned explanations, we decided to study a selection of chosen cases from our fieldwork.

Age-gapping queer projects

To paraphrase Judith Butler's (2006) quote, "I like my boys to be girls", some lesbians like their women to be boys or girls while others prefer them like well-matured wine; age is what attracts both of these groups (at least partly, or sometimes) to each other. It does not mean that an age gap is a necessary difference for lesbian desire, any more than, for instance, butch-femme. Rather, we propose that age offers new possibilities – not requirements – for lines of desire. Although age encompasses much, since it is everywhere, it seems to remain a "different difference" (Segal 2014, 17), very often over-looked in writing on lesbian desire. In what follows, we want to show how this particular choice of the object of one's desire matters and affects how the relationship is lived, experienced, and dis-played.

We draw our discussion on this complex desire(d) field of criss-crossing differences and sameness from two major mixed-method research projects. The first project, *Families of choice in Poland* (2013–2016, PI: Joanna Mizielińska), was a complex study on non-heterosexual families and their challenges in everyday life. The project had an interdisciplinary character and combined quanti-tative and qualitative approaches. It contained a survey with 3038 respondents in same-sex relationships, 53 biographical interviews, an ethnographic study on 21 families, and 22 focus group interviews.[6] The chosen case comes from an interview with a lesbian couple with an age difference of 12 years, in which both partners were interviewed separately. The second project, *Wills and Inheritance in Sexually Marginalised Groups* (2014–2019, PI: Antu Sorainen), equally relied on qualitative and quantitative data.[7] It consisted of two surveys in multiple languages with members of diverse European queer communities (N=1007) and legal professionals (N=112). The data was supported and complemented by 25 ethnographic interviews and kin diagrams.

The chosen Finnish case concerns a 42-year age difference where the senior partner, artist Rauni, had just died at the age of 80+ before an interview with her younger partner, an emerging artist Telle (mid-30s) took place.[8] Telle was married with kids when she met Rauni, and lived with her children and (now ex) husband. In contrast to what in conventional heteronormative terms is a two generations wide age gap, the Polish case involves a significantly smaller age difference of "only" twelve years: Ewelina (49 years) and Edyta (37 years) had been together for five years at the time of the interviews (2014), and both had previously been married. Ewelina divorced her husband about 3 years before the interview took place and moved out. For Ewelina, it was her first same-sex relationship, while Edyta, who never formally divorced her husband, lived with her previous female partner when the couple met.

The two E's live separately in nearby apartments in the same settlement. Both were financially independent. Ewelina is an accountant, and Edyta is a businesswoman who runs a restaurant with her husband. They both had one child of the same age (twelve years then), but of different gender, neither of whom knew about their mothers' relationship. Edyta planned to tell her daughter, and talked about it a lot during her interview. Ewelina respected Edyta's decision but did not plan to tell her son about the relationship, since she thought he was not ready

---

[6] For more on methodology see Mizielińska & Stasińska 2021; Mizielińska 2022.

[7] For more information see the website: www.antusorainen.com

[8] For ethical reasons, to secure the safety and anonymity of our informants and their partners, we both use fictional names.

for such news. To make matters more complicated, their children were friends, so telling one without telling the other would put a strain on their friendship. Therefore, Edyta kept postponing her disclosure.

In the Finnish case, the older woman Rauni was a celebrated artist. In her will, she left a considerable estate to Telle. As a consequence of this, Telle's children literally lived *in* a curiously manifested "family secret" (Smart 2007): their mother bought a bigger flat with the inheritance, and decorated this new family home with Rauni's furniture. Telle's children did not know the nature of their relationship, whereas the ex-husband was aware of the truth but chose to keep living in the household. To the outside, it looked like a "normal" heterosexual family that somehow came upon a fortune.

Drawing on our empirical findings, in the following part of the article, we study how age difference works as an erotiser in lesbian relationships, an attractor that might increase desire between women but that can also influence its character. By doing so, we also show how lesbian desire gets entangled with other important social factors, not only the geopolitical locations but also cultural and social constructions of gender and family. Further, we approach the age gap as a decisive difference in many diverse areas of everyday practices in lesbian relationships. Moreover, we are queering the very concept of the age gap by pointing out that it is contingent and contextual. It keeps changing over the life course and depends on queer time in terms of how long each of the partners has been out (Halberstam 2005). In thinking about the lesbian/queer age, we believe it is not always in sync with chronological age and the reproductive age (Halberstam 2005; Traies 2016), but it often goes sideways (Stockton 2009).

Age as a concept varies geopolitically; that is, "lesbian age difference" might mean something entirely different in a post-socialist country (such as Poland) than in a Nordic welfare country (such as Finland). Both of these nations come with different queer temporalities and histories of the LGBTQ+ movement or the recognition of LGBTQ+ rights than those of the UK or the US from where the dominant cultural and theoretical discourses as well as silences surrounding the topic arise (Mizielińska & Kulpa 2011).

Age as an attractor

"What difference does it make 'what' and 'who' we are orientated towards in the very direction of our desire?" asks Sara Ahmed (2006, 1). Her question needs to be rephrased for our purposes. It takes the following form: what happens when we orient our desire to an object which is doubly prohibited or stigmatised in our culture – i.e., the "same" sex and, in the case of a significant age gap, also a too different age regarding the cultural expectation of 'sameness' in terms of lesbian desire? What happens when mutual attraction between two people transgresses both these prohibitions or cultural expectations?

In McKenzie's study (2015), the interviewees seldom use their age difference either to emphasise the uniqueness of their relationship or to explain their mutual attraction. However, in our cases, age was very present in the narration about the beginning of the relationships. For Telle and Rauni, it was a clearly articulated attraction for both partners. Rauni shined as an inspiring experienced intellectual mentor in Telle's path towards an artist's life: this exceptional position in life, Rauni's acquired experiences, as well as her ageing, fascinated Telle. According to Telle, also Rauni was "sexually and emotionally explicitly happy to find intimate adventure and pleasantries at the last phase of her life". Rauni had had lesbian relationships and networks, decades before Telle was born. Rauni's unique historical knowledge of lesbian sexuality was one factor that made her attractive to Telle.

Ewelina's and Edyta's narratives about the specific features that attracted them to each other reveal that their mutual attraction was also connected with age. For example, Ewelina described the younger woman as more "alive, spontaneous, and social" and contrasted her with her then-husband, with whom she often felt lonely, missing contact with other people. Being younger than her, Edyta also got associated in Ewelina's mind with bigger sexual needs. It created distrust at the beginning of their relationship, heightened by Edyta's problems with alcohol. Ewelina said:

> When she was with her friends, I had nothing against it, only fears that under the influence of alcohol, things could happen. I did not trust her for a very long time [...] I value her sincerity. Sincerity, spontaneity, willingness to help ... And that she is full of life.

Then again, Edyta described her partner as more experienced, well organised, wiser, settled, and motivating her to introduce changes in her own life. It was thanks to Ewelina, for example, that Edyta joined the AA program.

One might claim that these personal characteristics could have nothing to do with age, since it is easy to imagine that the older partner could be more social – or sexually active – and the younger one more settled or professionally successful, although it might be less common. We do not want to deny that mutual attraction is always the outcome of complex factors but rather to claim that age-related differences might be an overlooked factor, and be more crucial than has otherwise been acknowledged. In our opinion, lesbian desire *is* about difference (while it is *also* about certain sameness), much along the lines that Ahmed (2006, 99) argues:

> Lesbian desire involves differences, which take shape through contact and are shaped by past contacts with others. [...] Lesbian desire is directed toward other women, and it is 'given' this direction that such desire encounters difference. Other women, whatever our differences, are other than ourselves.

Ultimately, the diversity of lesbian desire always boils down to the geographies and politics of space in terms of sexuality, emotions and gender expressions (such as butch/femme). Moreover, it intersects with other crucial factors (class or conventional life trajectory), which makes writing about lesbian desire challenging. We will show how the age gap as a range of possible differences and attractors in lesbian relationships is never an isolated phenomenon. Instead, we can understand the intersection of the three modes of temporality that we call biographical time, queer time, and historical/LGBTQ+ community time. With this approach, we can see how what we call the lesbian age gap works as an erotiser that is both contextual and fluid, dependent both on time and space, and how it is also a transgression that challenges conventional logics of development, maturity, adulthood, and responsibility (Stockton 2005; Halberstam 2005).

"The lesbian seducer" – and her seducer

The most common assumption associated with the lesbian age gap is the image of an older woman as the more experienced sexual seducer of a younger, "innocent" woman. This phantasmal narrative was popular among early sexologists such as Havelock Ellis. Radclyffe Hall applied the storyline in *The Well of Loneliness*, first published with Ellis' foreword. In this and other ways, the 19th century male sexologists' imaginary world has had a long legacy on the configurations and imaginations of lesbian desire and culture.

To contradict this odd legacy, we suggest – along with Halberstam (2004) – that lesbian desire often provides creative energy for younger women who challenge the heterosexual normative script of "proper" behaviour. When we take a closer look at our cases, Ewelina had no sexual experiences/encounters with women before she met the younger woman, and for a long time, she misread Edyta's attraction towards her for friendship. At one point, she even declared: "Had I realised that IT COULD BE SOMETHING, then probably never in my life would I have let that relationship happen."

Rauni and Telle started a sexual relationship only after Telle had formally divorced her husband. It was Rauni who urged that they should not enter a registered partnership as she was afraid that Telle would be perceived as a gold digger, seducing a famous, wealthy, and (assumedly) vulnerable older woman. This normative (and in Rauni's case, feared) assumption of older people as victims of the young has been problematised by the feminist and lesbian scholars of *New Ageing Studies*. Segal (2014) claims that life could and should be lived creatively – also sexually – to the end. Traies (2016, 222–223) describes older UK lesbians who want a future that includes personal growth and joy, framed on feminist principles, based on their experiences in their youth in the lesbian feminist and Consciousness Raising groups.

However, problems often occur from the rooted assumptions and social norms about age and the narrowing down of ideal possibilities for older women who attempt to live at full speed to the end of their lives. Segal (2014, 60) describes this as a fear that "eats the soul as threats of redundancy, disregard, abandonment and isolation routinely dampen the spirits of most people as they age, even when they remain economically privileged." We do not know how much such fears influenced Rauni's choices. However, as she had no capable close relatives and was often lost in her mind when on and off from different wards during her last years, she benefited from Telle's caring commitment in terms of her safety and health.

On the other hand, Edyta and Telle were, in some respects, both more experienced than their older partners. Before starting the relationship, Edyta lived with another female partner for whom she had left her husband. Because of such previous knowledge, she knew that she was attracted to Ewelina from the beginning. Hence, the relationship could not have been just a friendly one for her. When she reflects on the beginnings of their acquaintance, she vividly describes her attempts to "get" Ewelina:

> I remember when I first saw Ewelina in the kindergarten, it was Christmas Eve. I immediately turned my attention to her because she was such an ATTRACTIVE WOMAN! Moreover, she always walks so straight up so you feel she is even arrogant and looks down on the world. […] And that made me even more intrigued. And later I decided – "I'm coming closer to you, do you want it or not, and I will break this brick wall of yours."

Telle was also at least as active as Rauni in the seduction phase. She was 19 when she first met Rauni, then a teacher at an art course Telle attended. From then on, she kept following Rauni around, visited her home for Rauni's "long nightly private lectures", and let Rauni phone her continuously at home to listen to her professional and private worries. Telle also assisted Rauni in her artwork, intentionally befriended Rauni's elderly lesbian circle, took her for walks when she was in poor health, and even accompanied her to a hospice to say goodbye to Rauni's ex-girlfriend. Telle was persistent in getting close and intimate with Rauni; in all possible ways, she became the most important aid to her.

In the Polish case, the older partner was possibly more vulnerable at the turning point of her life. Edyta had already left her husband and lived with her daughter, while Ewelina, after 20 years of marriage and two years of a love affair with Edyta, decided to leave her husband but did not have a place of her own to live. Therefore, knowledge and understanding of the younger partner's situation was precious.

Hence, we see in both cases complicated sexual and emotional power dynamics, where the younger partner is (also) the seducer and the older is (also) the seduced.

Ideas of the lesbian age gap, which are often taken for granted, tend to privilege the older partner as the more experienced in life and the lesbian community and as economically more stable. However, we would argue for a more complicated scene of desire where the power dynamics between the partners is constantly shifting, depending on diverse factors such as social and cultural geographical contexts, lesbian age and queer time, class, marriage and reproductive status, economic independence, the particular moment of one's life trajectory, access to feminist, lesbian and queer communities, and even artistic talent and success.

The political geographies of
age-differential lesbian desire

In Poland, the younger partner usually helps the older one through the process of coming out, possibly leaving a straight relationship and introducing her into the lesbian culture (Mizielińska 2022). Younger people have a better ability to function "out of the closet", since they have grown up in a less discriminatory society than middle-aged and older people. Consequently, the younger Polish lesbian generation who have older partners are able to lead them through some of the most challenging moments in their life, and in this sense, they function as their "biographical caretakers"[9] (Mizielińska 2022). However, as said, such power dynamic shifts all the time.

In the Nordic context, where LGBTQ+ movements and the successful struggle for LGBTQ+ rights have an established history, it is arguably more likely that the older person "has moved through the tumultuous early stages of the coming out process, developed a sense of identity pride and honed the ability to navigate between lesbian and straight worlds" (Bruns 2008, 269). The more experienced partner could thus introduce the younger one to the lesbian world, and its emotional and sexual practices and function as a transmitter of queer culture.

Queer time, however, is not vertical but spiral, in that new lesbian and queer generations have often lost contact with the previous generations in their endeavour to create novel queer worlds, and, accordingly, queer age is not chronological; it keeps fluctuating. For example, when the senior partner is 42 years older than the younger partner, and has spent half of her life in a legal closet, like Rauni (in Finland, same-sex acts were decriminalised only in 1971), the picture Bruns so nicely painted above becomes more complicated – but also more politically relevant. The older women might have had a strong community and made their coming-outs decades ago, as Rauni did. Then again, the recent LGBTQ+ movement in Western countries has put much pressure on marriage rights instead of public sex or non-heteronormative public space and living experiments, such as lesbian/queer bars, activist or community spaces, art collectives, book shops, radical research communities, communes, publishing companies, gal-

---

[9] The concept was coined by Anselm Strauss to describe the help given to individuals at the turning points of their lives. Usually "biographical caretakers" give advice, help to solve problems, etc. Since Polish non-heterosexual persons often cannot rely on close relatives, parents, LGBTQ+ communities (partly because of their weakness in Poland), institutional guardians, and/or LGBTQ+ experts, in the majority of cases, partners become the source of support and care for each other (Mizielińska 2022).

leries, consciousness raising groups, communal education, non-profit lesbian enterprises, free-of-charge counselling and legal advice, political property (for example, lesbian lands), and such like. This means that many younger lesbians of Telle's age have not necessarily had any experience of what it means to have a lesbian network or culture outside of the Internet or their relationships. Therefore, interestingly, Telle and Rauni met in the curious limbo of the pre- and post-lesbian geopolitical space in Finland.

In contrast, in Poland, where LGBTQ+ communities started to organise formally after 1989, the post-socialist generation grew up with wider access to LGBTQ+ organisations than the previous one. Therefore, they are the ones who might take the lead at the beginning of the relationships, especially when their older partner came out later in life and did not have the time to work through the inevitable conflicts between how her life had been, on the one hand, and her new lesbian identity, on the other. For example, while recalling the early stage of their relationship, Edyta mentions Ewelina's struggle with her self-acceptance:

> As she said to me, "Listen, for me the traumatic experience was when I kissed you and glanced in the mirror and I saw that I kiss a woman. TRAGEDY! Jesus Christ, what am I doing? Not only do I betray my husband for the first time but I also betray him with a woman. Younger than me by about fifteen years."

In fact, their age difference is "only" 12 years. However, this over-statement speaks volumes about Ewelina's personal struggles and her inner conflicts – and maybe also about a more significant "lesbian" pattern to both play down and heighten the significance of (biological) age. It also says much about cultural norms of a) being faithful, b) being heterosexual, and c) having relationships with older people if one is a woman. In Ewelina's case, she transgresses these three "cultural taboos"; she is torn between desire and social convention.

The lesbian desire for age (difference)

Research on heterosexual couples with an age gap shows that both partners tend to minimise their age difference. Factors other than age influence their relationships more, and they usually claim that their "real age" was younger or more mature than their chronological one (McKenzie 2015). In contrast, Traies (2016, 28) noticed that in the case of older lesbians, age cohort was rarely the most useful categorisation, since chronological age was usually less significant than the age of "coming out", and ultimately, their lesbian histories: "Multiple intersecting processes of advantage and disadvantage can make the stories of two women of the same age very different from each other."

In the Polish case, age was present in the narratives of both partners. However, only the younger woman tended to think that "age is just a number", while, for the older partner, their age gap was perceived as a fundamental emotional obstacle with which she struggled. Edyta, the younger partner, says:

> [Age] did not matter to me at first, but it did matter to her. And it was also one of her arguments that this relationship made no sense, because the big age difference …

In the Finnish case, the age gap was so substantial, and Rauni already seriously ill in the final phase of her life, that the question of whether the biological age mattered was curiously both extremely relevant and irrelevant. Nevertheless, the age gap became a more complex dimension in the intellectual and erotic exchange between the two women. The mutual artist inspiration and sexual desire drew Telle to an intimate situation where a final caretaker role and the death of the older partner were soon to be expected. Transgressing into a spiritual age was a way out for Telle; she created and experienced a novel phase where the relationship continued posthumously, after Rauni's death in another space, in a sort of ether. For her, the relationship lived on in another form after Rauni's corporeal death as an esoteric existence; she was in a constant dialogue with Rauni inside her mind.

In both cases, the age gap was apparently more stressful for the older partner, but for different reasons. Ewelina's worries concerned their future primarily and resulted from the anxiety felt by many other older lesbian partners who do not want to become a burden for the younger ones:

> This difference in age is NOT about now, but what will be LATER! In ten years, when she will be forty-two, and I will be fifty-four, well, it is such a gap. You know, I will not be able to follow her and she will feel obliged to be with me, it would be unbearable for me. So, I was afraid that, for example, they would laugh at her, that she has a GRANDMOTHER as a partner, people can be cruel.

In Finland, a 54-year-old woman is not commonly treated as particularly old, and many lesbians of this age and older are highly active. Perhaps Ewelina's fears might be somehow connected to the Polish gender role expectations and healthcare system? In Poland, the average age of women giving birth for the first time is 27.7 years, lower than the Finnish average of 30. Also, the role of the grandmother is culturally more important in Poland than in Finland where women, on average, are more equal in the job market, are more educated, while the welfare state –with respect to kindergarten and the pension system – primarily takes care of children and elderly women. Consequently, kinship roles and family are somewhat differently crucial in reproduction, survival, and the final care concerns for Finnish and Polish women, including lesbians.

Rauni shared Ewelina's fears of somehow influencing the younger partner's future negatively. Her worry was not so much about her rapidly declining health but the broader issues of sexual politics (a too early and too queer widowhood prospect for Telle) and an urge to protect Telle's children from negative publicity. Rauni feared that by going public with their relationship, Telle would compromise her future as an artist and a mother. Rauni did not count on the Finnish public fully understanding the attraction between an older renowned lesbian artist and a much younger, not-so-well-off woman as something mutually enjoyed and anticipated, or, indeed, as mutual sexual desire.

These fears of older lesbian partners in two different European countries in different "lesbian age phase" situations reveal that while lesbian desire has specific and substantial power to subvert cultural scripts of age, it is always embedded in the geopolitical realities of the society in which it is lived out. As certain anxieties on the part of the older women influenced both relationships, it was so for somewhat different politically, culturally, and socially framed emotional reasons. Therefore, we now turn our analytic gaze into the emotional space and place concerning such realities in lesbian age-difference relationships.

Beyond happy future

Different feelings may accompany similar types of (lesbian) desire in different geographical contexts. When we fall in love or start relationships based on love, the dominant Western expectation is not to speculate about the future but rather to immerse oneself in "uncontrollable" emotions (Berlant 2001). Love is seen as blind and irrational. In both cases, however, age and the political situation around the age gap and queer sexualities were something that prompted the women to think about the future – or, in Rauni's case, about her after-life future in terms of her inheritance and artistic legacy (both left in Telle's hands in Rauni's will).

In the Polish case, Ewelina gradually learned how to concentrate on the present and decided to look with less fear at what the future might bring. Nevertheless, a different framing of time, the past and the future was still a cause of disagreement between her and Edyta. For Ewelina, the future seemed to be connected with her past and biological age. She tried to explain this to her younger partner. According to Edyta, the conversation looked like this:

> For a long time, I could not understand why she was so afraid to take her bag and get out of there [husband's apartment]. "But what's the problem?" I told her. "I did exactly the same thing. I did not want to live with my husband, so I took the kid under my arm, the bag, and I moved out, so why can't you do the same."

"Because you were twenty-six or twenty-seven years old and the whole life was ahead of you, and I am forty-something, and I do not have forty more to build my life, I have relatively fewer years, and it is harder." "I still do not understand." "Because I invested in this apartment twenty years of MY hard work, MY money, MY sacrifices, MY paintings, MY scrubbing of floors and such things, and you in yours only a year. SO DO YOU SEE THE DIFFERENCE?"

Both Es thus defined and envisioned their future in terms of age, and also the material, in particular related to the efforts to build one's own domestic property brick by brick, so to say, counted in years of one's life. When ageing is perceived as a multi-layered cake, where every year adds one safe material layer, it becomes more difficult to decide to change one's life in a profound and unpredictable way. It is not easy to abandon the philosophy of the future understood in terms of "years of investments." Here, the big contrast between Ewelina and Edyta lies in the ways they imagined their future, depending on the affective investments towards the future in one's past. Although Ewelina counted this in biological years (twenty years of marriage and living in the same apartment), the scope of her emotions was much broader. It included the rage that she had invested so much and was now left with nothing, the fear of not being able to start a new life of her own, the resentment towards the younger partner who did not understand this because of her age, the doubts that it might not work out, and the melancholia related to the time lost when younger. For Edyta, things seemed much more straightforward, or at least, she expressed a less broad scope of emotions.

In Rauni's case, as she is dead and was not interviewed, we must rely on what Telle told us about Rauni's thoughts and emotions and the 'knowledge' provided by Rauni's artwork, media interviews, and appearances at lesbian events. Based on these, it occurs to us that she mastered both the modernist expression of personal and, more specifically, lesbian fears and energies of exclusion and outsiderness. At the same time, she had resources to worry for the younger partner instead of demanding "normally" assumed benefits of an age gap relationship for herself, such as trying to deploy official relationship status to secure caretaking from the junior woman. Unfortunately, we cannot say much more about Rauni's authentic or real concerns and potential feelings attached to a much younger lover near the closure of death.

However, this much could be proposed: if there is not much future left in terms of biological age, perhaps there is also less anxiety about one's own future as a person (identity issues) in an age gap relationship, and, therefore, less anxiety transferred onto the younger partner's future? At least, when Telle divorced her husband to start a serious relationship with Rauni, it was Rauni, not Telle, who objected on registering their relationship because she was worried that Telle would adopt a social role of a "widow" too early in her life, and thereby missing out on something important. According to Telle, Rauni wanted her to stay "on the side of the living" in terms of social and cultural expectations, whereas for Telle, official widowhood would actually have been a welcomed future role. Because of Rauni's refusal to register their partnership, since she wanted to protect Telle from assuming a "wrong" status (widowhood) and her children from unwanted publicity, Telle had to keep living without social recognition of her loss and mourning, thus she created and experienced an after-life relationship in her own private imaginations.

The fact that the two described couples did not focus on a happy future reveals another (darker) side of any relationship, particularly the age dissimilar ones. We might consider lesbian age gap relationships as ones that resist the current health-normative culture, which "requires that we ignore vulnerability, unhappiness and loss and instead look for a bright future with ever-new accomplishment" (Lykke 2015, 85). Here, the Danish feminist scholar Nina Lykke refers to queer widowhood and mourning, writing after the death of her fifteen years older female partner. She beautifully captures the essence of what we would like to claim here: that certain "unhappy" feelings are present in these kinds of relationships, making the lesbian age difference specific and subversive, but essentially also troublesome. Saying this, we do not want to imply that lesbian age difference relationships are unhappy *per se* but that they are fundamentally different, built on different kinds of expectations, where death is always already present as a constant reminder of not growing old together or not staying alive simultaneously. This takes us to our following line of analysis, namely, the ways in which the lesbian age gap, when enacted in the closet or the political space – both in the domestic and public sphere – become connected.

Emotions, politics and disclosure

Different political and social environments advantage or disadvantage divergent attitudes towards displaying lesbian affection in public and "coming out" to friends and relatives, and also in terms of the age difference. For example, having had bad experiences with social attitudes already in the 1950s and the 1960s (before the decriminalisation of homosexual acts in Finland in 1971), Rauni retained a suspicious view of the goodwill of the media and heterosexual people around her. She did not trust them to understand the genuine nature of a sexual relationship between two women separated by four decades of biological age.

Telle adjusted to Rauni's closet arrangements of keeping their relationship out of the public eye but also out of her private family scene. She hid the relationship from her children even though she invested her time and energy in Rauni more than in her own children and home, i.e., staying several days per week at Rauni's place before Rauni passed away. She also dedicated a lot of her time to taking care of Rauni in her final month when she was seriously ill, feeding her and taking her in and out of hospitals, and finding a lawyer to take care of Rauni's will and calm her down. Telle also sorted out the funeral arrangements and emptied and sold Rauni's flat (which she inherited). She also inherited the copyrights and took care of archiving Rauni's artwork. Telle described her situation as socially invisible and vulnerable, since she was not ready to face the potential accusations of using the opportunity to find a fortune:

I had no role models; there is not one social category or culturally known character I could identify with – I needed to negotiate all this in my own head only. Also, now that Rauni is dead would her friends still want to be my friends, too? I am not sure about this, as they are so much older than I am. I have only a few friends who knew anything about our relationship.

In Poland, the younger partner, Edyta, who had had relationships with women for a longer time than Ewelina and thus also had had the time to accept her sexuality more fully, grew up in times of greater visibility of LGBTQ+ people than her partner, whose early adulthood experiences date back to the socialist regime. Because of all this, she was more willing to tell friends and her child about her relationship with Ewelina. However, because Ewelina insisted, she has not told her daughter yet. Also, probably under the influence of Ewelina's preference to keep their relationship hidden from the family circle, Edyta has not told her mother that they are more than friends, even though she came out to her a long time ago:

> However, I introduced Ewelina to my mom as my married colleague from work… I don't know if my mother guesses as much, I do not ask. I told her about my sexual orientation when I lived with my former partner; the response was, "I have heard you, but we're not going to talk about it."

Ewelina was more concerned about expressing her feelings in public or in her everyday affairs:

> My friend, whom I have known for many years, does not know about Edyta and me. I don't know how she would react or whether she would accept it. I'm a little rebellious because, on the other hand, is it my duty to tell everyone that I live with a woman or that I live with a man?

The "not naming things" policy is characteristic for Polish women of an older generation, shaping their attitudes towards disclosure (Mizielińska, Struzik & Król 2022). As Edyta says, Ewelina does not see the need to "make someone happy by naming things." However, this "no need to tell" stance influences the couple's everyday life. Nobody from Ewelina's family knew about her relationship with Edyta, including her own son. The need to keep the relationship unnamed and unknown also involved the decision of not living together. Edyta, who had lived with her previous female partner, did not exclude this option and tried to convince her older partner to move in together. Nevertheless, finally, she was persuaded by Ewelina and gave up. Interestingly, one of Ewelina's arguments against living together was related to her anxiety about the age difference between the partners. According to Edyta, Ewelina told her:

> "Listen, I lived in my husband's apartment for twenty years, and when I wanted to change something in my life it turned out that I did not have a roof over my head and now what? I will live with you five, ten, fifteen years… something might change between you and me, and then what? I will start again when I am sixty-five years old? How often will I start my life again from the beginning? Because actually building a roof over your head is the beginning of an adult's life". And that convinced me.

Arguably, such fears are also connected to the political history and social security system in Poland. The older Polish generation who experienced the sudden crash of the political regime and the uncertainties of housing would probably have more fears connected to losing their home than their Finnish lesbian counterparts to whom the housing system would offer a roof, for as long as they are raising children.

Haunting kinship and lesbian age gap

Contingent and complex political frameworks shape the terms of queer kinship practices, including specific state institutionalised legal practices, such as inheritance arrangements, marriage or civil partnership, possible offspring and everyday support and care arrangements, duties and relations. Therefore, it is vital to contrast how kinship gets formulated or incorporated in lesbian age gap relationships in these two cases, to see more nuances in how the geographies and discourses of desire influence the politics of emotions.

In Finland, Rauni ignored her bloodline in leaving almost all her estate to Telle in her will written just before her death, with the assistance of a lawyer whom Telle summoned. Rauni's close relatives "could not have taken care of her, because some had dementia and others were too busy or too distant", says Telle. Rauni's will is not known to the public, but Telle's ex-husband, with whom she lives in a new bigger flat, which was bought with the inheritance, knows about the relationship and the origins of her newfound wealth. He accepted the situation and participated in childcare in the shared domesticity with Telle. Thus, the ex-husband, who is kin to the children, was not only an inherent part of Telle's support group but he also benefited from Telle's queer inheritance in terms of living in a bigger home and keeping his family together for the straight public eye. However, the children did not know who the "ghost kin" – whose furniture surrounds them at their new home – actually was for their mother. The kids lived in a seemingly normal heterosexual family where the mother's deep and continuing emotional engagement with her dead lesbian lover was expressed in their everyday material surroundings – without them knowing about it.

In Poland, both partners considered the other partner as their family, but they had different ways of (dis)integrating their family of origin and their own family. Edyta writes that "Ewelina's parents do not accept certain things. So she pretends in their presence that they don't exist. But as a result, the parents are not a part of our life."

In contrast, Edyta's parents liked Ewelina, often inviting her to various family occasions. In the opinion of many LGBTQ+ people in Poland, being invited together to a family meeting is often taken as the final proof of the recognition of their blood family (Mizielińska, Abramowicz & Stasińska 2015). Nevertheless, in this case, the recognition was suspended and the nature of the relationship was hidden; Edyta's parents did not know that Ewelina was her intimate partner. Moreover, only by not naming the actual nature of their relationship could Edyta connect the two crucial entities in her life – the family of her own and her family of origin – that otherwise should have to be separated. In this way, they were not "out" as a couple, but nor were they completely "in the closet"; the closet door is never fully open or closed. According to Edyta:

> We even manage to spend the holidays together because my parents are very fond of Ewelina, so she spends just part of the holiday with her parents, and then packs and comes to me, to my parents, and there we all eat together. I do not think that I care a lot to name certain things, play with formulas such as "my partner" or "yes I'm a lesbian, and this is my partner." No. It is just Christmas, and this is someone the closest to me and someone whom my family and my surroundings accept. And this does the job.

Contrary to the distinction between families that LGBTQ+ people create and those from which they come, strongly present in the Anglo-American queer kinship studies (Weston 1997; Weeks, Heaphy & Donovan 2001), non-heterosexual families from geographical environments where family is a primary value tend to build their families not in separated from their families of origin, but integrated. It is mostly because they must depend on them in their daily struggle for recognition and against homophobia, which results in very complex interdependencies with their families of origin (Mizielińska & Stasińska 2018; Zhabenko 2019; Uibo 2021; Mizielińska 2022).

In Poland, facing a lack of rights and unable to find sufficient support within the almost non-existent local queer community and scattered LGBTIQ+ organisations, lesbian mothers, in particular, see their families of origin as the only refuge and source of potential acceptance. Therefore, they express a need to be included in the "traditionally" understood kinship structure as queers, and good relationships with their families of origin are fought for even more stubbornly, even if the toll might be very high (Mizielińska & Stasińska 2018; Mizielińska 2022). In Edyta's case, the emotional price to be paid for the relatives' support is a suspension of the true nature of her relationship. Only in this way, Edyta was recognised as somebody close, and the couple could be together on such significant occasions in Polish culture as Christmas and Easter. A similar strategy was employed when the couple manoeuvred between different forms of (non)recognition (as friends, as couples, and as mothers of their kids), deceiving their families for their own celebration of Christmas. They started to organise Christmas dinner for their friends (of which only some know about their relationship), husbands, and children a few years ago when Ewelina was still married and lived with her husband. Even now, they continued to do so, inviting their former husbands to participate in this ceremony.

The ex-husbands, children, and blood kin were thus integrated in the care and support network both in Poland in Finland in multi-layered ways. These involve intimate and partly esoteric emotional investments, family secrets, material resources, cultural codes, political realities, and even ghosts in different proportions and combinations. In a word, when it comes to lesbians and the age gap, kinship arguably gets even more "messy" than it always already is (Butler 2000). How then, in the midst of such a complex web of private and public secrets, vulnerable emotions, and care commitments, could one look ahead?

Visions in lesbian age gap relations

When queer people talk about their ageing, there is usually a lot of fear and anxiety around facing heteronormativity in care institutions (King 2013; Westwood 2016; Traies 2016). For several reasons, these emotions might be even stronger in the case of age dissimilar couples. Firstly, they know that their ageing process will not be simultaneous, and the prognosis is that the older partner will die first. Secondly, in Poland, the prevailing model of social policy is based on "private familialism" (Szelewa 2015): the obligation to take care of an elderly person relies on their relatives. Usually, women are expected to perform this role; consequently, "private familialism" is very gender specific. A similar ideology is emerging in Finland, where recent right-wing governments put more stress on private care in families, and targeted women as family caretakers in different methods (Sorainen 2018).

Consequently, younger lesbian partners in age gap relationships are always attached to some degree to the role of the final caretaker and may also feel obliged to take care of their older relatives. At the same time, they might have – often as strong and autonomous women who grew up at the fringes of the heterosexual system – problems with being cared for by a partner. In Telle's case, it was never an option that she would not be the caregiver, for it was clear from the beginning that Rauni was already very sick at the last short phase of life and her kinfolks were not at hand. In the Polish case, the age gap was not so big, but it was inevitably at the back of the heads of both partners, not just Ewelina, who articulated some of these worries when she pushed Edyta to AA. We could also see that the fear of being older and not "keeping up" with the younger partner was there from the very beginning. However, the fear of dependency, "being ball and chain," was prevalent also in other stories in Poland, particularly those collected during the focus groups with lesbians over 55 years old (Mizielińska, Struzik & Król 2022).

In Poland, where there is no partnership law, the younger person's role as partner and queer widow would not be recognised at all. The same happens in many countries, where not only queer life but also queer death and mourning for same-sex partners often stay unrecognised and out of public view (Bauer 2017; Alasuutari 2020, 2021). This is also what happened to Telle: almost no one, not even her own children, knows that she is Rauni's widow. Even in the funeral that she organised for Rauni, the latter's relatives had no idea who Telle was, taking her for a hired maid.

In Poland, lesbian mourning is not recognised by society. In Finland, the prevailing law on same-sex marriage offers, recently, more official space for queer widowhood. However, there are still such instances where the law and the lived lesbian realities do not converge, as in the case where Rauni's mistrust of the benevolence of the heterosexual society towards Telle's widowhood prevented Telle from becoming officially widowed. Instead, Telle created in her mind an esoteric queer space where no one but she and Rauni's spirit have direct access, but where the society does not really want to enter either, as queer widowhood is still not fully recognised in Finnish culture.

Another fear that the age gap lesbian couples often express is related to the specific geopolitical locations and the lack of sufficient – or any – LGBTIQ+ relational rights concerning inheritance arrangements, will-writing options, and possible inheritance tax discrimination by the law (Sorainen 2018). Interestingly, these exact problems (death, mourning, inheritance, lack of relationship regulations) were completely absent from the narratives of Edyta and Ewelina – as if they were not there yet. And yet they were present as very urgent problems in the narratives of older Polish lesbians from focus groups interviews that were conducted (Mizielińska, Struzik & Król 2022).

Then again, for Telle, it was obvious from the beginning that she would become the final caretaker. Also, from early on, Rauni made it clear that Telle would be the primary beneficiary of her will. They also negotiated several times whether to register their partnership or not (same-sex marriage became legal in Finland only after Rauni had died). However, they decided to ignore this legal option out of fear of potential anti-lesbian and other adverse social reactions towards Telle as a much younger heiress of the wealthier and artistically more famous woman. This shows that age gap relationships, their concerns, and affects change and show different prisms when we look at them through the lenses of a couple's life trajectory, the prevailing social attitudes, the political sphere, and changing legal landscapes.

Conclusions

In this chapter, we have argued that the age gap is an important element of lesbian desire and is a factor, which from the onset influences diverse areas of lesbian relationships in complex ways and in different geopolitical and legal contexts. The age gap affects how the relationships are lived, experienced, and displayed. However, the question of age gap is silenced in feminist and lesbian/queer writings, possibly because it might be read as a sign of difference, which is also associated with power and inequality in negative, uneducated, and overtly generalised ways. Understood as one definitive lesbian desire, the age gap might haunt the conceptualisations and configurations of lesbian relationships based on assumptions of equality and sameness in similar ways to how butch/femme does, in that it challenges the idealisation of "sameness" between two women (Hollibaugh & Moraga 1983; Nestle 1992, 2003; Dahl 2009). This is one possible reason for its exclusion and tabooing in the lives and social relations of women in such relationships, but also in academic literature.

Queering the very concept of "age gap" makes it a contingent and contextual term, changing over the course of a life and depending on queer time in terms of how long each of the partners has been out. Age gap lesbian relationships are about *many other* differences and they transgress the common preconceptions about such intimate configurations: queer age versus chronological age; community age (the years as being out – or back in); reproductive age; *the age of law* in terms of recognised kin and relationships; age as it relates to the financial situation; the age of intellectual property; how age relates to class and status along with many other factors, all complicating the taken for granted power dynamics in such intimate configurations.

The lesbian age gap also poses a question of temporalities in the understanding of queer communities – not only is there a multiplicity of communities but also multiple reasons to reject or desire community or be a part of it. In this way, our close reading of the two chosen case studies shows that the microdynamics of power in lesbian age gap relationships is defined by many other factors than have been recognised. Some age gap relationships also challenge the happiness duty in our late-capitalist culture, given that such relationships always immediately confront the partners with the possibility of loss and mourning.

The age gap is just one of many differences that can generate new lines of desire and shape what we can do, where we can go, and how we are perceived. We propose that it should not be dismissed but rather studied more closely in various geo-temporal locations.

Only then can we begin to truly understand the transgressive power of desire and love that still, or again, does not dare to speak its name in many countries.

References

Ahmed, S. 2006. *Queer Phenomenology: Orientations, Objects, Others*. First Edition. Durham: Duke University Press Books.

Alasuutari, V. 2020. *Death at the End of the Rainbow – Rethinking Queer Kinship, Rituals of Remembrance and the Finnish Culture of Death*. University of Turku: HUMANIORA, Turku. https://urn.fi/ URN: ISBN:978-951-29-8074-1

---. 2021. "Tied Together by Death – Post-Mortem Forms of Affective Intimacy in LGBTQ People's Stories of Partner Loss." *NORA – Nordic Journal of Feminist and Gender Research* 29 (3): 203–15. https://doi.org/ 10.1080/08038740.2021.1903554.

Bauer, H. 2017. *The Hirschfeld Archives: Violence, Death, and Modern Queer Culture*. Philadelphia: Temple University Press.

Berlant, L. 2001. "Love, A Queer Feeling," in *Homosexuality and Psychoanalysis,* Dean, T. & Lane, C., eds., 432–451. Chicago: The University of Chicago Press.

Bruns, C. M. 2008. "May–December Lesbian Relationships: Power Storms or Blue Skies?" *Journal of Lesbian Studies* 12, no. 2–3: 265–81. doi: 10.1080/10894160802161448.

Butler, J. 2000. *Antigone's Claim: Kinship Between Life and Death*. New York: Columbia University Press.

Butler, J. 2006. *Gender Trouble: Feminism and the Subversion of Identity*. 1 edition. New York: Routledge.

Dahl, U. & Del LaGrace Volcano. 2009. *Femmes of Power: Exploding Queer Femininities*. First Edition. London: Serpent's Tail.

Ellis, H. & Symonds, J. A. 1897. *Sexual Inversion*. London: Wilson and Macmillan.

Halberstam, J. J. 2005. *In a Queer Time and Place. Transgender Bodies, Subcultural Lives*. New York: New York University Press.

Hall, Radclyffe 1928. *The Well of Loneliness. With an Appreciation of Havelock Ellis*. London: Jonathan Cape.

Herdt, G., ed., 2009. *Moral Panics, Sex Panics: Fear and The Fight Over Sexual Rights*. New York and London: New York University Press.

Hollibaugh, A., & Moraga, C. 1983. "What We're Rollin around in Bed with: Sexual Silences in Feminism," in *Powers of Desire*, A. Snitow, C. Stansell, & S. Thompson, eds, 394–405. New York: Monthly Review Press.

King, A. 2013. "Queering Care in Later Life: The Lived Experiences and Intimacies of Older Lesbian, Gay and Bisexual People," in *Mapping*

Intimacies, T. Sanger and Y. Taylor, eds., 112–29. London: Palgrave Macmillan.

Lehmiller, J. J. & Agnew, C. R. 2011. "May-December Paradoxes: An Exploration of Age-Gap Relationships in Western Society," in *The Dark Side of Relationships II*, W. R. Cupach & B. H. Spitzberg, eds., 39–62. New York: Routledge.

Lykke, N. 2015. "Queer Widowhood." *lambda nordica* vol. 20, no. 4: 85–111.

McKenzie, L. 2015. *Age-Dissimilar Couples and Romantic Relationships. Ageless Love?* London: Palgrave Macmillan.

Mizielińska, J. & Kulpa, R. 2011. "'Contemporary Peripheries': Queer Studies, Circulation of Knowledge and East/West Divide," in *De-Centring Western Sexualities. Central and Eastern European Perspective*, R. Kulpa & J. Mizielińska, eds. Farnham and Burlington, VT: Ashgate.

Mizielińska, J., Abramowicz, M. & Stasińska, A. 2015. *Families of Choice in Poland. Family Life of Non-heterosexual People*. Warsaw: IP PAN. familiesofchoice.pl.

Mizielińska, J. & Stasińska, A. 2018. "Beyond the Western Gaze – Families of Choice in Poland." *Sexualities* 21 (7): 983–1001. doi: 10.1177/ 1363460717718508.

Mizielińska, J. & Stasińska, A. 2021. 'Frame Story Approach in Mixed and Multimethod Study on Non-Heterosexual Families in Poland': *Sociological Research Online* 26 (4): 792–809. doi: 10.1177/13607804209 72121.

Mizielińska, J., Struzik J. & Król, A. 2022. "Queer Kinship, Queer Ageing – Perspectives from Poland." *Gender, Place & Culture* 0 (0): 1–23. doi: 10.1080/0966369X.2022.2042210.

Mizielińska, J. 2022. *Queer Kinship at the Edge? Families of Choice in Poland*. Routledge, available Open Access: https://www.routledge.com/Queer-Kinship-on-the-Edge-Families-of-Choice-in-Poland/Mizielinska/p/ book/9780367860387

Nestle, J., ed. 1992. The Persistent Desire: A Femme-Butch Reader. 1st edition. Boston: Alyson Publications.

–––. 2003. A Restricted Country. 2nd edition. San Francisco: Cleis Press.

Oboler, R. S. 1980. "Is the Female Husband a Man? Woman/Woman Marriage among the Nandi of Kenya." *Ethnology* 19, no. 1 (Jan.): 69–88.

Rubin, G. 1992. Of Catamites and Kings: Reflections on Butch, Gender, and Boundaries. In *The Persistent Desire. A Femme-Butch-Reader*, edited by Nestle, J., 466–482. Boston: Alyson.

Segal, L. 2014. *Out of Time – The Pleasures & Perils of Ageing*. London and New York: Verso.

Sorainen, A. 2007. "Moral Panic! The Figure of the Paedophile and Sexual Politics of Fear in Finland," in *Youth, Gender and Pornography*, S. V. Knudsen, L. Löfgren-Mårtenson, & S. Månsson, eds., 189–203. Copenhagen: Danish University of Education Press.

Sorainen, A. 2018. "How the Inheritance System Thinks? – Queering Kinship, Gender and Care in the Legal Sphere," in Agha, P., ed., *Law, Politics, and Gender Binary*, 81–103. London: Routledge.

Stockton, K. B. 2009. *The Queer Child, or Growing Sideways in the Twentieth Century*. Illustrated edition. Durham: Duke University Press Books.

Szelewa, D. 2015. "Polityka rodzinna w Polsce po 1989 roku: od familializmu prywatnego do publicznego?" [Familial Policy in Poland after 1989: from private to public familialism], in *Niebezpieczne związki. Macierzyństwo, ojcostwo, polityka [Dangerous Liasons. Motherhood, fatherhood, politics]*, R. Hryciuk & E. Korolczuk, eds., 105–132. Warsaw: WUW.

Traies, J. 2016. *The Lives of Older Lesbians. Sexuality, Identity & the Life Course*. London: Palgrave Macmillan.

Uibo, R. 2021. *"And I Don't Know Who We Really Are to Each Other." Queers Doing Close Relationships in Estonia*. Stockholm: Södertörn University.

Wekker, G. 2006. *The Politics of Passion: Women's Sexual Culture in the Afro-Surinamese Diaspora*. New York: Columbia University Press.

Weston, K. 1997. *Families We Choose: Lesbians, Gays, Kinship*. Revised edition. New York: Columbia University Press.

Westwood, S. 2016. "Ageing Sexualities in UK Regulatory Contexts," in *Ageing and sexualities: Interdisciplinary perspectives*, E. Peel & R. Harding, eds., 33–52. Surrey: Ashgate.

Zhabenko, A. 2019. "Russian lesbian mothers: Between 'traditional values' and human rights." *Journal of Lesbian Studies* 23 (3): 321–335.

9. Mourning with Rainbow Kin: Approaching Queer Kinship from New-Materialist Perspectives

Nina Lykke

Queer kinship studies show that the beginning and end of life make up contexts where queer and (hetero)normative kinship relations may clash in significant ways. Political and theoretical debates around assisted reproduction (e.g., Franklin 2013; Dahl & Björklund 2014; Lie & Lykke 2016; Andreassen 2019) have made the point in relation to procreation. The minefield of affects surrounding queer kinship relations, when questions of death, dying, mourning, afterlife and continuing bonds enter the picture, has been discussed as part of queer HIV/AIDS debates (e.g., Pearl 1999). Debates on the queering of death are also proliferating in tandem with the unfolding of the broad field of Queer Death Studies (Radomska, Mehrabi & Lykke 2019, 2020), which among others include important efforts to queer understandings of continuing bonds with the dead (Alasuutari 2021).

Drawing on my autophenomenographic,[1] poetic-philosophic research on death, dying, mourning, afterlife and continuing bonds in queer and new-materialist perspectives (Lykke 2015, 2018, 2022), this chapter discusses how corpoaffective bondings, crisscrossing between biological and chosen relations may take on special meanings and agencies in the context of queer widowhood and the performing of queer mourning within a framework of rainbow kinship relations.[2] I define these bondings as based on

---

[1] Autophenomenography (Allen-Collinson 2010) is a method, closely related to auto-ethnography, and, like the latter, is based on the use of the researcher's own experiences as material and an entry point for scholarly analysis. In autophenomenography, the approach is phenomenological, and the focus is bodily, sensuous and affective dimensions of experience. I have further developed the method within the framework of a posthuman phenomenology of mourning, while also using poetic writing as a method of inquiry (Lykke 2022).

[2] In the chapter, I use the term queer kinship to overall theorise non-normative kinship relations. However, when I refer specifically to individual family members to which I became involved in kinship relations through my long-term lesbian relationship, i.e. my

corporeally and affectively grounded feelings such as compassion, love, sympathy, friendship etc., which emerge from many kinds of togetherness, intimacies and desires to be with and for one another, but which are not necessarily based on biological kinship or other kinds of conventionally confirmed family relations. My aim is to contribute to a rethinking of queer kinship on new-materialist grounds which implies that I reflect on the agencies and roles of embodiment, affects, material situations and relations that transcend the individually bounded body, emerging for example from shared temporalities, spatialities or other kinds of transcorporeal entanglements, connectednesses and intimacies. Against this background, I critically-affirmatively transgress the popular LGBTQ+ studies notion "families of choice" that, since Kate Weston's influential work (1991), has been widely used as an umbrella for non-normative family building (e.g., Weeks, Heaphy & Donovan 2001). Weston's term has been useful. Still, it is too limited insofar as it leaves the discussion of queer kinship on a discursive and voluntaristic level. From that point of departure, it is impossible to take into account the bodily and transcorporeal materialities of queer corpoaffective bonding, as well as the ways in which biological relations, including blood ties, perform queer, posthuman agencies of their own in rainbow families. The latter issues are crucial – when it comes to reflections on, inter alia, queer kinship in relation to death, dying, mourning, afterlife and continuing bonds, all of which are the focus of this chapter.

In accordance with the method of autophenomenography (Allen-Collinson 2010), and my further development of it within the framework of a posthuman phenomenology of mourning (Lykke 2022), my analytical material in this chapter is autobiographical and poetic texts (an excerpt from a longer autobiographical essay and a poem). They explore intense corpoaffective moments, related to my beloved lesbian life partner's cancer death some years

partner's children, their children and wives, as well as her siblings, I use the term rainbow kin to avoid confusion. The individual members of my rainbow family do not necessarily identify as queer or live queer lives. As I argue in the chapter, I have stopped using the once popular LGBTQ+ studies phrase "family of choice" (Weston 1991) as generic term, because I find it insufficient.

ago. With a starting point in these texts, I discuss queer corpo-affectivity among rainbow kin. I try to come to terms with the ways in which the bonds between my rainbow kin and I intensified through the shared process of mourning our much beloved partner/mother/grandmother/mother-in-law/sister/friend's death.

Queer kinship circles

The need to understand my queer kinship relations to my rainbow family in a new-materialist and corpoaffective sense beyond the framework offered by the concept, family of choice, arose for me in connection with my partner's death. As articulated in my autobiographical story, *Your Moment of Death,* and the poem *Mourning Circles,* intense corpoaffective bondings – mourning circles – emerged among those who gathered around my beloved, when she died.

YOUR MOMENT OF DEATH[3]

Suddenly you looked different. The skin of your face became even more transparent, and it was as if your mouth, until now wide open, closed partly in a smile, while your eyelids opened a bit so that we saw your dreaming eyes. But at the same time, it was also as if your countenance congealed. 'I think she has died!' Eigil said hesitantly. Then we saw two big waves under the skin of your neck where your artery was. So you had not died, we said affirmatively to each other. We tried to check your pulse. We listened to your mouth. But no more breaths came. The only sound left was the mechanical murmur of the oxygen apparatus. We kept standing with our arms around each other, looking at your smiling mouth and your almost closed eyes. For a very long time. We were as if in a trance – in an unbreakable circle, you, Eigil and me, in a moment which would last forever. At some point we understood that we had to extend the circle. We turned off the oxygen apparatus and called Uffe, Rikke and Naja,

---

[3] This autobiographical story is an excerpt from my essay "Queer Widowhood", first published in the open access journal *lambda nordica* (Lykke 2015: 91–92).

who had gone to bed a bit earlier. We said to each other that it was good that you had found peace.

I phoned the night nurses, who returned and confirmed that you had died. They took out the catheter and morphine drips, and we lowered the bedhead so that you were lying flat. As I wished, your hands were put casually on your duvet, not folded in a Christian gesture. The nurses suggested that we light some candles at the bedhead. But I gently rejected this suggestion. You hated candles due to the polluting particles they emit. Instead, I took a big painted stone from the table in the corner – the one Asker, the rainbow grandson whom I have known for the longest time, found at the beach and painted when he was three years old, that time when, many years ago, when we took him on a vacation together with us for the first time. We put the stone next to your pillow. The nurses left again. We sat down around your bed – and we sat like this for a long time. For a very long time. An endlessly closed circle.

MOURNING CIRCLES[4]

1.
Many are the kinship circles
that spring to life
in times of mourning.

2.
A son sits at a table
with his dying mother and the widow-soon-to-be.
They tell him the prognosis,
and take his hands
united in unfathomable sorrow.
Another son
comes rushing back from Mexico.
The dying mother climbs laboriously

---

[4] The poem "Mourning Circles" is, in agreement with the publisher, Bloomsbury Academic, London, reprinted from my poetic-philosophic monograph *Vibrant Death* (Lykke 2022: 188–190).

out of her deep morphine sleep
to greet him home one last time.
A snapshot from his cell phone
shows mother and son hand in hand.

3.
A son and two old friends arrive
the moment they are called to help
the widow-soon-to-be,
who recognises
that her dying beloved
needs more than one prosthetic extra body
during her final days.

4.
A brother comes to see his dying sister,
bringing her an old and yellowed photo
of him and her,
from the time when they were kids.

5.
A rainbow daughter,
since long divorced from the partner
who first introduced her to the family circle,
but still belonging closely to it,
arrives to say a last goodbye.
For a long, long time
she sits next to
her dying
rainbow mother
whom she has known since she was very young.
Shared tears of grief flow,
when she and the widow-soon-to-be
embrace each other in the hallway,
before she travels back
to where she lives.

6.
So they flock around the deathbed,
sitting there for many hours,
taking turns in holding hands,
and from time to time,
they moisten the lips and mouth
of their beloved
partner, mother, rainbow mother…
In the kitchen, another rainbow circle member is making
a delicious coq au vin
to strengthen the resilience of the mourners.
They watch and care, alternately, for the dying,
taking breaks to eat,
and then return to watch again,
till Death arrives.
After that they sit together, lingering,
around the bed of the deceased.

7.
Three grandchildren stand in silence,
looking at their dead grandmother.
Another grandchild draws a mandala wheel
as a gift for the deceased.
Yet, another rainbow circle member phones a female undertaker.

8.
Then they gather around the table in the living room,
a multiple rainbow kinship body,
united in bereavement,
planning a funeral ceremony together,
which will widen the mourning circle even further.

9.
Yet more mourners take part in the rituals
of fire, air, water, earth, and body,
celebrating all kinds of friend- and kinship bonds,
bringing many gifts to the deceased

with a strong collective wish
that they may be useful for her
when she now transitions
into the unknown.

10.
A sister brings a huge bouquet of tulips
to her dead sister's casket,
and commemorates,
the much beloved and admired elder sister's
magic powers
to fill their childhood games
of a long gone past
with pleasurable horrors.

11.
A widow kisses her dead beloved's casket passionately
covering the lid with many, many dark-red roses.
When the female undertaker drives the hearse away,
the widow follows it,
as long as she can,
blowing thousands of kisses from her fingers:
"My love, my love, we'll meet again!"
A sister puts her arm around the widow,
standing now abandoned,
still waving to the disappearing car.

12.
Two brothers embrace each other, sobbing,
when the hearse leaves with their dead grandmother.
With their arms full of flowers,
two other brothers run home,
so that the January garden, now in full bloom,
can welcome the multiple group of mourners
returning from the funeral ceremony
as one great body,
made up of many rainbow kin- and friendship circles.

Your Moment of Death and *Mourning Circles* address the ways in which mourning in the days around my beloved's death took shape around a collective practice that I performed together with my rainbow kin and friends. To make my argument about the corpo-affective bonds and queer kinship relations, from which this practice emerged, I take a point of departure in a brief summary of the autophenomenographical and poetic-philosophic analysis of death and mourning, which I unfurl in my monograph *Vibrant Death* (Lykke 2022).

I understand death along the lines of Deleuzoguattarian immanence philosophy as a process of "becoming-imperceptible" (Deleuze & Guattari 1988: 279) – a process that implies a "disruption of the self," a "dissolution of the subject," and a "merging into the eternal flow of becomings," i.e., into the flux of dynamic and generative inhuman forces, *zoe* (Braidotti 2006: 252). I build on this immanence philosophical framework. But I also make the point that even though immanence philosophy radically reontologises death as becoming-imperceptible, the movement into imperceptibility/death is still considered from a conventional, philosophical point of view: the subject of enunciation is the philosopher-"I", speaking with hir own death/becoming-imperceptible as horizon. In *Vibrant Death* (Lykke 2022), I give attention to a different position of enunciation. My focus is the speaking position of a mourning "I", who is not occupied by worries about hir own future death, but who laments the death of a beloved, and is absorbed by desires, through love-death, to follow hir to the world of the dead. This alternative position of enunciation adds complexity to the issue of becoming-imperceptible. Different types of existential questions are raised, and different corpoaffective registers come into focus, when the vantage point is shifted from the subject who imagines hir own vanishing, to that of a passionately mourning companion. Framed from this position, the existential questions are not so much related to death as a catastrophe of the subject, but linked to the mourner's quest to navigate the limbo of utter devastation, while the corpoaffectivity requiring attention is framed by desires to reconnect with the dead beloved.

In my book (2022) I have contemplated my journey of mourning from the devastating experience of bouncing against a wall of deadly silence, raised by my beloved's becoming-imperceptible, to spiritual-material openings of new kinds of ongoingness and corpo-affective bonding with the seascape where her ashes are scattered, and the watery assemblages with which they are now merged. What I shall pursue in this chapter is another dimension of my mourning. Namely the experience of an affective void opening, when the huge fund of affectivity and compassion, which my partner had embodied to all of us who gathered around her death-bed, vanished relentlessly the moment she died. As articulated in *Your Moment of Death* and *Mourning Circles,* I co-experienced the violent opening of this void together with my close rainbow kin, when my partner became imperceptible – i.e., when, from one moment to the next, she stopped subjectively beaming affect back not only to me, but to us all. My partner's two sons and their wives were present in our house the night my beloved died, as well as the days right before and after. Even though we all had our individual relations with my beloved and, therefore, no doubt mourned her differently, we nonetheless co-experienced the excruciating pain of her becoming-imperceptible that tore open a black hole in our universe, which absorbed all our affects without letting any recognisable human emotions return to us. I felt that this experience also somehow applied to the broader circles of rainbow kin, including my rainbow grandchildren, gathering in our house soon after to prepare for the funeral ceremony - and to the even broader circles of mourners (friends, other rainbow kin, my biological kin etc.) who came to participate in our self-invented funeral ceremony. If, twisting Spinoza (1996), we ask not only what bodies can do, but what *dead bodies* can do, it is obvious that dead bodies are powerful agents within the bigger or smaller circles casting them as grievable (Butler 2004). Along these lines, the dead body in the midst of our mourning circles was acting forcefully, absorbing us all into a void, which the process of the subject's becoming-imperceptible had violently opened.

However, we also responded to the situation. The first paragraph of *Your Moment of Death* voices a "we" (I and my close rainbow kin) who co-experience the becoming-imperceptible and form an intensely affective and intimate circle around the dead body. *Mourning Circles* differentiates mourners, and individualises mourning perspectives, but the last stanza makes all the mourners turn into one big collective body. In this way, both texts articulate a collective response to the opening of the void. I use the metaphor, circles, in both the story and the poem to articulate the intense and intimate corpoaffective bonding, which was called forward by the being-together around my partner's dead body, and by collectively preparing, inventing and jointly practicing a non-Christian funeral ritual. We form embodied and symbolic circles, made up of corpo-affective intensities and transcorporeal feelings of relatedness, intimacy and belonging, criss-crossing the borders between bio-logically related and chosen kin. I strongly felt that these circles emerged because the mourners who participated in them desired to fill the void, which had been opened by our beloved's death. Or in other words, the mourning circles came about because we tried to trace in the bodily and affective presence of each other, what we all missed so much: our beloved partner/mother/grandmother/mother-in-law/sister/friend's strongly corpoaffective presence and being-there for us.

Rethinking "families of choice"

The experience of a collective, corpoaffective process of mourn-ing, which I have described in the previous section, pushed me beyond an understanding of my rainbow kin as a mere "family of choice". It showed me that I needed more materially grounded conceptual frameworks to come to terms with my gut feelings of intensified corpoaffective relations to my rainbow kin. Until my partner's death, I had defined our rainbow family constellation as a "family of choice" (Weston 1991). My experience of it back then was, for example, resonating well with the comprehensive analy-sis of "non-heterosexual" families, carried out by LGBTQ+ studies scholars Jeffrey Weeks, Brian Heaphy and Catherine Donovan during the mid-1990s, in the UK (2001). These scholars define "families of choice" as a diversity of self-created "life experiments" (2001: vii) in family building among non-hetero-sexuals, characterised in consciously vague and open-ended ways as "something broader than the traditional relationships based on lineage, alliance and marriage, referring instead to kin-like net-works of relationships, based on friendship, and commitments 'beyond blood'", which, however, may "incorporate selected blood relatives" (2001: 9). In a chapter dealing with parenting (2001: 157–180), Weeks, Heaphy and Donovan present several stories of co-parenting lesbian couples, where one or both women had children before they met. These families seem to resemble that of my partner and me. In them, the researchers note a certain difference between the biological mother and the co-mother. The former is taking the main responsibility for the parenting, while the latter is balancing between taking responsibility and not wanting to appear as an intruder to children, who basically did not choose a family situation, which came about because the grown-ups chose to become a couple.

I recognise the difference between mother and co-mother, discussed by Weeks, Heaphy and Donovan. My partner always felt a special, deeply corpoaffective bond to her two children, due to the fact that she had given birth to them and been their main caretaker from the start. The sons, too, have always had a deep affection for their mother, grounded in these intimate bodily and affective bonds. I definitely did not want to act as an intruder to this relation-ship, so my partner's and my relations to the sons have always been different. I got to know my partner's biological sons when she and I became lovers, and I moved in with her and them over 45 years ago. The sons were 5 and 9 years old back then. They eventually accepted me as a co-mother. But as long as my partner lived, she acted as the main parent in relation to them (more important also than the biological father). I performed as a queer co-mother, and saw us all as a family of choice in the broad vague sense that the term is used by Weeks, Heaphy and Donovan (2001). This way of relating continued, when the sons grew up, married, and got child-ren themselves, who are now also grown-up, one of them having two kids with his partner.

While Weston's (1991) concept of a family of choice worked for me as a useful analytic until my partner died, it fell short once I had started to contemplate the significant changes, which my beloved's death called forward in my relation to my rainbow kin. When I began to reflect on these changes as part of my autophenomeno-graphic and poetic writing on death and mourning, it became clear to me that new theoretical approaches were needed. Excess meanings started to proliferate for which the framework, family of choice, had not the conceptual capacity to account. Retrospectively, I also began to acknowledge that excess meanings had been on the agenda earlier – without me really putting focus on it. My relationship to the grandchildren, daughters-in-law, and also to the biological siblings of my partner had already earlier corpoaffective dimensions in excess of the understanding, produced by the discursive and voluntaristic framework, family of choice. It dawned on me that I had not reflected this thoroughly, while my partner was still alive. It was the collective process of navigating the void of imperceptibility into which I and my rainbow kin became palpably pushed due to my partner's death, and my urge to try to understand the process philosophically, which generated a need for alternative theoretical approaches that could account for the intense corpo-affective bonds of the emerging mourning circles.

The corpoaffective states and bondings, calling for other theoretical frameworks than voluntaristic discourses of "choice" and "life experiments" (Weeks, Heaphy & Donovan 2001) were related to the process of collective mourning, discussed with *Your Moment of Death* and *Mourning Circles* as a pivot. I shall end this part of my discussion of mourning with rainbow kin, digging a bit further into the alternative theoretical frameworks that I suggest. However, at the same time, I want to avoid imposing explanations and theorisings on my rainbow kin, paying respect to our differences. Because even though we shared the need to mourn together, there were and are existential differences between our entrance points to the quest for navigating and making sense of the affective void, opened by my beloved's death. Therefore, I only take the contemplation of my own urge and attempts to navigate the void further – here and, more elaborately, in my book (Lykke 2022).

For me an important entry point to the void is based on my contemplations of my compassionate companionship with my partner (2018, 2022). This companionship unfolded as a corpoaffective attunement, which I define as "an intense sensitivity to the other's body and affective condition, based on what the philosopher Ralph Acampora (2006: 76), in a Spinozist sense, called *symphysis*" – i.e., a bodily co-experiencing "implying that the subject, in a material, corpoaffective sense, is affected by and co-experiences the ways in which hir significant others are bodily affected" (Lykke 2018: 116). Co-experiencing my partner's corpoaffective relation to her biological children, and their families, I deeply co-suffered with her profound feelings of grief when it became clear that it was not in her powers anymore to avoid causing them (and us all) intense grief through her death. The intense co-suffering with my partner during her years of illness awakened corpoaffective desires in me, as best as I could, to make up for the sons' and their children's deep corpoaffective experience of loss of their mother's/grandmother's embodied subjective presence and being-there for them. I think that it is these desires that made me wish to embody and enact more aspects of the parental relation that my partner had had to them than I had done earlier, when I still saw us as a family of choice with me as the co-mother. I so to speak started to feel an urge to corpoaffectively embody the space of the mother, while humbly acknowledging and in my enactments of it taking fully into account that I am different from my partner, and have to embody this space in my own way.

Along the lines of these reflections, the process of change vis-a-vis my rainbow kin to which my partner's death committed me can be described as a move from *co*-mothering to more fully desiring and in practice trying to corpoaffectively embody the mother/grandmother/great-grandmother space in the intergenerational rainbow family constellation. It stood out to me that these desires and the process of trying to materialise them in practice through new kinds of transcorporeal bondings could neither be reduced to a voluntaristic question of choice nor understood exclusively on a discursive level. What emerged was deepfelt queer desires to become as corpoaffectively connected to my rainbow kin as my partner had been in her capacity of mother – desires which was certainly not guided merely by choice.

Corpoaffective temporalities of queer kinship formations

To deepen the autophenomenographic analysis of my intense queer corpoaffective bonding with my rainbow kin in the wake of my beloved's death, this last section will zoom in on an incident, which was triggered by my first publication of the mourning story (*lambda nordica* 2015: 4), relating in particular to the second paragraph of *Your Moment of Death*. After having read this text, my younger rainbow son made me aware that my use of the phrase "our oldest grandson" (Lykke 2015: 92) (now rephrased to "the rainbow grandson whom I have known for the longest time", this volume) reproduced a temporal normativity with exclusionary effects. In a gentle, but still hurt way, my rainbow son told me that, with the label "our oldest grandson", I excluded two of my rainbow grandchildren who were older than the one to whom I referred. My younger rainbow son's wife had three children with an earlier partner, and two of them were in their preteens and teens, and still living together with their mother, when my younger rainbow son moved in with the family. My younger rainbow son and these two boys developed a strong bond to one another, and they started to call my partner and I "grandmothers." These two boys were both some years older than the eldest son of my older rainbow son, i.e., the grandson who as a 3-year-old painted the stone I placed on my dead partner's pillow instead of following the night nurses' suggestion to light candles. Against this background, the phrase "my oldest grandson" was exclusionary, implying that I did not include these two children in my inner and most intimate circle of rainbow grandchildren.

I became very sad when my younger rainbow son made me aware of this, and my sadness prompted me to reflect upon my use of the phrase "our oldest grandson" in the *lambda nordica*-text. Had I just reproduced a conventional phrase that imitated hetero-normative kinship relations? Indeed, vigilant self-criticism and resistance to the cannibalising logics of heteronormative kinship discourses, built on intersections of biology and lineage, is indeed necessary when trying to establish queer, non-normative kinship relations. It would be naïve to assume that such self-critical reflections would not be needed even in situations where all parties desire to establish queer kinship relations and make them work in non-normative ways. I consider an opening of spaces for discussion, negotiation and reflection to be an important aspect of the queering of kinship relations. Such relations are established and developed in a continuing practice, not just jumping out of blue air as a deus ex machina.

So, I welcomed my younger rainbow son's critique. But it also made me sad and upset that I might have acted in an exclusionary way, and more so, because it was too late to change the text in the first publishing of it. I had, indeed, earlier, before submitting the text to *lambda nordica*, put much weight on sharing it with my rainbow sons to make sure that I did not transgress boundaries of intimacy, regarding their deceased mother, with which they would not feel comfortable. I saw it as an ethical obligation on my part to include them in decisions on publication, since my memories and images of my partner and our rainbow family, which I interpellated in my texts, were touching upon their memories, too. However, due to specific circumstances, related to another dramatic death in our close rainbow kinship circle, my younger rainbow son did not get to read my text properly until after it was published.

The speculations that the situation triggered kept circling around the question: what was at stake for me in this particular text? Did I use an exclusionary phrase because, uncritically and unconsciously, I imitated heteronormative kinship relations and their underlying prioritisation of blood ties, lineage, and temporalities related to them? Or were other meanings and associations at stake? And if so, how were they related to the grandson who had painted the stone, which I put next to my dead partner's head? The painted stone, indeed, had many meanings. Firstly, it was a relic, memorialising the first of many vacations that my partner and I went on with the grandchildren. The memory of this particular vacation, which took place in the late 1990s, was emotionally tinged by the fact that it was the first time that this grandson, back then only 3 years old, was away from his parents for a week. Such a long period of being away from one's parents can be tough, when you are that young. So, my partner and I worked really hard the whole week to do the grandmothering work, which also was new to us, in a way which could make this 3-year-old kid feel happy, and not become too home-sick. The memory of the vacation, metonymically embodied by the painted stone-relic, was thus very emotional. It reflected my partner's and my sharing of our first experience of grandmothering without parental interference, as well as our intimate, long-term relationship to the grandson.

Secondly, my grabbing of the stone was related to my first act of protecting my beloved's dead body from being submitted to Christian-tinged norms surrounding death. The grabbing of the stone was a spontaneous response to the night nurses' suggestion that we lit candles, when they came to our home right after my partner had died to help me to relieve her body of the catheter and other devices. In the hours and days after my partner's death my gut feeling told me to resist and disrupt all the Christian normativities, which well-meaning people, such as the gentle and friendly night nurses, impose on you in this situation. During the days after my partner's death, these normativities - and an alertness to the ways in which they tended to sneak behind my back - became more and more conscious to me. The spontaneous grabbing of the stone, however, was the very first of these acts of resistance, at the time prompted by a mere gut feeling. I was so devastated by my partner's death about an hour earlier that I did not reflect very much, but rather let myself be led by gut feelings, which strongly prompted me to keep Christian symbols and gestures out of the picture. Like me, my partner was a feminist atheist, who definitely did not want to have her death inscribed in any gestures and rituals of a deeply patriarchal religion such as Christianity.

When I wrote the text about my partner's death for *lambda nordica* a year later, I was retrospectively aware of the grabbing of the stone as an act of resistance to Christian normativities. By that time, I revisited the stone as an alternative, strongly affect-laden, queer kinship-related relic. But again: why did I use the phrase "our oldest grandson" (Lykke 2015: 92)? While contemplating this issue after my younger rainbow son had taken me to task for it, it struck me that I had not given that particular phrase much attention, when I wrote the text for *lambda nordica*. However, another thought came to my mind as well in this moment of retrospective, self-critical reflection. Namely, that strong corpoaffectively grounded temporalities, actually, were at stake for me here. I have known the grandchild who painted the stone as a 3-year-old longer than my other rainbow grandchildren, even though he by age is younger than the rainbow sons of my younger rainbow son. My younger rainbow son and his wife started their relationship several years later than my older rainbow son and his wife had their two children. Therefore, in terms of time duration, I have had a queer kinship relation to my older rainbow son's children longer than I have known my two older rainbow grandchildren, the rainbow sons of my younger rainbow son. Moreover, I have known the rainbow grandchild who painted the stone, intimately, since the day he was born. My partner and I were invited to visit all the grandchildren who are blood-related to my rainbow sons, when they were newborn, and we have had the privilege of holding all of them in our arms from the very start of their lives. What struck me when contemplating these relations as a background for the phrase "our oldest grandson" is that it is important to think through how temporalities become agents in the forming of queer kinship relations. Corpoaffective intimacies, built up over time, tinge queer kinship relations in specific and meaningful ways. As other relations, queer kinship relations hold the potential to deepen with time, when you (the parties engaging in them) are mutually committed to establish an intimate companionship of being there for one another.

Against the background of these retrospective reflections, I came to the conclusion that my phrase "our oldest grandson" had thoughtlessly popped up in my text, and I should, indeed, have reflected more critically, before using it. But that said, it did, indeed, resonate with an important corpoaffectively grounded temporality that characterised my relation to this rainbow grandchild. He was the one, with whom my partner and I had established intimate bonds in terms of our first grandmothering experience. Moreover, we had known him over a time period, which spanned his entire life. To come to terms with these temporalities, it makes sense to speak about him as the rainbow grandchild whom I have known the longest. The changed wording, which I use in the text excerpt reprinted in this volume, allows me to ethically address my younger rainbow son's legitimate complaint about my first thoughtless phrasing, while, at the same time, also recognising how temporalities do play a role in relation to the emergence of queer corpo-affective bonding.

Conclusion

In this chapter, I have discussed the significance of corpoaffectivity in queer kinship relations with a focus on death, dying, mourning, afterlife and continuing bonds. Through an autophenomenographic approach, based on poetic, autobiographical explorations, I have contemplated corpoaffective experiences of changed and intensified relationships to my rainbow kin, which emerged in the wake of my lesbian life partner's death.

Based on a Deleuzoguattarian analysis of death as a becoming-imperceptible, I have suggested that my partner's death made my rainbow kin and I co-experience an affective void, to which we responded through collectively shared, albeit individually differently situated processes of mourning. In my analysis of our collective mourning practices, I have addressed the ways in which we formed mourning circles, trying to trace in the bodily presence of each other what had vanished from us: the subjective being-there for us of our beloved partner/mother/grandmother/mother-in-law/sister/friend. I also discussed how this process for me meant that my relations to my rainbow kin intensified in ways that made the classic LGBTQ+ Studies notion, "families of choice" (Weston 1991), fall short. Contemplating my corpoaffective move from identifying as a lesbian co-mother to desiring to subjectively fill the mother space that had become void through my partner's death, emphasised the necessity of a corpoaffectively, new-materialist grounded understanding beyond the discourse-theoretical and voluntaristic concept, families of choice. To further qualify the new-materialist and affect-theoretical approaches to the analysis of queer kinship relations, the last section of the chapter focused specifically on the agency of temporalities in the formation of inter-generational rainbow kinship.

I hope that my autophenomenographic analysis has shown how new-materialist and affect-theoretical entry points to queer kinship can open important analytical horizons beyond the concept of families of choice.

References

Acampora, R. R. 2006. *Corporal Compassion: Animal Ethics and Philosophy of Body*. Pittsburgh: Pittsburgh UP.

Alasuutari, V. 2021. Tied Together by Death – Post-Mortem Forms of Affective Intimacy in LGBTQ People's Stories of Partner Loss. *NORA. Nordic Journal of Feminist and Gender Research*, 29 (3): 203–215.

Allen-Collinson, J. 2010. Running Embodiment, Power and Vulnerability: Notes Towards a Feminist Phenomenology of Female Running. E. Kennedy & P. Markula, eds. *Women and Exercise: The Body, Health and Consumerism*. London: Routledge, 280–298.

Braidotti, R. 2006. *Transpositions: On Nomadic Ethics*. Cambridge: Polity.

Butler, J. 2004. *Precarious Life. The Powers of Mourning and Violence*. New York, London: Verso.

Dahl, U. & Björklund, J. 2014. Kinship & Reproduction. Special Issue. *lambda nordica* 19: 3-4.

Deleuze, G. & Guattari, F. 1988. *A Thousand Plateaus: Capitalism and Schizophrenia*. New York, London: Continuum. Transl. Brian Massumi.

Franklin, S. 2013. *Biological Relatives: IVF, Stem Cells, and the Future of Kinship*. Durham: Duke UP.

Lie, M. & Lykke, N., eds. 2016. *Assisted Reproduction Across Borders. Feminist Perspectives on Normalizations, Disruptions and Transmissions*. New York, London: Routledge.

Lykke, N. 2015. Queer Widowhood. *lambda nordica*. 2015: 4: 85–111.

Lykke, N. 2018. When Death Cuts Apart. On Affective Difference, Compassionate Companionship and Lesbian Widowhood. T. Juvonen & M. Kohlemainen, eds. *Affective Inequalities in Intimate Relationships*. Routledge, New York, London: 109–125.

Lykke, N. 2022. *Vibrant Death. A Posthuman Phenomenology of Mourning*. London: Bloomsbury Academic.

Pearl, M. 1999. *Alien Tears. Mourning, Melancholia, and Identity in AIDS literature*. Warwick: Warwick UP.

Radomska, M., Mehrabi, T. & Lykke, N. 2020. Queer Death Studies: Death, Dying and Mourning from a Queerfeminist Perspective. Special Issue. *Australian Feminist Studies*, vol. 35, Issue 104.

Radomska, M., Mehrabi T. & Lykke, N. 2019. Queer Death Studies: Coming to Terms with Death, Dying, and Mourning Differently. Special Issue. *Women, Gender and Research*, 2019 (3-4).

Spinoza, Benedict de. 1996. *Ethics*. London: Penguin Books.

Weeks, J., Heaphy, B. & Donovan, C. 2001. *Same Sex Intimacies. Families of Choice and Other Life Experiments*. London, New York: Routledge.

Weston, K. 1991. *Families We Choose: Lesbians, Gays, Kinship*. New York: Columbia UP.

10. Yours in Struggle: Baltic Dialogues

Ulrika Dahl & Joanna Mizielińska

Baltic battles

The Baltic Battle-party has taken place every year since 1978. The first one was organised as the official opening of the – at that time – new clubrooms in the Old Town and was a joint venture with MSC Finland. Because our Finnish brothers would travel across the Baltic, the party was named The Battle of the Baltic Sea (in Swedish) with the English translation Baltic Battle added.

From the very first party, in August 1978, it was a big success. It included a boat trip around the southern neighbourhood island and the main party took of course place in the new premises. Tom of Finland was specially invited and showed how his drawings were created, these who later become world famous. MSC Finland brought a jumping leather jack toy as a gift, which is framed behind acrylic glass in our current clubhouse.[1]

As the above story drawn from Baltic gay male leather culture suggests, queers have met and formed affinities and relations across the Baltic Sea since before homosexuality was declassified as an illness in Sweden in 1979 and Finland in 1981.[2] Indeed, the party described above, organised by and for leather men, points to a queer history of regional interconnectedness, one that is also reflected in decades of migration and centuries of changing national borders and rule around the sea. It also points to how (queer) affinity is not only constituted in reproduction but that "brotherhood" can also be made in "battle", and kinship ties formed through (sex) partying, including before the so-called fall of the Iron Curtain. Approaching the Baltic Sea as a body (of water)

---

[1] https://www.balticbattle.se/; last accessed 2022/01/04

[2] For more discussion about the history of homosexuality in Finland, see Moring this volume.

that both separates and joins us, it is clear that gender and sexual politics remain at the centre of both affinities and politics.

While queers continue to travel and migrate across the sea for love, labour and livelihood, there is also a long and complex Baltic legacy around reproductive sexual politics. Swedish women travelled to Poland for abortions in the 1960s when the Polish law was more "liberal" than the Swedish one. Today, as Polish women take to the streets to defend the right to abortion, Swedish feminists advocate welcoming Polish women to Sweden. Swedish women travel to Finland and the Baltic states to achieve pregnancy and acquire donated gametes and both Swedish and Polish women travel to Denmark to obtain donated sperm, while growing numbers of sperm donors in Denmark are reportedly recruited among students from Baltic and Eastern European nations.

If the Baltic battle described above points to a transnational queer community of sexual outlaws and gender transgressors, to a certain kind of visibility politics and to a geopolitically defined sense of kinship between queer men, *Queer(y)ing Kinship in the Baltic Region* as a research project not only built on this kind of shared and divergent history, it also aimed to depart from and create a differently related form of Baltic interconnectedness, namely that between four differently situated queer feminist researchers (that is, a Swedish queer fem(me)inist ethnographer trained in the US with a focus on intersectional analysis of queer family making and critical approaches to the biopolitics of assisted reproduction (Ulrika), a Polish interdisciplinary queer scholar with deep roots in and commitment to the lived experiences of LGBT people in Poland and a commitment to decentring Western theoretical hegemonies (Joanna), a Finnish anarchist and queer anthropologist with a long term interest in the historical dimensions of queer relationalities and legal systems, in how heteronormative kinship structures inheritance, and in how queer forms of will-writing reflects alternative forms of kinship (Antu), and an Estonian sociologist and gender studies scholar with a core commitment to rethinking practices of care and closeness in the context of Estonian neoliberal precarity (Raili). For nearly a decade now, and with a broad shared orientation, this team has navigated and discussed everyday challenges and dilemmas of doing research in communities to which we also belong in different ways. Departing from different geotemporalities, we have navigated in politically tumultuous times, where LGBTQ+ issues, including queer kinship and family-making have often been central to what can only be described as a conservative turn both within and between our different nations that we have both experienced and analysed differently.

Arguably, this broader conservative turn is most visible in Poland, where the ruling Law and Justice party has advocated a decidedly anti-LGBTQ+ agenda and built its nationalist-conservative discourse around casting LGBTQ+ families as a threat to the traditional Polish family and to the nation (Graff & Korulczuk 2021). In a speech at the party convention in Katowice in 2019, leader Jarosław Kaczyński insinuated that same-sex couples want the right to adopt children because of their desire for sexual gratification and stated that his party would never agree to marriage and adoption by same-sex couples. Commenting on the prohibition of sex education in schools, Kaczyński declared that "this has nothing to do with tolerance, but the affirmation of same-sex couples to whom we say no, especially when it comes to children. Hands off our children!"[3]

Meanwhile in Estonia, a nation that only a few years ago was the first post-Soviet state to propose a same-sex partnership law, members of the populist Estonian Conservative People's Party have instead called for a referendum on marriage and keeping it as a union between a man and a woman. Speaking to *Deutsche Welle* in 2020, interior minister and a deputy party leader Mart Helme said in response to a question about whether the partnership law would flood the Estonian nation with gays: "Let them run to Sweden. Everyone is there, everyone looks at them more politely,"[4] and stated that he personally had a decidedly unfriendly look on gays.

---

[3] Onet.pl. 2019. 'Jarosław Kaczyński: Wara Od Naszych Dzieci. Fala Komentarzy – Wiadomości'. 2019. https://wiadomosci.onet.pl/kraj/jaroslaw-kaczynski-wara-od-naszych -dzieci-fala-komentarzy/tyx6hqs; last accessed 2022-10-01.

[4] https://estonianworld.com/life/estonias-interior-minister-let-our-gays-run-to-sweden/; last accessed 2022-01-04.

While prime minister Jüri Ratas denounced Helme's statements, the threat that queers and queer relationalities seemingly pose to the Estonian nation is noteworthy, as is the need to clearly distinguish Estonia from the nation across the Baltic Sea.

In Finland, although the legal landscape on queer kinship issues has been even cutting edge in recent years (see Moring, in this book) the increasing popularity of True Finns and other right-wing conservative voices amongst the voters has made the proper establishment of Trans Law politically very difficult.

At the same time in Sweden, like in the Nordic region as a whole, the last decade has not only seen progress for LGBTQ+ people, but also an overall conservative turn in gender politics, the anti-immigration and staunchly family-conservative party Sweden Democrats becoming the 2nd largest party in the latest election in 2022 (see also Möser et al. 2022). Material inequalities have grown exponentially, in great part thanks to the continued privatisation of the welfare state, most notably healthcare and including reproductive medicine. While not quite oligarchy, it is certainly problematic that taxpayers are now contributing to filling the pockets of the elite. At the moment of writing, it is unclear what "progressive" LGBTQ+ politics actually means in the different nations around the sea, but undoubtably, questions of (gay) marriage and family have, in the words of Judith Butler (2002, 21) "become sites of intense displacement for other political fears, fears about technology, about new demographics, and about the very unity and transmissibility of the nation, fears that feminism, in its insistence on childcare, has effectively opened up kinship outside the family, opened it to strangers."

As participants, we have worked around and with these challenging times, while simultaneously bringing in a range of understandings of the core concepts of family and kinship, and how we are to understand the ways that queers live and make family and what it means to this project. Perhaps it is not so much a battle but a series of productive tensions in this project, where the queer geopolitics of knowledge production has animated our work. At the same time, our own bodies, working conditions, and personal lives have been differentially impacted by the times in which we live. In order to capture some of the core tensions and the lessons from them, this closing chapter is a dialogue between Joanna Mizielińska (JM) and Ulrika Dahl (UD) that explores rather than seeks to solve some of the core epistemological and geopolitical differences between us, in order to see how they have come to matter in this project and to the contributions and interventions we have sought to make.[5]

The conversation is divided into thematic sections. We begin by discussing how we arrived at studying queer kinship in this constellation and the context in which we began the research. In the following section we discuss what we mean by queer kinship. This is followed by the central section where we explore questions of temporality and geopolitics and how our own distinct positions, both intellectually and geopolitically, matter for what we do. The chapter ends with a brief discussion about what we have learned during this project and where we want to go next.

Arriving at queer kinship as a research question

UD: As Sara Ahmed (2012, 2) puts it, "[e]very research project has a story, which is the story of an arrival." Kinship is at the heart of gender, sexuality, race and nation, a kind of organising metaphor, and to ask questions about kinship thus involves asking core questions of identity, belonging and affinity. Perhaps we can start with how we arrived at researching *queer* kinship and family making or cross- and intergenerational intimacies more broadly?

JM: I started to think about a project on queer kinship in Poland around 2010. At that time, there was no research on this topic at all, no books, no articles except those that mostly translated Western findings into Polish. When I presented some of my pilot studies based on interviews with lesbian mothers I was treated with disbelief and ignorance because queer families and parenthood

---

[5] The dialogue began as a set of questions circulated to all four members via email but because Uibo was completing a doctoral thesis and beginning postdoctoral life, and due to Sorainen being on medical leave, it ended up being completed as a dialogue between Mizielińska and Dahl. All project members have however provided feedback on this version.

were perceived as something that did not exist in Poland, only in the "rotten West." At that time, complex, mixed and multi-method research was urgently needed in order to also undermine the heteronormative Polish vision of the traditional family (see Mizielińska 2022; Mizielińska & Stasińska 2020b).

When I started, I was mostly influenced by the approach of British "new family studies." Instead of assuming how non-hetero-sexual people live or taking for granted that they do not build families – a tendency that has been prevalent in every public opinion poll and most of books and publications within the canon of the sociology of family in Poland (Adamski 2002; Tyszka 2005) at that time – I wanted to ask the members of such families how *they* define their family, how they construct its composition and meanings through their practices and activities, what they need and in which way they would like to have their relationships recognised (in social or legal terms). Inspired by new family studies (NFS) (Gubrium & Holstein 1999; Levin 1993; Cheal 1993; Bernardes 1997; Gabb 2008) I have focused on the process and practices of doing families (Morgan 1996).

This approach helps to reverse the attention from an essentialist and normative vision of family as a static entity and starting point of research to a landing point allowing to embrace all kinds of human relationalities and intimacies, which was more than needed in the context of Polish family studies at that time. However, as an approach developed within Anglo-American academia, it might be considered as a part of a hegemonic universalist perspective and cannot be applied uncritically. In my analysis I acknowledged its epistemological and geographical situatedness and tried to be very sensitive towards local perspectives and other epistemologies. For instance, what doing and displaying families means in Poland might be completely illegible from the UK perspective where queer families are recognised, legally protected, and have become a part of the social landscape, in terms of their visibility, among other things (Mizielińska & Stasińska 2018, 2020a). I also reached for concepts and ideas from non-Western contexts, notably coined by academics working in the CEE, such as the "transparent closet" and "family closet", developed by Slovenian scholars Roman Kuhar and

Alenka Švab (2014), which have been useful for describing a very specific type of reaction that families of origin have to non-heterosexual coming out/disclosure, namely a strategy of passing over this fact, ignoring it (transparent closet) and not mentioning it to other family members and friends (family closet).

In my theoretical inspiration, I also find postcolonial scholarship on marginalised queer families (Acosta 2018; Decena 2011; Moore 2011) useful. In general, in postcolonial works, there is a tendency to question Western dominant explanatory models of queer lives that do not capture the experienced realities of Non-western locations. Many works question the validity of identity categories and coming out imperatives, showing that in other places where the meaning of family is different, people find other ways to negotiate their sexualities. For instance, in Decena's (2011) ethnographic study of Dominican gay men, he presents their tacit negotiations of the closet. In their attempts to sustain kinship bonds that they find particularly significant, they develop tacit ways to express their gayness, rendering redundant the Western coming out imperative.

UD: It is interesting how the cold war rhetoric of "the Rotten West" lives on and acquires new meaning, and it reminds us of the centrality of LGBTQ+ questions to national and European politics in the 21st century. Your story here also points to core questions in the project, namely how to study queer families in their distinct locations without getting caught in rigid comparative frameworks, but also to how some concepts are helpful and others less so as they "travel." To my mind the tradition of "new family studies" or "doing family" (British or not) is an excellent way to capture the meaningful everyday family making practices in which queers engage, their gendered forms of labour if you like, and it is no surprise that it's been very much used to study lesbian families, for instance.

In terms of how I arrived at studying queer kinship, several stories – intellectual, political and personal –intersected and pointed me in that direction. I was trained by feminist anthropologists and science and technology scholars in the US in the nineties, so in a sense kinship and reproduction was at the centre of all my training. I was early on introduced to Weston's (1991) and Newton's (1979) work on how queers made kinship and gender and to Lewin's ground-breaking (1993) work on lesbian mother-hood, and my early work on sexual and reproductive rights had also led me to Strathern's (1992), Haraway's (1997) and Franklin's (1997) work on assisted reproduction. As questions of kinship, family and reproduction are central for theorising and under-standing gender, sexuality and race, my training also pushed me to think them as central concepts and organising principles for how we think about (feminist) knowledge. So, in a sense kinship and reproduction have always been at the heart of my thinking.

My arrival at proposing *Queer(y)ing Kinship in the Baltic Region* as a project had much to do with time and place. I had done work on gender equality and regional identity building in the context of Sweden's entry into the EU, on the geopolitics of Nordic gender studies, and on the figure of the queer and lesbian femme and the politics of femininity; all of which involved kinship and repro-duction in different ways and I wrote about the new family law and the initial refusal to tackle the question of insemination in 2003 (see Dahl 2003; Nordqvist 2006). Here it also matters that in Sweden there is a tradition of queer scholarship that goes back to at least the mid-nineties, and that moreover LGBTQ+ rights are central to the national self-image, to the extent that it is not impossible to get support and funding for queer research topics.

On a more personal note, I also belong to the first generation of LGBTQ+ people who have had marriage and reproductive rights in fertile age and for whom having children was imaginable. Following the changes in family law and access to assisted repro-duction in Sweden in the early 2000s (see Dahl, this volume), there was a literal baby boom in my own queer generation and com-munity, and with that came new research, especially on lesbian parents (Ryan-Flood 2005; Nordqvist 2006; Malmqvist 2015). I was fascinated by the many different paths, rationales and struggles queer people went through and described around me, and above all, by the stories of relatedness that emerged. To some, known donors were important, whereas to others, anonymous donors were favoured and they were of no importance to the family (Polski

2013), and at the same time, the Swedish state made clear that only registered and approved donors who could be found would be approved. While some actively chose multi-parent models, others struggled to re-make motherhood through rethinking biology and care. It seemed that at the intersection of an increasingly privatised public health sector and a growing global fertility industry, there were many possible paths, and yet, each came with its own set of legal conditions, and far from all were able to achieve their dreams. At the same time, people made their own sense of the new legal and technological possibilities and found very different models of family, often in relation to their own complex family stories. In some respects, the queer families around me (with or without children) were similar to Weston's (1991) insofar as people both seemed to "choose" and make complex families, often involving friends, exes, co-parents, and at the same time, the legal frameworks seemed also to increasingly define and constrict what counted as family and kinship. I found that increasing numbers desired having "their own" children and were entangled with their biogenetic families.

My own queer politics and personal disinterest in reproducing myself made me ambivalent about both the assimilationist tendencies of the law (that is, the state's investment in creating a normative order in a queer chaos of reinventing relatedness) and about how the law increasingly seemed to create and structure power relations between parents (see also Nordqvist 2006). What is really queer about queer reproduction, I wondered. What is being reproduced in queer reproduction? In some ways it seemed that queers were being coerced into reproducing normative national values.

I was both interested in how the law reinscribed biogenetic and heteronormative kinship and the importance of fathers (and thus the regulation of donor-conceived families) and also struck by how often the queer dream of family "failed" (Dahl 2014); that is, getting married and having children, did not quite provide the "happy ever after" it was expected to do with many getting divorced. For some, this led to even more complex queer families, and for others to quite challenging battles around defining parenthood; all of which pointed to the complex and often contradictory workings of understandings of kinship that blood and law provide. Considering all these issues, I was also struck by how much of the emergent scholarship tended to focus on the white majoritarian population and their struggles with heteronormativity. Focusing on queers of colour in Sweden, I wanted to contribute to what Acosta (2018, 407) has called "queerer intersectional family scholarship" that "attends to how race, gender, class, and sexuality shape material reality rather than relying only on the experiences of the White middle-class to build family theory."

Like you, I have found a lot of the work on queer families conducted within the sociological tradition of "doing family" helpful and this work also echoes with how (queer) anthropologists have challenged conventional kinship models; even if for anthropologists the question of what it means to care for others also centrally includes questions of what it means to be related. I too draw on queer of colour scholarship, including the work of Eng (2010), Acosta (2011, 2018), Rodriguez (2014) and others, both because it points to the limits of those queer kinship studies that focus on and depart from white middle class subjects' experiences and because of the great need to attend to how legacies of colonialism and histories of race relations shape categories and experiences of gender, sexuality and family and for intersectional analysis and critical analysis of the nation state as a framework. So maybe what you mean by "Western" here is actually white hegemony?

JM: Not really. What I mean by Western is more complicated than that. It is true that most of the time it means Anglo-American because there are differences within "the West" to which we need to pay attention. But I speak from a very particular position that is neither West nor East. I speak from the periphery and this periphery has different power dynamics too, with its own exclusionary practices, and its own underdogs and scapegoats. On the other hand, it is important to note regarding your point about whiteness that there is a certain hierarchy here too. Some scholars aim to prove the use of racist language in relation to CEE and argue that "Eastern Europe might appear as being functionally on the side of the colonial and racial Other" (Melegh 2006, 39). Melegh, for instance, shows how racist language and racist scaling appear in the contemporary discourse on the East-West slope. Others show rather racial ambiguity towards CEE and talk about functionalist and cultural racism in operation. They point out that already in the 19th century, the founders of scientific racism perceived Eastern and Central Europeans as racially inferior and in need of being governed (Boatcă 2006; Kulawik & Kravchenko 2020; Melegh 2006). In her study on German colonialism, Kristin Kopp demonstrates that popular and scientific discourses presented Polish Eastern provinces of Prussia as a colonial space. There were no differences in the concepts used to describe the colonised lands in Africa and the Poles (Kopp 2011). Also, the Nazi politics were rooted in the classification of both Jewish and Slavic people as members of inferior races. More recent work on post-Yugoslavia shows the whole region as deeply embedded in the transnational formation of race (Baker 2018).

UD: Yes, it is entirely true that histories of race are central to the making of European enlightenment and also that the history of racial science is full of hierarchies of whiteness that also at times map onto persistent "East"-"West" rhetoric (something that Brexit made very clear). I think for me the point is that questions of race (at times masked as nationality) are central to reproduction and kinship, as the literature on third party assisted reproduction and the global fertility market makes clear. Privileged white Westerners frequently make use of donated eggs and surrogate arrangements in the former East (including the Baltic States and Ukraine) where treatments and arrangements are "cheaper", while at the same time creating and drawing on racialised ideas of likeness and difference and yet again while encountering homophobia. We may also add the gendered politics of labour migration here, with significant numbers of care workers in Western Europe from CEE countries.

What is queer about queer kinship?

UD: As we outline in the introduction, we all had stakes in decentring the Western, Anglo-American dominance of feminist and queer kinship studies as they relate to national identity, community making and social life, and ambitiously, we have aimed to intervene not only with empirical insights from different national contexts, but also on the level of theory. In some ways, this is about how we understand the different questions, methods, literatures and discussions we locate our work in. As we glean from our arrival stories above, a crucial question for us in the project, like in the field at large, has been how to think about what is queer about queer kinship; a theme that you, Joanna, have become a leading scholar of in recent years.

JM: In some way kinship is always already queer or at least it carries a queer potentiality because people always transgress the rules and norms of kinship in some ways or others. They do not live according to kinship norms either. However, their hegemony influences ways of thinking about kinship and its right forms. For me, queer in queer kinship is something that always questions the normative ways of forming relationships and living one's life; it is about opening a range of possibilities. But what is queer depends on the context – its gender, sexual and relational norms that govern people's decisions about the right (and wrong?) types of relationships. Queer is about subverting these norms, but this subversion does not need to be overt, quite the contrary it could be very subtle, tacit even. Again, depending on the context. In one context holding (or even touching) a hand of a loved one in a public space might be a queer gesture, in others it is just a normal way to express one's intimacy (Stasińska 2020). Queer in kinship also means something very obvious – transgressing the heteronormativity and its norms regarding the right family/kin forms with strict gender roles.

UD: I agree that in a way everything and nothing is queer about kinship, at least on a conceptual level. If kinship is always already queer because kinship is ultimately rules and norms that concern positions and relations, and that never quite define how people live and practice relations, then (heteronormative) kinship, like the genders and sexualities it organises and is organised by, is perhaps an ideal that we aspire towards but never quite live up to. We are all imposters in kinship, if you like. Add to that the way that assisted reproduction as such certainly queers heterosexual reproduction, while same-sex love also queers the core kinship symbol (intercourse) and we have ourselves a clearly queer phenomenon. At the same time, the growing legal regulation of "same-sex" kinship in Sweden illuminates the limits of "queering" kinship insofar as it also reinscribes an emphasis on knowledge about biological origins as in the best interest of the child.

Indeed, the pull of kinship as a theme or phenomenon to study, I think, has to do with its significance for regulating and organising the population through human reproduction and thereby also gender and sexuality, and by extension, identity. As you say, kinship is a kind of cultural terminology, a set of names for positions (wife, mother, sister, daughter, niece, etc) that define relations and that as such always have to be narrated, upheld in stories. As rules these kinship positions (derived from heterosexual reproduction) are powerful (and hegemonic); they are both the basis for laws and logics and are defined by those. A cultural logic where heterosexual reproduction is understood as the basis for "real" kinship and other forms, including "adoptive," "social," and "bonus" kin always refers to this allegedly universal original. At the same time, the nuclear heterosexual family is obviously a modern historical invention. In Sweden, the emphasis on (biological) fatherhood is relatively recent; it was not until the 1930s, when it became in the interest of the state to ensure that (biological) fathers supported children financially that an idea of knowledge about biological heritage began to be emphasised. Ironically, this also led to heightened stigmatisation of single mothers in the 1950s (Nordqvist 2006).

Does queer kinship, the kinship created by queers, unsettle this logic? I am interested if, how and when queer kinship, understood as a challenge to binary gender relations and reproductive heterosexuality as the origin of culture and the family, might or does unsettle the relationship between family and nation, and by extension in how reproduction is crucially always about race and gender. In other words, to my mind, queer kinship is not only a question about how to make family outside of the gender and sexuality norms or the law, but given the context in which I am working, if and how the existence of queer families actually alters broader societal conceptions of family and kinship. On the one hand, raising children outside of the idea of mommy-daddy-child unsettles the very idea of how the nation is reproduced. On the other hand, as long as queer families fit into the overall demographics of the population they are tolerated more. As you can see, I am very influenced by Butler's (2002) discussion about the possibilities and limitations of desiring recognition and legitimacy from the state. I am also in a sense less interested in recognition as such and more interested in what difference the (legal and cultural) organisation of kinship makes, to the formations of both subjects and states.

JM: Well, I guess we speak from two very different positions because in my geotemporal locations all queer families are put outside the state imaginary, even worse, they are made into a public enemy, a scapegoat even, by the same nation state to which you refer. So, I am rather speaking about unrecognisable queer kinship. And although I am also inspired by Butler, I am probably more interested in recognition than you are, again because of this difference in location (see Rich 1994). I wonder what it means to live recognisable lives as queer families in countries with inclusive legislation and recognition of queer families and parenthood, as opposed to struggling with one's own invisibility and precariousness as queer families in every step you make, because you want to "lead a good life in a bad life" (Butler 2012). This is precisely why I have used the term "family" in my project despite the debates and doubts about usefulness of the term "family" within Anglo-American queer theory (Roseneil and Budgeon 2004) I was familiar with. Because the term "family" is so mythologised and overloaded with heteronormative assumptions in Poland, I have opted for using it and claim its political importance in given (Polish) circumstances. For instance, when I did presentations and/or gave interviews in Poland the use of the term "family" was often criticised. Introducing my project, I was asked "How many of *that* do we have in Poland?" It was as if the one who asked this question couldn't say the word "family" in the context of non-heterosexual relationships (and he was/is not the only one). This is precisely why I thought it important to retain the term, stick with/to it even. In a country where "family" is strictly reserved for the nuclear model, and other models are openly refused to be called families daring to reach for such a sacred word, using it in the context of same-sex relational life was in fact a political gesture and aimed to change the mainstream discourse as well as the self-perception of LGBTQ+ communities.

UD: That makes total sense. Indeed, it is clear that geopolitics matter and the question of recognition is of course not irrelevant; perhaps the conceptual point from Butler (2002) here concerns the paradox of recognition itself, where on the one hand living without it causes immense suffering and on the other, achieving recognition inevitably tends to lead to new forms of hierarchies and exclusions. So, it seems that it matters which terminologies we use and we have stakes in those we chose for specific intellectual and political reasons. We are both navigating a kind of borderland, where on the one hand we want to make interventions into the political and scientific contexts in which we work, and on the other hand, we want to make interventions into the broader international field of research. Like you say, each research project needs to specify what makes kinship queer, and that means that work on queer kinship always needs to provide "thick description" (Geertz 1973), including historical and cultural context. I find what Jenny Gunnarsson Payne (2016) calls the grammars of kinship and the ways people tell and retell their stories of relatedness quite fascinating and it's something I would like to attend more to.

Different temporalities = different positionalities?

UD: *Queer(y)ing Kinship in the Baltic Region* was conceived in a moment of veritable explosion of research on queer kinship and family making, particularly in Euro-American scholarship and from a shared desire to both gather empirical data and to intervene in the debate on the level of theory. Yet, while queer kinship, family-making and reproduction are clearly timely research topics that we as project members have grappled with over time and in different research time arrangements, they are also entangled in multiple temporalities, both personal, historical and geopolitical. How can we unpack the different positions from which we have understood the field and our own positions? How do we conceptualise geopolitical and geotemporal location as they relate to doing research on queer kinship? Our goal was not "comparison" as such, but rather to think together about different themes that came up in our respective projects, and yet we have frequently ended up comparing our contexts. We do live and work in different nations with different histories related to both LGBT+ movements and research on these topics. Add to that our different trainings and methodologies and our relations to the international field of interdisciplinary queer studies. What are your thoughts on this?

JM: I am always reminded of from where I speak, especially during international conferences where I am frequently the only person from CEE. I always remember that "I am where I think", to repeat Walter Mignolo's (2011) statement, paraphrasing Cartesian "Cogito ergo sum." It is the perfect exemplification of a decolonial approach to the geopolitics of knowledge production, and it explains my understanding of knowledge as always already located. As Madina Tlostanova (2015, 48) puts it, "the geopolitics of knowledge refers to the local, spatial and temporal grounds of knowledge. The body-politics refers to individual and collective biographical grounds of understanding and thinking rooted in particular local histories and trajectories of origination and dispersion. Locality here is understood not merely as a geo-historical location but also as an epistemic correlation with the sensing body, perceiving the world from a particular local history."

To me it is clear that there are different temporalities between "West and the rest"; and the imposition of Western temporality forecloses full recognition of difference in LGBTQ+ movements and rights and how these differences influence thinking about queer kinship. It also dictates the way debate is held internationally as well as its content. In popular historiographical accounts of the sexual liberation in the West, we have the narration that spawns from 1950s and 1960s homophile days, through 1970s gay liberation, 1980s AIDS, to 1990s queer times. In the book *De-Centring Western Sexualities*, which I edited with Robert Kulpa, we used concepts of the "temporal disjunction" and "knotted temporality" and contrasted the Western conception of "time of sequence" with

CEE "time of coincidence" to describe differences in teleological development of sexual politics. For the CEE, "history" (the "new" Western history, which, from 1989, is supposed to be a universal one) happened almost "overnight." We argue for distinguishing between Western and Eastern geotemporal modalities. What we meant is not that there has been no development or change of "events" in the sexual politics in the "CEE" (both in the past and currently). What we meant is that 60 years of Western history is squeezed and is supposedly to be "reworked" in the "CEE" over only a few years, hence the feeling of immediacy and "all at once" mobilisation. But also, that there is ignorance about the CEE present, as it is seen as Western past. And only recently there are diverse attempts to bring back this forgotten post-socialist past, to debunk the myth of the near-total isolation of CEE during the Cold War and bring back some of the forgotten histories of homosexuality in the Eastern bloc, which might be read as a further step in this de-centralisation we asked for. For instance, in his very inspiring book *Transnational Homosexuals in Communist Poland* (2017), Łukasz Szulc shows that only by dehistoricising homosexuality in CEE, was it possible to present the whole region as homogenous, essentially homophobic, and in need of transition after 1989 (Szulc 2017, 7). As he rightly points out, some Eastern bloc countries decriminalised same-sex acts before many allegedly progressive West countries. For instance, Poland decriminalised (or in fact never criminalised) same-sex acts before many countries of the allegedly more progressive West, including Denmark (1933), Sweden (1944), England (1967), Canada (1969), West Germany (1969), Austria (1971), Finland (1971), Norway (1972), and the U.S. (entirely in 2001). It questions the teleological development of sexual politics and its unidirectionality and its taken-for-granted progressiveness. It also challenges the genealogies of origins as always already located in the West.

UD: Yes, I certainly hear you on these points! I wonder why it is that LGBTQ+ rights and movements, especially when placed on a global scale, are always cast and caught in a teleological progressive temporal framework that is really at odds with the reality of political change. At present, LGBTQ+ questions are increasingly central to contemporary political tensions, between nations and transnationally, including in 'anti-gender' movements (Kuhar & Paternotte 2017; Graff & Korulczuk 2021) and in this sense, I don't think we can see a smooth progress narrative at all, rather, we see questions pertaining to reproduction, gender, and biopolitics and movements for rights that are differently entangled with larger logics of neoliberalism, privatisations of welfare states and global fertility industries.

I share your commitment to a decolonial approach to knowledge production, one that certainly has to do with geopolitical location and that I have come across both within my US training (through Black, Indigenous, Latinx and Chicana feminisms) and through studying European gender studies for a long time. All of this for me is centrally related to European colonial and imperial projects that go back at least 500 years and also of course to the cold war of the 20th century, which means it is largely about different ideological approaches to how the state should relate to and perhaps, regulate, capitalism. If you find yourself coming up against temporal fantasies of what the East is like, I always have to challenge the deeply held fantasies of Sweden as social democratic paradise, as progressive, as a paradise of gender and sexual rights, devoid of colonial legacies or racism. Furthermore, and I suppose in part because I have worked within Baltic and CEE area studies, I also see a lot of productive travel between and conversation (and scholarly mobility and exchange) around how to understand the impact of these histories on contemporary intellectual and political work.

To my mind, considering LGBTQ+ issues solely in geopolitical terms, that is, using the nation as a taken for granted entity, inevitably involves grand generalisations and often seems to need "straw figures" to argue and position ourselves against. In the book you mention above, Łukasz Szulc (2017, 4) critiques the tendency "to blend fact and fiction, and thus, individually and collectively, perpetuate recurrent myth," not only of CEE but also of the so-called West. Indeed, the three geopolitics myths that Szulc identifies within the larger discussions about the globalisation of sexuality (in particular questions of identity, rights, and movements) include the myth of homogeneity whereby "both CEE and the West are all too frequently created as relatively uniform geopolitical entities adopting relatively uniform approaches to gender- and sexuality-related issues" (2017, 5), which as he contends, requires that we ignore differences within and exaggerate differences between regions, in order to make grand sweeping generalisations that also tend to flatten out complexity and ignore connections. He points to the problems of casting the West as "essentially progressive, that is, post-racial, post-feminist and post-gay, and CEE as essentially backward, that is, racist, sexist and homophobic" (ibid). Importantly, Szulc here points to the temporal myth whereby capitalism is cast as a political and economic system that brings about liberal stances towards gender and sexuality and whereby the East is lagging behind and at best able only to imitate what has already happened. All these myths rely on an idea of the "East" as isolated pre-1989, which as you point out, Szulc's own work on homosexuality and exchanges across borders clearly disputes.

Following Szulc, I find it interesting to track not only how LGBTQ+ rights became a global issue in the early nineties through a Western dominated Human Rights discourse and being placed on both UN and EU agendas and spurring a range of different objections due to their entanglements in Western neoimperialism (Szulc 2017, 26) but equally importantly, how neoliberal capitalism, or queer liberalism has shaped demands made by LGBTQ+ movements in different places.

Whilst "homosexuals" in Sweden have long had families and children (often conceived in heterosexual "relations", but not only), I am not so sure that legal changes and recognition is only thanks to the LGBTQ+ movement's "success" in rendering "us" visible. Rather, it seems to me that the emergence of new reproductive technologies and the onset of a global fertility market in the nineties, coupled with particular understandings of gender equality and children's rights to an origin and to access to two parents have been equally important. Clearly, the Swedish state has a vested interest in regulating reproduction and kinship for all sorts of reasons, including ensuring that a child is provided for by two parents (or else the state becomes a stand in parent), but it has also created different laws for differently conceived children, making the "easiest" path to joint recognition is to conceive via state health-care whereby the state also decides who is a suitable donor and what gametes to use. I would argue that a century of Social democratic welfare state building profoundly shapes how LGBTQ+ questions have been treated and how activism and demands have developed. Relatedly, it doesn't make sense to me to understand Swedish recognition of LGBTQ+ rights (especially to marriage and kinship) simply as "progressive" by comparison to some imagined homophobic other (indeed that is part of Swedish homonationalism). Rather, I think that Swedish homonationalist politics are deeply entangled with questions of immigration and demographics, and also reflect a distinct form of biopolitical regulation of national reproduction, with differentiated outcomes for differently situated people; far from all have access to these rights and far from all queers are allowed to reproduce the nation.

It seems clear across our empirical research that the struggle for rights is not a linear process that achieves all-encompassing inclusion, but rather, LGBTQ+ movements both work within and beyond the nation, they are entangled with party politics, economic development and a range of other forms inequality. In that sense, how people actually live and practice kinship and the networks and relationalities they are entangled in and draw on to achieve dreams of family, cannot simply be reduced to geopolitical location. An intersectional approach to queer kinship that attends to how material conditions, racial positions and citizenship are entangled with sexual orientation and family making in different geopolitical localities that are in turn shaped by complex historico-political processes is needed in order to challenge simple dichotomies of East and West.

JM: That is why it is perhaps important to distinguish between Western and Anglo-American geotemporalities, which influence our positions towards and against them as queer academics. I cannot speak in any other name but myself. My position as a queer/sexuality researcher is strictly connected with CEE position of being in between, as part of the contemporary semi-periphery (to use a concept developed by a Serbian philosopher Marina

Blagojevic), always trying to catch up with the more advanced "centre". Blagojević (2009, 34) argues that the semi-periphery is fundamentally "transitional, in a process of transition from one set of structures to another set of structures, and therefore it is unstable, and often has characteristics of the void, chaos, or structurelessness". This in-betweeness is particularly visible when as a CEE academic I try to translate concepts and theories that originated in the Anglo-American context and check their usefulness in the CEE. This process of translation demands mitigating different obstacles and challenges from both Anglo-American and Polish contexts. It also demands an understanding of cultural and social borders and acknowledging/respecting local epistemologies. And this is probably completely different for you as a person trained in the Anglo-American context but working in Swedish academia.

UD: It is interesting to consider training, it is a bit like "childhood", isn't it, assumed to shape us forever. I have been a practicing academic in Sweden for 20 years now, yet in some people's views I am "American" in my way of thinking. Yes, there is no denying that my training has influenced my thinking, but I think this has more to do with where I trained and with whom than with some generalised idea of the US. For sure, there is a long history of debating the hegemony or dominance of Anglo-American concepts in the Nordic region as well (see Dahl et al. 2016; Mulinari 2001; Widerberg 1998). Yet, what I always found fascinating here in Sweden is that by assigning geopolitical belonging to certain concepts (for instance, it is commonly stated that "race" and "queer" are American concepts) they can also be disavowed as not useful. When I reviewed the history of Nordic gender studies (Dahl et al. 2016; Dahl 2011), it was very clear that concepts that challenge the progressive story of gender equality, or perhaps rather, that question the "primary" focus on gender (as opposed to an intersectional approach) were not warmly welcomed and have since often been cast as "additional perspectives."

JM: Interesting what you say about "disavowing concepts" because I do not have such experience. From what I observe, the discussion about the dominance of Anglo-American concepts in the CEE (but also beyond the Western academia) is not so much about disavowing but rather about showing how certain concepts work differently in different circumstances, like I explained with the concept of the family at the beginning. But also with the concept of what queer might mean in different circumstances or the concept of whiteness (and racism) and scales of Europeanness based more on ethnicity and religion than race in the region (Boatcă, 2006). Since in the past I had been interested in the politics of translation of queer theory in the Finnish context in my queering Moominland project I remember that my queer interviewees there did not question certain concepts to save their privileges but rather to show their complicated functioning there.

UD: Sure, concepts work differently in different locations, but if we take questions of race and racism for instance, questions that many white feminists have been quick to dismiss (through statements such as "I don't see colour" or "race is an American concept, we don't have race here" or "it is also difficult to be an immigrant from a different European country", etc.), it not only makes it difficult to address racism, it also basically refuses to acknowledge the work of many, many critical race, postcolonial, and black scholars *in* the Nordic region who use these concepts (and others) in their work. At many international conferences, people frequently assume that the North of Europe, Scandinavia/the Nordic region, is one homogenous region, and moreover, that it is a sexual and gender utopia where gender equality is achieved, marriage is gender neutral and recognition of parenthood is not reduced to contributions of sperm and egg/womb. To me this is not only a reflection of a kind of progress narrative, it is also a fantasy and my research has found that people don't necessarily walk around with a warm feeling of being recognised and affirmed. It also seems to me that in an era of neoliberal capitalism, all nations are involved in various forms of "catching up" (catching up to *what* exactly, is a bit unclear at this point). Again, I would say that it is not so much the historically social democratic nation state as it is the privatisation of large sections of the public good, including housing, care, education and so on, a neoliberalisation on a large-scale including individualisation, that has pushed the advances in LGBTQ+ rights;

that is, rights become obtainable through individualism and that market logic. This by no means makes me a fan of neoliberalism, quite the contrary, I am deeply sceptical of the (neo)liberal discourses of rights. So, what do we mean by catching up? What scale are we talking about, who is it that needs to catch up and to what? It seems to me that the whole machinery of thinking about history as progress has ended, certainly with the acute climate crisis and the overall destruction of the planet, but also with the current shift to the right and the rise of massively conservative movements across Europe and the world.

JM: Maybe it ended in some (queer) academics minds but it did not disappear totally. And in writing about "catching up" I have tried with Robert Kulpa to reconstruct the dominant narration about CEE regions and its "delays" in developing sexual politics. This narrative uses Western LGBTIQ gains (ignoring that there is still a lot to be done in the so-called West) as a litmus paper for the democratic credentials of CEE. And I do believe following other scholars from the region that thinking about CEE in terms of time and not place (see for example Tlostanova 2012, Kulawik & Kravcenko 2020) is often responsible for ignorance of CEE local specificities or simply an expressed lack of interest. As Tlostanova (2012, 132) rightly writes, "the almost overnight vanishing of the second world led to a typical Western understanding of the post-Soviet as a time, not as space. It is the time after socialism and not the dozens of millions of rendered irrelevant lives of those who inhabit the post-communist space." It means that the specificity of the East European perspective and the post-socialist conditions tend to disappear, including the specificity of queer lives there. The whole region starts to be perceived as dislodged, a semi-periphery similar to the West but not similar enough. Not completely Other but not the same either. As a consequence of such disappearance, CEE functions as "Western's Europe incomplete self" (Boatcă 2006, 100), slowly catching up with the more advanced "centre," particularly regarding its sexual/reproductive politics and LGBT activism (Mizielińska & Kulpa 2011).

It has also consequences for production of knowledge about queer kinship. Seeing contemporary CEE concerns as Anglo-

American/Western past overlooks differences. It also means that the Anglo-American scholars dictate what is considered the most pressing and cutting-edge issues concerning queer (kinship) studies, as Pako Chalkidis also rightly observes in this volume, pointing towards its preoccupation with reproduction. For instance, now when the West has entered its post-marriage phase, the scholarly debates focus on homonormativity of queer reproduction, often not acknowledging the importance of fighting for recognition of queer families in Poland, because they are seen as reminiscent of problems the West has already solved. Consequently, possibilities of profound articulation of the specificity of the CEE position showing that the so-called old Anglo-American/Western problems might function differently elsewhere, resulting in different resistance practices, are not so interesting for Western academia, or, if they are then they are just treated as yet more case studies for a long–known phenomena (see Mizielińska 2020, 2022).

UD: Yes, I agree that there are all kinds of stereotypes and mainstream political fantasies of CEE, but when it comes to *our field*, I keep wondering who you are referring to and where this narrative of dictation happens? It seems to me that what you are saying here is a problem about both national and European (re)unification, identity-building and integration; it is a project that has been going on for centuries. Certainly, in popular culture and dominant EU discourses for example, there are ideas about how "progressive" or "modern" different nations or regions are or of "how far we have come" in various places and of course, like all stereotypes, those feature in academic debates as well. A different take might be to say that since 1989, CEE has become incredibly interesting and important for, for instance, Sweden, demonstrated, among other things, in the amount of funding for research that aims to understand the "new" Europe in all its different specificities, its joint histories, its common futures and shared problems. Maybe you are trying to capture a feeling, or an impression of being placed in a particular way, attributed to a position?

JM: You know that you have just questioned the whole bunch of decolonial works which point out the hierarchy in knowledge production, or what you have just called "narrative of dictation", right? And the fact that CEE becomes "incredibly interesting and important" to understand proves exactly my points. Interesting for whom and why? Another case study? Another exoticised "tamed savage"? Attila Melegh, in his book *On the East-West Slope. Globalization, Nationalism, Racism, and Central and Eastern Europe* (2006), tries to capture the paradox traced in the dominant discourses on CEE. On the one hand, 1989 marked the end of the distinct "Eastern" category within Europe and the slow disappearance of the whole East-West divide (in terms of CEE). On the other hand, this divide is still present, although debated with regard to different, geographically, and politically understood contexts. Whenever CEE fails on its Western development path, it causes lamentation about the impossibility of transplanting certain "Western" practices or transcending certain developmental phases (Melegh 2006, 9), and an outbreak of experts searching for the real cause of this failure. Usually, they use arguments of still unfinished transition (i.e., CEE are in the "state-building" phase whereas Western states have entered the "post-nationalist" era) or return to their new/old stereotypes about true Eastern nature, i.e., "East is East" arguments and/or discourses of the so-called Soviet/Balkan mentality (Melegh 2006).

UD: OK, I understand that what you are hearing is dismissal, perhaps that is part of the challenge here. I am not at all saying that our present, including our scholarly conversations, are not deeply marked by the past century in ways that position us differently, nor am I dismissing the profound insights offered by much feminist scholarship from the region. What I *am* saying is on the one hand that due to historical changes that are far beyond the control of academics, we have now had at least 30 years of rich knowledge exchange and production (some of which has happened through collaborative efforts, like ours) and that I do think this makes a difference, and on the other hand, simply that I am not always sure that all epistemological differences can be reduced to geopolitics of location, rather, I think they are also often theoretical and political. Some of the most important psychoanalytic theorising, for instance, certainly comes from "Eastern Europe", to give but one example. Indeed, the current rise of fascism and right-wing extremism all over Europe can hardly be reduced to an East-West divide. I remain interested in thinking about capitalism, neo-liberalism, socialism and social democracy as historical ideological forces with intense material effects.

But if we get back to our own field, to my mind what we might call interdisciplinary queer studies is very heterogeneous, both theoretically and methodologically; it consists of scholars and traditions asking specific questions to specific locations or data sets from particular points of view. For instance, I'm not sure there is such a thing as a "post-marriage phase" (and I agree that is a grandiose and unhelpful descriptor). For whom? Where? Rather, there are ongoing theoretical and political debates around marriage as a mode of recognition and different takes on what is queer about it. Theoretical and political debates around its significance seems to me related to the core fact that so many rights, including rights to citizenship and immigration, reproduction and kinship recognition, care and divisions of labour, and so on, are tied to marriage. If we think of queer theorists who are critical of marriage as the "one size fits all" solution to gay respectability, they are by and large critical of queer liberalism as a paradigm (e.g., Duggan 2002; Eng 2010; Eng & Puar 2020). The work of queer scholars of colour and decolonial scholars also points to the limitations of these liberal models of recognition, especially in settler colonialist nations but I would also include rapidly dismantling welfare states under late capitalism, such as Sweden and other Nordic countries. To my mind, there are no "solved" issues when it comes to kinship and reproduction; rather, these issues reflect particular national histories and take on different meaning in different times, to differently positioned bodies. Our task as researchers is to analyse and make sense of complexity and attend to details. I think we do and should challenge the teleological narrative that you describe.

JM: Of course. I couldn't agree more. But when I say "post-marriage" stage I refer to a scholarship that discusses this problem and also names it as such taking marriage right for granted. Let me give you an example. Look for instance at *Queer Families and Relationships After Marriage Equality* edited by Michael W. Yarbrough, Angela Jones and Joseph Nicholas DeFilippis. It collects papers presented at the conference held in 2016 entitled "After Marriage: The Future of LGBTQ Politics and Scholarship." The main aim of this book is to analyse the situation of queer relationships in different countries in what they call that after marriage-period that they presuppose we are all in. The book focuses on the question what are the impacts of same-sex marriage on queer family formations: does it push them into normalisation and resemblance of heterosexual marriages and if so, what happens to those queers whose relationships do not fit into this homogenous marriage model? Although it presents interesting and diverse international articles, ranging from empirical papers to interviews with activists, it still lacks the perspectives of those countries, like Poland, where same-sex marriage or partnership is a highly contested option, probably not available for queer people in the nearest future. In the West/Anglo-American contexts, the way I see it, reproductive freedom and queer parenthood are recognised and ARTs and surrogacy are available, which of course does not mean they are available to everybody and in the exact way/proportion. There are still all sorts of inequalities and discussions about abuses and exclusionary practices of these reproductive freedoms along with those around the reproduction of homonormativity and racism, the need for trans rights, etc. In Poland, when we asked in our survey about methods of having children in the future, most of the younger generation said that they would choose ARTs with an anonymous donor (women) and surrogacy (men). In reality, people mostly have kids from previous relationships with men and/or through finding semen via the "black market," since from 2015 ARTs is reserved for heterosexual couples (married or cohabited). And surrogacy is forbidden. The reproductive problems of Polish queers might look like old Anglo-American/ Western problems whereas in fact they are not. Because they currently include reproduction in their life trajectory in comparable ways as Western queers and the lack of choice and reproductive rights does not stop them from pursuing their plans (i.e., having children). However, their ways or what I call tactics in my new book (Mizielińska 2022), are different, because they are often forced to circumvent the law, finding the loopholes in the system, etc. Therefore, the question of choice as taken for granted in many Anglo-American/Western debates (focusing on possible abuses/failures, reproduction of race, homonormativity) is less central for them and for me in my attempts to understand their daily practices because they rather struggle with limits of choice (see Mizielińska 2020).

UD: Hm. This is an interesting and quite generalising narrative of the West that also speaks to Szulc's myths that I talked about above. I think we can usefully distinguish between modes of reproduction and forms of recognition of parenthood. Certainly, in Sweden there is "reproductive freedom" in the sense of free and available abortion and contraception and those with wombs who under a certain age can pass the tests of mental health and have the socioeconomic means, and that it is possible to have children through ARTs and that surrogacy happens within a global fertility market. Of course, the "inclusive" family law sends an extremely important message, no denying that, but neither signal "availability", but rather at best "possibility" and each comes with a complex legal procedure through which the state regulates kinship, with deeply biopolitical results. I read the literature you mention as in part concerned with Butler's (2002) questions concerning what kind of qualitative difference same-sex parenting and marriage might make to our understandings of kinship, and in turn to gender and sexuality. To my mind, it is possible to read Poland's current position on this matter as pointing precisely to the centrality of LGBTQ+ issues to nation building; if only through vehement refusal of what you yourself has shown is a sociological fact; queer families already exist.

The point of discussing those "abuses" you mention, is to question the idea of "universal" rights, to call attention to the global dimensions of power and to how reproduction and family-making involve dimensions beyond sexual orientation, often depend on a market logic and a neoliberal idea of what makes a good life, and that far from all can obtain what perhaps *appears* available for those who desire a reproductive futurity. Yet, the discrepancies that you describe are everywhere in my work too; far from all can realise their dreams. What I call a "fertile" generation that comes of age in an era of rights (Dahl 2018a, 2018b) imagines family life in accordance with what is available to them and at the same time, the way that people actually live with children and make family is not simply as same-sex headed nuclear families with "their own" children. I would strongly argue that what you describe as "choice" here is itself indicative of a market logic – quite far from what, for instance, Weston (1991) was talking about.

Choice is overrated as a term with which to think reproduction and family; in fact, my own research has taught me that few people actually simply have "families of choice," they have multiple forms of kin relations and quite flexible grammars to describe these by and for many people. Kin is not chosen, nor does it always recognise one's own family. In my work, I've tried hard to understand what queer kinship "is" or "does" beyond what the state sanctions or what is obtainable in the market and then retroactively fought to have recognised (such as in the case of transnational surrogacy). It is clear from the survey that I discuss in another chapter in this book that "equality" is far from achieved for all LGBTQ+ people in Sweden, that many struggle with their families of origin, and also the fact that recognition from the state also comes with subjection to its regulations. Is that reproductive freedom? I don't know. Justice? Not really. Are all forms of "chosen families" or queer parenthood recognised? Most certainly not. So when I read your work, I certainly don't think of the queers you work with as being in a different time or fighting for something that has already been "achieved", in fact, I often see similarities in how differently situated queer subjects negotiate and articulate "feelings of kinship" and that all queers live, in a sense, global lives and imaginaries. It seems to me that what Butler (2002) meant when she discussed the dilemmas of "desiring the state's desire" in "Is Kinship always already heterosexual?", namely that with every legal change and inclusion, there are new exclusions and boundaries drawn around what counts as legitimate relations, is an ongoing question for all of us and that the fantasy of linear progress must be disputed. We must ask freedom and recognition for whom, when, where and how?

JM: I agree. But I think that we ask similar questions from different geo-political locations and it matters. It seems to me that we also deal with different types of biopolitics and ways of regulating queer lives. When in CEE queer subjects/families are governed by punishment/prohibition and non-recognition, in Sweden they are controlled by inclusion on the condition that they will reproduce the right version of the nation. And this conditional inclusion gets idealised by CEE queers who, for instance, do not understand the critique of commercialisation of Pride parades because in their geopolitical contexts one can be put into the prison for hanging the rainbow flag on the statue and/or heavily beaten by wearing the rainbow badge.

UD: Fair enough. And those differences, as you say, matter profoundly in the everyday lives of queers. I think I am also trying to make a distinction here between analytical frameworks and empirical data, even if that distinction is extremely difficult to make, especially when we are also entangled in these political projects in different ways…

Queer methods: Living and researching queer kinship

UD: One of the great benefits from this project has been learning from one another's methodological approaches and working with mixed methods. What have been some of the gains and insights provided from studying queer kinship in both quantitative and qualitative ways, and what does it mean to study queer kinship in our respective locations?

JM: As my points above illustrate, also in thinking about the project methodology one has to take into account specific local contexts. In the Anglo-American context, where there has been plenty of research on LGBTQ+ families, one can concentrate on smaller scale projects "to create strategically illuminating set of facets in relation to specific research concerns and questions, not a random set, or an eclectic set, or a representative set, or a total set" as Jennifer Mason explained while writing about the facet approach she promotes (Mason 2011a: 77). This single phenomenon approach makes more sense there than in the Polish context where, so far, there have been no larger and mixed-method projects regarding LGBTQ+ families and relationships. In my project we had to gain the general knowledge first (that's why we used quantitative survey first with more than 3000 respondents) and only then to start to deepen it by use of diverse qualitative methods (biographical interviews, participatory observations for 30 days, interviews on family maps, important photos/objects, focus group interviews see Mizielińska & Stasińska 2020, Mizielińska 2022). In a way we tried to make up for "delays" in the CEE knowledge production, to do "everything at once," which, from the beginning to the end, as we applied many methods and tried to cover all spheres of family and intimate life of non-heterosexual couples in a relatively short period of time (3.5 years), was very demanding and challenging.

UD: I find the question of how methodologies and research questions relate to geopolitics quite fascinating. Most research, certainly in anthropology and sociology, starts from the idea that one should either study a population that has not been studied before or that one should ask a new question or employ a new method (cf Dahl & Gabb 2019). Like much work conducted by queer scholars, "Families of Choice" has not only provided ground-breaking empirical research but also been politically motivated and that is important. Yet, I see a paradox in your reasoning here. On the one hand, you criticise the idea that CEE is "behind" and on the other, you propose that you need to make up for a "delay," an absence. It makes me wonder again what the measuring stick is, so to speak. Could it be that it depends on our research questions, that different methodological approaches and theoretical apparatuses are more or less useful, depending on what we study? Relatedly, I am wondering to what extent we are constrained by different disciplinary conventions and expectations?

JM: And you have caught me here! Because it is and it is not contradictory. When I said "delays" in the CEE knowledge production I express the insider perspective which reflects my in-between-ness. Namely, that I know the field and I know what has been produced here and there. So, on the one hand, I am overwhelmed by these wonderful and insightful works which makes me feel inferior, always not good enough. And on the other hand, facing "the emptiness" in the Polish context makes me at least want to map the territory, put something on the almost empty table. However, I also wanted to underline that our research questions are always already shaped by work that has been done before us, so I guess our starting point is different.

UD: I understand and recognise the struggle of "in-betweenness"; we certainly always have to speak to many audiences at once! However, I don't necessarily see a contradiction between small-scale qualitative research and larger quantitative ones, nor do I see them as sequential. Rather, I think they reflect different scales, on the one hand, and research traditions, on the other. Of course, the question of what kind of research gets funded is a political one, both in Sweden and in Europe at large. There is a lot of (straight) gatekeeping by researchers on the different research councils and those assessing research applications. Perhaps there is a longer tradition in some settings of viewing small-scale qualitative research as valid and worthwhile forms of science? I cannot say that it always makes much of an impact, and it can clearly be dismissed, as the overall attack on poststructuralism (and queer) at the moment attests to. Clearly, you identified a need to point to the existence of LGBTQ+ families in relation to both "conventional" Polish family research and in relation to a state that does not recognise LGBTQ+ people, but that doesn't necessarily mean that what you call a "single phenomenon" project is a "Western" thing. Rather, to me it suggests that your stakes are clear and you draw on certain kinds of disciplinary and methodological traditions in order to realise them. Every project on LGBTQ+ livelihood in Poland from now on has to refer to your work; and that can hardly be said of mine…

JM: I guess that is one of the advantages of having done pioneering work in the context where literally nothing existed but where there are the disadvantages I talked about before. I have never said that small-scale projects are not important and invalid, because I think quite the opposite. In making the distinction here I refer more to the plenitude of work being done in the Anglo-American academia, both large scale and small scale, and the feeling of dealing with "nothingness". And I think this simply shapes you and your research questions, i.e., you cannot be polemical because there is nobody to argue with except very heteronormative family studies scholars, at least at the time I started the project. But of course, I see your "in-betweenness" in relation to Swedish academia and work on LGBTQ+ families being done there.

UD: I understand the need to be polemical and to figure out to whom to address one's critique, and I get that yours then becomes the wider (queer) academic world, in which you are geopolitically positioned. One entry into thinking about queer kinship in Sweden for me came from reading the 2001 state sponsored public investigation (called an SOU) on "Children in Homosexual families," which laid the ground for changing family law around adoption (see also Nordqvist 2006). In Sweden, significant policy and legal changes (always reflecting political ideals of their time) often begin with state-initiated scientific investigations to lay the ground for, and to enable researchers and politicians to propose legal changes. This one found some hardly surprising results: gay people do raise children and same-sex parenthood does not mess up the gender identity and psychosocial development of children! Its starting point is clearly profoundly heteronormative; heterosexual parenthood is the ideal, norm and point for comparison and it sets the stage for a conditional "inclusion" of queer parents; yet, only insofar as biogenetic origins ("fatherhood" in particular) is not hidden and to the extent that these families are *like* heterosexual ones in gendered but also classed and racialised ways. While I certainly understand that for many LGBTQ+ people there is a strong desire to be "normal" (whatever that means beyond feeling belonging in one's tribe so to speak) as a kinship theorist, I find it fascinating how the "inclusion" of new family forms by the state actually serves to secure rather than trouble biogenetic parenthood as the foundation for family and belonging.

This investigation does not rely on any significant empirical data on gay families in Sweden, but on previous research conducted elsewhere. As far as I know, there are no surveys done on families in Sweden that ask about how people define family, or any empirical data collected that comes near to what you have done in Poland (other than the one I did thanks to working with you and that I discuss in this book). Perhaps what this suggests is that in fact, Sweden is "behind"; we still do not know how many families there are or what their thoughts are.

JM: But it was partly what drove me to do the survey, that these very heteronormative questions were asked in the Polish national polls without even taking into account even the possibility of the existence of LGBTQ+ families or queer subjects in general. So, in my survey I repeated some questions that have been asked to representative group of Poles in heteronormative national surveys, I simply reshaped the questions and added some less heteronormative responses as options (for more see Mizielińska, Abramowicz & Stasińska 2015).

UD: It is clear that we face different challenges in different locations. From very early on when I presented my research through ethnographic examples and complex stories of kin-making, I have frequently been met with questions of validity: questions about the size of my data set and how "representative" my analysis or my examples are. Objections seemed particularly salient when I pointed to significant silences in the literature, or to inequalities and norms within the fertile part of the LGBTQ+ population and how it was being studied. In particular, when I addressed how queers of colour I have interviewed understand and create family within a hegemonically white society, how families that do not fit within the couple and dual parenthood-based model understand relatedness, and how changing relations between adults involved in raising children might alter understandings of parenthood, I was often met with objections or told that my examples were exceptions. Reading previous research and following cultural representations, it has become increasingly clear that the nation and its majoritarian (white) population is often taken for granted, rather than interrogated and in the case of Sweden, the history of welfare state biopolitics was often ignored in discussions of how LGBTQ+ people make families in a historical context of increasing rights. Making this argument, I am frequently met with numbers that point to the progressiveness of the Nordic states, or told that family-making via access to assisted reproduction is a right upheld by a social democratic welfare state and its state-funded healthcare will "democratise" reproduction. Learning about your survey made me curious about what numbers might tell us and they did not exactly show "equality." It made a huge difference, so thank you!

Queer futurities: Where do we go from here?

UD: As we finalise this project, and thus our many years of collaboration, what do you think we have learned from our conversations? Have we managed to further the discussions within Baltic and Eastern European Studies or within queer kinship studies? What kinds of questions are we left with and what do we study next?

JM: For me it was important to be in a dialogue with all of you, to share our knowledge, sometimes argue too, because as Sarah Schulman rightly notices, conflict is not abuse (Schulman 2016) and particularly in our turbulent time we need to differentiate between harm and different/polyphonic visions which might be productive. In Poland I often feel very "homeless" in terms of academia and academic disputes. I lack community, community of interests, shared political visions, sensitive to all kinds of exclusions. It was also a productive dialogue because while sharing my data and analysis with you all, I could see them through different eyes and deepen my perspective. So "shareness" and queer solidarity are what I value most. But of course, it was an intellectually very inspiring dialogue too. Particularly, when we were all in one place for a short while. For instance, when we were in Stockholm, Antu Sorainen and I started to think about lesbian relationships with age differences as an important and largely ignored topic in queer kinship literature (see our chapter in this book). I agree with Pako Chalkidis's point (in this volume) that nowadays queer kinship is so focused on family making through the reproduction that neglects sexuality, but I would add that it also ignores its other possible forms and that family means diverse forms of relating and as such does not have to be focus on the child.

So, I do hope that our piece will encourage other scholars to develop projects concentrating on age differences in queer relationships. I also think that thanks to this inspiring dialogue between the four of us we are better equipped to undertake future projects, in different configurations and with different foci but with the same intellectual (and queer) generosity, which is more than needed in such difficult times in all of our present locations.

UD: I agree that it was incredibly important to have time to meet, work closely, and engage in conversation. To that end, all our meetings, also in Warsaw and Helsinki, and at various conferences have been very important. A long slow conversation, in which there is also room for the body, for our lives at large, and for our partners and kin. Interestingly, I did start out wanting to have a much more open definition of family (one that did not centre so much on children) but the "baby boom" in Scandinavia and all the complexities of the different laws that regulate parenthood depending on modes of conception sort of took over. Antu Sorainen's work on queer will-writing and inheritance (especially among queers who do not have children "of their own") has been profoundly significant for my thinking about queer lineage and family and I'd like to think more about this (see Sorainen 2014). My research assistant Johan Sundell conducted interviews with gay/queer men of different generations, many of whom insisted on other forms of family than through procreation as well, and I have met many radical queers who make kin rather than babies (to paraphrase Haraway, 2016, 137). Yet, I remain fascinated with how (white) lesbians have become mothers and thus central to reproducing the nation, but very rarely seem to rock the boat (or do they? I guess time will tell!) Trans parents on the other hand, along with multi-parent families, meet much more resistance as do transgender and nonbinary children.

I think a crucial part of our project has been Raili Uibo's (2021) thesis project on *Queers doing close relations in Estonia*. Raili set out to study the context for and consequences of Estonia being the first post-Soviet state to introduce a same-sex partnership law. Yet, what she found as she started doing research on families was that perhaps more than anything else, the livelihoods of queers in

Estonia were shaped by extreme neoliberal austerity politics under which the care of others took very different shapes. I have learned a lot from Raili's work on care and in particular from her notion of opacity and how queers neither hide nor separate their queer lives but rather opaquely incorporate queerness in their lives. Her work has contributed both significant data on queer lives in the Baltic region and made important theoretical contributions. In addition, she is a very skilled researcher and editor, as work on this book as well as in my new project on assisted reproduction across Scandinavian borders, where she designs surveys and preps for research, testifies.

For myself, I suppose I am still interested both in the relationship between (queer) kinship and nation building and in the conditions under which LGBTQ+ people are able to form recognisable families. I also remain interested in queer kinship practices, that is, how we address what Butler (2002, 15) calls the "fundamental forms of human dependency, which may include birth, child-rearing, relations of emotional dependency and support, generational ties, illness, dying, and death (to name a few)" in a complex time marked by growing nationalism and conservativism, on the one hand, and queer liberalism and late capitalism, on the other. To that end, I am frequently drawn to art, to the work of filmmakers, podcasters, writers. I am also drawn to constellations in which life, work and kinship merge in different ways. I think it is true that while in many respects it is difficult to distinguish kinship from friendship and community or from state definitions, kinship and reproduction as core organising concepts has far from lost its significance; in fact, it remains at the heart of geopolitics and of what it means to live a liveable life.

References

Acosta, K. L. 2011. "The Language of (in)Visibility: Using in-between Spaces as a Vehicle for Empowerment in the Family." *Journal of Homosexuality* 58 (6–7): 883–900.

Acosta, K. L. 2018. "Queering Family Scholarship: Theorizing from the Borderlands." *Journal of Family Theory & Review* 10: 406–418. doi: 10.1111/jftr.12263

Adamski, F. 2002. *Rodzina. Wymiar Społeczno-Kulturowy [Family. Socio-Cultural Dimension]*. Kraków: Wydawnictwo Uniwersytetu Jagiellońskiego.

Ahmed, S. 2012. *On being Included: Racism and Diversity in Institutional Life*. Durham: Duke University Press.

Baker, C. 2018. *Race and the Yugoslav Region: Postsocialist, Post-Conflict, Postcolonial? (Theory for a Global Age)*. Manchester: Manchester University Press.

Bernardes, J. 1997. *Family Studies. An Introduction*. London; New York: Routledge.

Blagojević, M. 2009. *Knowledge Production at the Semiperiphery: A Gender Perspective*. Belgrade: Institut za kriminološka i sociološka istraživanja.

Boatcă, M. 2006. "No Race to the Swift: Negotiating Racial Identity in Past and Present Eastern Europe." *Human Architecture: Journal of the Sociology of Self-Knowledge* 5 (1): 91.

Butler, J. 2002. "Is Kinship always Already Heterosexual?" *differences* 13 (1): 14–44.

Butler, J. 2012. "Can One Lead a Good Life in a Bad Life?" *Radical Philosophy* 176: 9–18.

Cheal, D. 1993. "Unity and Difference in Postmodern Families." *Journal of Family Issues* 14 (1): 5–19. https://doi.org/10.1177/0192513X93014001002.

Dahl, U. 2003. "Inseminationsfrågan som kom bort." *bang* 1: 15–17.

---. 2011. "Queer in the Nordic Region: Telling Queer (Feminist) Stories," in *Queer in Europe*, L. Downing & R. Gillett, eds., 143–157. London: Ashgate.

---. 2014. "Not Gay as in Happy, but Queer as in Fuck You." *lambda nordica* 19 (3–4): 143.

---. 2018a. "Becoming Fertile in the Land of Organic Milk: Lesbian and Queer Reproductions of Femininity and Motherhood in Sweden." *Sexualities* 21 (7): 1021–1038.

---. 2018b. "(the Promise of) Monstrous Kinship? Queer Reproduction and the Somatechnics of Sexual and Racial Difference." *Somatechnics* 8 (2): 195–211.

Dahl, U. & Gabb, J. 2019. "Trends in Contemporary Queer Kinship and Family Research." *lambda nordica* 24 (2–3): 209–237

Dahl, U., Liljeström, M. & Manns, U. 2016. *The Geopolitics of Nordic and Russian Gender Research 1975–2005*. Stockholm: Södertörn University.

Decena, C. U. 2011. *Tacit Subjects: Belonging and Same-Sex Desire among Dominican Immigrant Men*. Durham: Duke University Press Books.

Duggan, L. 2002. "The New Homonormativity: The Sexual Politics of Neo-liberalism," in *Materializing Democracy: Toward a Revitalized Cultural Politics*, edited by R. Castronovo & D. D. Nelson, 175–194. Durham: Duke University Press.

Eng, D. L. 2010. *The Feeling of Kinship: Queer Liberalism and the Racialization of Intimacy*. Durham [NC]: Duke University Press.

Eng, D. L. & Jasbir K. P. 2020. "Left of Queer: Introduction." *Social Text* 38 (4): 1–24.

Franklin, S. 1997. *Embodied Progress: A Cultural Account of Assisted Conception*. London: Routledge.

Gabb, J. 2008. *Researching Intimacy in Families*. Basingstoke; New York: Palgrave Macmillan.

Geertz, C. 1973. *The Interpretation of Cultures. Selected essays*. New York: Basic books.

Graff, A. & Korolczuk, E. 2021. *Anti-Gender Politics in the Populist Moment*. Abingdon, Oxon; New York, NY; Routledge.

Gunnarsson Payne, J. 2016. "Grammars of Kinship: Biological Motherhood and Assisted Reproduction in the Age of Epigenetics." *Signs: Journal of Women in Culture and Society* 41 (3): 483–506.

Haraway, D. J. 1997. *Modest_Witness@Second_Millennium:FemaleMan© _Meets_OncoMouse: Feminism and Technoscience*. New York: Routledge.

Haraway, D. J. 2016. *Staying with the Trouble: Making Kin in the Chthulucene*. Durham, NC: Duke University Press.

Holstein, J. A. & Gubrium, J. 1999. "What Is Family?" *Marriage & Family Review* 28 (3–4): 3–20.

Kopp, K. 2010. "Gray Zones: On the Inclusion of "Poland" in the Study of German Colonialism," in *German Colonialism and National Identity*, M. Perraudin & J. Zimmerer, eds., 33–44. New York: Routledge.

Kuhar, R. & Paternotte, D. 2017. *Anti-Gender Campaigns in Europe: Mobilizing Against Equality*. 1st ed. London: Rowman & Littlefield International, Ltd.

Kulawik, T. & Kravchenko, Z., eds. *Borderlands in European Gender Studies*. Abingdon; New York: Routledge, 2020.

Levin, I. 1993. "Family as Mapped Realities." *Journal of Family Issues* 14 (1): 82–91.

Lewin, E. 1993. *Lesbian Mothers: Accounts of Gender in American Culture*. Ithaca, NY: Cornell University Press.

Malmquist, A. 2015. "Pride and Prejudice: Lesbian Families in Contemporary Sweden." PhD thesis, Linköping University.

Mason, J. 2011. "Facet Methodology: The Case for an Inventive Research Orientation." *Methodological Innovations Online* 6 (3): 75–92.

Melegh, A. 2006. *On the East/West Slope: Globalization, Nationalism, Racism and Discources on Eastern Europe*. New York: Central European University Press.

Mignolo, W. D. 2011. "I Am Where I Think. Remapping the Order of Knowing," in *The Creolization of Theory*, edited by F. Lionnet & S. Shih, 159–192. Durham: Duke University Press.

Mizielińska, J. 2020. "The Limits of Choice: Queer Parents and Stateless Children in Their Search for Recognition in Poland." *Gender, Place & Culture* 29 (2): 153–176.

Mizielińska, J. 2022. *Queer Kinship at the Edge? Families of Choice in Poland.* Routledge, forthcoming.

Mizielińska, J., Abramowicz, M. & Stasińska, A. 2015. *Families of Choice in Poland. Family Life of Non-Heterosexual People.* Warsaw: IP PAN.

Mizielińska, J. & Kulpa, R. 2011. "'Contemporary Peripheries': Queer Studies, Circulation of Knowledge and East/West Divide," in *De-Centring Western Sexualities. Central and Eastern European Perspective*, R. Kulpa & J. Mizielińska, eds., 11–26. Farnham; Burlington, VT: Ashgate.

Mizielińska, J. & Stasińska, A. 2018. "Beyond the Western Gaze: Families of Choice in Poland". *Sexualities* 21 (7): 101–23. doi: 10.1177/136346071 7718508.

———. 2020a. "Negotiations Between Possibilities and Reality: Reproductive Choices of Families of Choice in Poland." *European Journal of Women's Studies* 27 (2/4): 1–16.

———. 2020b. "Frame Story Approach in Mixed and Multimethod Study on Non-Heterosexual Families in Poland." *Sociological Research Online* 26 (4): 792–809. doi: 10.1177/1360780420972121.

Moore, M. R. 2011. *Invisible Families: Gay Identities, Relationships, and Motherhood among Black Women.* 1st ed. Berkeley and Los Angeles: University of California Press.

Morgan, D. 1996. *Family Connections: An Introduction to Family Studies.* 1 edition. Cambridge, UK: Cambridge, MA: Polity.

Mulinari, D. 2001. "'Race'/ethnicity in a 'Nordic' context: a reflection from the Swedish borderlands," in *Svensk genusforskning i världen: globala perspektiv i svensk genusforskning och svensk genusforskning i ett globalt perspektiv*, A. Johansson, 6–24. Gothenburg: Nationella sekretariatet för genusforskning.

Möser, C., Ramme, J. & Takács, J. 2022. *Paradoxical Right-Wing Sexual Politics in Europe.* Cham: Springer.

Newton, E. 1979. *Mother Camp: Female Impersonators in America.* Chicago: University of Chicago Press.

Nordqvist, P. 2006. "Att tala om familj: Lesbiskas berättelser om planerat föräldraskap." *lambda nordica* 11 (4): 63–81.

Polski, A. 2013. *Ingen av betydelse. Mödrar från samkönad familjebildning talar om spermadonatorn.* Master's thesis, Lund University.

Rich, A. 1994. *Blood, Bread, and Poetry: Selected Prose 1979–1985.* Reissue edition. New York, NY: W. W. Norton & Company.

Rodriguez, J. M. 2014. *Sexual Futures, Queer Gestures, and Other Latina Longings.* New York: NYU Press.

Roseneil, S. & Budgeon, S. 2004. "Cultures of Intimacy and Care Beyond 'the Family': Personal Life and Social Change in the Early 21st Century." *Current Sociology* 52 (2): 135–159.

Ryan-Flood, R. 2005. "Contested Heteronormativities: Discourses of Fatherhood among Lesbian Parents in Sweden and Ireland: New Parenting: Opportunities and Challenges." *Sexualities* 8 (2): 189–204.

Schulman, S. 2016. *Conflict Is Not Abuse: Overstating Harm, Community Responsibility, and the Duty of Repair*. Vancouver: Arsenal Pulp Press.

Sorainen, A. 2014. "Queer Personal Lives, Inheritance Perspectives, and Small Places." *lambda nordica* 19 (3–4): 31.

Stasińska, A. 2020. "Tender Gestures in Heteronormative Spaces. Displaying Affection in Public by Families of Choice in Poland." *Gender, Place & Culture* 29 (2): 177–200.

Strathern, M. 1992. *Reproducing the Future: Essays on Anthropology, Kinship and the New Reproductive Technologies*. Manchester: Manchester University Press.

Szulc, L. 2017. *Transnational Homosexuals in Communist Poland. Cross-border Flows in Gay and Lesbian Magazines*. London: Palgrave Macmillan.

Švab, A. & Kuhar, R. 2014. "The Transparent and Family Closets: Gay Men and Lesbians and Their Families of Origin." *Journal of GLBT Family Studies* 10 (1–2): 15–35.

Tlostanova, M. 2012. "Postsocialist ≠ Postcolonial? On Post-Soviet Imaginary and Global Coloniality." *Journal of Postcolonial Writing* 48: 130–42.

Tlostanova, M. 2015. "Can the post-soviet think? On coloniality of knowledge, external imperial and double colonial difference." *Intersections. East European Journal of Society and Politics* 1 (2): 38–58

Tyszka, Z. 2005. *Rodzina We Współczesnym Świecie*. Poznań: Wydawnictwo Adama Mickiewicza.

Uibo, R. 2021. *"And I don't know who we really are to each other." Queers doing close relationships in Estonia*. Stockholm: Södertörn University.

Weston, K. 1991. *Families we Choose: Lesbians, Gays, Kinship*. New York: Columbia University Press.

Widerberg, K. 1998. "Translating Gender." *NORA: Nordic Journal of Women's Studies* 6 (2): 133–138.

Yarbrough, M., Jones, A. & DeFilippis, J. eds., 2018, *Queer Families and Relationships After Marriage Equality*. London; New York: Routledge.

List of Contributors

Pako Chalkidis is a Social Anthropologist. Their research interests focus on anthropology of gender and sexuality, anthropology of kinship and family, queer theory, sexuality and institutionalization, digital methods for Social Science, and Greek ethnography. Over the last decade they have participated in several EU funded projects, undertaking research on sexual and gender politics, new reproductive technologies and kinship, and migration policies along with issues of institutional injustice. Previously, Aspa was a Marie Skłodowska-Curie Postdoctoral fellow (co-funded with IAS) at the University of Warwick.

Ulrika Dahl is a Cultural Anthropologist and Professor of Gender Studies at Uppsala University in Sweden. Her interests are feminist and queer politics and theory, critical race and whiteness studies, decolonial pedagogies, femininity, affect, and queer kinship and reproduction. Ulrika was senior editor of *lambda Nordica- Nordic journal of LGBTQ studies* from 2009–2020 and she has published extensively on Nordic queer studies, gender studies and on the figure of the femme. She was Project leader for the project "Queer(y)ing Kinship in the Baltic Region" (funded by the Foundation for Baltic and East European Studies) and currently works in a Forte-funded research project (with Rikke Andreassen) entitled "Scandinavian Border Crossings: Race and Nation in Queer Assisted Reproduction" with a focus on biopolitics, race and nation in contemporary queer family making. She is also beginning new research on the conservative turn in (Nordic) feminism and gender studies and their relation to "gender critical" feminism and anti-gender movements. With a passion for creative writing, Ulrika is currently also working on her second book in Swedish, a lyric essay on queer kinship, desire and embodied knowledge.

Jenny Gunnarsson Payne is professor of Ethnology at Södertörn University in Sweden. She has published widely on issues of gender, reproduction and kinship, as well as on feminist, anti-feminist and populist mobilisation. Her work can be found in journals such as *Signs: Journal of Women in Culture and Society, Journal of Political Ideologies* and *Critical Policy Studies.*

Suraiya Jetha is a Mellon Fellow at the MIT Press in Boston, USA. She holds a PhD in Anthropology and Feminist Studies from the University of California, Santa Cruz. Her doctoral studies were supported by the Norway-America Association (NORAM), the Department of Social Anthropology at the University of Oslo, the UCSC Office of the Chancellor, the UCSC Dean of Graduate Studies, and the UCSC Department of Anthropology. She also holds an MA in Anthropology from the New School for Social Research, an MA in Migration and Diaspora Studies from the School for Oriental and African Studies, and a BA in Anthropology from Yale University.

Nina Lykke is Professor Emerita of Gender Studies at Linköping University, Sweden, and Adjunct Professor at Aarhus University, Denmark. She is also a poet and writer, and has recently co-founded an international network for Queer Death Studies. Her current research interests include feminist theory; queering of death, and mourning in posthuman, queer feminist, new material-ist, decolonial and eco-critical perspectives; autophenomenogra-phy, and poetic writing. She has recently published in journals such as *Australian Feminist Studies; NORA; Catalyst. Feminism, Theory, Technoscience; Environmental Humanities; Social Identities; Kerb Journal; and lambda nordica* . She is also the author of numerous books such as *Cosmodolphins* (2000), *Feminist Studies* (2010), and *Vibrant Death. A Posthuman Phenomenology of Mourning* (2022). Website: www.ninalykke.net

Anna Malmqvist is Associate Professor in Social Psychology at Linköping University. Her research has extensive focus on LGBTQ+ families, including focus on paths to parenthood and everyday family life experiences. She has published a book on lesbian motherhood (2016), gay fatherhood (2022), and co-edited the first Swedish textbook in LGBTQ+ psychology (with Tove Lundberg and Matilda Wurm, 2017).

Joanna Mizielińska holds a D.S.s (habilitation) in sociology, from the University of Warsaw and a Ph.D. in Feminist Philosophy, Institute of Philosophy and Sociology from the Polish Academy of Sciences. Currently, she works at the Institute of Sociology, Collegium Civitas. She was the Principal Investigator of the project *Families of Choice in Poland* (2013–2016), which was the first multi-method project on non-heterosexual families in Poland and the Co-investigator in an international Erasmus + project *Doing Rights. Innovative Tools for Professionals Working with LGBT families* (2017–2020) and "Queer(y)ing Kinship in the Baltic Region" [dir. by prof. U. Dahl, Södertörn University, 2016–2021]. She has been an expert in LGBTIQ issues for almost 20 years, conducting qualitative and quantitative research. She is an author of books and articles on gender, sexuality, queer kinship, including *De-Centering Western Sexualities. Central and Eastern European Perspective* (co-edited with R. Kulpa, 2011). The findings of her recent study include the books *Families of choice in Poland. Family life of nonheterosexual persons* (with M. Abramowicz and A. Stasińska, 2015), *In Different Voices. Families of Choice in Poland* (with J. Struzik and A. Krol, 2017) and *Different or Ordinary? Families of Choice in Poland* (2017) – and numerous academic articles. Her book entitled *Queer Kinship at the Edge? Families of Choice in Poland* (2022) has just been published by Routledge and is available open access.

Anna Moring, PhD, works as leading specialist of the Network of Family Diversity. Her work for the past ten years has been to gather information on family diversity for the purposes of legislative work and family politics. She is currently also the leader of "Law and Diverse Families", a Finnish Government funded research project on law and family diversity. She has previously published on family ideals, the legal rights of diverse families, parental leaves, and the legal status of LGBTIQ+ families in Finland. The research from which the chapter in this book took place during a period of postdoctoral research within the project "CoreKin – Contrasting and Re-Imagining Margins of Kinship", an Academy of Finland funded research project 1.9.2016–31.8.2020, grant number 297957 (Director: Antu Sorainen).

Michael Nebeling Petersen, PhD, is Associate Professor in Gender Studies at the Center for Gender, Sexuality and Difference at the Department for Scandinavian Studies and Linguistics at the University of Copenhagen, Denmark. He has worked extensively on homosexual culture and citizenship, new technologies of reproduction and kinship as well as digital media and mediated cultures of intimacy – with a firm interest on the formations of and intersections between sexuality, gender, whiteness, and national belonging. Currently, he is Project leader for the collaborative project *The Cultural History of AIDS in Denmark*, that examines how AIDS emerged, became signified and became embedded in Danish culture during the period 1981–2021.

Antu Sorainen PhD, is Docent in Gender Studies, working as Principal Investigator at the University of Helsinki. She was the Director of the research team "CoreKin – Contrasting and Re-Imagining Margins of Kinship" (Academy of Finland, 2016–2020). Her current research project focuses on Protolesbian Personal Histories and Nationalist Sentiment in the 1920–30s Finland (The Cultural Foundation of Finland, 2019–2024). She has conducted empirical studies in queer sexualities, especially in the legal field. She is the co-author of a book on the conceptual history of "Sittlichkeit", and publishes on queer kinship and inheritance practices. Sorainen was an Academy Fellow at the Academy of Finland and the Project leader of the research project entitled "Wills and Inheritance Practices in Sexually Marginalised Groups" (2014–2019).

Raili Uibo holds a PhD in Gender Studies from Södertörn University. Her PhD project was part of the international research project "Queer(y)ing Kinship in the Baltic Region" and explores how

LGBTQ+ people in Estonia are doing close relationships, care and intimacy. She received her MA in Gender Studies from Lund University and BA in Sociology from Tallinn University. Her research interests are queer and feminist theory and activism, post-socialist and decolonial Studies.